CW01337458

LONDON'S DISTRICT RAILWAY

Volume Two: Twentieth Century

LONDON'S DISTRICT RAILWAY

A History of the Metropolitan District Railway Company

Volume Two: Twentieth Century

M. A. C. Horne FCILT MIRO

Capital Transport

Title page: **A contemporary colour representation of a typical District motorman at the controls of his train.**
Roy Allen collection

First published 2019

ISBN 978 1 85414 430 0

© M. A. C. Horne 2019

Published by Capital Transport Publishing Ltd
www.capitaltransport.com

Printed by Parksons Graphics

CONTENTS

INTRODUCTION TO VOLUME 2 AND ACKNOWLEDGEMENTS

Volume 1 ended whilst steam haulage of District trains was still the only means of propulsion available, although the directors fully realized it was unsustainable on an underground railway where competing electric lines were being built. This volume picks up that story and explains what the District proposed to do about electrification (which was a problem because the company was in such a state it could not raise the money required) and how it happened that an American team came to save the day. The story continues by explaining how this team later adapted and extended the District and its associated lines to create what would become the Underground system familiar today.

This history really finishes in 1933 when the District company surrendered its business to the newly formed London Passenger Transport Board, but even by then practical control had been in the hands of the holding company that had originally electrified the railway; the District was in reality just one of several associated Underground lines that were already operated as a single system. When London Transport took charge in 1933 it made little difference. In Appendix 1 I have very briefly carried the story forward to today, to make it easier to relate the state of what is today's District Line with that found in 1933 when the District Railway handed its railway over.

I would like to thank Brian Hardy and Jim Connor for assistance with images and in particular to thank Roy Allen who made available many items from his extensive collection of District material. I must also thank John Liffen for reading the manuscript and making a number of helpful suggestions as well as discovering typos and other errors. Jim Whiting must also be thanked for his continual support and forbearance during this lengthy project, and again has supplied numerous images. The staff of the LT Museum library and photographic collection must be thanked for the work they have done in supplying quite a large number of images and access to certain other records. None of this would have been possible without the assistance of the National Archives and London Metropolitan Archives whose extensive collections of railway material have been available for research but where, it seems to me, their value and coverage is not being exploited judging by the small number of people I have seen using them. These collections deserve more use and there is still a great deal more history to be revealed.

ABBREVIATIONS

BET	British Electric Traction Co Ltd
BPCR	Brompton & Piccadilly Circus Railway
BTH	British Thomson-Houston Company
C&WR	City & West End Railway
CLR	Central London Railway
CSLR	City & South London Railway
ECC	Electric Construction Company
ELR	East London Railway
E&SHR	Ealing & South Harrow Railway
GCR	Great Central Railway
GER	Great Eastern Railway
GNSR	Great Northern & Strand Railway
GWR	Great Western Railway
H&MR	Hounslow & Metropolitan Railway
H&UR	Harrow & Uxbridge Railway
LBSCR	London, Brighton & South Coast Railway
LCC	London County Council
LCDR	London, Chatham & Dover Railway
LGOC	London General Omnibus Company
LER	London Electric Railway
LMSR	London, Midland & Scottish Railway
LNER	London & North Eastern Railway
LNWR	London & North Western Railway
LSWR	London & South Western Railway
LT	London Transport (and the London Passenger Transport Board)
LTSR	London, Tilbury & Southend Railway
LUT	London United Tramways
kW	kilowatt
MDR	Metropolitan District Railway
MDETC	Metropolitan District Electric Traction Company
Met	Metropolitan Railway
MW	Megawatt
N&SWJR	North & South Western Junction Railway
NUR	National Union of Railwaymen
SER	South Eastern Railway
SECR	South Eastern & Chatham Railway
T.O.T.	Train-Omnibus-Tram (promotional slogan)
UERL	Underground Electric Railways Company of London Ltd
W&BR	Whitechapel & Bow Railway
W&SR	Wimbledon & Sutton Railway
WLR	West London Railway (and West London Extension Railway)

Chapter One

FACING UP TO ELECTRIFICATION

The need to electrify

Towards the end of the Victorian era the District employed 1600 staff, ran 560 train trips to or through Mansion House daily along 39 route miles of track, only 13 of which were wholly owned by the District. The signalmen in the busiest box made 7000 lever movements daily and sent 3150 telegraph messages. About 115,000 passenger journeys were made each day on ordinary tickets, and another 52,000 on seasons. 70 per cent of passengers were third-class, 21 per cent seconds and 9 per cent firsts. The average fare was 2.18d. All this was a very commendable example of what could be done with the existing technology, but it did not represent much progress from the passenger's viewpoint.

For thirty years the operation of the District changed in no important respect. The same locomotives hauled the same carriages in the same grimy conditions. This was utterly unsustainable—the District was out of date and wearing out and public expectations were rising as clean, new electric railways were emerging elsewhere in London. There was no cheap solution, but steam-age technology made it impossible to increase services further.

This cartoon represents a crowded District carriage in 1897, at about the time the need for electrification began to command attention. There was seating for ten in each compartment, but an equal number standing was not unknown. *Windsor Magazine* November 1897

Electric railways, like the Central London whose construction began in 1895, seriously threatened to undermine traffic on the parallel District. Improving bus and tram services had already inflicted damage, requiring painful fares reductions. Something had to be done, but financially the District was in poor shape. Existing shareholders had virtually given up hope of any dividend and raising money for new investment was going to be very difficult.

Electric traction in a primitive form was known in the 1880s. Magnus Volk's short electric railway opened in Brighton in 1883 and in 1883/4 two Irish electric tramways came into operation. These were all narrow-gauge systems and whilst the Irish lines were several miles long they were really only demonstration systems that showed electric traction was feasible. It was in 1890 the City & South London Railway became the first standard-gauge electric railway in Britain and proved that the technology worked at a practical scale (it also proved deep tube tunnelling worked). The Liverpool Overhead (electric) Railway opened in 1893 and several American railroads were employing electric traction shortly afterwards. After 1890, new London local lines were promoted in large numbers, all expected to be electric, and this piled on the pressure.

The Queen's Silver Jubilee year (1887) had been a particularly low point for District receipts and in desperation the idea of using battery locomotives was contemplated, which would provide a cleaner and livelier form of haulage. This proved quite impractical. The idea flowed from the technology first developed by a Mr Elieson on part of the West Metropolitan Tramways in 1883, and subsequently elsewhere. An agreement was made with the Met to test an Elieson locomotive but the company running the trial could not get it to work and this discouraged the District which had been watching with interest. On paper, large savings were possible but without a working locomotive, nothing more was heard.*

By the late 1890s the existing steam operation was becoming very unsatisfactory. A former District driver recalling his steam days in 1929 says:

> People who grouse about rush-hour congestion on the District to-day haven't the faintest idea of what things were like in the past. I remember once, when strong complaints were being made that there were not sufficient trains to cope with the traffic, that checks were taken of the number of passengers some of the trains actually carried. One train at Walham Green was found to have over 1,000 people in it, and I don't think that this figure was anything very exceptional. You were not only crushed in those days, but you were nearly suffocated as well by the smoke and the steam in the tunnel sections. ... The old times are all very well to talk about, but you can take it from me that there wasn't anything very pleasant in being jammed twenty-four into a compartment of the old steam trains, especially at night, with only one dismal gas-lamp in the compartment.

There is likely to be substance to this recollection: in 1904 even the shareholders were told that there was probably nothing more uncomfortable than travelling in a District Railway train.[1] These complaints about the conditions of the District were not new but the problem was that fourteen years after electric traction was shown to be practicable still nothing had been done and conditions continued to deteriorate.

---

* It is reputed the Metropolitan trial failed because of the difficulty of creating a vacuum for the braking system without a steam locomotive, rather than a failure of the drive mechanism. The batteries were only to demonstrate what the locomotive could do and on any commercial system current collection from continuous conductors would have been necessary.

The Pond Affair

Although disaffected directors had been evident throughout the District's life it was during 1896 that the most persistent episode began: an episode indirectly leaving its mark on today's Underground diagram.

During 1896, the name Charles Pond becomes significant. It was he who fronted what became known in the press as the Bloomsbury Syndicate, a shadowy group of entrepreneurs and frustrated District shareholders who used an office at 2 Bloomsbury Street and who ostensibly wanted changes instead of talk. Pond had no previous association with the District and, to give him a voice, he purchased £100 nominal value of District stock in June 1896, costing under £30 and giving him access to shareholder meetings.[2] Pond had once been a member of the Stock Exchange but after several financial misfortunes had become a noted music hall *artiste* who, the previous year, was reported playing Shylock at the Gaiety theatre. Although it is not clear how he was selected to do battle with Forbes he knew stockbroker Murray Griffith and chosen he was to present a new way out for the District.

Earlier that year a group of District shareholders conceived a scheme for a deep-level electric express railway between Earls Court and Mansion House and intended to function quite independently of the steam railway. By running directly underneath the existing railway, new property required would be minimal and stations would be shared, vastly reducing costs. Benefits included an attractive, clean and fast route to the City and a mechanism to help block other tube proposals that might threaten the District (such schemes were already emerging). At this stage it is not clear whether it was a ruse to increase the depleted share price with the illusion of action or whether it was a genuine attempt to provide a modern, clean relief tube at low cost, for the idea was perfectly plausible. The press hinted it might be a 'rig' where continual buying would artificially raise the share price, so allowing those then selling to make a handsome profit, but the circumstances suggest this was unlikely.[3]

What we do know is that those involved realized that Forbes would never support such an apparently speculative scheme unless he were under pressure to do so, and that meant exercising a significant amount of voting power. In the name of the Bloomsbury Syndicate, large quantities of cheap District stock were purchased, with the inevitable result that the price went up. The District had over £4 million of voting stock and by September the syndicate owned nearly £750,000 of ordinary stock which, whilst quite insufficient to exert control, was more than enough to capture the attention of the directors.

Pond then wrote to the District board explaining the proposal and offering £1 million to finance the construction of the deep level line and other improvements. Pond claimed to represent an unheard of group calling itself the Metropolitan District Railway Shareholders Association but he did not indicate this was the Bloomsbury Syndicate, which owned the newly-acquired shares purchased just for this purpose. Pond proposed to pay cash for £1 million 4% District Second Preference stock not liable to pay any interest until the 5% Preference Stock had been paid and a 5 per cent dividend paid on the ordinary stock. Since the District had rarely paid anything at all on its ordinary stock, this seemed a very high-risk proposal since the prospect of making any return seemed to be absurdly low. On discovering the terms *The Railway Times* called them ridiculous and that anyone investing only £100 would be an imbecile.[4]

Pond disclosed some of the principal shareholders involved, who included the stockbroker Murray Griffith and entrepreneur Whitaker Wright. Four other major buyers were associates of Pond, and the stockbroker, a gentleman called Welbore Ellis, had shares in his own right. On the basis of the proposal and its influential backers a meeting was quickly arranged with the District directors who agreed to have a proper engineering survey undertaken by the eminent engineer Sir Benjamin Baker (though the Association was expected to meet the cost—perhaps to see if they were serious). We shall deal with the engineering survey shortly but, suffice to say here, Forbes felt compelled to run with the scheme and see where it went, notwithstanding personal doubts.

While the deep-level scheme took its course during 1896-7 Pond carried on purchasing more District stock. It then emerged that some of the syndicate had been buying and selling this stock to line their own pockets and when it was discovered that Ellis himself had been dealing on his own account, to the disadvantage of the others, Whitaker Wright and Murray Griffith, both clearly major players, cashed up and left the syndicate.* During this time Forbes watched with interest, suggesting to other shareholders that Pond and his anonymous association were unlikely candidates to fund a new railway, even if the scheme were viable. We must note that while events were unfolding Pond was still on the stage. He presented his 'Shylock' at the Duke of York's on 25th June 1896 for charity, he played the lead role as Othello at Covent Garden Theatre on 30th July 1896 and parts in three more Shakespeare plays for a charity presentation at Charing Cross Hospital on 28th November. The bemused Forbes must have known how his challenger was spending his time.

It was necessary to obtain parliamentary powers for the line, for which submitting a bill involved substantial costs. Forbes insisted that the association should pay for this (as offered in its letter) and so prove its ability to raise the capital, but events took a different turn.

During October 1896, Ellis discovered that Pond was an undischarged bankrupt in the name of Zachariah Pattle and had formally changed his name to Pond in July 1887—though there is some evidence this was his earlier (and more satisfactory) stage name anyway.† This made Ellis nervous about further dealing and whether he was going to get paid a large sum already owed by the syndicate, effectively run by Pond. Whether this was material to what happened next we shall probably never know, but the day after Forbes had put Pond on the spot about paying for the parliamentary expenses, Ellis, without telling Pond, told Forbes he could probably find the money himself. In any event the parliamentary notice went in and Ellis paid a contribution on his own account. Ellis meanwhile sold a large shareholding to recover cash spent, much to Pond's annoyance, and each attempted to sue the other, Ellis coming out of things slightly better. This raised some fascinating technical points of law that went all the way to the House of Lords.

By 1897 Pond was no longer the force he had been, but this did not discourage him from becoming a frequent and vocal thorn in Forbes's side. The syndicate still held an amount of District stock, so he had to be heard, and it is reasonable to suppose he wanted it to do well so he could maximise its gain when he eventually sold it, though in fact the price remained stubbornly unresponsive and he probably got little more back than he paid, and perhaps a little less.

---

* Murray Griffith later became a long standing and much respected District shareholder, whilst Whitaker Wright was found guilty of fraud in a quite unconnected matter and poisoned himself.

† *The Era*, 5th June 1886, for example, finds him under the name Pond playing the Sea Captain in 'Twelfth Night' at *The Gaiety*. Prior to 1880 Pond (then Pattle) was a member of the stock exchange but got badly into debt. Made bankrupt, his debts were liquidated in 1880, and eventually the whole £9000 or so was fully paid. He went back into business as financier in 1889 at 31 Lombard St. He took over a coal concession in Mexico (which attracted some other business too) but they didn't work out and he was bankrupted again.

Pond campaigned by means of circulars seeking support, presenting his ideas and castigating the directors. At shareholder meetings he criticized the way the company was run and highlighted its shortcomings. He was vocal about Forbes's inability to focus on the District's problems because of his involvement in so many other businesses. He attempted to put his own choice of directors forward instead of re-electing long-standing directors that did nothing. Some of these encounters were heated and very bad tempered, but Pond was invariably put in his place by Forbes. Actually Pond did have support for some of his ideas and even Murray Griffith (the District's largest shareholder) was sometimes supportive, but the immovable Forbes was dismissive and was backed by the much-respected Robert Perks (Murray Griffith's cousin) who reminded shareholders of all the good things the existing board had done.

Pond made a conciliatory speech at the February 1899 meeting and referred to certain changes the District had made, including various station improvements, which he approved of. Pond did not appear at the August 1899 meeting, and we hear no more of him. Was he and his ephemeral shareholders' association really so content? District shares had mysteriously rallied towards the end of December 1898 rising from 29 on 22nd November to nearly 35 on 29th November. Some of this was put down to buying by the London & Globe Finance Corporation (under Whitaker Wright's control), but the existence of a wider clique was mooted. District stock remained at around this level through much of December, though heavy buying and selling made it volatile. On 23rd December the *Financial Times* suggested recent movement was not being controlled by Pond, and that Pond and his syndicate had sold out two weeks earlier, presumably profiting on the stock built up over the previous three years. The most recent buying had been by brokers acting for some of the larger railways, and District prices continued to creep up.

District Railway Share Buy Price (date reported)

1 Feb 96	28	2 May 96	29	1 Aug 96	28
1 Nov 96	32	1 Feb 97	28¼	1 May 97	29
31 Jul 97	30	1 Nov 97	30	29 Jan 98	31¼
1 May 98	27¼	30 Jul 98	30¼	29 Oct 98	27½
28 Jan 99	34¾	29 Apr 99	39¾	29 July 99	32¼

After this, Pond found his talents were best directed towards the stage. He died on 15th October 1931, having spent thirty years or so both as a reputable actor and as a music hall artist where he wrote and played a cockney character of his own devising, which was well-regarded but not very lucrative. His obituary indicated he was good company with an eager, droll and original mind and a good raconteur. He had much to reveal.

The Main Line Railways look to the District

While Pond and others were trying to energize the District, other interests saw an opportunity. During 1899 several of the main line railways, having observed the District's studied inaction, came to the conclusion that the line might be more successful as a conduit for their own trains (doing, in fact, what had originally been proposed in 1864). The idea was for the Great Central Railway (GCR), Great Western Railway (GWR), London, Chatham & Dover Railway (LCDR) and South Eastern Railway (SER) to lease the District jointly. The District was already in communication with south London railways via the East London Railway (ELR) and the then-authorized Whitechapel & Bow Railway (W&BR) would give access with east London. New east- and west-facing curves at Victoria would link with the LCDR. The GWR (and via that railway the GCR) would make a connection with the District near Acton. Cross-London paths for suburban and freight traffic would be shared amongst the lessees. By May, the idea became blighted by the feeling that Parliament would never allow such an arrangement and that in the meantime an attempt should be made to put main line directors on the District board. The timing was not good, for by coincidence others were now looking to do the same thing, as we shall see shortly. There is evidence that certain main lines were buying up District shares; these were probably those shares released by Pond and friends and the purchases were rumoured to be the cause of their rising price, but no more was heard of the scheme.[5]

Forbes must have been involved in all this from his control of the LCDR, and its association with the SER, and the idea was explained to the shareholders in vague but verbose terms in March 1899, though he described discussions as confidential; it was only with prompting Forbes mentioned in August that he 'thought' discussions were still taking place 'from time-to-time', hinting that the impetus was no longer very great.[6]

The long term impact on the District would have been tremendous. Clearly, the operation of many foreign through-trains, all steam-hauled, would have greatly impacted on the electrification options. It is very questionable whether the District would have had the capacity for all this, and the thought of busy flat junctions at Victoria is intriguing. The scheme was intended to benefit the main lines, apparently without thought of the consequences for the existing traffic. We can only speculate what this scheme would have done for the future of the London Underground.

A Deep Level District

We must now return to the District's deep level line, initiated by Pond but quickly shifting beyond his control: we re-join it at the point Benjamin Baker was asked to investigate the scheme from the technical point of view. It was perhaps a surprise to Forbes that Baker's report was so positive and it put him in a difficult position. Forbes did not believe the tube scheme was sensible and thought that there was no alternative to electrification of the whole District system which, when done, would render the deep level line unnecessary. On the other hand there was clearly pressure to be seen to be doing something and the opportunity for a large amount of affordable funding could hardly be turned down unless it could be demonstrated beyond doubt that the syndicate was unable to do as it claimed (he referred to the whole scheme as a chimera). He therefore played along with the proposal, no doubt waiting for the syndicate to falter, which it did.

The report about the route and how it might be delivered was dated 13th October 1896. It was tight timing to get everything ready so that a bill might be submitted in November, but this was achieved and parliamentary powers were obtained without much difficulty in August 1897. Wisely, the Act also authorised electrification of all or any part of the District Railway and those parts jointly owned with the Met (with its consent). The Met was not then seeking electrification powers and it may have appeared there was a real risk of the District being forced by circumstances to electrify to Mansion House, but not beyond, and also having to endure the Inner Circle's steam trains west of Mansion House. To say this would have been unsatisfactory would hardly describe matters and with this prospect very real, it made sense to have a quite separate all-electric route to the City available as a 'plan B'.

The initial scheme was for a completely independent railway with stations beneath the existing ones at Earls Court, Charing Cross (Victoria had been considered instead) and Mansion House. Baker considered that it would be better if trains rose to the surface just east of Earls Court, and that a connection be made with the existing system, allowing through trains to operate. At this stage, through operation appeared to call for the steam locomotives to be exchanged for electric ones at Earls Court, depending on what additional parts of the District were electrified. Changing locos in the platforms would have caused intolerable delays and he suggested building a 176yd-long covered way near the deep-level tunnel mouths and changing the locos there. The location was on a gradient and Baker proposed the train braking be augmented by some kind of rack brake system at this point. It seems always to have been intended to build the tubes at a size of around 12ft 6ins, so if through trains to the District's western branches were to be run, tube-type rolling stock would have to be used throughout. How this was to be achieved with existing steam locomotives was not gone into. East of Earls Court, the opportunity to run express trains to the West End and City would have reduced running times enormously and been a very attractive alternative to the omnibus and rival tube upstarts preying on what the District felt was its own traffic.

Baker described the line beginning about half way between Earls Court and Gloucester Road and falling at 1:42 for about 300yds, partly under Cromwell Road before taking up the line of the District, above. At Charing Cross the deep level would be about 63ft beneath the existing line, and at Mansion House 71ft. Hydraulic lifts and stairs would link the two District platform levels and existing station buildings and entry and exit stairs would be used. The suggested rolling stock would comprise ten 'full-powered' electric locomotives and 80 long American-type carriages; it was expected to operate eight trains in service and land would be required for the shops and stabling yard necessary. A generating station would be needed, as close to Earls Court as possible, and the land in the triangle west of Gloucester Road was recommended if covenants concerning its use permitted it.[7]

Costs were expected to be: Tunnelling £745,440, track £30,860, stations £25,000, contingency £80,100, land £118,600, electrical installation and rolling stock £264,000, professional fees £189,000; this totals £1,453,000.

The main departure between the Baker plan and the line as authorized was to build the power station in Fulham. The Act scheduled three possible sites. One was adjacent to Walham Green station, another comprised land close to Parsons Green station, and the third was on land at Eel Brook Common. The Act allowed the District to raise £1.2 million for the deep level line and £500,000 for electrification and general improvements on the rest of the line. Despite flexibility being given in terms of what kind of shares could be issued, the reality was that, with the Bloomsbury Syndicate having fizzled out, the District would have great difficulty in raising any money through shares as it was still unable to service much of its existing shareholding adequately, or at all. It was the worst of all positions to be in. Without modernization the District was effectively doomed at some point, but piling on more debt to that already incurred (and which was already crippling) required more than an act of faith that all would come good at some point in the future.

Rival Tube Threats

1897 was a busy year for tube schemes and, as Pond had suggested, schemes were emerging that had an adverse bearing on the future of the District. One of these was a very grave threat: this was the City & West End Railway (C&WER), which proposed a deep level tube railway between Hammersmith and Cannon Street via Kensington High Street, Piccadilly Circus and Fleet Street. It was arguably a better route than the District and would have siphoned off a great deal of traffic even without factoring in that it would be a clean, smoke-free environment. The line was to have had a depot and power station at Hammersmith and the promoters had gained experience with their involvement in the Central London Railway, another excellent route, then under construction.

Yet another new tube promoted in the same session was the Brompton & Piccadilly Circus Railway (BPCR), proposing a line from South Kensington to Air Street, near Piccadilly Circus. No running connection was contemplated with the District (or the deep level line) and the platforms were to be east of Exhibition Road, under Thurloe Street, a little to the north of the District tracks. A station building was to be erected at the south end of Exhibition Road and a passenger connection was planned between the new tube and the District by means of the Exhibition subway, which passed nearly above the end of the projected tube. Interchange was planned at Piccadilly with another proposed tube line and a 3-minute train service was conjectured at busy times and 5-minutes at others. A power station was planned on the banks of the Thames in Fulham, at Chelsea Creek, and this will become important later. This was to be linked to the new tube by means of an extremely long duct (the word 'pipeline' is used in the Act) running under the streets from the power station at Lots Road to South Kensington.

The BPCR was no threat to the District and was thought likely to help develop traffic as well as discouraging further tube schemes in the vicinity; to this end the District was disposed to support the BPCR wholeheartedly and oppose the C&WER; it would be very unlikely both schemes would have been permitted owing to the long common section of route. This prognosis was entirely correct and the BPCR was authorized in August 1897 with the other scheme thrown out.

It was hoped the line would be built for £385,000 by Mr George Talbot, who had built part of the Central London Railway, and who expected to complete the civil engineering in 2½ years; a provisional contract had been entered into on that basis. Track, signalling and rolling stock would cost £144,000. The chairman was Charles Grey Mott, who was the power behind the City & South London Railway, over whose station at King William Street the BPCR offices were located.

The BPCR was authorized to raise £600,000 in £10 shares and subscribers were sought in July 1898, but the response was rather poor and the company decided not to allot any shares. Soon afterwards, the District took advantage of the situation and agreement was soon reached for the District to take practical control. On 25th November 1898 most of the Brompton directors were replaced by District directors, Forbes taking the chair.* The agreement was ratified in the BPCR's 1899 Act, which also authorized the District to subscribe £200,000 of the £400,000 additional capital now felt required.

Importantly, the 1899 Act authorized the BPCR to build a connecting line between the District deep level route east of South Kensington to meet the BPCR under Thurloe Square; this would enable through electric trains from Earls Court to proceed either to Piccadilly or to Mansion House.

As electrification of the whole of the District became more likely, albeit painfully slowly, so the utility of the original District deep level scheme became marginalized. More useful were the prospects of through a tube route from Earls Court to Piccadilly using part of the deep level line and the BPCR; this might generate extra traffic whilst helping to fend of potential competition. The District renewed its BPCR powers in 1900 but an attempt to extend the line to Angel in the 1901 Session was thwarted by a legal technicality.

We will see shortly what use was to be made of the District's interest in this line.

* The exception was Sir Joseph Dimsdale, who stayed on to serve the new board.

The Metropolitan Factor

The Metropolitan was in nothing like the same dire financial position as the District, but had some similar challenges. Within central London its railways were of similar character to the District, but were even older. Importantly, the threats to traffic being lost to more up-to-date rivals was just as acute and the public was already complaining vocally about filthy, overcrowded accommodation. Doing nothing was not an option. But the Met was of a very different character to the District outside the inner circle and its connecting lines and by 1897 comprised a trunk route extending well beyond Aylesbury and with plans for developments elsewhere. The Met therefore concentrated on how to electrify the inner area but always with an eye to extension much farther out, which the same electrification system might have to cater for—there could hardly be two systems. Powers for electrification were obtained in 1898.

This was mixed news for the District. On the one hand it meant the whole of the inner circle and other joint sections could be electrified, overcoming the risk of entertaining mixed operation, but on the other it meant having to come to terms with the Met about the technical detail of electrification as, clearly, each company's trains would have to be able to operate over the other's lines.

With electrification now inevitable, on 26th May 1898 the District board authorized the appointment of two specialists to go into the details of what was required. With Met agreement, it was now felt necessary to carry out experiments jointly to determine the best system and to identify and resolve the issues that would need to be overcome. The consultants were Sir John Wolfe Barry and William Preece*, who were to represent both companies. £20,000 was authorized to pay for the experiments, half to be paid by each company. At this stage it was imagined that it would cost about £500,000 to electrify the whole of the District.

The Great Experiment

The *Railway Times* observed towards the end of 1898 that Forbes was at last showing evidence of action after years of procrastination. One factor had been a lengthy coal strike and lockout in South Wales during 1898. The District had always used the best quality coal to reduce the level of smoke and fumes to the bare minimum, but during the strike coal prices had shot up and they had to make use of indifferent coal. As a result the stations and tunnels became choked with fumes, describes as 'abnormally disagreeable', and felt to be making passengers switch to the buses.

As neither railway had direct experience of electric working, the consulting engineers suggested it would be helpful to find out what the best system would be, given the limited British experience at that time. The plan was to carry out experiments between Earls Court and High Street Kensington, each company contributing £10,000 towards the costs. This 1500-yard section was representative of the challenges to be faced, but was not heavily used and in the event of mishap the consequences could be confined to a limited area.

To assist them, the consultants employed the engineer Thomas Parker and the Electric Construction Company (with which he was associated) to arrange for and carry out the installation of equipment. Parker had supplied all the electrical equipment for the successful Liverpool Overhead Railway, which began operation in February 1893, and

* William Preece was electrician and engineer in chief to the Post Office and Sir John Wolfe Barry an eminent consulting engineer (one of whose clients was the Metropolitan Railway). Preece became a Knight Commander of the Order of the Bath in the 1899 Birthday honours.

had just been awarded the contract for the electrical work on the City & South London Railway extension. Some elements of the press were hostile to the idea of experiments and wondered why the companies just didn't get on with the main job, but the response was that it was important to discover how to electrify an existing line where access was going to be very limited, as well as to determine what equipment was suitable. Shareholders were told that one of the complications was the need to accommodate the trains of other railways, which would be steam hauled, at least for a while: it was not a matter to be rushed into, shareholders were told, with no irony intended. It was not even clear whether the District would be better off with electric locomotives or one of the technically more advanced systems that did not need locomotives.

What happened next is not known precisely, but the practical effect was that on 10th November 1898 the Met board asked Parker to undertake quite separate experiments for them. The District board minutes suggest that (for some reason) Parker had withdrawn from the joint scheme at Earls Court, following which the consulting engineers instead appointed Siemens Brothers & Co, of Woolwich. Parker undertook electrification experiments at Wembley Park using a disused contractor's railway leading to the part-built Wembley Park tower. Current was obtained by using power from a steam engine, mounted on blocks, which was connected to a dynamo. A trial electric trip for the Met's directors was held as early as 24th October 1899, long before the Earls Court experiment was ready. The Met was sufficiently impressed with Parker to retain his services for some years.

There is little evidence of intimate co-operation between the Met and District in this period since not only did Parker, as a result of his Wembley experiments, make a formal recommendation to the Met in December 1899 about how they should proceed with electrification but the Met board, in February 1900, agreed Parker should co-operate with Messrs Westinghouse to survey the railway and obtain estimates—all before the so-called joint experiment at Earls Court had even started.

The District had been less put out by the change in electrical contractor and acquiesced to the installation of twin conductor rails along the chosen section, one either side of (and slightly higher than) the running rails. The use of four rails rather than three was due to the speed with which they could be laid. Four rails avoided unnecessary bonding of the existing running rails to accommodate return current, with the attendant risk of electrical leakage and interference with the telegraph circuits it would cause, neither being worth tackling for a mere experiment. Electrification using direct current was then felt the only practicable system, and the only one in which there was already appropriate experience. Although the technical press, as early as November 1898, stated that the two conductor rails would become part of the 'permanent' installation, it was decided quite quickly that on any final system one of the two current rails would be centrally located between the running rails; this could not be done for this experiment as it would foul the apparatus of the Railway (previously Station) Indicator Company which hung below the carriages to make contact with the treadles used to update the on-board train indicators.

The conductor rails were of 75lb per yard channel section and made of a form of mild steel that had improved conductivity. These rails were carried on porcelain insulators fixed to the sleeper ends and were described as being 'of telegraph pattern', probably because these were easily available. A piece of leather was interposed between the insulator and underside of the rail to reduce vibration and insulators with anchors were placed every 100 yards to prevent the current rails creeping.

Plans were prepared, and contracts let, before year end, with installation work taking place during 1899, at an apparently leisurely pace. Final costs were £25,700, each company paying half even though the estimate had been exceeded.

A 6-coach train was ordered from Brown, Marshalls & Co to which was fitted electric traction equipment by Siemens, the two railways each owning half of the train. The end vehicles were motor coaches equipped with driving cabs, weighed 54 tons and carried four traction motors each. The intermediate four coaches, weighing 18 tons each, were of ordinary construction with compartments. Only the leading coach was under power in either direction, the rear car being hauled dead. Each train was designed to seat 312 passengers (80 first, 96 second and 136 third class), though it is doubtful if they were ever called upon to do so during the experiment. Internally, electric lighting was employed, using incandescent lamps connected in groups of four-in-series across the traction supply.

The four compartment type coaches were made 3-inches wider than ordinary District coaches and were comfortably set out, though the third class smoking compartments lacked seat cushions. The end coaches were built as small saloons as the large driving wheels made the conventional door arrangement impossible; these coaches also had compartments for the driver and guard.

The heart of the equipment was the controller at each end of the train. It was mounted centrally in the cab and was bulky, having to carry the whole traction load (*The Electrician* described it as resembling the steering wheel of a small yacht). It had twelve power positions, but only three of them were ordinary running positions, the remainder were for the accelerating stages only. The three running positions were: all motors in series; or, two pairs of motors in series with each series pair paralleled; or, all motors in parallel. The cab was equipped with more instruments than was later considered usual, but this was primarily to assist the engineers monitor train performance as part of the experiment.

This shows the type of generator used at Warwick Road. The 3-cylinder Belliss engine (at rear) drove the dynamo via a large flywheel. The dynamo was of Siemens HB27/40 type considered very suitable for railway work. These sets were known for their constant speed in spite of very variable load. *Electrical Review* 16th June 1899

Looking east at Earls Court, the experimental electric train is about to depart towards High Street Kensington. The rear motor car is idle, the front car providing all the power. *Tramway & Railway World*, Author's collection

Each Siemens motor was built onto an axle of the motor car and was rated at 110hp, though intended to provide a maximum of 200hp when required. The train was fitted with fourteen spring-loaded collector shoes, seven (positive) along one side and seven (negative) along the other; all the shoes along each side were electrically connected by buslines running along the length of the train and the train could draw power if only a single shoe of each pole was in contact with the conductor rail. The need to provide pickup shoes on each carriage was to make sure traction current was always available, particularly over all the gaps at Earls Court (the longest being 225ft). The equipment was capable of accelerating the train at 1¼ mph per second at the lower end of the speed range, but the small power plant could not sustain this in the full parallel position. The maximum speed obtained was about 38mph.

The train was fitted with sanding apparatus whereby sand could be blown under the wheels as required. This used the same air supply as the brakes, the compressed air produced by pumps (found to be rather noisy and soon replaced). Ordinary steam drivers were employed to do the driving, those selected quickly becoming proficient in using the electrical equipment.

This shows one of the spring-loaded pick-up shoes on one of the cars, making contact with the channel-section current rail. Vertical movement of the shoe is constrained by the vertical slot. The mechanism is apparently slung from a pair of insulators attached to a substantial mounting attached to the axle box.
The King 2nd June 1900

Electric power was supplied from generating plant near Warwick Road, about 250yds west Earls Court station (next to the pump house). The installation was only ever intended to be temporary and was housed in a corrugated iron shed. Inside were two Babcock & Wilcox water tube boilers feeding steam at 160lb per square inch to a pair of directly coupled Belliss-Siemens generators each capable of generating 360hp.* The maximum output was 385 Amps at 550 volts dc and power was fed to the end of the conductor rails outside the power station. A steam ejector was used in order to carry away the smoke from the boilers to minimize inconvenience to people living nearby. This was a wholly inefficient way of delivering electricity as the power station had to be in steam whenever the electric service was running, but was only called upon to deliver current for about three minutes in every twenty. Without any general system of electricity supply in the area, it was all that could be done.

Trials of the equipment and trains are first known on the night of 7-8th November 1899 and were repeated on other nights (and during the Sunday church interval) when trains were not running.[8] Tests during traffic hours began in February 1900, the first run being made on 8th of that month. The train operated as required between Earls Court and the District side of High Street Kensington. Board of Trade inspectors, Colonels Trotter and Yorke, inspected the installation on 3rd April and gave formal approval on 2nd May. Although there was a press run on 18th May, it was only three days later that

* The steam engines were Belliss type TEC4 coupled to Siemens 2-pole drum-wound generators described as 27x40 and the same type used by the recently opened Waterloo & City Railway.

Above: **The experimental train in the siding running alongside the curve between Earls Court and High Street. On the right, the triangle of land (formerly brickworks) is entirely wild and was for some years let out for growing trees and shrubs.** *The Electrician*, 25 May 1900

Below: **View at north side of Cromwell Road triangle looking towards High Street Kensington. On left is the siding, on extreme right (just visible) are the Met's tracks and Cromwell Curve 'A' signal box is ahead with Cromwell Curve itself just behind the box making its junction at the tunnel mouth.** *The Electrician*, 25 May 1900

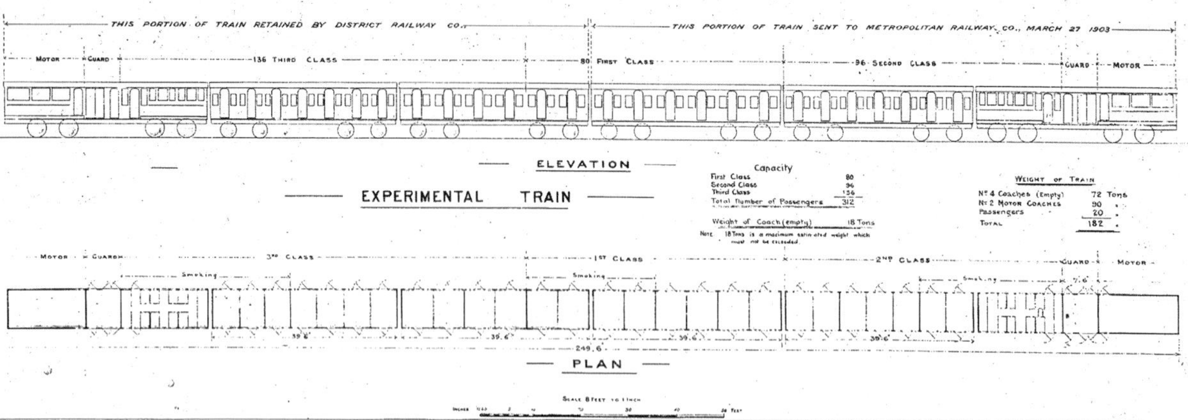

Above: **Diagram of the experimental electric train showing general arrangement.** Author's collection

Below: **Diagram of the motor car showing the driving compartment and controller (at left) and saloon (behind) with under-floor equipment.** *The Electrical Engineer* 25th May 1900

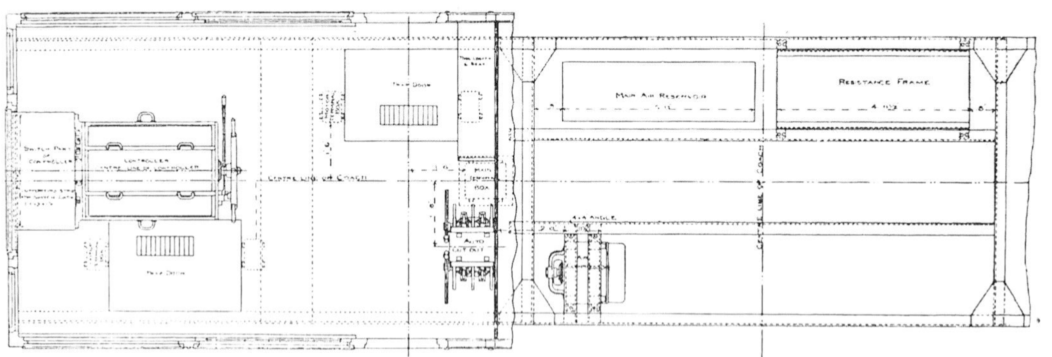

FIG. 5.—Plan of Locomotive, showing Position of Controlling Gear.

the train actually entered passenger service, after which it ran daily. An attempt was made to charge a shilling for its use, but the public felt this exorbitant and after only a week ordinary fares were again charged.* The electric service was withdrawn from 6th November, the trials having evidently proved successful, but the working expenses were too high to warrant continued running.

William Preece (Sir William from June 1899) remarked to the press that the testing had included starting the train on the 1:43 gradient, which it achieved effortlessly; Preece was sure that a steam locomotive with a similar load could not have done this. Intriguingly, he also referred to a tug-of-war that had been arranged between the electric train and a steam locomotive, the latter being very much the loser.

* Normal fares were 2d, 3d or 4d depending on class.

A very rare image of the passenger compartment within one of the 1900 motor cars. This was a second class car but is still quite plush. *The King* 2nd June 1900

While testing was in hand, the Met instructed Parker to inspect the trial installation and make a detailed report to its board, the inspection taking place on 9th June. Parker's report, penned the same day, expressed some unease caused partly by not being able to inspect everything he had hoped. His main concern was the weight of the train, which was about half as heavy again as comparable Liverpool equipment capable of carrying the same load. He felt this would proportionately increase electricity consumption and needlessly waste power station fuel. In addition he understood the unsprung weight on the motor axles of the experimental train would be about 8½ tons compared with 3½ tons on the Liverpool cars and this would be ruinously destructive to the track. He also thought the amount of potential passenger space taken up by the equipment was excessive and was not clear how the current rail potential was going to be maintained at +250 and -250 volts (to minimise risk of electric shock) without it becoming a 3-wire system requiring rail bonding.[9] These observations caused some concern to the Met directors and required Wolfe Barry and Preece to respond, apparently addressing the suggested shortcomings to everyone's satisfaction, given it was only an experimental system.

ORDINARY CARRIAGE OF THE EXPERIMENTAL ELECTRIC TRAIN OF THE METROPOLITAN DISTRICT RAILWAY.

Elevations of the trailer carriage and motor carriage used in the electrification experiments: the latter shows the enormous size of the driver's compartment. Author's collection

MOTOR CARRIAGE CONSTRUCTED FOR THE EXPERIMENTAL ELECTRIC TRAIN OF THE METROPOLITAN DISTRICT RAILWAY.

At about the same time, the District board felt the test should be enlarged by extending the electric tracks to Putney Bridge. Unfortunately, when this was investigated, the power station was considered unable to handle the larger load required and, together with the additional rails, would cost a further £15,000, so the matter was dropped.

Once the tests had been completed, the District put the cars away somewhere. There seems to have been no great hurry to do anything more with them and it was not until March 1903 that the District's engineer reported that he had recently handed over the Met's three cars at High Street Kensington.* The three District carriages went to Mill Hill Park works where the electrical equipment was removed and the vehicles sold to the Colne Valley & Halstead Railway (which became part of the LNER in 1923); the carriages are known to have been tested on the Colne Valley railway on 22nd October 1906 and at least two

* The Met's cars were: a third class motor car, a third class trailer and a composite trailer. The two trailer cars were adapted for locomotive haulage and became part of the Metropolitan's carriage fleet.

One of the experimental 1900 District coaches at the end of its life at Stratford Works in 1953 (it had been seen in service in Cromer the previous year). It entered service on Colne Valley & Halstead Railway in April 1908. Author's collection

lasted long enough to be taken over by British Railways upon nationalization. The vehicles were refitted and Stone's electric lighting was installed after which the two bogie carriages became for some years the mainstay of the passenger service and the former motor car was used as a van.

Next Steps

In the meantime the Met and District formed an Electric Traction Joint Committee, comprising six members, half from each of the two railways.* Its initial purpose was to review the results of the experiments but it was continued in order to make recommendations and supervise the selection of suitable contractors. In late summer, it was in a position to issue tenders for a complete electrification system.

While the experiment was still in hand, the consulting engineers began thinking about how the wider system might be electrified, the logistics of doing this being complicated. On 20th August they produced a report recommending the railway be electrified in stages beginning by gradual introduction of electric trains on the Inner Circle service and then gradually substituting electric locomotives for steam on the other services. This, of course, meant retaining existing coaching stock, some of which was elderly. Events were to take a dramatic change of course.

Anticipating that the trial would be a success and that electrification was imminent the District applied for powers during the 1899-1900 Session to construct its power station and lay in the necessary supply mains. By now the company had concluded that the three sites it had already earmarked as possible locations in its 1897 Act were not suitable and

* The members were: J.S. Forbes, Sir Charles Dalrymple and Major Isaacs from the District, and Captain Davey, Colonel Mellor and Charles McLaren from the Metropolitan.

that the location selected by the unbuilt Brompton & Piccadilly Circus Railway was much better. This was adjacent to Chelsea Creek, in the strip of land bordered on the north by Lots Road. Use was subject to some or all the land not actually being needed by the BPCR, but since that company was now owned by the District this was not a problem. The location was remote from the District's network so powers were also needed for a cable tunnel to convey the high tension mains to Earls Court; this was authorized to run via Lots Road, Kings Road, Gunter Grove, Finborough Road and Warwick Road, the cables being encased in cast-iron 'boxes' 15 inches by 9 inches, laid 2ft beneath the streets (the mains were eventually laid very differently). An alternative route was also authorized alongside the West London Extension Railway (WLR) between the power station and West Brompton where the main (which had to cross under Chelsea Creek) was to be laid in hermetically sealed pipes at the margin of the railway's property, but the District always seemed less keen on this option. The advantages of the new site were ability to bring in sea-borne coal by barge and ability to use cooling water from the creek.[10]

Which System?

It is perhaps revealing that while the experimental train was being tested the editor of the *Railway Magazine* travelled on it as a guest and asked about Sprague's multiple unit system of electrical control, already successfully in use in the USA. He was surprised to discover that none of the engineers present had heard of it.[11] The systems had been fully described in contemporary international engineering journals and this suggests a degree of British inward looking that might have influenced the way the specification for an electrified system was written, evidently not taking into account existing technology let alone emerging technology, as we shall see.

The specification for full-scale electrification required a significant speeding up of services and much-improved headways. At this stage, either a 3-rail or 4-rail direct current system was considered equally suitable, but while it was obvious electricity could be utilized to great advantage there were various different systems available and neither party wished to prejudge the best equipment to adopt. The joint committee was finally in a position to go out to tender on what it described as a non-prescriptive basis and sent out invitations on 3rd August 1900. It considered the responses on 3rd December.

The essential requirement to be met was that 220 train-miles per hour be operated by trains covering the 13 miles around the inner circle in 50 minutes including 27 stops. This was equivalent (so we are told) to sixteen trains of a capacity of 430 per train but they would have to interwork with other trains that would not necessarily be electric. The number 430 corresponds approximately to the existing steam stock. Sixteen trains implies eight in each direction, approximating to a 6-minute service. It is not at all clear how the trains to the District branches were to be handled and this would perhaps have been achieved by a variation to the inner circle tender once agreement with the Met had been reached about the system to be adopted.

Compliant proposals were received from:[12]

British Companies

1. The Electric Construction Company Ltd

This was the company with which Thomas Parker was associated, with roots dating back to 1889. The company was involved in heavy electrical engineering and equipped and operated the electric Liverpool Overhead Railway.

The ECC proposed a 5-wire direct current system of the type used on the City & South London Railway (CSLR). One conductor rail would be provided on each track, one 600V positive and the other track 600V negative, producing 1200V between the conductors and maintaining the running rails more or less at earth potential. Two 'outer' conductors would be at a 2400V potential and motor-generators would keep the whole lot in balance (the high outer voltages were to minimise losses). Substations would be needed at South Kensington (or Gloucester Road), Edgware Road, Farringdon Street and Blackfriars. Current would also be supplied directly at the power station, and batteries were proposed to augment the supply. Locomotive haulage was proposed, with retention of existing carriages.

2. Dick, Kerr & Co Ltd

This was a Scottish company with offices in London and was a combination of interests dating back to 1883. The company was involved in heavy engineering as well as electrical work and more recently had become involved with tramways. The company had constructed some motor cars in 1899 for the Waterloo & City Railway. Dick, Kerr were the sole agents for the English Electric Manufacturing Company.

This company proposed that current should be generated at Chelsea Creek at 5000V and distributed to three substations for conversion to 500V. Current would be picked up either from a single conductor rail (with running rail return) or by two conductor rails (the proposal suggested one could be situated above the other one at side of the track). It was proposed to use three motor and three trailer cars, using the multiple unit system.

3. Brush Electrical Engineering Co Ltd

This was established in 1880 as an electrical engineering firm to work certain American patents in the UK. It was heavily involved in lighting and power supply apparatus and then moved into tramway engineering. It later expanded into production of tramcars and railway carriages.

This curious proposal involved a stud contact system where a conducting strip would be affixed to the sleepers and a large brush would make contact with it as the train progressed. Presumably one or more brushes would have been connected electrically to ensure a continuous supply of current. We can only guess at how pointwork would have been negotiated. A 3-wire distribution arrangement was proposed with 750V at the studs and 1500V between the outers (the centre wire, or return, being at earth potential). Two generating stations (Chelsea and Kings Cross) would feed at 1500V and no substations were required, though small booster stations might have been necessary, as on the CSLR. Locomotives would be used with existing carriages.

Brush was very uncomfortable putting forward a priced proposal based on details it had to work out itself and hoped its bid would be regarded as an estimate and that a proper specification would then be given. They were not successful.

4. British Thomson-Houston Co Ltd

This firm was first established in 1886 to work the patents of the Thomson-Houston company of America, later the (American) General Electric Company. After reconstruction in 1896, it took the above name. BTH in the UK was at first heavily controlled by American influences. BTH came to represent major heavy electrical engineering capabilities, including tramways and railways.

BTH proposed to generate centrally at 6500V (3-phase) and distribute to substations at same locations as proposed by ECC, converting to 500V dc. A 3-wire distribution system was proposed with 1000V between outer conductors (one track having conductor rail at +500V and the other at -500V with central earth). The conductor rails were to be arranged as on the Earls Court line, but on each track one of these was at earth potential and bonded to the corresponding conductor on adjacent track. The advantage of doing this was to provide a low resistance return path without having to bond the existing running rails. Substations were proposed at Farringdon Street, Blackfriars, South Kensington and Edgware Road. A 4-motor locomotive was proposed with existing rolling stock.

5. British Westinghouse Electric & Manufacturing Co Ltd

Until 1907, this company was a British subsidiary of the Westinghouse Electric & Manufacturing Company, of Pittsburgh. It was established in the UK in 1899 and was partly (later wholly) British owned. It was intended to exploit in the UK the massive capabilities of Westinghouse in the US. It opened a manufacturing plant in Manchester in 1902 so at the time of bidding for the District electrification the company's UK capabilities were untried.

British Westinghouse also proposed a generating station at Chelsea Creek, generating at 11,000V (3-phase). Current would be distributed at high voltage to substations at Westminster, Baker Street and Aldgate for conversion to 650V dc on the usual 2-wire basis. Either one conductor rail (with running rail return) or twin conductor rails were possible. Completely new open saloon rolling stock with two motor coaches on the multiple unit system, and five trailers, was the preferred solution but it was possible to adapt the proposal to use existing stock if required.

6. Siemens Brothers & Co Ltd, with Mather & Platt Ltd and Thames Electrical Engineering Works (a division of Thames Ironworks, Shipbuilding & Engineering Co Ltd)

Siemens was a very old firm based in Woolwich, the English branch being established in 1858. Although involved in some heavy electrical engineering its main business was in cables, telegraphy and lighting, which led to involvement in power generation and then tramway work. Siemens was responsible for devising and installing the District's trial electric system at Earls Court and had built a small shunting locomotive for the Waterloo & City Railway. Mather & Platt Ltd was a Manchester-based company involved in electrical engineering, which had equipped the original CSLR in 1890. Thames Electrical Engineering Works was based in Blackwall and was part of the Thames Ironworks group of heavy engineers.

Mather & Platt's experience with the CSLR meant it was no surprise to see it, too, proposing a 3-wire system with common wire neutral. Three power stations were proposed, at Chelsea, Wapping and Praed Street (on Paddington canal), and these would directly feed the tracks. Three balancing stations were proposed at High Street Kensington, Kings Cross and Charing Cross, where the usual motor-generator sets would transfer loads from one track to the other if current consumption (and hence track voltages) were unequal. A working pressure of 520V was proposed, supported by batteries. The use of existing rolling stock was proposed with gearless 4-motor locomotives using the same principles as used on the Central London Railway.

Continental Suppliers

7. Ganz & Co, Budapest

Ganz was founded by Abraham Ganz (a Swiss) in Buda, in the Kingdom of Hungary, in 1844, the company developed from an ironworks to a major engineering and shipbuilding company that included electrical engineering, tramway work and railway locomotive and carriage construction. Ganz once employed Nikola Tesla, the famous physicist who invented the polyphase electricity distribution system, and Ganz was an enthusiastic developer of successful 3-phase motors and high voltage distribution systems, and was perhaps somewhat ahead of its time. When the bid was submitted, they had an experimental line in operation using 3-phase induction motors and an overhead wire supply system using two trolley wires.

Ganz proposed generating at 12,000V (3-phase) and distributing to five transformer substations at South Kensington, Praed Street, Kings Cross, Aldgate and Charing Cross. Current would be transformed down to 3000V, still at 3-phase, with one conductor bonded to the running rails and earthed. The other two conductors would form twin overhead catenary wires with current picked up by trolleys or similar devices. It was suggested the existing rolling stock would be used, with new motor coaches at each end of the trains, each carrying four 300hp motors. This was the lowest tender, partly because the substations were inexpensive and few in number and partly because of reuse of the existing stock.

8. O. L. Kummer & Co, Dresden

Oskar Ludwig Kummer, a Prussian naval engineer, began his business near Dresden in 1888 and began producing electrical apparatus, including electric motors; production later expanded to include much heavy electrical engineering work including tramcar apparatus. Having overstretched itself, the company became insolvent in 1901, shortly after expressing interest in the District electrification work.

Kummer proposed to generate at 5000V (three-phase) from a central power house to two substations, at Temple and between High Street and Gloucester Road, where power would be reduced to 600V dc. The supply would be supported by batteries. Trains would comprise two new 4-motor cars at each end using the multiple unit system and existing carriages between. Trains would pick up current from a contact wire somewhere in the '6ft way' via a trolley and return via the running rails.

9. J.G. White & Co Ltd

A company established in London in 1900 to take over the business outside the USA of J.G. White & Co of New York, a firm of electrical engineers and contractors. White was quite active with tramways technology. Proposals from this firm included an association with Frank J Sprague, who devised lift, and then train, control systems used by the latest US lines but not yet in London. White was an engineering consultancy and had no manufacturing capacity and the arrangements by which a fully functioning system would be delivered are not clear.

White proposed generating at 6600V (three phase) centrally and distributing to three (unspecified) substations for transformation to 425V ac and conversion to 650V dc using rotary converters. Trains using the Sprague multiple unit system were recommended and where foreign trains had to be accommodated two motor cars could be coupled back to back to function as a locomotive. The use of existing rolling stock was indicated but it is not clear whether new motor cars would be provided (and it is unlikely there were sufficient existing cars unless new motor cars were provided).

Other companies are reported to have made (non-compliant) bids including Crompton & Co Ltd, Schuckert Electric Co, AEG, Felten & Guilleaume, Brignett Electrique Co, Houtin & Leblanc.[13]

The British Westinghouse proposal consisted of an offer to build the power station, electrify the railway, provide the rolling stock and maintain the whole lot on an ongoing basis as if a contract were in place. So novel was this at the time that Westinghouse applied for parliamentary powers to carry this out, there being doubt about whether they could carry out the scheme without them. Equipment and services would be provided to the District, Met and LSWR over those sections which the District and Met operated. This was also the only bid to include lighting the stations.[14]

Viewing the tenders with a modern eye, some of them are very unadventurous and the proposals to transmit power using lengthy direct current cables seems a bit outdated when the new Central London Railway was using high-voltage alternating current distribution with some success. The idea in some proposals for multiple power stations seems particularly inefficient. The popular idea of using existing rolling stock (some of it by now very old) also seems odd and one wonders if this was done purely to make electrification affordable. Kummer's proposal for a single conductor wire and just two substations must at least be doubtful on technical grounds as the voltage drop would have been tremendous (and would still have been excessive if, as appears possible, a third track feed direct from the power house had been made). The Brush proposal was conceptual with no detail and the company was only geared up to produce equipment to a tight specification and did not want to engage with large scale commercial risk.

The tender responses were considered by the electrification joint committee during December 1900 and by January rumours were already emerging that the favoured contractor was Messrs Ganz with its 3-phase system using overhead wires. The *Railway News* in January 1901 reported that no decision had yet been made but it was already clear that there were credible contractors who could do the job affordably, probably for a lump sum price. This was a formidable line up of electrical contractors, many of whom had proved themselves perfectly competent at electrifying railways. However the technology was developing fast and it took the consulting engineers a full year to come up with a final recommendation.

The two most plausible responses were investigated in detail. One was the Thomson-Houston direct current (dc) system operating at about 600 volts and the other was the Ganz 3000 volt, 25-cycle 3-phase alternating current (ac) system (using twin overhead conductors) from Budapest. On paper this looked an exceedingly good proposal (it was £200,000 cheaper than its rival), but although experiments in Hungary tended to support the theoretical advantages it hadn't yet been installed on a passenger railway anywhere, although an installation was in hand. This was a major concern and, on 9th January 1901, Preece and Wolfe Barry were requested to inspect the trial system in Budapest and at the same time inspect the factory to see whether it was capable of undertaking a work as large as the District's electrification. As a result of this visit, they were fully satisfied that it worked and that Ganz could do the job.

Following the return of the engineers, all six members of the joint committee met on 7th February and agreed to recommend to their respective boards that the Ganz system be adopted and that their tender should be accepted. On 13th March, at another meeting of the committee, a resolution was read from the Met's board that approved the recommendation, together with a draft letter to Messrs Ganz, for consideration by the District. This was discussed and after some adjustment was sent to Ganz on 22nd March. It was, in effect, an acceptance of Ganz's tender subject only to the approval of the Board of Trade, which was required to approve the electrical installation.[15]

The press was excited when, during February, Wolfe Barry resigned, accompanied by rumours (later denied) that the directors declined to accept his advice. In fact, the committee's job was done and the recommendation had been made. Wolfe Barry had just been appointed to Lord Rayleigh's committee looking into the vibration problems on the Central London and was fully occupied.[16]

The next step was for the joint secretaries of the committee to write to the Board of Trade seeking approval for the proposed electrical system, the reply being made on 8th May. This indicated that the officials, on the advice of the chief inspecting officer, could 'support the proposal so far', but the reply then reminded the committee that Major Trotter (of the Inspectorate) had already discussed the Ganz system and felt that he could not make any recommendation until a trial section of the District had been equipped and shown to be satisfactory. In addition, the Board of Trade was only prepared to consider the system for use on the inner circle, and not on any other part of either railway. It may fairly be said that the Board was not very enthusiastic about this new technology, mainly because it was untried in conditions remotely similar to those on the inner circle. The two railway companies knew that Major Trotter had said that if the Ganz system was to be used then he would want to see it tested on a representative piece of line *before* approval was given, so this response cannot have been a surprise. Neither company was keen to spend yet more money equipping a representative experimental section and, more importantly, the delay would be at least six months and more likely a year.

In parallel with the technical discussion, the District attempted to organize finance. The proposal to accept the Ganz tender in January was preceded by an extraordinary general meeting two days earlier at which Forbes (now 78) obtained the authority of his shareholders to issue new ordinary shares for the full £500,000 that Parliament had authorized in 1897, plus another £166,000 in the form of debentures. It is worth recording the sombre mood of the meeting where shareholders knew they were overstretching but, as one shareholder put it, they would probably be in the hands of a receiver anyway within a couple of years.

On the face of it, in May 1901 the District was now poised to embark on a scheme of electrification if it could overcome two major hurdles. First, it had to convince the Board of Trade that using a completely new technology would be safe and prudent and secondly it required people to come forward to buy shares in a barely solvent company seriously over-reaching itself, which even Forbes realized would be very difficult. We will never know how all this would have unfolded because events transpired to completely change this course. It is now necessary to explore what happened and why the required testing of the new technology on the District system did not take place.

Chapter Two

THE AMERICANS

Yerkes in London

The last decade of the nineteenth century coincided with a particularly difficult period for raising large amounts of capital in London. Amongst several unbuilt tube lines, the exasperated promoters of the Charing Cross Euston & Hampstead Railway (usually just called the Hampstead tube), authorized as long previously as 1893, had nearly given up hope of raising the necessary money in Britain. Having been given to understand that capital was more freely available in the US, the promoters, Thomas James Reeves and H.H. Montague Smith,* ventured to Chicago in July 1899 and succeeded in obtaining an appointment with the financier and traction magnate Charles Tyson Yerkes to whom they explained the details underlying the intended tube railway and the difficulty they were having raising capital. Reeves indicated that the promoters would consider selling the rights if Yerkes would commit to building the line and honouring commitments already entered into. Intrigued by the opportunity, Yerkes agreed merely to consider what he had been told.

In fact Yerkes was more than intrigued. He was a regular visitor to London, then the world's largest city (by some way), and he was already familiar with its transport shortcomings and the curious attitude towards improving matters, such as forbidding street-cars (trams) from entering the central area. If the railway could be built at a sensible cost, he could see it should be profitable. He sent a trusted railway expert, Henry C. Davis, to London to investigate the position and after inspecting the route he reported back to Yerkes in encouraging terms. Yerkes then sent his right-hand man, DeLancey Louderback, who made a very detailed examination of the position in March 1900 and he, too, made a very encouraging report indicating that with the restriction on tramways the underground railway would have the traffic to itself. Significantly, he met Sir William Preece who, as already indicated, was one of the specialist engineers looking into the electrification of the District. Louderback

Charles Tyson Yerkes. LTM

* Henry Herbert Montague Smith, a Westminster vestryman with an interest in transport matters (he had been a patentee in connection with rope tramways). Reeves represented a large engineering contractor.

Sir Robert Perks MP in 1902. Author's collection

claimed Preece told him that anyone who obtained good underground franchises would have a gold mine, though this cannot have been supported by much evidence to date.

Suitably encouraged, Yerkes decided to visit London himself. Existing business commitments meant he could not set sail until the end of July, arriving at Southampton on the 26th, amidst rumours (denied at the time) that he had come to consolidate London's railways into a giant electric system. Certainly the visit confirmed his view that he should build the new tube but Davis, who was accompanying him, had arranged for him to meet Robert Perks, who was a large District shareholder (we encountered him earlier). Whether this actually initiated his interest in the District, with its unaffordable but essential electrification plan, seems unlikely, for Yerkes had privately indicated to Montague Smith in 1899 that his interests were wider than the Hampstead tube; it is likely that the meeting with Perks paved the way for progress to be made. By the end of 1900 Yerkes resolved to buy heavily into District Railway shares as the start of the necessary process of gaining control.[1]

Yerkes buys into the District

Yerkes moved rapidly, using in part funds released by sale of his interests in the Chicago elevated railways and buying shares anonymously through the brokers Messel & Co. By February 1901 he had invested $3,000,000 (about £617,000)*; this was a very substantial holding, but not quite sufficient to give him control.

Further shares were bought in an alliance with other investors, notably Perks, and this strengthened Yerkes' position. The *Railway News* for 16th March reported that Yerkes (who had just returned to England) was already claiming to have a controlling interest in the District. It was not until 6th June 1901 a special shareholders' meeting was held at which Yerkes and Perks announced that they were now in control of the company and intended to carry through the long-awaited electrification and modernization plans.† Most of the shareholders enthusiastically approved the proposals, though a small number of xenophobes made clear their dislike of American methods and their railway being turned over to what one shareholder openly claimed to be 'unscrupulous Yankees'.[2]

When Yerkes arrived in March, he brought his engineer, James Russell Chapman, with him to begin examining the technical aspects. Evidently without consulting the District, he was already expressing his view that 'electrolysation' of that railway would be carried

* The equivalent value today might be of the order of £70 million.

† In all, Yerkes bought £500,000 worth of stock at 25 and £450,000 at 35 as well as a substantial holding of second preference stock and debentures.

NUMBER 1

SHARES 10000

THE METROPOLITAN DISTRICT ELECTRIC TRACTION COMPANY, LIMITED.

INCORPORATED UNDER THE COMPANIES ACTS 1862 TO 1900.

CAPITAL £1,000,000

DIVIDED INTO 50,000 SHARES OF £20 EACH.

SHARES £20 EACH.

This is to Certify that Charles Tyson Yerkes of 54 Wall Street New York is the Registered Proprietor of Ten Thousand Shares of £20 each in THE METROPOLITAN DISTRICT ELECTRIC TRACTION COMPANY, LIMITED, numbered 1 to 10,000 inclusive subject to the Memorandum and Articles of Association thereof.

Given under the Common Seal of the said Company this thirtieth day of August 1901.

Directors.

Secretary.

NOTE. No transfer of the shares comprised in this certificate or any portion thereof will be registered until this certificate has been delivered at the company's office.

A share certificate of 30th August 1901 representing one of Yerkes' holdings in the Metropolitan District Electric Traction Co. Photo in Roy Allen Collection

out by British Westinghouse, a firm which, in the UK, acted as agents for America's General Electric company. Yerkes had already despatched a British engineer he was working with to America to study their systems (this was H. F. Parshall, engineer of the Hampstead tube, which Yerkes had acquired). It is evident from all this that Yerkes was not accustomed to hanging about.

The Traction Company

For his part, Yerkes indicated that he would finance the new work entirely and bring over a complete team of American engineers familiar with this kind of modernization as there seemed to be no experience available in Britain. To address the finance issue he established on 15th July 1901 a Metropolitan District Electric Traction Company (MDETC) to build the power station, raise the capital and carry out the works on behalf of the District. It was intended to raise £1 million in the form of 50,000 £20 shares.[3]

Yerkes himself took 16,800 shares, many of which were then allotted to his own business colleagues, including Murray Griffith, now a District director and one who, as we have seen, was pro-electrification (and because of his family connection with Perks he was probably considered reliable). Of the remaining shares only 3150 shares were subscribed for in London, all at first in the hands of Messrs Govett, Sons and Company of Throgmorton Avenue. Just over 30,000 were subscribed for by 25 American business and financial interests (the largest single subscriber, the Maryland Trust of Baltimore, taking 4000 and acting as the clearing house for U.S. transactions). Yerkes became chairman of the traction company* and both he and Perks sold their personal District shareholding to that company (as did some other shareholders). The initial call on the shares was just £5 and by March 1902 there had been some slight shifting around of the shares with Yerkes' portion having reduced to £11,950.[4]

* The other directors were: Walter Abbott (of Boston), Patrick Calhoun (of New York), C.A. Grenfell (London) and Murray Griffith (London), though the latter was not a founding director and was appointed subsequently.

Forbes remained as chairman of the District, perhaps a surprise given his apparent lack of energy in attending to the railway's serious challenges, but probably regarded as a safe pair of hands for managing the last days of steam operation: all the new works were to be done by the Americans.

However, as events unfolded, it became apparent that there were benefits in consolidating a wider range of schemes in order to carry them out at the same time; to operate a coordinated programme would be quicker and cheaper. Already there was the Hampstead tube to build, and the District itself had powers to construct its deep level line and the BPCR, which it now owned. Meanwhile the entirely independent Baker Street & Waterloo Railway had been partly built, but the finance and construction company responsible for building it failed at the end of 1900 and the rate of construction reduced to a mere crawl before being stopped completely later during 1901. An American syndicate showed an interest in taking it over but Yerkes was quicker in dealing with the liquidators (or more persuasive) and finally obtained all the rights to the line and the part-completed works in March 1902. There was then the unbuilt Great Northern & Strand Railway (GNSR), with powers to build a line from Wood Green to Aldwych. This had also been unsuccessful in raising capital and by 1901 it was apparent that there would be benefits in linking the line with the BPCR tube to produce a cross-London route. In fact the BPCR purchased the GNSR construction powers in September 1901.

To achieve all of this would hopelessly outstrip the combined capital resources of the MDETC and Yerkes and Perks. The obvious option was simply to increase the capital of the company to about £10 million, but bringing further investors on board meant a dilution of the profits to themselves, about which expectations had already been raised. Yerkes came up with a scheme to protect their own personal positions which involved the company issuing a form of security called a deferred certificate, the amount to equal the capital actually paid in and Yerkes and Perks between them would receive half. The benefit arose through the certificates entitling their holder to a proportion (according to their holding) of the profits of the company after the 5 per cent bond holders were paid. Since the company hoped to generate revenue well in excess of its commitment to bondholders, this would be very lucrative to Yerkes and Perks.

Perks liked the idea but, being a solicitor, had to point out that the traction company had no power to issues securities of this type. The easiest solution was to create an entirely new company with authority to raise all the capital required and to issue securities that would meet the founders' personal financial expectations.

The 'Underground' Company

Raising the enormous additional capital needed was a huge task requiring very special expertise and Yerkes approached the banker and financier Edgar Speyer, a senior partner in his family's banking house. Speyer was a cautious man and went through all of the prevailing proposals in great detail. Evidently satisfied that these were sound, Speyer helped Yerkes form his new company, the 'Underground Electric Railways Company of London Ltd', with a much-enlarged capital. The arrangement effectively gave the bankers control, though Yerkes was left in charge subject to various constraints, not least of which was that the bankers nominated the majority of directors for ten years, a position Yerkes was unused to. The bankers very much liked the idea of the deferred certificates and decided to take a slice of these too, to the annoyance of Perks and greater annoyance of Yerkes, out of whose share they would be taken. Nor did Yerkes care for being put on a salary rather than being able to use more imaginative methods to remunerate himself, according to the need of the moment. Perhaps he also resented being 'managed' by a much younger person with no knowledge of the electric traction business. Speyer, though, was exceedingly competent and Yerkes needed him.

Edgar Speyer. LTM (originally *Illustrated London News*)

The Underground Electric Railways Company of London, Limited was registered on 9th April 1902, by Bircham and Company with a capital of £5,000,000 in the form of 500,000 £10 shares. The stated objects were to acquire the undertaking of the Metropolitan District Electric Traction Company, to promote the adoption of electric traction for railways, light railways and tramways in the United Kingdom, to construct and maintain works, buildings, rolling stock and conveniences for providing, working and maintaining electric traction, and particularly works for the generation, distribution, accumulation, application and use of electric energy, to acquire any railways, light railways or tramways, or rights in relation thereto, to equip the same with electric or other traction, and to carry on the business of electrical, mechanical and general engineers, suppliers of electricity for light, heat, motive power and telegraphic, telephonic and other purposes, company promoters, financiers, guarantors, contractors.[5]

In practical terms this meant finding the money, building the power station, building the tube lines and equipping the District, all of which was roughly estimated as costing about £16 million. It will be seen that there was a substantial financial hole to be filled. The subscribers to the company, with one share each, were E. S. Speyer, 7 Lothbury, E.C., banker; W. H. Brown, 7 Lothbury, E.C., banker; A. N. Smith, 27 Carlton Hill, N.W., clerk; H. G. Leith, 35 Hans Road, S.W., clerk; C. T. Yerkes, Hamilton House, Victoria Embankment, W.C., gentleman; W. E. Mandelick, Hamilton House, Victoria Embankment, W.C., gentleman; A. J. Kent, 8 Cross Road, South Wimbledon, accountant. As with the earlier company it was not intended to make any public issue.

The number of directors was not to be less than three or more than seven. The subscribers were to appoint the first directors subject to the right during the first ten years of Speyer Brothers of London, Speyer and Company of New York and The Old Colony Trust Company of Boston, U.S.A. to nominate a majority of the directors for the time being.[6]

So far as the takeover was concerned, the proposal was for the shareholders in the MDETC to be recompensed with 100,000 of the new £10 shares exchanged for 50,000 of the MDETC £20 shares. However £15 had by then been called on the latter (valuing them at £750,000) and it was arranged to return £250,000 to shareholders in cash (worth £5 per old share) and treat the balance of £500,000 as the first call of £5 on the new shares, thus leaving shareholders in the same financial position as they had been before. Perks seems never to have had either Traction or Underground shares and remained a director (and for a while chairman) of the District. He received a consultant's salary of £4500 a year backdated to 1st July 1902 for his effort and co-operation. This was even more than

Murray Griffith in 1901. Griffith is a name not widely known but he was influential in improving the District Railway. London Underground's Griffith House is named after him. *Railway News* Vol 76 1901

Forbes used to get! The bankers arranging the various shares offers also did rather well out of it.

Forbes Departs

James Staats Forbes had presided over the District Railway for nearly thirty years when he resigned on 5th September 1901, giving way to a rather different management style where actions rather than words mattered. Forbes had already been eased out of the South Eastern & Chatham confederation* and had secured a role as an adviser for the huge sum of £3000 a year for ten years, an amount so vast in proportion to its apparent importance that shareholders began to ask questions about why such a sum was apparently hidden in the accounts and that, surely, it actually represented a pension (and this at a moment when the company was in serious debt and had just borrowed more). Forbes indicated that he was far 'too big a man, and too proud, to be a pensioner', and perhaps we see here a glimpse into his character.[7] At his own request he remained chairman of the London, Chatham & Dover Railway until his death, though this was a hugely reduced role since the creation of the joint management committee with the South Eastern.

It does not appear Forbes had intended to go, but his departure from the District was inevitable once the Americans had the measure of him. At the shareholders' meeting on 16th August 1901 (chaired by Forbes), Murray Griffith observed that the District was entering a new era and he felt that the board should be reconstituted, the directors being required to give effect to such a proposal. This clearly orchestrated move was carried and at the next board meeting Lucas and Wyld resigned and Robert Perks and Murray Griffith were appointed, the new board comprising Perks, Griffith, Forbes, Isaacs, Dalrymple and Law. At the conclusion of the meeting, Forbes stood down as chairman and Perks took over the responsibility.[8] Perks, we have already noted, had been engaging with Yerkes over the previous couple of years and was a safe pair of hands during a time of impending change.

Forbes was pleased to accept the post of 'advisory director' for four years on lucrative terms, though in fact he rarely attended board meetings and departed on 17th February

* The South Eastern & Chatham Railway was the name usually given to the joint management committee set up in 1899 to operate as one system the South Eastern Railway and the London, Chatham and Dover Railways, reducing competition and some costs. These two companies retained their legal identities but the public was presented with only one system.

1903. He died on 5th April 1904, at the age of 81, at his home on Chelsea Embankment, leaving a fortune largely abstracted from the railway industry.*

Though often credited as being a good administrator and manager it has been difficult to find very much in the press that actually praised Forbes's wisdom and leadership as a railway director: rather the reverse. The *Railway Times* was usually fairly direct in its opinions of Forbes. In 1900 it was commenting on a District shareholders' meeting and was minded to observe:

> At Thursday's meeting of the Metropolitan District Railway Mr. Forbes promised us a 'revolution in the finances of the company' in the next few years. A year or two ago Mr. Forbes told us there was nothing like the 'good old humdrum way.' And, truth to tell, he and his companies have acted up to that preaching for many weary years. But if his next 'revolution' is to give no better results than the Chatham-South Eastern upheaval, then let the unhappy District stick to the evils it knows of rather than rush into the unknown under such a leadership. Mr. Forbes may be the great railway expert that he would have us believe, but it is singular that no undertaking with which he has been connected has ever flourished—at least not so far as we can remember. What is the reason of the seeming blighting influence of his presence![9]

In a later item about Forbes's railways several fairly pointed remarks were made about his abilities wherein he was actually accused of being a 'ghastly failure', adding that his railways have gone from bad to worse whilst others have prospered, and had become 'a standing disgrace'.[10] And this was in 1900, the year before the District's first half year was described by Forbes himself as the worst half-year ever, and complaining that there was 'really very little the District could do'. In an inspired snipe early in 1901 the journal suggested that Forbes might make himself very rich by buying large amounts of stock in the companies he presided over and then retiring, so to enjoy the instant profit as the shares soared.

Was the Forbes era all bad? Certainly in the early days a completely hapless District board was glad to have someone join them who actually knew about railways and could set the operating regime along the right course after the Met was ejected. The District obtained a fine reputation for service and reliability under very difficult circumstances and some, perhaps much, of the credit for this is down to Forbes. Moreover, Forbes understood some very basic issues and the options they suggested. Building in the centre of London had latterly cost over £900,000 a mile and had nearly bankrupted the company whilst building in the suburbs was less than £100,000 a mile and usually much less, perhaps only £50,000 a mile. It was therefore sensible to build up extra traffic by expanding into the suburbs. It was even cheaper if District trains could run over someone else's tracks. To describe this as 'policy' would be too grand a term, but it is what the District, under Forbes's guidance, actually did.

Less good was the expensive City Lines venture and the equally miserable involvement with the ELR, each of which made a loss that had to be made good by the Met and the District, the latter quite unable to spare the money. Worse, was the clear understanding by the late 1890s that the District had to modernize, at which point years of inaction in overcoming its high fixed costs came home to roost as the District could not raise money. The challenge was not an easy one, but it was surely an impossible task for someone like Forbes who had so many other calls on his time, who was in his 70s, showed no great inclination to delegate and was rarely challenged (except towards the end by exasperated

* The estate was valued at £135,368. Establishing today's equivalent value is fraught with assumptions, but in employment value terms it would be worth nearly £50 million.

shareholders—Forbes incidentally was only a nominal shareholder and had not suffered the considerable losses which the original shareholders had). The overriding impression is of a man who showed no sense of urgency whilst in office but was content to accept his fees from the companies he presided over, which were considerable.

His efforts as chairman of 'Ediswan' lighting followed the familiar pattern but in this case some unexpected major costs led to the discovery of some serious problems and irregularities and the suspicion the company was not being effectively managed; two directors were required to resign to make way for shareholder representatives. Forbes was one who departed—he resigned on 19th July 1901 claiming pressure of work and domestic bereavement (his wife had died on 1st July) but he would have had great difficulty in hanging on in the circumstances.

He was felt to have been more successful at the National Telephone Company, but there were still critics. The *Electrical Review* felt that the telephone company was one of the few he had been associated with where the shareholders felt some gratitude.[11] On resigning as a director of the National Telephone Company in November 1901 he was also able to secure a role as general adviser under similar circumstances with a fee of £1000 for 5 years. Towards the end of his stint he had been much engaged with giving evidence to a hostile parliamentary select committee in 1898 and then the antics of the postmaster general in establishing a rival telephone system in London.[12] This was all very time consuming for a man who was supposed to be finding a way of electrifying the District at the same time.

His longevity is, by repute, largely down to his diplomatic skills and excellent chairmanship at meetings that could sometimes be quite difficult. He was regarded as knowledgeable and amiable which must have helped. These skills are referred to in most of the reports of shareholders' meetings. There is no doubt that he was in some respects very capable, but he was also very expensive and perhaps after addressing the initial causes of his appointment (usually imminent bankruptcy) it would have been better to have given way to someone who could give more energetic attention to the task of developing the railways for the future.

The following comments from newspapers probably reflect typical views:

> (From *Pall Mall Gazette*) Mr. Forbes was at his best in dealing with a recalcitrant share-holder or taming an unruly meeting, but his success has not been conspicuous in other directions, and railway investors have no particular reason to shed other than crocodile tears over his departure.
>
> (*Sunday Sun*) Though undoubtedly a power, especially when dealing with a turbulent meeting or a recalcitrant shareholder, Mr. Forbes's resignation will be viewed with equanimity. An able and tactful speaker, a just and level-headed man of business, respected by all, and yet by no means a brilliant railway manager, Mr. Forbes has filled the chair of the District Company for close on thirty years. No one will claim that the management of the Chatham and District lines has founded Mr. Forbes's reputation as a railway magnate. Time, energy, and labour has he lavishly expended in his work, but he never managed to steer the ship out of its sea of difficulties into smooth water. As a kindly personality and a gentleman he will be regretted, but as a manager his departure should be welcomed.

Many have drawn attention to the rivalry between Forbes and Sir Edward Watkin where the Met and the SER competed with the District and LCDR, the press pumping up the various arguments between the opposing companies as though they were in fact personal between the two men. Watkin was also involved in several companies and was an MP and just as distracted as Forbes. If Forbes was tactful and played the long game (sometimes a very long game) then Watkin was more direct, perhaps rather impetuous and appearing rather aggressive (not necessarily intentionally) to those who did not know him well. It is natural they might see and react differently to unfolding events. In my researches, I can see that many of the court cases were justly brought through genuine misunderstandings around poorly-drafted contracts or Acts of Parliament and that it was essential that terms be clarified. As far as I can see there were relatively few instances where annoyance might have been personal.

Was Forbes straightforward? This seems very unlikely and a certain slipperiness is evident. It is most unlikely, for example, that he ever had the slightest intention of merging with the Met but he always indicated he was willing to talk and gave the impression it would one day happen. His successors spurned a merger too, so his inclination might have been quite correct; it is just that he was saying something different. Perhaps he just liked keeping his options open.

The Electrification Controversy

In the last chapter we left the District and Met in 1901 agreeing to proceed with electrifying their systems using the Ganz system but with progress stalled because the Board of Trade was insisting on further lengthy and expensive tests (and the District had no money). The decision about the electrification system pre-dated practical control by Yerkes, the man who was to finance the electrification. Yerkes brought an entire team with him which was very experienced in American methods but found this new-fangled alternating current system a complete mystery, a mystery compounded by the fact that there was no existing system on which to draw experience. From a business point of view this presented an extremely serious financial risk that was difficult to mitigate. The direct current system, though perhaps mundane and no longer state of the art, drew on a wealth of experience, had proved that it could do the job, its installation could be costed reliably and the American engineers knew exactly what had to be done.

The emerging American influence during the spring of 1901 soon caused some cooling of enthusiasm with Ganz, which understood only too well what the Americans were up to. The Met watched with horror as the electrification scheme started to unravel. At a meeting on 29th June 1901 the District (now under Yerkes' influence) indicated it wanted to deploy the dc system, as used in Chicago, using 6-car trains (the end cars motored) and to split trains in half for the quiet midday service. Yerkes already knew in some detail exactly how he wanted the District electrification to work and understood there was an interesting discussion to be had with the Met. Yerkes and Perks sought to mollify the Met by offering to electrify the Met's system for them, subject to agreeable financial terms, but the Met would not entertain such an idea and stuck to the recommended proposal to install the Ganz system. This caused Yerkes to revisit the Ganz proposal, about which a lot of work had already been done, and during the summer he visited Budapest to investigate the system personally. He was irked to find that the experimental line had been dismantled and despite examining the technology came away more thoroughly determined than before not to adopt that system. Although he was being told that the system was fully tested and satisfactory it was obvious on closer inspection that lots of very significant modifications were still being made and it would not be possible to see a passenger line actually in action for some while yet.

Probably another factor in all this was the gradual bringing together of the various tube railway schemes which, because of their nature, were compelled to use a dc traction system on the 3-rail or 4-rail system as there was not room in the tunnels for overhead lines. Again for practical reasons, Yerkes would not want to install two completely different types of technology at the same time if it could be avoided. Whether inter-running between the tubes and the District was contemplated at this early stage one cannot tell, but the fact that fitting out and heavy-overhaul of Piccadilly tube stock was undertaken at Mill Hill Park when the tube railway opened, and ran there under its own power, suggests a common electrification system had useful possibilities not lightly to be brushed off.

Before the Traction Company could embark upon electrification of the District it was necessary to have a formal agreement in place and confirmation of that agreement in an Act of Parliament. A bill proceeded through the 1901 Session and the final agreement, dated 18th July 1901 was appended to it. During its progress various interested parties aired their views and the Met voiced its opinion. The Met had been content with the Ganz recommendation for electrifying the inner circle but resented the Americans increasing the scope and the costs, which seemed to be dragging the Met along with it. The District (articulating the traction company's views) contended that the Ganz system was selected on the basis of a bid to electrify the inner circle only but the District now wanted to electrify the whole of its railway and had no confidence in the Ganz system to do the job.

The views were irreconcilable and the select committee dealing with the bill obtained the agreement of the companies to accept arbitration. It was settled that if, after one month of the date of the Act, the parties could not agree about the method of electrification then the matter could be referred to the Board of Trade who would appoint a tribunal. This would be led by an arbitrator (who would not be an electrical engineer) and two engineers, one appointed by each company, to hear such evidence as was required. The tribunal would report to the Board of Trade which would make a binding award.[13]

The Act received the Royal Assent on 9th August 1901 and it is no surprise that, in September, the Board of Trade was asked to convene an arbitration tribunal. Although each party would meet its own costs, it is revealing that half the Met's costs were met by Ganz, desperate not to lose a very large contract. Alfred Lyttelton QC was appointed to lead the tribunal, which sat for twelve days during October and November and heard evidence, not only from the interested parties but a range of technical experts.* Ganz put up a strong performance but the tribunal seems mainly to have been swayed by the fact there was no working example of the overhead concept whilst the dc system was tried and tested.

The system Ganz was proposing worked on the cascade principle, capable of regenerating about 9 per cent of current on braking. On each of the two motor cars 3-phase power at line voltage served a main motor at 3000V whilst current taken via slip rings from the rotor powered the auxiliary motor at 300V; the accelerating rheostats were connected to the output of the auxiliary motor. When the train reached about half speed the auxiliary motors were cut out and hauled dead, the main motors being sufficient to accelerate the train further. On braking, the auxiliary motor was reconnected, producing a dragging effect down to half speed, below which it was cut out. The complete train was expected to weigh 150 tons and with four 300hp main motors performance should have been more than adequate. On starting, the auxiliary motors would produce a further 1200hp (ie 2400hp in all), which would have contributed to some very lively acceleration

* The other members of the tribunal were Thomas Parker, nominated by the Metropolitan Railway Company and H.F. Parshall, engineer, of 8 Prince Street, London, E.C., nominated by the District Company (Parshall had been responsible for the electrical system on the recently opened Central London Railway and was known to Yerkes). They heard the evidence of the two parties, and the arguments and speeches of the counsel on their behalf, on 7th October and eleven subsequent days.

Rare picture of the Ganz trial line in Budapest. The Met & District electrification consultants saw this in operation but it closed shortly before Yerkes paid a visit. The body was mounted on a huge sample bogie with two massive motors. *The Graphic* 16 March 1901

(2.6ft/second/second was threatened). Top speed was claimed to be only 25mph but the target was to run 2500ft start to stop in 92 seconds.[14]

During the evidence some interesting issues emerged. For example, the Ganz system had been proposed purely to address the requirement to electrify the inner circle but the District wanted to electrify the whole of its railway and the Met explained that it might well wish to extend its own electrified area. The experts explained that 3-phase motors were constrained to operate at a specific top speed, although with more complicated control gear a half-speed option was possible. However, extended running at any intermediate speeds was rather inefficient. This was not a problem on the inner circle where a motor designed for (say) 25mph operation would be satisfactory, but it would not do on the outer sections of the railway with long inter-station distances where speeds up to 40mph might be called for. Direct current motors, on the other hand, were much more versatile.

Another fascinating technical difficulty was also aired. On double-track sections of line the various crossovers and reversing points made it essential that the twin overhead lines were electrified with the same phase in the same position on each track, for example phase 1 on the northern wire and phase 2 on the other wire. This arrangement was necessary not only to reduce dead sections at junctions and crossings but more importantly because if the phases were swapped over above a moving train the motors would reverse direction; this would be a problem at crossovers and had to be avoided. This was carefully explained to the Inquiry because the phenomenon gave rise to a fascinating problem. If electric services expanded beyond the inner circle, several triangular junctions would be encountered. At such junctions it was impossible to avoid the problem at one of the three apexes where the wires along one leg met the wires across the junction where the phases were in the opposite position. In such a circumstances a train travelling at speed would discover the phases suddenly reversing, throwing the motors into reverse with catastrophic consequences. Nobody had yet invented a mechanism that could automatically rearrange the motoring circuit at junctions like this without risk of damage. It was not that the problem was insuperable: it was that it had not hitherto been considered and heightened the potential risk and opportunity for delay if the Ganz system were adopted.

The overhead wiring arrangements were misunderstood by many, but at junctions were hardly more difficult than on a trolleybus system. Bow collectors were to be used, with insulation half way along to separate the phases. Two bows, near the ends, were needed on each motor car to avoid gapping at crossovers. There was an issue about clearance in some sections of tunnel and this emerged as a challenge in a few places. There was some excitement expressed about the proposed use by Ganz of liquid rheostats where circuit resistance was altered by moving electrodes in and out of an electrolyte; Ganz eventually had to consider adding a cooling system to stop temperatures running away but the technical press wondered why on earth they had adopted this approach in the first place. More worrying was the stream of major changes to the proposal in the original tender (for example in relation to the number of substations) which filled nobody with confidence.

The technical evidence given was interesting and detailed and one cannot help feeling that some of this ought to have been gone into by the electrification experts brought in originally to guide the Met and District and that perhaps Preece and Wolfe Barry had not been the best choices for this particular job.

All in all, the dull but robust American system could hardly fail to win the day. The Met accepted the decision with good grace and was now very keen to make up for lost time. Another helpful proposal by the District to supply the Met with electric current was declined (perhaps unwisely), and each railway built its own power station.

Meanwhile, the Ganz system was deployed on the 67-mile and steeply-graded Valtellina Railway in Italy from 4th September 1902 with such conspicuous success that it was soon widely replicated elsewhere on the Continent and the dc-orientated American General Electric Company enthusiastically promoted the system in the USA. This steeply graded, sharply curved and many-tunnelled line used equipment very similar to that proposed for the District but operating at 15 cycles rather than 25. Although Ganz made no money out of it and lost enthusiasm as small unexpected setbacks (all resolved) ate into profits, technically it did all work rather well; the Valtellina line was ideal for a 3-phase system where stations were few, gradients were steep and speed was constant. The District was ideal for dc traction, and that is what it got.

The Ealing & South Harrow Trial – Electrical Equipment

The American engineers were familiar with automatic signalling in the USA, where there were at least ten systems in use, the earliest one (on the Southern Pacific) dating back to 1885.[15] Yerkes recognised that improved services could only be operated with electric trains and automatic signalling introduced together. There was experience of doing this in Boston and something similar was proposed for London, but the conditions were slightly different. The Yerkes team therefore decided to conduct a large-scale trial to understand how the electrification system, trains and signalling worked together. Noted earlier, the E&SHR had been completed but not yet opened and this line offered a convenient opportunity to try out the new technologies; the District had assumed full control from 1st July 1900.

The line had been inspected by the Board of Trade on 27th March 1901 when construction was complete. Nothing remarkable was noted about the five stations, two viaducts, nine underbridges and eight overbridges that were examined. Track employed 87 lb per yard rails and ballast of broken brick, burnt clay or coke breeze. The Board of Trade appeared uneasy about how this might consolidate and imposed a blanket speed limit of 25mph, which persisted for a couple of years after eventual opening. There were six signalboxes (including a new one at Hanger Lane Junction) and it was intended to employ Sykes block instruments but they had not yet been fitted. The inspector noted that the section south of Hanger Lane ran all the way to Mill Hill Park as Ealing Common box was disused and the signal arms had been removed. Station nameboards and clocks had yet to be fitted and the inspector required all signals out of sight of their signal box to be repeated in the box.

80 RAILWAYS.

THE DISTRICT RAILWAY,

EITHER BY ITS OWN LINE
OR BY ITS CONNECTIONS, SERVES
THE WHOLE OF THE
PLACES OF AMUSEMENT,
INTEREST, AND ATTRACTION,
IN AND AROUND LONDON.

It is the most direct and quickest means of conveyance between

EAST END, CITY, & WEST END,

and it connects with the
TERMINI OF ALL
THE RAILWAYS RUNNING INTO LONDON.

The Extension to North Ealing, Perivale-Alperton, Sudbury Town, Sudbury Hill, and South Harrow, will be opened early in 1903.

Through Bookings are in operation between the
DISTRICT LINE AND ALL STATIONS IN
LONDON AND THE SUBURBS.

Always ask for Tickets "via DISTRICT RAILWAY."

The "DISTRICT RAILWAY" MAP of LONDON, and the "DISTRICT" MAP of GREATER LONDON and ENVIRONS, are obtainable at the Company's Booking Offices, at Station Bookstalls, and of the Principal Booksellers throughout the Kingdom.

Price 6d. (on Paper), 1s. Mounted (in Stiff Cover), 3s. 6d. Mounted, Rollered, and Varnished.

A District advertisement from unknown journal, perhaps late 1902, promoting virtues of the District. With some optimism it hopes the South Harrow line will soon be open. Significantly, there is not yet expected to be a station at Park Royal. Roy Allen Collection

During 1902 and early 1903 experimental electric and signalling equipment was installed. Two 100lb per yard, low-voltage power rails were laid, one (outer) positive and one (centre) negative. In the US, the electric lines were mainly the elevated railways running across the city centres and these were carried on massive steel structures that provided a well-earthed and low-resistance return circuit for the electric current, so that only a third rail was required for the electric power. In London, no such return circuit was available and the Board of Trade had very strict rules about how much current leakage could be tolerated from the return circuit via the running rails. The complications around managing the return current inclined the American engineers to select a 4-rail system where the running rails carried no traction current at all.

As a point of historical importance, the positive rail was not where it had been installed on the Earls Court line (located 12¼ inches outside each running rail) and there was some discussion about whether the District should adopt the suggested British standard that was being contemplated, which was 19¼ inches from the running rail.* The Met thought this new standard would be used and began to plan its electrification on that basis. However, by early 1902, the Yerkes team wanted to be able to run District and Piccadilly trains along the same tracks because the tube stock needed access to Mill Hill

* Perversely this 'standard' was only employed by the Lancashire & Yorkshire Railway.

The signal box at Perivale-Alperton was never commissioned although it was fully-equipped and survived for some years. Located at the north end of the station, One Tree Hill is visible in background. Alan A Jackson collection

Park car sheds. The Piccadilly, being in tube tunnel, was in a very confined space and the maximum distance that the positive rail could be from the adjacent running rail was only 16 inches. In consequence, this had also to be the distance used on the District. Because the LSWR lines used by District trains had to follow suit, it also meant that the London main line railways had later to employ this arrangement when they electrified, as they still do today. It was a while before the Met discovered this and, though much irritated as it had already begun installing conductor rails at the larger spacing, accepted the decision.[16]

A temporary power station was erected about half way along the electrified line, near Alperton, using equipment recovered from the experiment at Earls Court. This was located in the north-east quadrant where the railway crossed the Grand Union Canal, from which cooling water was obtained. The roof of the L-shaped building was the same level as the viaduct allowing aerial power lines to pass onto the viaduct and connect directly to the current rails. The reused plant included the two Belliss-Siemens generator sets and two Babcock & Wilcox boilers. However, the power demands of the E&SHR were greater than at Earls Court so some upgrading was necessary. A 400 amp-hour set of batteries was installed, and a Highfield booster, which allowed batteries to top up the peak load whilst recharging when the extra power was not required. Four 6kW motor generator sets were installed to supply current to the signalling system at 110 volts. The generator building outlived the experimental line and was still standing in the 1930s, having been absorbed into a factory. The positive supply was at about 550 volts and the negative was near earth potential and earthed at various points.

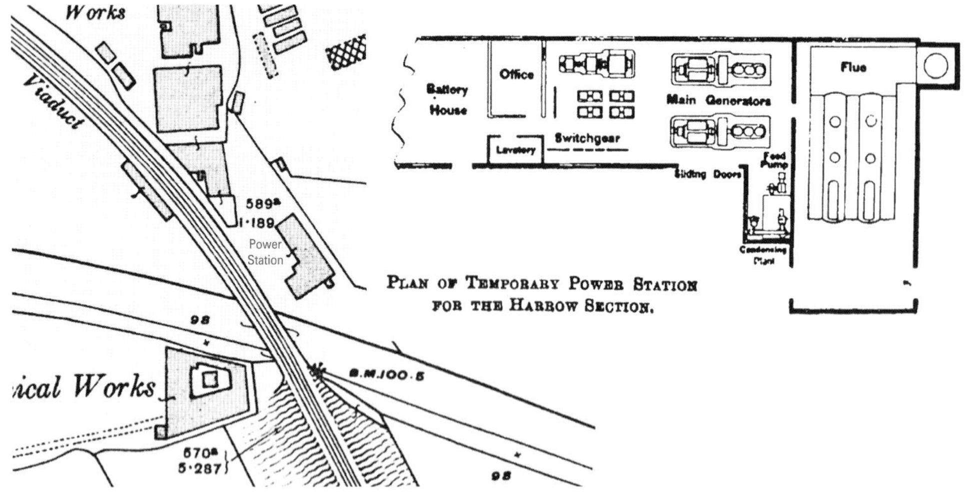

Sketch plan and location map of the temporary power station at Alperton in 1903. Author's collection

The cables required for the current supply, telephone and signalling were laid in a trough between the two tracks and made provision for the subsequent laying of the cables between Lots Road and a permanent substation planned at Sudbury Town.

The electrification of the branch caused Wembley Urban District Council to express concern about safety at the two footpath crossings on the line, north of Sudbury Town. The District responded that guard boards had been fitted at the break in the positive rails making it difficult for users to come into contact with it and the negative rail was near earth potential; even so 'permanent provision' was in mind (the crossings were later replaced by footbridges).[17]

One of the experimental trains at South Harrow prior to the public opening of the line. The original mechanical signals provided here were not included in the experimental automatic system. Author's collection

Mill Hill Park around 1903. This shows the steam service layout (with engine shed) but some of the tracks have been electrified for the South Harrow service. Author's collection

The track circuit controlled automatic signalling was similar to that used very successfully on the Boston Elevated Electric Railway, but adapted for the more challenging 4-rail arrangement where false operation by stray traction current had to be guarded against. Although signal boxes and mechanically-operated semaphore signals had been installed at each of the original E&SHR stations, the signal boxes and crossovers were mostly stripped out and, except at the two ends, the existing semaphores were converted to automatic operation using small electro-pneumatic motors connected to the existing arms and rodding. In the Park Royal area extra

One of the mechanical signals converted to automatic operation in 1903. The actuating air motor is located low down, at top of the black base. This is probably Perivale-Alperton and the open countryside is all too evident. Author's collection

One of the gravity operated trainstops that Westinghouse explain they were using on the branch by early 1904.
Westinghouse Signalling Pamphlet No 7 in Author's collection

signals had to be provided as there had not been a signal box there when the line was built.

At each automatic signal location, on the right hand side of the running rails, was a small metal pivoted arm, the end of which was maintained below rail level when the signal was clear. When the associated signal arm was at danger the 'trip' arm rotated and projected upwards, just above rail level. In this position the 'trip' arm would engage with the handle of an emergency brake cock hanging down from the front of the train in a corresponding position, thus applying the emergency brake. Such a system ensured a train would be stopped promptly if a signal was inadvertently passed at danger. The arm became known as a 'train-stop' and the corresponding device on the train a 'trip-cock'.

Early descriptions suggest these trip arms were mechanically linked to the adjacent signal so that one motor controlled both functions (as in Boston) but a 1904 photo shows a trainstop arm with a separate motor mounted on the sleepers; this pushed the arm down and a large weighted arm on the opposite side of the track brought the trip arm back up again. It is possible the original mechanical linkages were unsatisfactory but attempts to resolve this have not been successful.

Signal boxes were retained only at South Harrow and North Ealing (the latter only intended for use in emergencies), though some of the unused buildings survived longer for other purposes. Since it was necessary to send the electric trains somewhere useful, the electrification was extended to Mill Hill Park so passengers could interchange with steam services to London. Shortly after the line opened, the District was delighted to experience (more than once) some serious flooding along the route with the rails partly under water but the signalling continued to function normally throughout.

The track circuits varied in length between 1400ft and 3500ft and there were eighteen automatic signals in use. The signalling supply was at 110 volts and reduced at point of use to 20 volts to operate the signal motors and provide track circuit potential of 8 volts. The air supply was obtained from compressors at Hanger Lane and South Harrow and distributed through an air main laid beside the line.

At South Harrow, the E&SHR tracks extended about 250ft north of the platforms to meet those of the Met, from the Uxbridge direction, at the Northolt Road bridge. These were part of the old H&UR scheme and were not brought into use when the Harrow-on-the-Hill to Uxbridge section opened on 4th July 1904 but lay derelict until the District decided to exercise its running rights in 1910.

The Ealing & South Harrow Trial – Test Trains

Cars and Car types

For the trains, Yerkes was keen to test alternative technologies to make sure the best available equipment was used in London and that the provisional proposals for operating an electric service were deliverable. Nevertheless, his American experience predisposed him towards use of methods that were clearly working in Chicago and Boston and it is no surprise that the design of the cars were based on the latest American practice even though they were built in Britain. Fourteen cars were ordered, each 49ft 10½ins over buffers, and these were designed as two 7-car trains. The cars were ordered from Brush Electrical Engineering Company, and each train comprised three motor cars and four 'trail' cars, as they were first called.[17] The motor cars each had one motor bogie one trail bogie. The end motors cars had a driving position at the outer ends, and the middle motor had driving positions at each end. The design was essentially American, with closely-spaced arched windows and a wide clerestory roof with ends sloping down at the car ends. Although the intermediate platforms were open, the car roof also extended over them providing some weather protection.

South Harrow Shed

The cars were delivered to South Harrow without electrical equipment and a 2-road corrugated iron shed was erected on the north side of the railway in which the cars could be kitted out and later maintained. The shed had capacity for just six cars and additional sidings were laid alongside.* So far as it can be established all 14 cars were delivered to South Harrow on 11th March 1903, whereupon the equipment was installed.[19] The engineer J.S. Thomson was brought over from Chicago to supervise construction at Brush and the equipping, testing and operation of the cars on the Harrow line.

Livery

Descriptions of the trains on delivery uniformly describe them as bright yellow, canary yellow or yellowy-green. However, photographs and one single report suggests that the car exterior included some varnished woodwork (perhaps confined to structural members) with very large coloured panels along the sides and front which were of bright yellow lined in red. A reporter was told that yellow was 'often used' for this type of car in the US as it was found very serviceable (though he felt the British might find it aggressive).[20] Both trains carried the name 'Metropolitan District Railway' in gold above the windows and photos indicate the words 'smoking car' were also painted above the end gangways on the cars concerned. We do not know how long they stayed yellow and there is evidence that by September at least some cars were red and others red with white upper panels, but yellow cars were still evident.[21]

---

* The shed and sidings are where today's sidings are located at South Harrow and the site had previously been used as a contractor's worksite.

Above: **One of the BTH-equipped cars at South Harrow; just visible through the driver's window is the large controller. Clearly visible here is the shoe-gear, at this time mounted at extreme end of leading bogie, and the van Dorn coupler.** Author's collection

Below: **Test train being shown off at South Harrow before opening, view looking north**. *Traction & Transmission* Vol 9, 1904

Above: **This is one of the BTH-equipped cars and of all the images examined appears best to show off the colour scheme where the (natural) wood is visible in places but large areas are painted yellow-green widely described in the press, with the edging emphasised by thin red lining. This view also emphasises the bow-shaped front. This view was probably taken in April 1903 to accompany an article in *The Electrician* of 24 April.** Author's collection

Below: **This shows a train (BTH car leading) outside the shed at South Harrow and gives a good impression of one of the early 4-car trains. Just visible between the first two cars are barriers to reduce risk of anyone falling between the cars.** Roy Allen collection

Seating and Class Distinction

Seating was mainly longitudinal (in line with the car sides) but some transverse seats were available. The seats were nearly all rattan covered but it was stated cloth had been tried on specimen cars. Rattan was chosen as being hygienic and easy to clean.[22] The trailers thus seated 52, the middle motors 48 and the end motors 38. *The Times* lamented the halving of seating capacity compared with steam stock, observing that the District's new owners assumed that because it was usual for passengers to tolerate standing in America it was going to be acceptable here. The longitudinal seating comprised mostly long undivided benches but at least one middle motor car (perhaps both) had squat wooden dividers making clear the number for which they were intended to provide, and these better suited the British preference. A nice touch was the fitting of hat and coat hooks to the window pillars.

When the cars were delivered, the District was still vacillating about whether to provide any first-class accommodation and there was no evidence of such a thing being provided, the only 'class' division being between smoking and non-smoking.[23] The possibility of a 'reserved' class was under discussion, but of this, more anon. When services began later in 1903 it is known some first-class had been made available on the ordinary trains, probably by designating a trailer, as that was easiest. Second class passengers were allowed to occupy first class seats on the Harrow service.[24]

Car Entrances and exits

All cars except the end motors had an open platform at each end of the enclosed saloon which was separated from the end platform by a sliding door; end motor cars had this arrangement at only the non-driving end. Half-height hinged iron gates protected the sides of the end platforms and at stations they could be swung open by one of the

This view looks south from footbridge near South Harrow station and shows the temporary shed (with doors closed) and some cars behind it. Author's collection

Above: **A rarely photographed Westinghouse motor car on a 7-car demonstration train just north of Sudbury Hill. The image appeared in the July 1903 edition of *Railway Magazine* and was taken before the railway opened.** Author's collection

Below: **Diagrams showing the three types of experimental car.** *Railway News* Vol 79 1903 in Author's collection

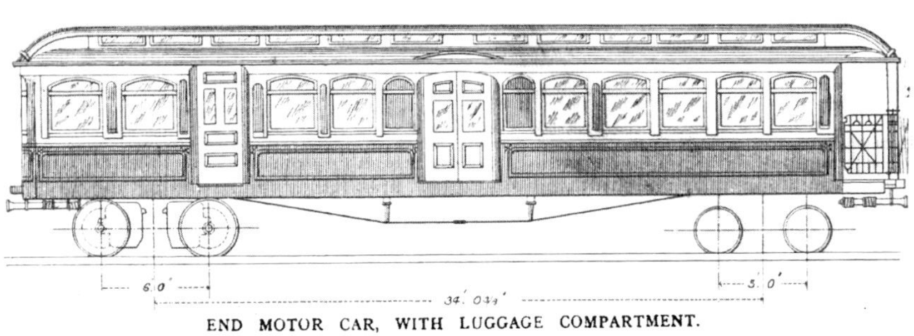

END MOTOR CAR, WITH LUGGAGE COMPARTMENT.

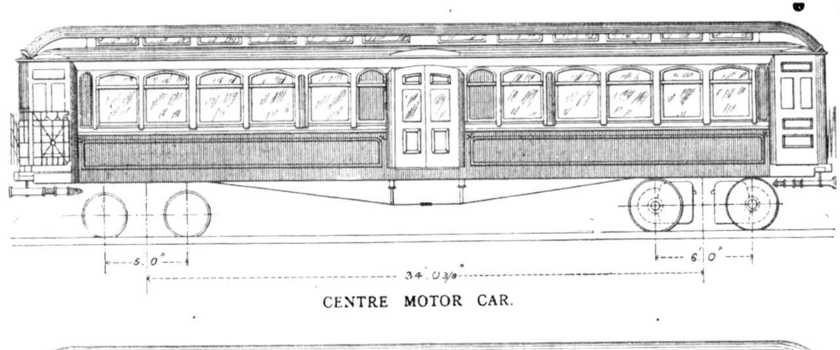

CENTRE MOTOR CAR.

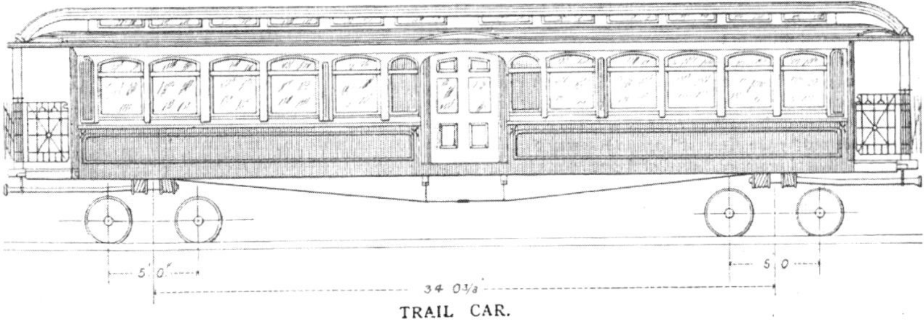

TRAIL CAR.

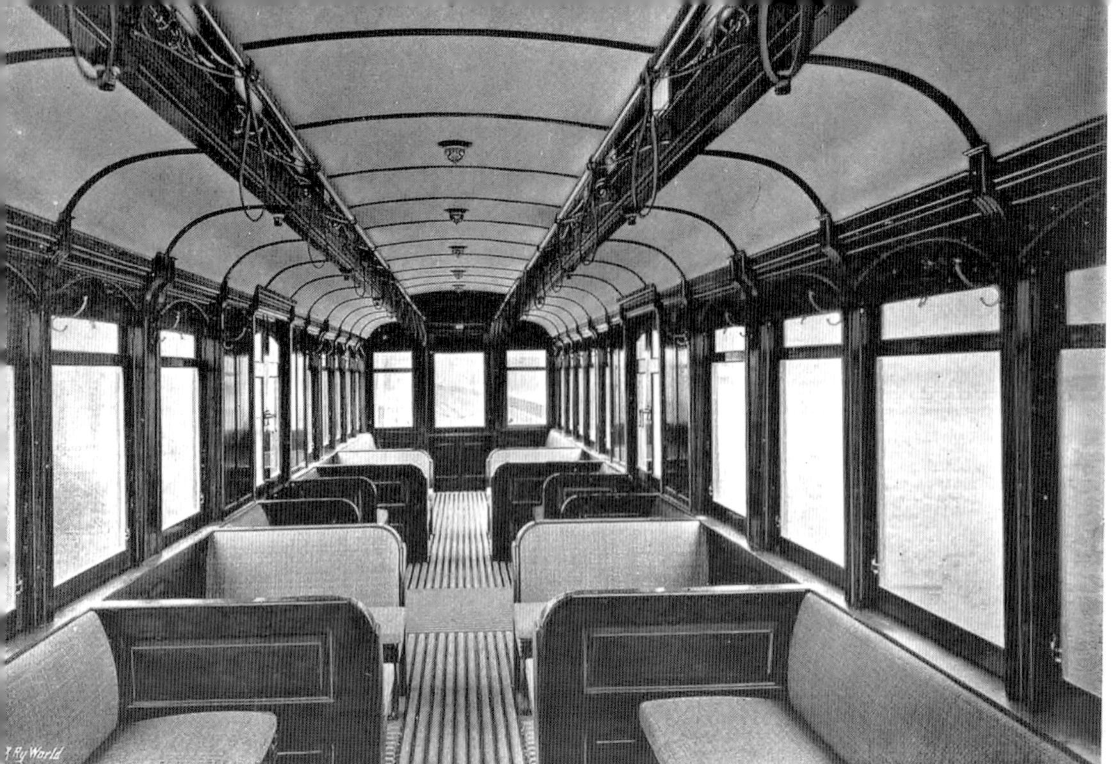

Interior of one of the 1903 cars showing interior detail. Author's collection

conductors, standing between the cars, manipulating the gates on the two adjacent cars simultaneously.[25] There was no passenger access from the extreme ends of the trains where there were no open platforms.

In addition to the entrances on the end platforms there were twin sliding doors along the centre of each car but the Board of Trade inspectors were told that there were no plans to use these in service except in emergencies, from which one might conclude they were locked shut.[26] The idea of centre doors was inspired by the new rolling stock on the Boston Elevated Street Railway, which employed centre doors to allow exit from cars and the end platforms to allow entry, it being felt (with some justification) that opposing flows at narrow doorways was a major source of delays at stations. The Boston system became busy very quickly and it was found the use of separate doors for boarding and alighting was a valuable feature, though rigid enforcement was necessary.[27] It is not a surprise to see that allowance had been made for its possible use in London, although it would require heavy staffing.

A novel feature was the provision of electric heaters, it being realized at the start that District trains spent much time in the open air. Sixteen heaters were installed in each car, and two in each driving cab. Each car boasted not only windows that slid downwards to open but also benefited from having internal sun blinds.[28]

Driving cabs and Luggage Compartments

The end motor cars had substantial luggage compartments at the driving ends and these gave access to the driving position. The controls were located in a half-cab arrangement located on the right hand side, unusual for Britain but normal in the US. Above the driving ends, a central headlight and two revolving roof-mounted tail lamps at the ends of the trains were copied directly from styles used on the Brooklyn and Boston elevated systems.

A postcard of a Harrow-bound 1903 experimental train in service not long after its introduction. The train is about to pass under the Creffield Road bridge (near Ealing Common) and just visible are the red and white painted trailers forming the two centre cars. Roy Allen Collection

The car ends were not flat but had a slightly V-shaped appearance (this was an Americanism caused by the ferociously sharp curves on the elevated lines, where it was necessary to provide extra clearance at car ends). This wedge shape may be the reason that the end-of-train access (presumably for emergency or staff use) was offset and took the form of two narrow inward-opening hinged doors occupying the whole of the nearside of the front of the train. Looked at this from today's perspective, it was odd since if two trains had to be coupled together in an emergency the doorways would not line up.

The middle motor cars also had right hand driving positions on each end platform. The driving controls were shut away when not needed by an ingenious system of hinged flaps, or doors, and manipulating these allowed the driver to create a segregated (if primitive) half-cab when required, whilst leaving the left-hand gate (on the platform side) available for passengers. The driving cars were equipped with pneumatic sanding equipment and audible warning devices described variously as whistles or 'sirens'.[29] The large luggage compartments on the end cars catered for accompanied and unaccompanied luggage and parcels but significantly reduced the space available for passengers. This area was separated from the passenger saloon by a sliding door.

The inspection report of 18th June 1903 especially mentions that the trains were to be operated in 4-car sets (two motors and two trailers) by a driver and three guards; such sets would weigh 90 tons.[30] Reports of this time are inconsistent in their use of the terms guard and conductor, but the latter seemed to be the favoured term for electric trains whilst 'guard' tended to mean someone used on steam hauled trains, the duties being significantly different.

Bogies

The cars were equipped with cast steel bogies, also built by Brush. These were of two types. A single motor bogie was provided at one end on each motor car, each carrying two traction motors. All the other bogies, the trailer bogies, were of lighter construction. Both designs were of cast steel and similar to designs used in Chicago. The motored wheels were of 36-inch diameter but all the other wheels were 30-inch.

Equipment

One train was fitted with British Thomson-Houston (BTH) control gear, GE68 traction motors rated at 175hp and the Christensen air brake, the other with control and air-braking systems by the Westinghouse Electric and Manufacturing Co and their own pattern of motors rated at 150hp.[31] The former system was similar to that recently introduced on the CLR whilst the latter had just been introduced on the Mersey Railway, with more success than it met with on the District.

The Westinghouse system made life very easy for the driver, who was provided with a miniature control panel with a small operating handle. By simple manipulation of this handle control wires along the whole train were energized, power being obtained at 14 volts from a small battery on the operative motor car. Depending on which combination of wires were energized, pin valves controlled a supply of compressed air to various pieces of apparatus on each motor car, including the line breakers (supplying traction power), reversers and a remotely-operated drum-controller. This latter controlled the supply of current through the starting resistors to the motors. The air supply was obtained from the compressed air needed for the braking system. The design was quite ingenious but had the advantage that acceleration was automatic. The system was used successfully on the Brooklyn Elevated system and the Mersey Railway.

The BTH system was a development of that invented by Frank Julius Sprague and involved the use of contactors under each of the motor cars that controlled the motor current. The contactors were operated from the several train wires running the length of the train, these being operated by a master controller on the leading car where the driver called for whatever power was needed. This system was not automatic and the driver had to manipulate the controller by hand as the train accelerated, to maintain an efficient rate of acceleration. The control circuits used a small amount of current from the traction supply rather than batteries, but this was not considered unsafe. The American version of this equipment was used on both the New York subway and on the Manhattan elevated system as well as the Central London Railway in London.

Both the trial systems (and those following for the next ninety years or so) used series-parallel control technology and included basic safety devices such as the cutting off of power if the emergency brake were applied. At first both motor cars were equipped with two sets of pick-up shoegear (one set on each bogie) and sockets at the ends of all cars allowed all the shoes of like polarity to be connected together along the train. However, photographs clearly show that after a short while the trailers were also fitted with shoegear. As soon as the trains arrived they were subjected to an extensive system of tests to compare actual performance against that expected. As the trains were wired differently, the cars could not be swapped between trains, though short trains could be run.

Ealing & South Harrow Operation

A trial trip for the benefit of the District's directors took place on 9th April 1903, when the press was told it was hoped to open the line on 1st May.[32] By early May, when the line had still not been opened, this had become 'a few weeks'. Unconstrained testing took place along the unopened E&SHR but it was more difficult to test the new equipment on the section between Hanger Lane and Mill Hill Park; this carried the existing steam service but the Sunday church interval provided a convenient opportunity for testing between 3rd May and 14th June.

The electric service was not ready until mid-June when the District announced it was to open the line throughout on Monday 22nd, to capture the traffic for the Royal

DISTRICT RAILWAY.

G.O. 27.

NOTICE TO STAFF

RESPECTING

OPENING OF SOUTH HARROW LI

1. The Extension of the Railway from Hanger Lane Junction (
is situated about midway between Ealing Common and Ealing Broa
Stations) to SOUTH HARROW will be opened for Passenger and Pa
Traffic on Monday, 22nd June, 1903.

2. The Station Initials and Names of Stations are:—

NORTH EALING and HANGER HILL.

PARK ROYAL (for Royal Agricultural Society's Show Gr and Twyford Abbey).

PERIVALE-ALPERTON.

SUDBURY TOWN (for Horsendon).

SUDBURY HILL (for Greenford Green).

SOUTH HARROW (for Roxeth and Northolt).

3. The Train Service over the Harrow Line will be formed part by Electric and partly by Steam Trains (for particulars see Working Noti 71/03 and others to be issued from time to time).

4. As there will be only two Classes on the Electrical Trains (vi 1st and 3rd), holders of 2nd Class Tickets must, when travelling betwe Mill Hill Park and any Harrow Line Station be allowed to travel 1st Cl without payment of Excess Fare. During the week ending 27th ins there will be no distinction of class on the Electric Trains.

5. The directions in the General Instructions Book applicable to th Ealing and Hounslow Lines apply to Harrow Line Stations, and attenti is drawn to the alterations made in Rules 48 (n) & (o) and 69.

6. The present stock of "All Stations" Staff Privileged Tickets w not be withdrawn, and although such Tickets issued by both District a Metropolitan Railways are NOT printed on the back as being available Harrow Line Stations they must be recognised thereat.

7. Workmen's Tickets will be issued up to 7.30 a.m., the back journey halves being available for return by any Train after 12 noon.

8. From date of opening of Harrow Line, Workmen's Ticket and from Ealing and Hounslow Line Stations will also be issued u 7.30 a.m. under the same conditions as Workmen's Tickets generally other parts of District Railway.

Cheap Early Morning Fares Tickets to and from Ealing and Houn Lines Stations will be issued after 7.30 a.m. by, and in connection wit 'ollowing Trains:—

From LONDON (East to West) BY TRAINS DUE AT		To LONDON (West to Eas BY TRAINS FROM	
'ng Broadway ...	8. 2 a.m.	Ealing Broadway ...	at 7.54
Ealing ...		Ealing ...	...
slow Barr		slow Barracks ...	

OYAL AGRICULTURAL SHOW, 1903.

9. From 23rd (Tuesday) to 27th inst. (Saturday), both days in- e, the ROYAL AGRICULTURAL SOCIETY will hold their First Annual in the Permanent Ground, Park Royal, which is within a few ites' walk of Park Royal Station.

10. Passengers should be directed to turn to the right on leaving Royal Station and to take the first turning on the right, which tter road leads to the Main Entrance to the Show Ground.

11. As Tickets may be issued to the L. N. W. Railway Show Ground ion (in which case Passengers have to change at Willesden Junction) must be taken, when Passengers ask for Trains to Park Royal, to t them according to the route shown on the Tickets they hold.

Those travelling by District Company's direct route must proceed r by Through South Harrow Trains or be directed to change at Hill Park, as the case may be.

12. Tickets issued to Park Royal from S. E. & C., or L. B. S. C. Railway Stations are NOT AVAILABLE for use over District Railway, nless printed as issued to Park Royal via Victoria and West Kensington.

13. In announcing South Harrow Trains mention must be made Park Royal, and in announcing any other Trains calling at Mill Hill rk "Change at Mill Hill Park for Park Royal" must also be announced.

W. E. SOAR.

TRAFFIC MANAGER'S OFFICE,
ST. JAMES' PARK STATION,
20th June, 1903.

Remnants of leaflet issued in connection with the opening of the Ealing & South Harrow line with electric trains. The leaflet anticipated opening of the whole line on 22nd June, but this was overtaken by events and only opened to Park Royal on 23rd with full opening on 28th. Author's collection

Agricultural Show at the new Park Royal showground, held between 23rd and 27th June 1903.[33] There had not originally been intended a station between North Ealing and Perivale-Alperton but showground traffic made it worthwhile constructing one and a mundane wooden structure was thrown up near Twyford Abbey Road, called Park Royal and Twyford Abbey.

Unfortunately, treacherous weather caused embankment slips further north which blocked the line and the public opening was postponed for two weeks. Nevertheless, the showground traffic was considered so valuable that by using the crossover at North Ealing a 15-minute train service was arranged between Mill Hill Park and Park Royal from 23rd June, running on a single line basis. Two trains were employed. Although the District did capture some show traffic, only 65,000 visitors attended, rather less than hoped; even so, the District was grateful for the traffic.

Better weather enabled embankment repairs to be completed faster than expected and on 28th June the whole line was opened as far as South Harrow offering an hourly service during slack hours enhanced during busy hours to irregular (but about 15-30 minute) intervals making connections at Mill Hill Park.[34] From the July timetable (beginning on 4th July) the basic train service on the South Harrow line was scheduled to be half-hourly for most of the day.[35]

Although it was mooted that part of the service would be run by steam trains when the line opened, newspaper and other reports of the events suggest that the trains were all electrically operated. There was a suggestion that only the BTH train would be available for some weeks but the sighting of more than one 4-car train suggests this did not happen. District shareholders were told on 6th August 1903 that four trains were available for use on the South Harrow line, though usually only two were actually needed in service. This is consistent with there being two 4-car and two middle-motor single cars available, at least in theory.[36]

There is some evidence that cars from one of the equipment manufacturers were unreliable. A District official told *The Financier* in May 1904 that: 'we had two trains running at first, but one of them developed certain faults, and we have taken it off the regular service, using it now and again, and then making a careful examination to see the reasons for the faults developed.' At some point, the unsatisfactory Westinghouse equipment was entirely replaced and it is possible this explains its absence.[37]

Passenger reaction to the cars in their original form was muted through want of their being many passengers. Such comment as the *Railway Magazine* obtained from a single reader claimed the lighting was poor and constantly flickered, the cars were draughty, the seats had no armrests and the cars jolted and swayed excessively. This is probably not a representative view but may reflect an enforced departure from a comfortable and cosy railway compartment of the traditional kind. The flickering was remarked on by others too and was said to have been caused by the new and dirty conductor rails, the problem soon disappearing.

On 1st July 1903 water-feed troubles at the power station at 7pm saw electric services suspended for four hours (a report describes a steam engine and single carriage bringing belated City passengers home).[38] Some similar kind of trouble happened later in the month; between 21st and 25th July, single cars were substituted for the scheduled 4-car trains. At about the same time, the minutes report that a horse on the line, between Park Royal and Alperton, somehow managed to come into collision with both single cars, putting them out of action for a day (we know not the fate of the horse).[39] From 18th October boiler repairs at the power station reduced power available and for several days it was again necessary to replace the trains by single cars.

The problem with the troublesome earthworks was evidently not cured when the railway opened to South Harrow. During November 1903, following a period of rain, there was a further subsidence affecting the embankment between the River Brent and Alperton viaduct and the whole of the branch had to be operated as a single line whilst works took place on the other. This failure was very serious. The situation was still ongoing on 12th December when an irate passenger wrote to *The Times* complaining that posters were still announcing a half-hour service towards Harrow but since the slip the train service had been reduced to hourly, 'the actual departure times being a complete mystery'.[40] The shareholders were later told the cause was damage caused by severe flooding along the Brent valley which had resulted in part of the line having to be reconstructed at substantial expense and maintenance on other parts of the line being higher than expected.[41] The stabilization work was not finally completed until 5th June 1904 and followed a period from March when contractors' trains consolidated the embankment using spoil from the excavations for the new depot at Mill Hill Park. Restoration of the line was just in time for the Royal Agricultural show of 1904 which operated between 21st and 25th June. Although the electric service remained half-hourly, it was augmented by through half-hour steam trains running direct from central London.

Even after all this, some more precautions were taken and in December 1904 the District determined to buy strips of land alongside the troublesome section so the slopes could be flattened, 2¾ acres being obtained.[42]

General Description of Line

When trains began running to South Harrow passengers found a line meandering pleasantly through open countryside, and around the base of unspoilt Horsenden Hill, towards the margins of Roxeth, a village at the foot of Harrow Hill. The only major civil engineering work was the substantial viaduct over the canal at Alperton from which a small cluster of houses (and the District's small power station) might have been seen; the only other cluster, at Sudbury, would have been invisible from the cutting.

South Harrow and North Ealing stations both had brick station buildings, each of two storeys with a pitched roof and of a rather domestic style. The upper storeys comprised the stationmaster's accommodation and at ground floor level centrally-located entrances from the forecourts led to the small ticket halls. At South Harrow the building was on the 'up' (London-bound) side and the booking hall led directly onto the platform (the other platform was accessible by means of a subway). Both platforms had substantially-built pitched roof awnings supported on columns. At North Ealing, the building had to be on the 'down' side and was higher than platform level allowing direct access to the overbridge to the 'up' platform as well as steps directly to the 'down' platform. Only the 'down' platform had awnings (similar to those at South Harrow), the other one had just a small shelter.

Sudbury Hill, Sudbury Town and Perivale-Alperton stations had large shed-like buildings that served as ticket offices. These structures were all similar and constructed of wood and corrugated iron. The large pitched roofs were adapted at each station to suit conditions, variously overhanging parts of the entrances or platform to provide some weather protection. In all cases the entrance was at the centre of the façade and inside

Alperton station as it appeared about 1910, but very little changed since opening day in 1903 for the Yerkes experimental service. The unused signal box is just visible, rendered unnecessary by the automatic signals.
Author's collection

Sudbury Town for Horsenden station looking south not long after opening, view from the unused signal box. Author's collection

was a gloomy wooden ticket office with fairly small, mean windows. At Sudbury Hill there were awnings on the 'up' platform and a smaller shelter with raked back roof on the 'down' platform. The station building was on the bridge and steps led down to each platform. At Sudbury Town the station building was at platform level and the roof was extended over part of the 'up' platform to provide sheltering, a separate small shelter being put on the 'down' platform. At Perivale-Alperton (the 'Perivale' was dropped

Below: **Park Royal and Twyford Abbey station was an afterthought provided for the Royal Agricultural Show and not originally expected to be a permanent station.** Author's collection

Even a few years after opening, the bridge at the north end of Park Royal station adequately demonstrates the lack of development going on in this tranquil area. This is Twyford Abbey Road, looking east. Author's collection

from 7th October 1910), the building was at road level and steps led up the platforms, awnings being provided on the 'up' line and the usual small shelter on the 'down'. All these platforms were at first of wooden construction, though by the 1920s photographs suggest they had already been replaced by solid construction with non-slip nosing stones.

Park Royal, being an afterthought, was in a rather different style with wooden platforms and a hut-like building erected on a trestle arrangement straddling the embankment on the 'up' side and a lengthy stairway leading down to the unmade street below. Both platforms had grim-looking shelters, that on the 'up' platform next to the ticket hall. Separate steps connected the 'down' platform and the road, but there was also a footbridge. Although Park Royal had been intended as a temporary station, it lasted nearly thirty years as the showground area developed as a major trading estate. Here, too, the wooden platform was later upgraded to stone. The station was later rebuilt on a new site.

The line was not busy. For some years virtually the only habitation was at South Harrow and people living on the hill were far more likely to use Harrow-on-the-Hill station with its better and more direct train service. At Sudbury Hill and Sudbury Town a few houses were built north of the line but there was nothing in any other direction (and a new electric tram route better served much of this area). There was very little development at Alperton, nothing at Park Royal & Twyford Abbey but North Ealing showed some promise, though it was right at the edge of the town and there was no development to the east. While the early train service intervals were maintained, train lengths were reduced and Park Royal station became for a while a request stop with restricted opening hours.

The Great Central interest

In 1898 the Great Central Railway (GCR) obtained powers to create a diversionary route between Neasden and Grendon Underwood, part of which was shared with the GWR. The new line had its own station at Sudbury Hill and crossed beneath the E&SHR line less

Above: **Exterior of South Harrow station a few years after opening. This was one of only two brick-built stations. The exterior of the other, at North Ealing, was nearly identical.** Author's collection

Below: **Postcard of South Harrow in early days looking towards London. The subway connecting platforms is just visible at this end of the awning.** Author's collection

than half a mile south of South Harrow. The GCR wanted a bridge here and was prepared to supply one with sufficient room for four E&SHR tracks in case they were ever required. However, the E&SHR owned a strip of land between 250ft and 300ft wide, adjacent to its line on the east side; this ran all the way between South Harrow station and Wood End Road and crossed the path of the GCR route at an angle. The E&SHR therefore obliged the GCR to provide a 600ft long covered way completely beneath this strip, at substantial expense, passive provision being made for later installation of an extra pair of GCR tracks below. The GCR route was constructed between 1901 and 1905 and the contractor's temporary line crossed over the E&SHR by means of a wooden bridge whilst the permanent line was being built underneath. The land above this covered way, even today, is just woodland.

During construction of this diversionary route the GCR and the District considered a running link between the two railways, allowing southbound GCR trains to access the District tracks towards London and vice versa. Plans were drawn up which made provision for a double line connection with a small goods yard at the GCR end and the earthworks were completed, the remains visible today. Powers for the two railways to agree joint running arrangements and provide goods yards were granted in the 1901-2 Session but no running connection was actually installed, probably because proposals for goods traffic at west end of the District were not pursued.

Plan showing the Great Central Railway Neasden-Northolt line (running left to right) and tunnel under the District, heading north towards South Harrow, shown towards right. The plan shows proposed link between the railways and interchange goods sidings alongside the GCR line. Author's collection

This looks south towards Sudbury Hill. In foreground, the Great Central Railway tunnel is being excavated beneath the District tracks but their contractors' railway actually crosses above the District (which has been opened) by the ramshackle temporary bridge. The cutting on the right was later removed to install a running connection between the railways (though track was not laid). Leicestershire Library Service

Improving Capacity west of Hammersmith

It should be recorded here that the LSWR-owned section of line between Studland Road Junction and Turnham Green was considered a possible source of congestion for the new electric services. This section was used by both LSWR and Met trains that would continue to be steam-hauled and was not amenable to the new electro-pneumatic signalling that would soon become universal elsewhere on the District. The solution appeared to be independent tracks, and powers to construct these were sought in the District's bill for the 1903 Session. The powers would have permitted separate tracks to be constructed on the south side of the LSWR lines to a point west of Turnham Green where a junction would be made with the existing Richmond line; the new District tracks would meanwhile sweep above the Richmond line to rejoin the existing alignment to Ealing. The LSWR objected to this scheme, which would deprive it of revenue, and the clauses were dropped. In exchange, the LSWR agreed to revise the arrangements between the companies giving the District more freedom. In particular, the District could now run as many trains as it felt necessary and fix all fares to its western stations (including Turnham Green and Ravenscourt Park) without reference to the LSWR. The new agreement was for ten years and the District could revisit the matter of widening if it proved impossible to run the number of trains required. The agreement did not improve prospect of sharing of the line with steam trains and the continuance of the mechanical signalling system.

Chapter Three
MODERNIZATION AT LAST

Deep Level Developments

We left the District's child, the dormant BPCR in 1900 with powers already obtained to make a junction with the District deep-level line at South Kensington and, if expedient, to use the District's powers to build the BPCR westwards to Earls Court. With District main line electrification being pressed forward it is evident the BPCR was taking priority over the deep-level duplicate District proposal. Allowing BPCR trains to reach the District's station at Earls Court would have made a rather inconvenient turning point and the possibility of BPCR trains running further west (or reduced-size District trains running onto the tube) cannot be discounted. In any event, the District would retain powers to run trains at deep level over the Earls Court to South Kensington section and there was not yet any suggestion the deep level line further east should be abandoned.

In 1901 the BPCR sought powers for a branch from South Kensington via the Fulham Road to Chelsea, at Stamford Bridge.[1] At South Kensington station very complex junctions were thought necessary to allow trains from this branch to run eastwards onto both the District main line and the District deep level, as well as the BPCR main line towards Piccadilly. Perhaps fortunately the bill failed.

The BPCR was one of many tube schemes that lacked any means of funding but Yerkes was aware of it through his interest in the District. By the time he became involved, Parliament was under pressure to consider numerous speculative tube railway bills and

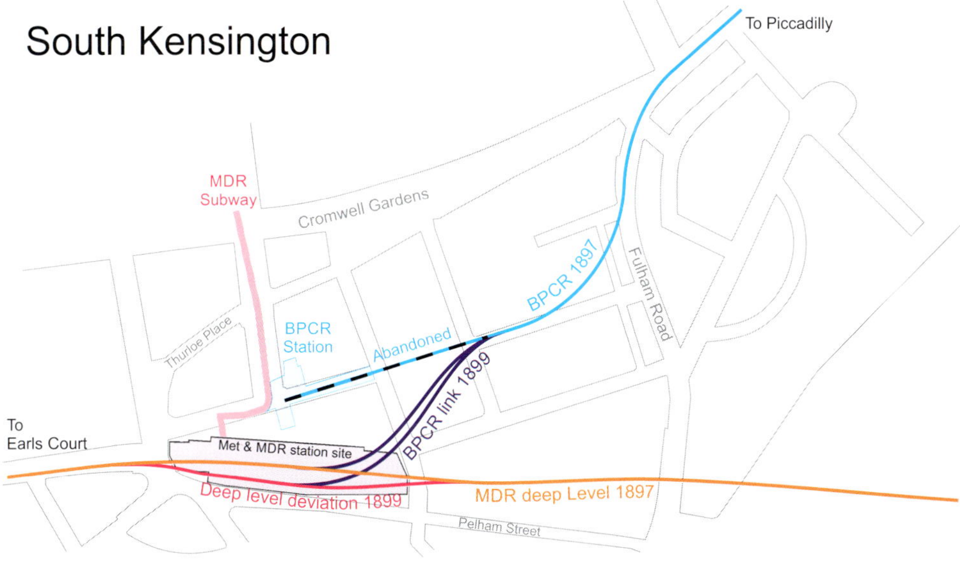

Plan of South Kensington showing relationship between District deep level line and the associated Brompton & Piccadilly Circus line. MACH

made it known it would avoid authorizing duplicative lines and wanted to see 'through routes'. Noted earlier was a decision by Yerkes to acquire the dormant GNSR in September 1901 and his team rapidly concluded a plan to build a connecting link between Piccadilly Circus and Holborn to produce a through route from Finsbury Park to South Kensington, Earls Court and stations farther west. This link was also included in the bill for the 1901-2 Session and had better success than the speculative branches at South Kensington.

In evidence given during the bill's committee hearing the BPCR's engineer (James Szlumper) specifically referred to each of the District's western termini as possible sources of traffic and the District's Robert Perks, in his evidence, thought the new line would bring a great deal of new traffic to the District and regretted it had not been possible to proceed sooner. Yerkes himself gave evidence and suggested through trains, of two motor cars and four trailers, would be operated along the tube section, and other evidence given suggests trains from Ealing and Hounslow would have run through 'to the north'. The Act also changed the name of the BPCR to the ponderously titled Great Northern Piccadilly & Brompton Railway, which will here be shortened to 'Piccadilly tube'.[2]

The 1902 Act excluded a proposed line linking the BPCR at Piccadilly to the deep-level line at Charing Cross enabling District deep-level trains to reach the City via either Piccadilly or the direct route; the committee examining the bill at first felt the curves were too sharp but although the railway agreed to ease them the arrangement of tunnels at Piccadilly was now found objectionable. It also found the preamble not proved for a direct line of 2 miles 32 chains from Knightsbridge via Fulham Road to meet the District west of Parsons Green, with running powers to Putney Bridge, which was also struck out.

The manner in which the Piccadilly tube was to be linked with the District was to develop further. For the 1903 parliamentary session the District proposed to extend the deep level railway from the site of the authorized connection at Knaresborough Place to the east end of Hammersmith station at the Great Church Lane bridge from where it would have run into the terminal platforms of the existing station. This would have given the Piccadilly tube trains a proper terminal whilst facilitating some kind of connection with the District. This did not survive the parliamentary process unscathed for the extension was chopped off at the west end of Earls Court station in new deep level platforms, which were presumably viewed as a terminal. The running connection with the District at Knaresborough Place, allowed for in the 1897 Act, was formally abandoned. However, the Act, passed on 21st July, included the agreement between the Piccadilly and District of 17th April 1902 where the District agreed to provide access on its own lands between the main line and the deep level lines to be used by the Piccadilly; the agreement did not commit itself to where this might be but simply stated that the District was under no obligation to provide this access more than 20 chains west of West Kensington station, suggesting the matter was subject to ongoing discussion. That a railway should be authorized in an agreement was rather unusual but it was wholly under District property and acquisition of compulsory powers was unnecessary.

Further reflection about what should happen to Piccadilly trains beyond Earls Court resulted in the District agreeing to accommodate Piccadilly tube trains at Hammersmith and to duplicate the existing line between Hammersmith and the point where the tube rose to the surface. Powers for the widening were obtained in the District's 1904 Act. The Piccadilly tube connection required a lengthy 1:50-graded ramp, contained within concrete walls, west of the tunnel mouth and reaching surface level just east of the Gliddon Road bridge. Further east, space for the extra tracks was achieved mainly by trimming back the slopes of the shallow cutting and building vertical retaining walls

In the background lies West Kensington station and the Ferris wheel in the District's exhibition grounds. In the foreground are located the new Piccadilly tracks (in the cutting) and the adjacent District tracks (on the right, taking up space once partly the back yards of the dwellings). Image taken early 1906. Just visible between the tunnel mouth and Great Wheel is the signal box controlling access to the Midland goods yard at West Kensington. On the left are the Piccadilly lay-by sidings; in the background may be seen the connection with the District so Piccadilly trains could access Lillie Bridge yard. Author's collection

on both sides, avoiding the need to obtain much extra land; the Piccadilly was to have use of the two extra tracks along the northern side. At Hammersmith the Piccadilly would occupy existing terminal platform space the District no longer needed. Running connections would be made with the District, but only for empty stock moves. The tunnel section from Earls Court and the ramp were formally vested in the Piccadilly tube whilst the widened District line was rented to the Piccadilly for £12,000 a year from 1st January 1905. The junction between the two was exactly 20 chains from West Kensington in line with the agreement.

The whole of the construction works between South Kensington and Hammersmith were placed in the hands of the engineer, Mr Cuthbert A Brereton, and the contractors for the widening work were Messrs Bott & Stennett. As part of this work 80 trucks and two locomotives were used to carry excavated material to Hounslow to build up land in the angle where the Hounslow Town branch peeled off.[3]

At South Kensington options to build some variation of the deep level line at a future date were left open by building junction tunnels west of the Piccadilly tube platform on the westbound line, and at the east end of the eastbound platform. It was also convenient to build a short length of District deep tube (westbound) platform at the back of the lifts. In 1927 this dead space was converted into a signalling school and later a wartime engineering headquarters, but is now part of the station subway network.

The District did not immediately give up all hope of building the rest of the deep level line although sharing the Earls Court–South Kensington section with the Piccadilly would have been very difficult. The District's 1903 bill included a deep level line by extension from the existing proposed terminus at Mansion House to just west of Stepney Green on the Whitechapel and Bow, thus completely by-passing the City Lines. This was not allowed to proceed and, after that, it was obvious that the deep level line served no useful purpose and that was the end of it. The line was formally abandoned by the District's 1908 Act.

Hounslow Line Developments

With the arrival of Yerkes and his team, the Hounslow branch perhaps stood out as a particularly dire example of a railway failing to develop new traffic. As things stood, the line was worked by the District but owned by the Hounslow & Metropolitan Railway (H&MR). Passenger traffic was so low that the District had great difficulty even in paying the H&MR debenture holders. Although the H&MR preference shareholders were 'guaranteed' payment, there was no money to actually pay them and the debts rolled over each half year, mounting up as they did so. The ordinary shareholders never received a penny, and were in good company with the District's own shareholders for whom this was normal.

While the District had to work and maintain the line it had no responsibility for investing in it. The H&MR was not motivated to do so either as its shareholders were not disposed to pour more money into this disastrous venture. Meanwhile the District was required neither to invest nor to throw good money after bad either. Costs were cut to the bone but the situation was most unsatisfactory.

The little-used line was offered for use as a testbed for a novel system of electrification in 1890. This was a scheme promoted by the Series Electrical Traction Syndicate who held patents for a variety of third-rail electrification where the electrical current travelled through successive trains in series. This challenge could only be met by breaking the traction current circuit at the point where each train was located and connecting each train's motor circuit across each side of the break. This meant somehow deploying pickups on each train that somehow disconnected the intervening piece of traction conductor. A moment's thought suggests any number of formidable technical challenges. The answer was a conduit below one of the running rails containing a very large number of connectors, wired in series, between which a pickup below the train ploughed its way, successively breaking the circuit. The company was only set up in 1887 but transformed in 1889 to the Series & General Electric Traction Company and although the heads of terms were agreed with the District nothing was actually done and the traction company went out of business soon after, being removed from the register of companies in 1893. The traction company appears to have undertaken to provide the equipment between Mill Hill Park and Hounslow at its own cost for demonstration purposes, using two District carriages and two special motor cars using 150hp motors.[4] The work required on an existing line would have been formidable, but I should add that this improbable system was actually deployed on a demonstration tramway in Northfleet and was shown to be feasible.

At a more mundane level, it would be fair to say that after the Hounslow Town branch closed in 1886 the unadventurous train services settled down to a bare minimum and little more was done. Lack of initiative to develop traffic meant that it remained very light and insufficient for the branch to pay its way. *The Railway Magazine* carried a vivid article on the Hounslow branch in 1901, part of which bears setting out below:

> The branch of the Metropolitan District Railway from Mill Hill Park to Hounslow Barracks is probably the most cheaply worked line in the kingdom. The staff at the stations consist of an inspector, a porter, and a youth, but as the time the stations are open extends over a large portion of the twenty-four hours, it frequently happens that not more than one of the staff is seen at the same time. During the greater part of the day the train service is performed by a train of five carriages, which makes one journey each way every hour, although in the morning and early evening trains run every half-hour. The line was opened to Hounslow on May 1, 1883, and the stations are, therefore, of a modem type, but the woodwork probably has not been repainted since the stations were first completed. There are signal-boxes at the stations, but the signals are not connected with them. The normal position of the signals is 'off', and they are apparently always in this position, although there is a legend that they are placed at danger after the passing of each train, and not again taken 'off' until the train rings an electric bell, by means of a rail contact when passing out of the block section. Starting signals are not provided; the posts are there, but no semaphores. The only engineering work worthy of notice on the line is the two-span lattice-girder bridge, carrying the railway over the Brent River Navigation and the Brentford branch of the Great Western Railway, which at the point of crossing happen to be side by side. As rigid economy is practised on the line, it is surprising to find that the train uses both the up and down lines. Why not work the branch as a 'single line'? The wear, tear and maintenance of one set of rails would thereby be saved, as well as the lighting of one of the platforms at each of the stations.
>
> As a matter of fact, the line is single on the extension to Hounslow Barracks (referred to later on), and this newer portion has been constructed in a less lavish manner, the station buildings being of corrugated iron, with but a short platform. The signal-box, which controls the single line, is used, but is not situate at the commencement of the 'single' portion. It is placed in a position to operate the signals and points in connection with the (now disused) line to Hounslow Town Station, the single line not beginning for about 160 yards beyond the box. The box is placed on the up side of the line (which, as we have already indicated, is double at this point), consequently the driver can deliver up the staff on the up journey to the signalman without the latter leaving his cabin, but how the staff is handed to the driver on the down journey is another matter.
>
> The district through which the branch railway from Mill Hill Park runs has developed but little since the line was opened eighteen years ago, the surrounding country being market gardens and orchards. The only thing liberal about the line is the number of the inclined blocks provided for actuating the station indicators in the train, no less than seven of these being provided on the up line at South Ealing, within a couple of yards of each other. By the way, the branch train is not fitted with the station indicators, but this is a mere detail, the intention is good.

The connections with the Ealing trains are very well arranged at Mill Hill Junction, the up branch and the down main line trains arrive almost at the same time, the branch train then runs forward, and the engine runs round the train, meanwhile the down train has left for Ealing, and the branch train occupies the down platform for its return journey, the up main line train arriving at the same time, so that passengers to and from the branch do not have any unnecessary waiting at Mill Hill Station.

The Great Western Railway to the north and the London and South-Western Railway to the south, pretty well absorb the traffic arising in the district, and now to make matters worse for the District Railway, electric tram lines have been laid down the Bath Road to Hounslow, and in a few days the trams will be running, so that the outlook is not improving.

The derelict line to the Hounslow Town Station is about half a mile in length, and was constructed in the most substantial manner with a double set of rails, about one-half of it being on a brick viaduct of over twenty arches. There is (or was) an imposing station, a signal-box, engine line with coal stage, engine pit, water tank and column, a complete system of signals, with interlocking, and, in fact, everything required on a first-class line of railway. But time has wrought havoc with the disused line, the flooring of the two platforms is gone (except under the covered portion), and the beams are fast decaying. Only one connection (the down) remains with the used portion of the railway, the points, and a short length of the up line, it is true, are still in situ at the junction, but the remainder of the rails up to the platform have been takes up, as also have the crossings and rails at the 'dead end' of the platforms. The station-house buildings are occupied as a dwelling-house, and the covered portion of the platform is used for hanging out the family washing, while a solitary cock fowl is to be seen strutting about on the platform, and is apparently 'monarch of all he surveys'. At any rate, we did not stay 'to dispute his rights'.

The station yard and some of the arches are let to the District Council for storing steam rollers, dust carts, and other articles for which the Council's offices are not adequately adapted.

The existing situation was untenable and looming electrification meant investment was unavoidable and it was time to sort out the ownership arrangements and bring the H&MR completely into the fold. The 1880 working agreement provided for the District to buy the line at its cost price (roundly £300,000), but since this was felt to exceed by a long way its earning value no attempt had been made to buy it sooner. The District now found it convenient to offer a price representing about half its construction cost, which was felt reasonable by both parties.

The District purchased the H&MR on 21st July 1903 (the date of the authorizing Act) and thereafter it was part of the District. Payment was made by the issuing of 3½% Hounslow Rentcharge stock to the value of £165,714, this being exchanged at face value for the H&MR's debentures and preference shares (with outstanding interest owed). The luckless ordinary shareholders got back rather less than 20 per cent of the face value.*

Interest on the rentcharge stock was secured on the revenues of the Hounslow branch, but arrears were secured on the whole of the District's earning. This was a good deal for those owning the guaranteed shares. The new rentcharge stock was soon rolled into a consolidated District rentcharge stock offering the same return.

One effect of the District's renewed interest in the branch once purchased was to re-open Hounslow Town station. This was a wasting though expensive asset, given its much better traffic position compared with the remote stations on the Barracks line. Some idea of its circumstances was given at a District shareholders' meeting when it was explained that Hounslow Town had been shut up for years, though it was understood chickens had been kept there and some platelayers had used the building as lodgings.[5] The District was already in the process of putting the station back into a good condition, which required a great deal of work. It was re-opened on 1st March 1903.

---

* At takeover there were £53,000 worth of 5% preference shares that were not receiving any return and £70,000 worth of debentures actually receiving the 4½% due. There was also £210,000 worth of ordinary shares.

CABS. Cabs meet the Trains at HESTON-HOUNSLOW and HOUNSLOW BARRACKS Stations, *but to prevent disappointment they should be ordered beforehand* by a communication addressed to the Station Inspector, Heston-Hounslow or Hounslow Barracks Station, as the case may be.

Cabs can also be obtained at EALING, MILL HILL PARK, and CHISWICK PARK and at PUTNEY BRIDGE (Fulham) Stations.

To help promote travel along the Hounslow line the use of cabs was promoted to help passengers complete their journeys. Author's collection

Having two Hounslow branches was awkward and the District felt the best way of serving both was to operate single trains to and from Osterley and send portions to each branch. In the up direction a 3-coach train from Hounslow Town arrived at Osterley and then drew forward to clear the entrance to the sidings located between the running lines. The 5-coach portion from Hounslow Barracks would then arrive and the engine would run forward into the sidings. The 'Town' portion would then set back into the platform and couple up before the whole train departed towards London. In the other direction the 'Town' portion was uncoupled, allowing the 'Barracks' portion at the country end to depart. An engine from the east end siding was then run through the station and backed onto the 'Town' portion ready for it to depart.[6]

This cumbersome system did not last very long and from 1st October 1903 the Hounslow Town service was reduced to a shuttle from Osterley, as in 1884. From 1st May 1904 the shuttle was taken off altogether in favour of working the trains alternately to each destination, giving them only an hourly service.[7]

Trams in on the Act

Life along the sleepy Hounslow branch might just have been busier soon after the Yerkes team arrived. The Metropolitan District Electric Traction Co promoted a light railway in November 1901, application being made to the Light Railway Commissioners for the appropriate order. The line was to run from Hounslow predominantly along the Bath Road via Colnbrook to Slough, stopping in the High Street, opposite Windsor Road. A branch was to run along the Ditton Road through Stoke Poges and terminating in Datchet, near the Manor Hotel. At the Hounslow end the line was to pass under the Bath Road near Hounslow Barracks station and form a junction with the H&MR immediately east of the station. The intention appears to have been to operate an on-street electric tram system between Slough, Datchet and Hounslow Barracks and then have some kind of interchange station. The powers would have allowed a through running connection to have been made but the light railway's engineer, Sir Alexander Binnie, explained that this was not contemplated owing to the difficulty of designing suitable rolling stock.

The scheme amounted to about twelve miles of line and was heavily opposed by the GWR and LSWR, the London United Tramways, the various urban district councils and Buckingham and Middlesex County Councils, the latter of which considered that preference should be given to a deal already done with the London United Tramways (LUT) to operate on the Council's behalf tramways in the county south of the Grand Junction Canal. Indeed the LUT made known its own (quite similar) scheme shortly before the public inquiry which was held in February 1902. Further difficulties arose as to how the line could get through the narrow high street in Colnbrook as the commissioners could not see how it could adequately be widened, which resulted in the proposal being refused consent.[8] As it happened, the LUT joined the UERL in 1902 but its own electric trams never got further west than Hounslow town centre.

The MDETC also promoted a Windsor and Maidenhead Light Railway at the same time as the Slough and Datchet proposal, but they were not to be interconnected. The Windsor line comprised 12¼ miles of line between Windsor and Maidenhead and a branch; Sir Arthur Binnie was again the engineer and explained it would serve as a feeder to the GWR. There was again an inquiry, this time at Windsor in February 1902, and there was again a great deal of opposition. The GWR opposed the line on the usual basis that it considered its own train services sufficient and the LUT was also vigorous in its disapproval even though it had neither nearby routes of its own nor plans to build any. Maidenhead Corporation opposed on basis it might build one of its own, though Windsor supported the scheme, as did many people along the route. Again the route was refused.[9] Why the traction company, with so much very important stuff on its plate already, was getting involved in schemes so remote from London and beyond where at that time it was unlikely an electricity supply could be supplied economically has not been established, but these two rebuttals caused ideas for its future tramway developments to be left to the experts at the LUT.

The LUT was keen to gain traffic and to support the District Railway by creating new journey opportunities through good interchanges and the availability of through tickets. In 1904 the LUT put forward a bill to allow its new electric trams to change from street running near Hammersmith Broadway and descend into a subway that would serve a below-ground terminus at Hammersmith at the same level as the District platforms; the terminus would be underneath the station ticket hall and the District supported the scheme. It was hoped to make the interchange with proposed new tramway services to Barnes and Mortlake, amongst other destinations. The London County Council scuppered this potentially very useful proposal on technical grounds by persuading the scrutinizing committee that the bill should have been presented as a tramway bill and not an electric railway bill, and that was the end of that.[10]

The District's Construction Agreements

The first agreement between the MDETC and the District was signed on 18th July 1901. This provided for the whole of the responsibility for electrifying the District, installing electric lighting, providing the rolling stock and providing or adapting necessary maintenance equipment and workshops to be the responsibility of the MDETC. The plans and specifications were to be agreed in advance with the District's engineers and works and equipment were to be completed to the reasonable satisfaction of the District's engineers. In the case of the City Lines the MDETC would provide the money required for the District to pay its proportion of the cost of electrifying that section.

The detail was complex and required the District to recompense the MDETC by issuing it shares to the value of the money advanced on the basis that the District would issue £500,000 of fully paid up ordinary stock reckoned at £25 for each £100 nominal (equal to £125,000) and £166,000 4% debenture stock (totalling £291,000). The MDETC would borrow the money required on the security of the shares, hoping to sell them after electrification at a higher price.

So far as the power station was concerned, the District was to acquire the Lots Road site and the MDETC would finance the District to do so. The MDETC would then, at its own cost, build and equip the power house and build the ducts to Earls Court and upon their completion they would be vested in the MDETC. The District would then be required to lease the power house for 999 years, paying an annual rental equal to 5 per cent of its actual cost (the land and construction cost was capped at £400,000) and 4 per cent of the financing costs up until the point the lease was granted. This arrangement left the District in possession of the power house (which it would operate itself) but also provided an income stream for the MDETC. The power house cost rather more to build than had been hoped; the land alone had been estimated at £80,000 but actually cost £165,000.

When the UERL superseded the MDETC it took over the existing responsibilities but anticipating the larger portfolio of railways that would be serviced by Lots Road some important changes were made by means of a supplemental agreement dated 21st April 1902. This voided the leasing arrangement and left the power house firmly in the hands of the UERL on condition that it provided an ongoing supply of electricity to the District and certain other railways at a fair rate, to be agreed. Instead of the 5 per cent lease charge would be a charge on some proportion of the whole cost of the land and building and this would be included in the electricity charge (this was because by now other railways would also be drawing a supply and would need to pay their own proportionate charge). On 23rd April 1903 yet another agreement was entered into with the UERL. This confirmed that the previous agreements still applied and also made provision for transferring additional shares between the District and UERL if additional costs arose. It was the intention to sell the District (and tube railway) shares obtained this way at some time in the future to recoup the cash expended on electrification and tube construction and make a profit from the uplift in prices. We shall see soon that this was not how matters played out.

These agreements were necessarily led by the District as this was the statutory company involved; perhaps inevitably it exposed quite complicated matters to the gaze of the London County Council which never sought to disguise its distaste for what it felt to be unfettered ambitions of the UERL, its American promoters and the feeling that it was subverting the will of Parliament in its financial control of its subsidiary railways.

Power House Plans

London in 1902 had only just begun to enjoy the benefits of electric light, and then not uniformly throughout the Metropolis. Each small district had been responsible for arranging its own supply, either by building its own generating station or allowing a private company to do so. Some areas had made faster progress than others and a few had only just begun a supply. Nobody was then expected to use electricity for heat or power so generating stations tended to be tiny. In 1900, it is doubtful if the whole of the installed plant in London exceeded 100MW and since few of the local suppliers were interconnected it was impossible to obtain a large load.* In short, there was nobody Yerkes could turn to in order to obtain reliable electricity on the scale needed so the only option was to construct a dedicated power house, sufficiently large to supply each of his own railways and also those sections of foreign railways over which District trains operated.

Yerkes' chief engineer (James Chapman) planned a sizable power house at the Chelsea Creek site, already identified, but not at first expected to supply more than the District

* An exception to the general development of the system was the London Electric Supply Corporation which did generate remotely in Deptford and transmitted to central London at high voltage but had a chequered history and even after the Yerkes system was finished was producing only 10MW. It might have worked out differently had Forbes, its chairman, not lost confidence in Ferranti, that company's far-seeing engineer.

and BPCR. No doubt suspicious of the ability of the British to deliver equipment on the scale required, Chapman approached the Westinghouse Electric Manufacturing Co of Pittsburgh in May or June 1901 to tender for traditional reciprocating engines, four high-pressure compound engines of 5200kW being specified (together capable of generating nearly 21MW). When the tender was returned it offered a selection of compound engines for consideration, including 3- and 4-cylinder versions. As an alternative four steam turbines were offered, suitable for generation at 25 cycles a second* with transmission at 11,000 volts. It appears that the turbines (but not the reciprocating engines) would be made in Manchester by the new UK manufacturing facility of Westinghouse, which was in course of construction.† A letter of intent was sent to Westinghouse in August 1901 for four turbines and associated generators, subject to the outcome of the expected arbitration about the electrification system. The generators were not only more efficient than the steam engines but were regarded as easier to keep in phase when supplying power in parallel with other machines. Even so, the building design retained the facility for the tall reciprocating equipment if ever required.

When it was known that the 4-rail dc system was to be adopted, and also that the tube lines would all need to be fed from Lots Road, the plan was changed with the building design considerably enlarged, requiring additional land. At first the plan was altered such that the order for the existing units was increased from four to ten turbo-generator sets, still generating at 25 cycles. This was later changed to eight, more efficient, machines rotating at 1000rpm instead of 750rpm, increasing frequency to 33⅓ cycles per second and uprated to 5500kW. A station capacity of 44MW was considered adequate for the time being and the provision for two further machines to be added later if demand required suggested an ultimate capacity of 55MW, at least.

There was criticism both at the time and later that so much electrification work was going outside the UK, but Yerkes said that where this was so the UK could either not meet the standard or the required delivery times. Whilst true that some of the equipment would be sourced in Pittsburgh, much of the electrical equipment at Lots Road would all be built by the Westinghouse British subsidiary or other British suppliers.

Plant Actually Installed

Although power house construction began in 1902 it was not possible to get access to all the land until the end of 1903, a huge inconvenience. In February 1904 Yerkes told newspapers that he hoped to have electric trains running by 1st January 1905 if the power house were complete.

Excluding the track owned by the Met, the route mileage of track to be electrified amounted to 41 route miles, either owned by the District or over which District trains ran. In addition were the tracks of the other tube and associated lines, which amounted to just over 33 miles. It may be seen that over half the supply of the Lots Road station would be needed for the District alone.

Like many power stations the live plant was divided into two sections, one for raising the steam and the other for actual generation. The steam raising equipment was arranged in the boiler house, which faced the Thames, and was 453ft 6ins long by 175ft broad and 140ft high. The four immense chimneys were built by Alphons Custodis Chimney

---

* Today we use a unit called the Hertz (Hz) to represent the frequency at that time defined by 'cycles a second'.

† This was called the British Westinghouse Electrical & Manufacturing Co but from 1907 American control waned and after ownership change the company became Metropolitan-Vickers in 1919.

The cable duct being laid as part of a new road. The cableway from Lots Road was a massive task involving wide and deep trenches into which the 64 individual ducts were installed. It was probably the largest electricity distribution main in London at that time. The ducts were laid in two groups divided by a central wall (prominent here). This view is from a jointing and inspection chamber. Author's collection

Lots Road in 1904. The as yet incomplete roof covers the high level coal bunker. Author's collection

HEIGHT
275 ft
INTERNAL DIAMETER
19 ft
On top of one of the Shafts
The largest pair of TWIN STACKS
IN THE WORLD
Chelsea Power House of the Underground
Electric Railways Company of London Ltd.
Built on their Patent System by the
Alphons Custodis Chimney Construction Co.,
119 Victoria Street, Westminster, London S. W.

Zachariah Ellis Knapp came to London with a reputation for building traction power stations and had a major role in the success of Lots Road. He became Yerkes' chief draftsman. LTM

As some of the largest chimneys thus far built, the Alphons Custodis Chimney Construction Co was proud to make known their involvement with constructing Lots Road Power House. Roy Allen Collection

Construction Co, a New York subsidiary of a German firm, and used German workers.* These 275ft high chimneys were arranged in pairs near each end. The adjacent, but smaller, generator house faced onto Lots Road and was the same length but only about 100ft high and 96ft wide. The vast building was steel-framed and employed both French and German steel.

The boiler house was designed to accommodate 80 boilers, though only 64 were installed at opening. These were Babcock & Wilcox steel water-tube boilers grouped in clusters of eight, some on the first floor and some on the second. This was said at the time to be a unique arrangement and done to save valuable floor space. Each boiler had a working pressure of 175lb per square inch. In normal circumstances, manual firing was unthinkable and mechanical stokers of the chain-grate type were installed, one for each boiler. By this means coal was fed into the boiler and burnt, the speed of feed being managed to match the quality of the fuel.

The coal was stored in a set of colossal bunkers running the entire length of the building just below the roof and were 20ft high, the whole lot (a massive weight even when empty) being supported by steel beams attached to the building's steel frame. The total capacity of the bunkers was 15,000 tons, said to be about three weeks supply at the

* This American company owned the rights to the perforated radial brick, invented by Alphons Custodis in Germany in 1869. This brick allowed chimneys to be built larger than with ordinary bricks. The Lots Road chimneys at 19ft diameter and 275ft height were said by the company at the time to be the largest stacks in the world.

expected rate of usage of 800 tons per day. From this height coal was delivered to the boilers by gravity. Coal normally arrived by barges directly into a specially designed dock in Chelsea Creek, divided from the tidal river by lock gates so the barges being unloaded remained afloat at low tide. Travelling cranes shifted the unloaded coal into a holding area from which mechanical conveyors lifted it to an entry point at the top of the building and further conveyors moved it to the required bunkers. The conveyors could shift 60 tons of coal an hour. It was also possible to obtain coal via the WLR, on the west side of the building. Here, the coal was unloaded from railway wagons into hoppers that fed a second bucket conveyor that took the coal to roof level from which it was dropped onto the belt conveyors.

In the other direction, ash from the boilers was directed by gravity into the basement where a narrow-gauge railway system allowing the ash to be moved about and stored in a bunker outside the building alongside a landing stage in the Chelsea Creek, from where it could be loaded onto barges. Battery locomotives, built by BTH, were used to haul self-dumping trucks into which the ash fell.

The turbo-generators were quite new in Britain at the time and even in the US turbines suited to high-capacity power generation were a fairly new development. The Lots Road machines were described as being the largest steam turbines so far built. Steam entered the turbine unit at 165 lbs per square inch causing the turbine to rotate at 1000 rpm. The steam was finally expelled at little more than atmospheric pressure and was sent to condensers cooled by Thames water drawn in via pipes from the centre of the river and returned several degrees warmer.

Each turbine was directly coupled to a generator set rated at 5.5MW and producing 3-phase alternating current at 11,000 volts, though the rated output was capable of considerable overload for short periods. Each of the eight generators passed through switchgear and fed a group of six or seven feeder cables, each feeding a selection of

Postcard showing the newly electrified tracks at Southfields, an LSWR station served by District trains. At extreme left is the station signal box. LTM

substations. There were fifteen substations associated with the District, and nine others serving only the tube lines, making 24 in all. In all cases, no adjacent substations were usually fed from the same generator so that failure of an individual generator would not result in failure of supply to the track.

The first two turbo-alternators were run in November 1904, but it was not until January 1905 before one was run under load. When electric services actually started in June 1905 there were still only four sets available, with a fifth from the following month. It was only in May 1906 that the last of the eight became available. Fortunately the small number of sets at first available was sufficient and in January 1907 Chapman observed that only three turbo-alternators were then needed to supply the full load of the District and two tubes. Even so, we shall see shortly that with the arrival of the Hampstead tube in June, and poor machine availability, supplies could sometimes be close to the wire.

The electricity had somehow to be conveyed between the power house and the railway and there was very little option but to take it under the streets. This was no small job—even before designs were complete it was clear that over 60 cables might be needed, all carrying heavy currents at 11,000 volts.

With the substantial increase in power output expected at Lots Road the large iron-pipe originally intended for the cableway was going to be hopelessly inadequate and a much larger structure was required, which also impacting on the route. The District was induced to add a second route in its 1902 Act, giving it the option to bring cables to the east end of Earls Court. The second route ran along Lots Road, Upcorne Road, Barnaby Street, Cremorne Road, Edith Grove, Redcliffe Gardens, Earls Court Road and Earls Court Gardens. In addition a connection between this and the earlier route was permitted along Richmond Road so that, if desirable, either of the southern routes could enter the railway at either end of Earls Court.

This route was evidently not considered satisfactory and in the District's 1903 Act a further revised route was adopted. This took the cables from the west end of the power house under Lots Road, Uverdale Road, across Kings Road and under land of the Royal Exotic Nurseries and under Fulham Road, Ifield Road, Adrian Terrace, Finborough Road, across Richmond Road, Warwick Road and onto the railway at the west end of Earls Court station where there was a substation; at the same time powers for the western route along Edith Grove towards Earls Court Road were revoked. One reason for this change was that a new road was being built along the horticultural lands and the cable tunnel could be built at the same time and at far less cost.

Although the connection between the power house and the railway was just over a mile it involved some 65 miles of cable, all supplied by British Insulated and Helsby Cables. The work of constructing the duct began only late in 1903 and took about six months. Callender's Cable & Construction Co Ltd actually built the ducts while the cable company installed and jointed the cables. The duct required a trench 6ft wide and varied in depth from 7ft to 16ft (depending largely on pipes and sewers that were encountered). Where cable joints were planned then chambers had to be built requiring a greater width. The trench was then filled with duct-ways, 64 being deployed in two groups of 32 astride a brick wall. Each duct-way was four ducts wide by eight high and the whole lot was embedded in solid concrete. The ducts, by Doulton, were of glazed earthenware of 4 inches internal diameter. The cables were all 3-core copper, paper insulated and with a thick lead sheath. At first, only 56 cables were laid in, leaving some spare ducts although a telephone cable was laid in one of them. One duct also contained a heavy duty copper earth cable to which the lead sheaths were bonded every 1000ft and one end of which was bonded to the power station's earthing system.

The duct route was legally owned by the District Railway but was also used by the feeder cables serving the various tubes and the District felt use of this wayleave by the tubes should be rewarded. Eventually the sum of £4500 was negotiated for the use of the ducts and cable runs with additional revenue for sharing the use of the substations at Charing Cross, South Kensington and Earls Court.[11] The District owned the cables feeding Campbell Road substation but which were only used to supply the LTSR and the latter were persuaded in 1907 to buy the cables outright, paying the District £18,110 for the cables and ducts.[12]

Power Distribution

Having been delivered to Earls Court station via the cable subway, the high voltage supplies had then to be distributed to the various substations. In the tunnel sections the cables were carried within continuous covered metal troughs (two cables per trough) attached to brackets along the tunnel wall, so the heavy cables were continuously supported. This was felt the best way of dealing with a tunnel design that made it awkward to suspend cables closer than every 12ft, as the lead cables sagged far too much for this spacing to be acceptable. About 1230 tons of steel troughing having a combined length of over 100 miles was required for this job. The most densely-packed section of tunnel was between Earls Court and South Kensington where 15 cables were attached to each tunnel wall, reducing to 14 per wall to Victoria, 13 to Charing Cross and so on.

A typical District substation. Although built by various different builders the designs were similar. Size varied according to the equipment for which it had ultimate provision. LTM

In the open air, the high tension cables were conveyed in ducts laid either along the lineside or in the so-called 6ft way, between the tracks. Manholes, 12ft long, were provided at intervals, within which cables could be jointed. Earthenware ducts were also provided at the stations in tunnel sections to allow cables to pass through stations below the platforms. All in all, over 90-miles of ducts were built in the open air and at stations, some ducts also being occupied by low tension cables.

Installing the cables could only be done at night with cables brought in on drums mounted on a cable-laying train. A proficient gang could install a 500ft cable in about ten minutes, but subsequent jointing would take a lot longer (two complete joints would take three nights). Because of the limited access times, installation took over six months. In the open air, more time was available, but it took longer to draw cables into the ducts. At the tunnel stations the installation of ducts under the platforms was coordinated with the replacement of wooden platforms by concrete.

Trackwork alterations and laying conductor rails could also only be done at night and the directors were proud to announce that for many months up to 1000 contractors swarmed onto the railway each night to get on with the job in the few precious hours during which trains were not running. So far as it has been possible to tell, train services were suspended on only one day throughout the process, and this was Sunday 28th August 1904. *The Railway News* reported:[13]

> When the last train had passed through Earls Court Station on Saturday night an army of navvies and platelayers set to work between that station and Warwick Road, and remained in possession till the weekday service commenced on Monday morning. During that period the whole of that important section of the line was relaid for electrical traction purposes. Passengers had been forewarned what was to happen. Passengers for Putney and Wimbledon were obliged to alight at Earls Court and walk to West Brompton. The officials placed a number of their staff on the route, whose business it was to point the way from one station to the other. All luggage was carried free. There was only one platform at Earls Court into which trains from the east could run. Before they could get away again it was necessary for them to be shunted twice—once to the inside 'up' platform and then to the outside 'up' platform. Yet in spite of these roundabout manoeuvres the traffic all day was fairly regular. It is believed that no further disturbance of traffic will be necessary.

The works were on such a large scale that the District had to borrow locomotives to operate the various trains servicing the construction works. The District's engineer, George Estall, was instructed to hire up to six locomotives from the Midland Railway for moving electrification materials.[14]

Each substation was equipped with the usual switches to select the required Lots Road feeder and power then passed to the transformers which stepped down the 3-phase supply from 11,000 to 370 volts. The current from each transformer then passed to a corresponding rotary converter which converted the alternating current to direct current at about 600 volts. The combined substation output was usually aggregated on low tension busbars from which the various track sections were fed as required. It had been the intention to supply trains at 550 volts but the UERL noticed that the Mersey Railway had been allowed to use the higher voltage and Board of Trade approval was given for the District to use it providing the positive rail was protected.

Substations varied in capacity from 800kW to 1500kW and had two, three or four sets of equipment, in most cases with capacity for at least one additional set to be installed later if needed. The four larger substations had four feeders rather than two. The District's substations were located at: Hounslow, Sudbury Town, Mill Hill Park, Ravenscourt Park, Putney Bridge, Earls Court, South Kensington, Victoria, Charing Cross, Mansion House and Whitechapel. Lots Road also supplied substations at Kew Gardens and Wimbledon Park on the LSWR and at Campbell Road and East Ham on the LTSR; these were staffed by the main line railways. Some of the substations also supplied the tube railways at or near joint stations.

The substation buildings were mainly of a similar style, though a variety of contractors were used. The block-like buildings had arched windows and pitched roof, with internal galleries allowing the heavy equipment to be on the ground floor and switchgear on galleries. Exceptions were at Mansion House, Victoria and Charing Cross. At the former two locations shortage of land resulted in substations being built over the tracks, supported on massive girders, while at Charing Cross the whole thing was located below ground in a vast subterranean chamber next to the eastbound platform.

The availability of extra power meant that when the LCC tramway system was laid down and electrified along the Victoria Embankment in 1906 the UERL was able to supply electrical power from its Charing Cross substation to get the system open before the LCC's own power supply became available, owing to its own substation being delayed.[15] Between Blackfriars and Westminster bridges the tramway tracks were entirely offset to the south of the District tunnels but a problem arose near Waterloo Bridge where a branch tramway tunnel was being built and where the tramlines had to cross directly over the District tunnel. The complication was the LCC's preference for using a conduit form of current collection where current rails were buried under the road in a conduit and a current collector device attached to the trams projected into the conduit via a metal-edged slot along the roadway, equidistantly between the tram's running rails. The conduit was bulky and its lowest point was 2ft below the road surface. During construction of the tramway in 1906 it was found the conduit fouled the crown of the District tunnel and some of the arch had to be removed. Since the LCC needed a large triangular junction here, the only permanent solution was to remove the tunnel crown altogether and substitute steel beams in this area, which were then floored over, all at the cost of the LCC.[16]

Along the District both signal and power cables were laid in the open air ducts but this was quickly found to be rather inconvenient and after the Great War new cabling work began using exposed cable runs using concrete posts from which cables were hung. As and when existing power cables were replaced these, too, were hung on exposed cable runs. The metal troughing in tunnels also proved very inconvenient in practice and during the 1920s the troughs were removed and the cables rehung from closely-spaced hangers suspended from heavy-duty metal bars attached to the tunnel walls which provided continuous support.

Following the installation already made on the Ealing & South Harrow line, current rails were installed in the centre of the track and 16 inches outside one or other of the running rails, usually the one on the nearside. The current rails weighed 100lb per yard, a great deal more than the running rails; this was required to provide adequate conductivity as it was important to minimize the voltage drop, particularly for trains under heavy load midway between substations. The steel used was high-conductivity and was at first hard to get in Britain, large quantities being brought in from Germany; the British Firm of Bolckow, Vaughan and Co eventually rose to the occasion and met about two thirds of the total requirement. Doulton insulators were employed to support the current rails, the negative rail being maintained just 1½ inches above the height of the running rails and the positive current rail 3-inches, as on the E&SHR line. By this means the collector shoes on the trains rode clear of the running rails at points and crossings. In correspondence with the Board of Trade in February 1902, Yerkes thought that if the District was at some time in the future re-laid with much heavier running rails that could carry traction current with low resistance then it might be possible to remove the centre conductor rail.[17]

At each substation, current was supplied to a 350ft length of track on each of the two roads called a 'train section'. Either side of each train section the current rails were continuous to the next substation (or the end of the line) and the various traction current sections were insulated from each other by providing gaps in the rails, short ramps being fitted to the rail ends to drop or lift the collector shoes to the correct level as they ran over the gaps. Except at train sections and termini, all traction current sections were fed by substations at both ends, minimizing the voltage drop. Cutting off current along a particular section of track had therefore, usually, to be done at two substations and required close co-ordination.

The reason for the train sections resulted from the train wiring, as all positive pick up shoes were connected together via substantial power 'bus-lines' that ran the length of the train, as were all negative shoes. This meant that full power was available if just one positive and one negative shoe, anywhere on the train, made contact with the current rails. This introduced the possibility that at current rail gaps a train might electrically bridge the gap either when there was a fault or if the current on one section were switched off: this could be very dangerous. By having a train section, which was always switched off when the traction current section either side were discharged, then bridging the gap was prevented.

For the traction supply system to work effectively good communications was essential both between substations and with Lots Road. A telephone switchboard was provided at Lots Road linked to every substation, the telephone cable running alongside the railway and through the Earls Court cable subway.

Although the District was stating as early as January 1905 that the electrical system was ready and the only thing that was preventing the start of electric services was the absence of any trains, it is evident that work at the power house was still not complete although it would not be too long before there was enough capacity to run a service. The South Harrow line was already electric and continued drawing current from the temporary power house at Alperton until Saturday 10th June 1905, from which date Alperton power station was permanently closed.[18] This coincided with train service improvements and the *Railway Times* notes the South Harrow train service had just improved from 30- to 15-minute intervals (though this frequency did not endure).[19] The enhanced service was an opportunity to test the newly-arrived trains in an operating environment prior to mainline service.

There was some discussion about introducing electric trains on the Hounslow line using power from Alperton had Lots Road not been ready. Although this was not necessary because of other delays, it is doubtful whether this was feasible owing to the enormous voltage drop that would have been apparent by operating a long branch so far away from the power station.

Not Without Problems

The technical risks taken by the UERL were great, but felt justified in view of the scale of change required. Aggravation with the neighbours was observed quite quickly (for nobody wants to live next to a power station) but the most common difficulty was smoke and this seems to have been a problem at some point with all of the early railway power stations. A very revealing case late in 1907 suggests that at least some of the complaints were marginal. Chelsea Borough Council, energized by sensitive residents, took out a summons against the UERL for the alleged emission of black smoke from the chimneys, contrary to some earlier understanding. The facts were briefly given by the council but the UERL prepared a response based on the most exact and up-to-date scientific data. This showed the company had employed the most modern equipment possible across the world and the smoke had not actually been black smoke (suggesting unburnt fuel) but brown; the result was that the magistrate dismissed the summons and directed that 300 guineas costs be paid by the council, adding that in his opinion the company were employing equipment at the works as perfect as science could possibly make them and suggesting the case should never have been brought.[20]

The decision to adopt these very large British Westinghouse alternators throughout the station was found to be an unfortunate one. Not only were they unable to supply the power that had been specified but they were relatively unreliable. For example the internal wiring had to be repaired on several occasions, in the first two years turbine blades were stripped off on eighteen occasions, the machines gave rise to so much vibration that the UERL was threatened with legal action by both Chelsea Council and the London County Council, and so on. Westinghouse went to some effort to remedy the faults, but with only partial success. In the meantime, the UERL withheld final payments for the equipment.

Finally, in exasperation, the UERL decided to replace half of the turbine units with new ones supplied by C.A. Parsons & Co. This resulted in new machines being installed with the existing generators during 1908. Whilst this was in hand, a second contract was let for the remaining four machines and by 1910 all the turbines had been replaced and the vibration and reliability problems disappeared. In addition the new equipment was rated at 6000kW per machine, providing a useful increase in real output compared with what had been promised, but rarely delivered, previously.

This move disconcerted British Westinghouse who now saw no prospect of getting paid the amount still owing to it and took the matter to arbitration under the terms of its original contract. The UERL responded with a counter claim for the extra coal and other costs that had been incurred and would have been incurred for the expected 20-year equipment life (an enormous amount) and the cost of the new turbines. The arbitrator once again was Alfred Lyttelton QC who heard the evidence during 1911. Westinghouse, incidentally, did not contest the £43,000 extra running costs that had been unnecessarily incurred, but took issue with projected extra costs for equipment that had been removed and the cost of the replacement turbines. After much deliberation, and obtaining the court's view about some legal points, the arbitrator pointed out that the decision to replace the turbines made commercial sense in its own right and claiming damages for excessive costs that might be incurred for equipment that no longer existed was quite unreasonable. Nevertheless the extra coal and some other costs were real enough and Westinghouse was required to pay the Underground the relatively modest sum of £15,394, less than four per cent of the UERL's original claim. Even so, Westinghouse appealed and the matter eventually ended up at the House of Lords.

Their Lordships considered the matter in detail and concluded that the Parsons machines, introduced to mitigate the losses being incurred, were so much more efficient than the Westinghouse ones that the savings outstripped the extra costs and existing losses and that the arbitrator had to set his award on one side. This set an interesting legal precedent still used today. The House of Lords also observed that had the UERL made its claim before changing the turbines then it would probably have been awarded significant damages, information that must have grated a little on a company that was not making itself rich from its enterprise. It is interesting that the Parsons turbines were not only more efficient and reliable than those from Westinghouse, but were also a great deal cheaper, such was the rapid progress being made in the field of steam turbine engineering.

Signalling

It had been intended to test a second automatic signalling system on the E&SHR, by the British Pneumatic company, with twelve block sections, but this was eventually considered unnecessary as the Westinghouse system had proved so admirable.[21] The new signalling arrangement on the rest of the District was therefore a development of the Westinghouse E&SHR equipment, a contract being agreed in February 1904.[22]

Below ground, there was rarely space to use semaphore signals and in any case intermediate semaphore signals would have been difficult to see. Instead, moveable coloured spectacles were installed at ground level in the space between the tracks, the spectacles being raised or lowered by pneumatic motors to present a coloured glass in front of a fixed lamp. When the track was clear, compressed air actuated a piston that raised the green glass in front of the lamp while occupation of the track released the air allowing the spectacle to drop under its own weight, putting the red glass in front of the lamp. The lamps were at first illuminated by gas from the main running along the tunnel, though each signal also had an Adlake long burning oil lamp in case the gas failed (the oil lamp could run for a week).[23] It was found the lamps had a tendency to blow out in the draughts and they were soon replaced by electric lamps, while still retaining the moveable spectacles.*

In the open air, the signals between successive junctions were also entirely automatic in operation but it was possible to use conventional semaphore arms made of corrugated steel; the usual glass spectacles were carried in a heavy casting at one end which avoided the need for a separate counterweight that ensured the arm always returned to danger. The arm operated in the lower quadrant and was supported by another casting containing the lamp bracket and air-motor. This improved design of air motor was very compact and operated at about 65lb per sq in, operating the signal arm by a short link. Pipework connected the motor to the controlling valve near ground level. The automatic signals were painted plain red at first but later had a narrow horizontal white stripe added to improve visibility.

Trainstops were provided at all automatic signals, this version using a spring to maintain the arm in the danger position and a compressed air motor to lower it, the motor acting in concert with the associated signal. Trainstops were not generally provided in sidings and there is circumstantial evidence that trainstops were not installed at the few mechanically-operated signals controlled by traditional frames (with some exceptions while the pneumatic signals were being installed).

The operation of junctions using electro-pneumatic power was another new development. The use of large mechanically-operated signal boxes was considered impractical, inefficient and hard to interface with the automatic signalling. A reduced-size mechanically-interlocked signal frame was more suitable, operated by miniature levers, and which accommodated electrical contact shafts and electrically-operated locks that prevented the levers being manipulated if the conflicting track sections were occupied. Mechanical locking prevented unsafe routes being set up. Air-operated motors were required to control the position of points at junctions and crossovers and again these were actuated by air valves electrically controlled by interlocked levers in the signal frame. Correct operation was proved mechanically by the interlocking and by electric locks within the lever frame which ensured points and signals had responded correctly

* The previous mechanical tunnel signals installed when the various sections of line opened were also gaslit and the new ep signals presumably made use of the same gas main.

to lever operations and that levers could not be moved if track circuits indicated that moving a lever would be unsafe.

A suitable miniature signal frame was manufactured by the Westinghouse Brake Company as its 'Style B' power frame and the District purchased a number of these over the years and found them very successful. At a few locations the existing mechanical signal frames were retained, with points mechanically operated and signal levers connected to circuit-breakers that normally kept the electro-pneumatic signals at danger (these signals operated automatically when the appropriate lever was pulled over).

To gain experience a large installation was introduced at Mill Hill Park early in 1905. This power frame had 47 levers of which 22 operated points and 17 signals, with some spare positions. The press was captivated by the signalman's track diagram which was back-illuminated to show all the track sections as a short illuminated strip. As trains moved through the area, the lamps along the associated track sections went out so the trains seemed to move along as dark shadows. The diagram was designed by the District's innovative signal engineer, Mr Bernard Hartley Peter. This was the first time a diagram like this had been deployed in Britain and the idea was felt necessary as, in the central area tunnels, the signalmen would not be able to see the trains.[24] It is recorded by someone who knew Peter that 'some difficulty' was found in producing these diagrams, which could be up to 9ft long. The problem was that the depiction of the track, signals, numbers, labels and other features had to be painted onto the back of the glass in reverse

This shows District tunnel signal as installed. It is raised, displaying a green aspect. The air motor and drive rod seen just behind the signal drive the train stop arm (hidden while signal not at danger). Author's collection

A trainstop employed in association with the automatic signalling, approach direction of train is from the left. The spring pushed the horizontal rod to the right, raising the small arm at the left of the image. When the associated signal was clear air was admitted to the motor on the right and this pushed the rod to the left, pushing the arm down, clear of the train. Author's collection

The first electro-pneumatic signal cabin, at Mill Hill Park, early in 1905 and some months before it came into service. *Tramway & Railway World* February 1905

and eventually the use was made of a signwriter experienced in painting legends on the inside of pub windows. Many years later the design was changed to a piece of card with the correct shapes cut out, and lettered right way round, sandwiched between two sheets of glass.[25]

The Mill Hill Park system was very successful and the whole of the District was equipped with track circuits and most of it with power-operated points. Some 410 track circuits and 488 signals were installed, with thirteen electro-pneumatic signal frames in new or converted signal boxes, a fourteenth was added in 1908. There were five additional boxes intended only for use in emergencies and eleven other boxes where mechanical frames and associated pointwork had been retained but (as with the emergency boxes) the signal arms were converted for electro-pneumatic operation. The power-operated signals controlled by a signalman (which the District as first called 'interlocked' signals) were red and had the usual white band painted near the outer end, as with their mechanical counterparts.

In the event of fog, semaphore signals could be very difficult to see. To reduce the number of track staff employed during fog to warn drivers they were approaching a danger signal use was soon made of Clayton's automatic fog machines which put a detonator on the line a suitable braking distance ahead of a signal at danger and removed it if the signal cleared.

East end of Mill Hill Park station showing new signal box and substantial signal gantry. In the far distance and almost unresolved are a mass of sidings on the 'up side' and a number of stabled trains. The London-bound platform shows signs of a very short extension having been added. Author's collection

As signalmen could rarely see the trains, they needed a means of identifying their destination prior to arrival so they could set up the correct route. An ingenious electromechanical system was devised which passed an indication to each signalbox of the destination of each train, enabling the signalman to set up the correct route with confidence. Unfortunately this equipment was not ready when the first swathe of electric signalling came into service and trains had to be described by the use of bell codes, no doubt with occasional errors.

It was but a small additional step to use these same circuits to provide passenger information by means of large indicators on the platforms and a scheme for fitting these was announced in November 1905, by which time at least one indicator was fitted, possibly a prototype. Most central area stations had a single indicator on each platform with the main destinations listed against which a number 1 or 2 or 3 could be illuminated, thereby denoting the destinations of the next three trains. As these were not available at first, and neither did the first batches of trains display destination boards, the staff had to carry on shouting and bawling the destinations for a while and probably carried on using the old painted boards on the platforms. Installation of this equipment was completed by mid-1906 and served the Underground into the 1980s and beyond.[26]

One of the new electro-pneumatic signals installed by the District. This one is near Mill Hill Park. The upper arm is operated by a lever in the signal box and the arm below is a repeater. At first the repeater arms were coloured red (like the stop arm above) but they were soon changed to yellow; the District was the first British railway to do this.LTM

The new train indicators were found to be an immediate success. The various destinations were displayed on enamel plates and the order of the next three trains denoted by numbers lighting up adjacent. The name painted out adjacent to Ealing is Uxbridge, as trains did not at first run further than Harrow. Addison Road was displayed for LNWR trains. Westinghouse brochure in Author's collection

Crucial to frequent and efficient train services was accurate timekeeping and the Americans favoured the system promoted by the Self Winding Clock Company (of New York). Two features appealed. The first was the ability of each clock to wind itself up each hour using an electrical ratchet system powered by dry cells. This avoided the tedious process of clock winding, usually done weekly with hand-wound clocks. The other feature was a synchronizing process that happened hourly. A master clock sent out hourly pulses exactly on the hour and this signal caused a synchronizer on each clock to adjust the minute hand precisely to its correct position. Clocks were provided in each signal cabin, and on station platforms and in booking halls.

New Rolling Stock

Prior to 1901 the District contemplated the possibility of using existing rolling stock in some way, perhaps with locomotives or new power cars, but Yerkes had no intention of trying to reuse the existing fleet and preferred to use new designs which had proved successful in the USA. This meant purchasing a large number of entirely new cars to operate the electric services. Yerkes remarked in 1902 that he thought 480 cars would be needed to run the expected services, a number repeated the following year and in 1904,[27] but the actual orders were for only 420 new cars, enough for 60 7-car trains to which must be added the 14 experimental cars that had already arrived in 1903.*

* 480 cars would have been sufficient for exactly 60 8-car trains but I have never seen reference to running trains this long so early and platform lengths would have been a big problem. It would also have covered 80 6-car trains but this would have been excessive by any measure.

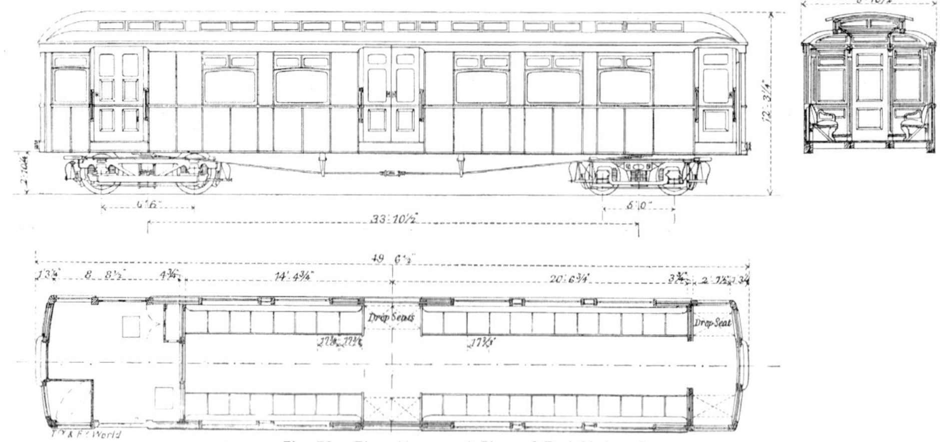

Plan and elevation of Brush motor car with luggage compartment. These cars had all-longitudinal seating but the trailers and middle motors had some transverse bays. Author's collection

The new cars were in many ways similar to those of 1903 but the styling had been updated to be slightly less wild-west looking and the end platforms were now fully enclosed. This did not mean the public was going to embrace them willingly and the press was distinctly sniffy about the design. The loss of seats was particularly remarked upon. The Americans felt, with some justification based on their own experiences, that for short journeys it was more important that the cars had a high capacity than the maximum number of seats. Of course, this meant that many more people would have to stand than was the case in the steam stock and handrails were installed, from which were hung leather straps, so people had something to hang onto (which the steam stock trains did not have). The 9-carriage steam stock trains could seat 400 whilst a 7-car electric could typically seat 348 which, given the more frequent electric service being promised, might have been thought a reasonable bargain, but that would not have been newsworthy.*

As with the 1903 cars, there were to be two end motor cars, a middle motor car and four trailers on a standard full length train. This time there were to be luggage compartments on only a proportion of end motors, creating a fourth type of car. The end motor cars with luggage compartments had seats for 40 persons whilst the other end motors could seat 48. In both cases seating was entirely longitudinal, the ordinary cushions being upholstered in plaited cane and seating positions separated from each other by wooden dividers bearing arm rests. The other coaches could all seat 52 people and included several bays of facing seats in groups of four, the seat finishes being similar to the longitudinal seats but lacking the partitions.

The total requirement was for 120 motor cars intended for use at the end of trains, 72 motor cars for use in the middle of trains, and 228 'trail' cars, as they were first called (though they soon became known simply as 'trailers'). The end motor cars had driver's controls just at the outer ends while the middle motors had control equipment at both ends. This time the driver's controls were on the left hand side, and all cars had end platforms (except those with luggage compartments, to which there was not supposed to be unrestricted passenger access). The enclosed end gangways did at first open directly

* This debate may strike a chord in the minds of Metropolitan Line passengers watching LU's S stock coming into service with 300 seats instead of the 442 seats of the stock being replaced.

into the car interior but sliding doors were soon fitted across the opening to reduce draughts and discourage passengers from riding on the platforms between stations.

Although most trains were intended to be of 'standard' formation the car mix allowed twelve of the sixty trains to have two middle motors and one fewer trailer, so that when uncoupled both a 4-car and a 3-car portion could remain in service (the idea of splitting trains at Mill Hill Park with portions for South Harrow and Hounslow was entertained but not in fact introduced at that time). On a 'standard' train, three cars could be detached at either end but the uncoupled portion would only have one driving cab and would have to be put away.

All the cars were of the same length, 49ft 6½ins between the ends of their rigid 'buffers', and were 12ft 3¼ins high, from rail level, and 8ft 10½ins wide between mouldings at roof level (the widest point). The slight shortening of the cars was achieved by reducing the tapered ends as they were not necessary on the District, which did not have the vicious curves used on the American system. Just twenty of the end motor cars (all those made by Brush) were fitted with luggage compartments and more will be said about this later. Exactly how it was envisaged these would operate is unclear but at the time of ordering the District carried accompanied and unaccompanied parcels and *Street Railway Journal* asserts that special accommodation was 'required by statute on a portion of the District trains'.[28] The compartment took up one end of the car, had its own doors and accommodated the driving cab in the nearside corner.

In 1902 Yerkes explained to the Board of Trade that he particularly wanted to use 150hp motors whose size required driving wheels of 36 inches diameter. In consequence the car floors could not be lowered below the height of the existing trains, which were ten inches above platform level. Yerkes explained such a step would seriously reduce boarding times which, after exhaustive tests, were found to be about eleven seconds where access were level. Yerkes wanted to raise all the platform heights at District stations so they were level with the trains and draw attention to the step at other stations by means of lights. The chief inspecting officer was appalled at the idea of increasing the platform height to 3ft 11ins, being worried about people falling onto the track, trains of other companies serving the stations and how difficult it would make things for bookstall attendants needing to cross the lines. These not altogether convincing reasons discouraged Yerkes from pressing the matter and it was not until around 2012 that platform and train heights were matched up.[29]

A surprisingly large number of car-builders were used. In February 1904, the District was proud to explain to shareholders that the majority of equipment orders placed so far were to British manufacturers and suppliers. Perks, the chairman, explained that 420 new cars had yet to be built and reported that:

> Tenders have been invited from seven or eight of the most prominent car builders in the country, and if there are any gentlemen who are extremely sensitive on the question of letting contracts go abroad, it will comfort them to know that the whole of these firms who have been invited to tender are British contractors, and that the works will be executed in this country.

This proved rather optimistic. In August 1904 Perks found himself having to explain that of the 420 cars required, orders for 280 had been placed on the continent. When the tenders had been returned it emerged that the prices quoted by the British manufacturers was 30-40 per cent higher than those of the continental manufacturers for the same specification. The UERL made every effort to get the prices of the British firms reduced, but they refused to do so. Immediately the contract for the 280 cars had been let on the

Rows of District cars being assembled in the Brush works at Loughborough in 1904. The all-wooden construction is very obvious. Author's collection

continent, the British manufacturers reduced their prices to match and contracts for the remaining 140 cars were let to British firms.

Brush Electrical Engineering Ltd of Loughborough and Metropolitan Amalgamated Railway Carriage & Wagon Co at Lancaster were the British suppliers, each for 70 car bodies with bogies. The continental order, for 280 cars, was placed with a French syndicate led by Les Ateliers de Construction du Nord de la France. The delivery times were tight as the cars were required by the end of 1904, which is probably why the orders were so widely split, though, in the event, none of the suppliers met the promised delivery date, in some cases by many months. When, subsequently, the UERL was asked why such large orders had been given to the French the answer was that construction costs were lower and joinery costs so very much lower that it was cheaper to buy in France, even given the extra transport costs (there was a great deal of wood in the District cars).[30]

The French syndicate comprised: Les Ateliers de construction du Nord de la France, where 60 cars were made at their works in Blanc Misseron; Ivry Port (Compagnie Français de Matériel de Chemin de Fer, 42 cars); Lunéville (de Dietrich et Compagnie, 68 cars); Pantin (Desouches, David et Compagnie, 42 cars) and St Denis (Compagnie Générale de Construction, 68 cars). The order for the bogies was organized differently and these were built by the Blanc Misseron works with 250 of the trailer bogies from the German firm of Wagon-Fabrik Actien Gesellshaft. British manufacturers contributed a number of motor bogies to this pool. The bogies must have travelled about quite a bit to allow all the cars to be delivered on their own wheels.

The construction work, including the wheels and bogies, was widely dispersed though all was made to UERL designs with components notionally interchangeable, but it must have been very difficult to manage consistent quality control with so many manufacturers involved. When complete, the British-built cars were conveyed by railway via the South Acton link to Mill Hill Park works where all the traction equipment was already waiting to be fitted. The French cars were delivered by ship to Tilbury Docks and then brought along the LTSR via Barking and Bow Road to Mill Hill Park.

As a result of the exhaustive tests conducted on the South Harrow line in the summer of 1903, the District quickly decided to equip the new trains with BTH control equipment, orders being placed as early as August; an order for all the motors (also from BTH) followed in January 1904 after further tests.[31] The materials were delivered to the new car sheds at Mill Hill Park to be married up with the car bodies when they arrived.

The BTH control equipment was the same system recently employed in New York and elsewhere and had shown itself to be very reliable. Each motor car had a series of contactors mounted underneath the car which controlled the current supply to the motors, all the equipments being operated from the master controller in the leading driving cab. The traction motors were of the GE69 type, rated at 200hp. These were large and heavy, at 6100lbs including the gears, and subsequently gave a fair bit of trouble only cured by constant attention and some modifications. The motor cars had a single motor bogie that carried two traction motors, so a train with three motor cars was rated at 1200hp.

Motor car underframes were of wood reinforced with steel, but those of the trailer cars were of wood only, in the belief that the stresses on those cars were rather less. This apparent economy gave rise to a great deal of trouble a few years later.

7-car train of new District stock under test on the South Harrow line just north of Sudbury Hill station in 1905, a Brush motor car is nearest. There are few houses in this area, but in background may be seen The Rising Sun pub (which is still there) and some work on the Great Central Railway. Roy Allen collection

Interior of one of the District's new motor cars at about time of delivery. Seats, lights and window blinds are still to be installed; blinds were fitted although curtains appear to have been considered. Author's collection

One of the new cars at Mill Hill Park sheds having had its equipment fitted and before entering service. The covers have been opened to allow the equipment to be admired. Removable destination displays are visible by trailing entrance doors but no provision has yet been made for front displays although the headlamps are prominent; these could be obscured by press-on hoods so that combinations of the white lamp positions could form a destination code so staff could see at a distance where the train was for. The small luggage compartment is visible through the open door and prominent are the footboards, at first installed only at door locations but later made continuous. The fussy gold lining is just apparent. *Tramway & Railway World*

In addition to the ordinary rolling stock the District acquired two electric crane cars for the use of engineers. These had similar equipment to the motor cars. Roy Allen collection

Bodywork was constructed mainly of Oregon pine and white ash with mahogany trimmings, all of which was subjected to the fire-proofing process of the Fire Resisting Corporation of Fulham, which made the cars virtually fireproof; some 250,000 cubic feet of wood was treated. The interior panels were of mahogany, flatted to a dull polish. The interior metallic fittings were all of bronze and the ceilings were of asbestos millboard, painted white and decorated in gold. Externally, the wooden bodywork was covered with aluminium panelling and painted bright scarlet, giving a most striking appearance.* The wooden doors, however, and some framing, were varnished rather than painted.[32]

The glazing was of heavy plate glass with brilliant cut decoration. The side windows were very wide compared with the 1903 cars and incorporated opening toplights for ventilation. Additional ventilation was available from vents along the side of the clerestory; these could be closed off by a member of staff operating a lever that opened or closed all the vents along each side. The minute book refer to each window having two pairs of curtains but a picture of a car so fitted has not been seen.[33] The seat frames and backs were of steel and the gangway between the opposing seat risers was 3ft 10ins, giving plenty of standing room. Beneath the seats were what was described at the time as Laycock's 'Gold' electric car heaters for use in winter; these were connected to the traction supply.

Each car had electric lighting comprising between 30 and 35 incandescent lamps of 16 candlepower and arranged in two rows along the car, either side of the clerestory. It was appreciated that with trains designed to run for much of the time in tunnel the lighting had to be of high quality, sufficient to allow people who were seated to be able to read newspapers. The electricity was obtained from the traction supply and distributed via a lighting main running along the train and fed to the lamps in groups of five 110V lamps in series with each other. The lights of each car were operated from two switches, each controlling half the lights.

* *Tramway & Railway World* described the colour as Royal Scarlet.

Instructions were issued that lights had to be switched on at all times in the main tunnel sections and at dusk elsewhere. In short tunnels beyond the central area it was good enough to switch just half the lights. In case of failure of the traction supply a small number of oil lamps were available and staff had to be ready to light these if the lighting failed.

Following experience, the UERL decided to use the 1903-style US motor bogie design on the 1905 cars but not the trailer bogie design which had evidently proved unsatisfactory. Another US type was selected which had been used widely on elevated lines and was of the equalizer-bar type. Unfortunately, when the design was adopted on the District it was also to prove unsatisfactory and gave a great deal of trouble. Again 3ft 6in wheels were used on the motor bogies and 3ft on the trailing ones.

The new trains were equipped throughout with the Westinghouse automatic air brake with which the District was already familiar. This was similar to the brake already tested on the 1903 cars and had proved entirely satisfactory in service conditions.

All cars were close-coupled by means of centrally arranged drawgear with a built in spring buffer. The coupler heads were of the Stearn and Ward type (named after the US patentees) which enabled cars to be coupled automatically simply by pushing the cars together.* This was usually just called the Ward coupler and was standard throughout the life of the District. The UERL did participate in a demonstration given at the LBSCR's Victoria station in December 1905 of the Darling patent automatic coupling but since most of the cars had been delivered or were under construction there was no enthusiasm to change, and the District stuck with the Ward coupler.[34] When the new cars were introduced the van Dorn couplers on the 1903 cars were replaced by Ward couplers so the cars could couple, if necessary.

The driver's control positions were novel by standards that we have become accustomed to now. Except for the few cars with luggage compartments, the driver's controls were installed in the gangways at the car end on the left hand side, this being a change from the experimental cars where the driver was on the right. The change was probably made because most of the platforms were on the left and it enabled the driver to look back along the train at stations to make sure it was safe to start. As on the 1903 cars, the controls were normally obscured by a large wooden door, thus enabling the platforms to be used by passengers. When the controls were in use, the wooden door was moved to create an enclosed half-cab for the driver. Where luggage compartments were fitted there was no end platform and the driver was given what was described as a 'collapsible' cab in the corner.

Disposal of the Steam Stock

The *Railway Times* of 5th August 1905 was among several journals carrying a notice advertising the disposal of 54 steam locomotives and 368 4-wheeled carriages, all fitted with Pintsch's lighting system except for one 9-carriage train fitted with Stone's electric system. 48 of the locos were broken up or sold, realizing just £15,480. One was broken up by the company to establish the scrap price. Four locos went to George Cohen at £410 each but the ten worst went to Samuel Isaacs with the remainder sold to R. Frazer and Sons.

Of the 395 carriages (many very old) two went to the War Office, three to Isaacs and 288 to Frazers with 200 sets of gas recipients removed and sold separately for six shillings each. The Taff Vale Railway purchased 40 of the third class coaches for £1200 for the use of workmen, according to a contributor to the *Railway Magazine* who spotted some lurking on one of that railway's mineral branches.[35] The remaining carriages were mostly

---

* This was the subject of US Patent No 737673 granted on 1st September 1903 to R.B. Stearns and F.D. Ward.

A line of disused steam locomotives outside Mill Hill Park works in 1906. Most were scrapped shortly after this. Author's collection

broken up, but a few survived as tool vans or other engineering vehicles and one survived as a hut at Whitechapel for many years. The District retained its 27 'joint stock' carriages thinking they might be useful for something but no purpose was in fact found.[36] These were offered for sale at the end of October 1907, also going to the Taff Vale Railway for £80 each.[37] In all, £7613 was raised from the carriage stock.

Example of a District newspaper label used to show that packages of newspapers carried by train had been paid for. Author's collection

Luggage and Parcels

When electric trains were being planned, the District had a thriving parcels service and we have already noted that parcels and unaccompanied luggage had to be accommodated on steam trains in addition to anything passengers might carry with them. That limited accommodation for this traffic was incorporated into the designs of the electric stock does not inform us about whether it was simply for carrying large and inconvenient passengers' luggage or whether it was at first intended to continue carrying the unaccompanied parcels traffic.

What we do know is that by the time the trains came into service the District had decided to abandon the carriage of unaccompanied luggage and parcels, the service last operating on 18th March 1905.[38]

The noxious fish traffic from Monument was also banned on District trains from 13th May 1905, shortly before the smart new electric trains arrived.

The following statement was made in the summer of 1904, which sheds some light.

> There is one little question with reference to the carriage of luggage. We have had to reduce the facilities for people bringing luggage upon our railway consequent upon the enormous number of electrical trains which we shall have to run over our line. We had to choose between two dilemmas—whether we were to have a rapid and cheap service, or whether we are to have our trains impeded by people bringing vast quantities of luggage to be conveyed upon our line. We have had to materially restrict the amount of luggage so carried, and Parliament has imposed upon us the obligation of running two trains carrying the statutory quantity of luggage each way per day. We shall endeavour, for the convenience of our customers, to run those luggage trains at the most convenient times of the day, but I think the arrangement we have come to is one which will meet the interests of the public at large, although now and then some individual may have to suffer, and may therefore complain.[39]

Instructions dated September 1905 observe that where a car has a luggage compartment the conductor in charge was required to ensure luggage was loaded and stored properly and put out at the right station, the luggage compartment being required to be placed at the west end of trains. This did not absolve the conductor from his regular duty of ensuring that all was clear before giving the signal to start. The door to the compartment had to be kept closed.

This is evidence that the luggage compartments were actually used as such for a while but because of the small number of luggage cars, the facility could only have been provided on about a third of the trains. It was thus chance if a train actually included a luggage car and contemporary reports indicate that on most trains the parcels were carried in the end motor car in the space by the offside centre doors amongst the passengers. Here, the conductor sorted them into the correct piles to be put out at each station, putting the pile for the next station alongside the nearside centre door and hauling it out onto the platform on arrival.[40] These special arrangements declined over the years though in 1915 staff were still being given guidance about stowing luggage.[41]

Mill Hill Park Depot

Lillie Bridge Works was highly unsuitable for the new electric stock, was difficult to expand and had only very awkward connections with the running lines. This called for a modern purpose-built depot within which all maintenance could be performed. Vacant land was found near Mill Hill Park station but this was at street level whilst the railway at this point was in a cutting, requiring a connecting ramp to be built. Work began in early 1904 and quite quickly steam shovels and 150 navvies got on with the job, at that time expecting rolling stock to be delivered in only eleven months' time.[42] Most of the spoil removed was despatched to Hounslow where it was dumped on District Railway land where the two branch lines diverged, raising the level of the land considerably.

The main component of the car depot was the covered accommodation, a series of connected buildings 800ft long by 216ft wide; we call them car sheds now, but the Americans who designed them often referred to them as 'car barns' and some early plans are so titled. The sheds had three main sections, these being the wood-working shop, the cleaning and repair shop, and the paint shop. Along the north-east side of the sheds (next to the 2-track wood shop) were a series of offices, stores and workshops, and there was space upstairs for offices. Within the sheds were eleven sets of railway tracks, most capable of holding two 7-car trains and together with a few outside sidings 25 trains could

Above: **Depot office at Mill Hill Park depot around 1905. The woman typing (on left) is Miss Armstrong. Interesting view of depot office life but unclear why the set of photos was taken.** LTM

Below: **Drawing of one end of Mill Hill Park Car Barns showing the 2-road lifting shop entrance and offices.** Author's collection

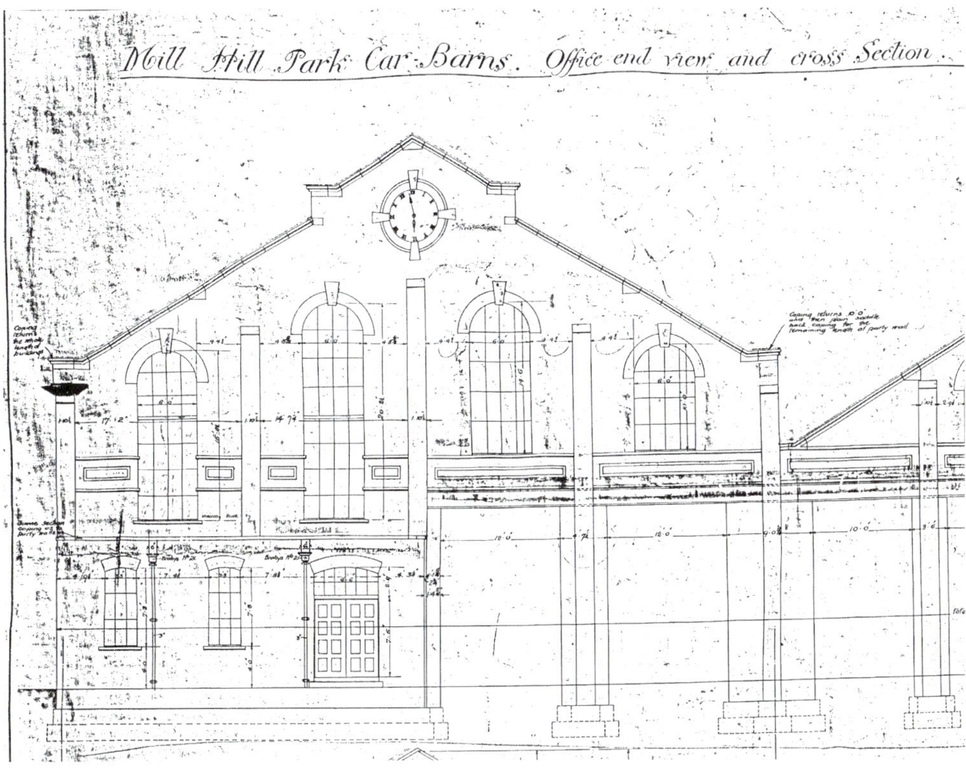

be accommodated in what amounted to 1½ miles of track. The 4-road paint shop occupied the south west part of the building and radiators were provided to help reduce the drying time required (in those days cars were painted quite frequently). Pits were not provided in the paint shop and the paint was stored in a separate building outside to reduce the risk of any fire spreading. The 5-road repair shop was in the centre of the building and 4ft-deep pits between the rails gave access to equipment under the trains. Two travelling cranes were provided which together could lift cars and move them about and facilities were provided to deal with all kinds of repairs, including rewinding of electric motors.

Realizing that it would be dangerous and inconvenient to have current rails in the car sheds, some means was required for getting power to the trains for testing and moving them about. The answer was an overhead railway suspended from the roof supports, each of the two rails carried on insulators and carrying traction current. A small 4-wheeled trolley was free to move along the rails and picked up the current supply which was taken to a pair of long insulated flexible power lines suspended from the trolley. At the other end of the lines was a single large plug that could be inserted into a corresponding socket on a motor car that connected with the train's power bus lines, providing the train with power. If the train were moved the trolley would be pulled along with it. It was, of course, crucial to remove the plug lead before the train was moved fully out of the shed or the trolley would be pulled off the overhead rails, an occurrence that was (and still is) not unknown. This arrangement had already been usefully employed in the shed at South Harrow.

North end of Mill Hill Park depot shortly after delivery of the cars began. Roy Allen Collection

On arrival of the new cars, the BTH electrical equipment was then fitted and tested. Because Mill Hill Park could not alone meet all the car stabling requirements, new sidings were also laid out in the triangle of land east of Earls Court and at East Ham, together with new sidings at Parsons Green.

The District's shed at South Harrow was soon removed once cars could stable at Mill Hill Park but a problem now arose with the Piccadilly trains that began turning up in autumn 1906 as the new sheds at Lillie Bridge were not ready, the contract for the work having been let only in November 1905. The Piccadilly trains were being equipped at Mill Hill Park but there was only very limited space for storage. The land at South Harrow was again found useful and in September a £900 corrugated iron building to serve as a temporary car shed was contracted with John McManus, to be finished within six weeks, and Piccadilly cars were stored there until Lillie Bridge could accept them.[43]

Track

Track was improved both in advance of electrification and afterwards when many connections not necessary with electric working were taken out. The track was thoroughly overhauled to make it suitable for the more punishing service expected and many of the rails were replaced as were all sleepers showing signs of excessive wear. Old sleepers were of hardwood but the new ones installed were all of Jarrah, felt to be even more incombustible and hard wearing.[44] The trackwork was closely coordinated with the

The complex junction at Warwick Road was a particular problem to electrify. This admittedly poor quality view looks west with the new substation in background and pump-house chimney just visible. This view is taken from the new signal box. *Railway & Travel Monthly* Volume 7

installation of signalling as it was necessary to bond joints in the so-called continuous rail while insulated blockjoints were required wherever automatic signalling was installed. These works saw the last of the flat-bottomed rail removed at the Warwick Road crossing in 1904 as it was previously thought too difficult to relay with chaired rails.[45]

Once the new train services had settled in it was discovered that track wear was far greater than had been expected. It was never conclusively proved exactly what the cause was, but a combination of more rapid acceleration, more powerful brakes and smaller wheels was implicated. In consequence the District opted to use a harder steel rail based on the Sandberg principle, which introduced more carbon and silicon. This produced a great improvement in rail life. At the same time manganese steel was introduced to check rails to reduce excessive wear.[46]

Apart from the rail problems, other defects were discovered under the punishing new conditions, particularly with the formation and drainage. Shareholders were told early in 1907 that it would be necessary to spend £50,000 on re-draining and ballasting works and that this was essential and could not be deferred. It was hoped to complete the work within a year.[47]

By 1909 many of the early problems had been cured but the battering at the rail ends was proving a serious problem on the District but not so on the tube lines. From this the engineer concluded that the old steam-age track was not sufficiently rigid and proposed to reduced sleeper spacing in order to improve matters.[48]

East London Line and District involvement

We noted the District's association with the ELR when the through connection was installed in 1884. It will be recalled that this railway was an entirely independent concern, though it was operated by a management committee of the six railways with which it was physically connected, including both the Met and District, both of which ran trains onto the line via the junction at St Mary's. The District ran into the LBSCR station at New Cross while the Metropolitan served the SER station. The GER ran trains from Liverpool Street to New Cross (LBSCR) and onwards to Croydon and the LBSCR was running trains from its own line as far as Shoreditch. Before District electrification, the ELR stations were managed and staffed by the SER.

In 1902 the Met and District encouraged the other ELR lessees to think that electrification would halt the declining traffic, but far from embracing the idea they felt that electrification was unaffordable, given the ELR's appalling financial position (which was even worse than that of the District). Neither the Met nor the District felt that it was feasible for either of them to undertake the work without all the other parties paying their share. In the circumstances the District withdrew its through trains on and from 1st August 1905 and the Met withdrew its steam trains to New Cross (SER) from 3rd December 1906. The SER introduced a local service from New Cross to Whitechapel to supplement the remaining GER and LBSCR trains, but clearly the services along the line now were less attractive than hitherto, doing nothing to bolster traffic.

Once through services between the City Lines and the ELR had been withdrawn, the connection with the ELR was severed at the ELR end and the Met converted the running lines beyond St Mary's Junction into sidings, used for a while to stable District trains. Agreement was reached with the District for the Hammersmith & City trains that had previously run onto the ELR to be diverted into Whitechapel (District) station, which had ample capacity and enabled Met passengers to interchange with the ELR via the tortuous link at ticket hall level.

Chapter Four

RUNNING THE NEW SERVICES

New Train Services Introduced

Yerkes had hoped to be running electric trains as the year 1905 opened, and at the January shareholders' meeting Perks, the chairman of the meeting, lamented that it had not been possible to do so, mainly because none of the car builders had adhered to their contractual commitments. Perks said only fourteen (English) cars had been delivered by end of 1904 when the whole of the rolling stock had been expected; but there were no new cars at all—these were the experimental cars.[1]

When the first of the main electric train fleet began to arrive it was tested on the South Harrow line, and several posed photographs were taken of a train along this section. The first attempt to operate an electric train east of Mill Hill Park on a full-scale trial basis was during the early hours of 20th January 1905. Unfortunately, it was found that the new cars fouled some of the station platforms and the trip had to be abandoned. It was not possible to resume testing until alterations had been made to provide adequate clearance. Another trial trip took place from Mill Hill Park to Bow Road and back without incident on 28th March and this allowed plans to be made for electric trains to begin in passenger service.[2] The train was minutely inspected by the press which was told journeys would be faster because of the much quicker acceleration and the reduced boarding times at stations, where it was hoped to achieve 20 seconds instead of the 35 seconds for the steam trains. The trial run itself completed the runs in each direction much faster than scheduled.

There was a very unfortunate incident on 28th February, while tests were being made with the current rails near Westminster Bridge station. The National Telephone Company had laid cables in the District tunnels as a convenient means of connecting exchanges without having to dig up the streets and this provided useful wayleave revenue for the District. Unfortunately, the installation of the railway's own power cables meant moving the lead-covered telephone cables and one had been temporarily dropped along the trackside. By chance, it made contact with the top of some metal troughing which in turn had been left touching a current rail. This was not a problem while the line was still dead but it became a very big problem when current was turned on for testing. The consequence was that it sent a huge current at 550 volts along the telephone cable, starting electrical fires at two central London telephone exchanges and interrupting 6000 telephone circuits in the City area. Lessons were learnt all round, but fortunately nobody was hurt.

The challenge of introducing electric trains needed careful thought because interworking steam trains and electric trains was complex and involved matters like staff training, train manning, locomotive changes, steam trains still serviced from Lillie Bridge whilst electric trains would be serviced from Mill Hill Park, and so on. In the end it was felt that specific service groups should be converted overnight and that the conversion should start while only a proportion of cars were available (even by 31st July only 268 of 420 cars had actually been delivered).

The Times, **30th March 1905.**
Author's collection

ELECTRIC TRACTION ON THE DISTRICT RAILWAY.

The first train to be run by electricity over the main line of the Metropolitan District Railway left Mill-hill-park early on Tuesday morning and travelled to Bow-road and back. This trial run, taken in conjunction with that carried out by the Metropolitan a week before, covers the whole of the Inner Circle with the exception of a few yards at Aldgate, and thus demonstrates that the electrification of the line is now an accomplished fact. When, however, the electrical service will be put into operation it is as yet impossible to say. The chief obstacle in the way of its immediate initiation is the absence of rolling stock, the builders being late in delivery, but in addition some of the machinery at certain of the sub-stations has still to be installed, and the new automatic signalling system is not yet complete all over the line. This last is a most important feature of the undertaking, for it is only by its aid that the frequent service of trains that is contemplated will be rendered possible. With the existing signalling methods the *maximum* number of trains in each direction is about 18 an hour, but the automatic system which is being introduced will, it is hoped, permit a *maximum* of 40 per hour, if required by the volume of traffic. Two interesting features of this system, which has been at work for a considerable time on the Ealing and South Harrow branch, are that distant signals will not be employed, all semaphore arms having the same value, and meaning stop when at danger, and that a mechanical device is provided which applies the air brakes and stops the train should the driver inadvertently overrun a signal standing at danger. At Mill-hill-park the main signal-box, which controls the sidings and car-yard, is fitted with power signals on the Westinghouse electro-pneumatic system, the operation of moving the signal and points being performed by means of little levers only a few inches long; this box also contains an illuminated plan of the area it controls, on which a dark shadow indicates the presence and movement of every train. Normally the trains will consist of seven coaches, three of them being motor-cars, with a seating capacity of over 300 and standing room for many more, but each can be divided into two shorter trains, of three and four vehicles respectively, for use when traffic is light. In general the coaches, which are nearly 50ft. long, resemble those running in the electrical trains of the Metropolitan Railway, but the accommodation, with merely rudimentary divisions between the seats (which, for the rest, are not unduly capacious), looks less inviting, and the exterior finish, with its bright red paint, is somewhat strange to English eyes. An important structural difference is the provision of sliding side-doors in the middle of the cars, in addition to the doors at each end; these are opened and shut by pneumatic pressure controlled by the conductors, and will doubtless be useful in facilitating the rapid entrance and exit of passengers.

District trailer car as delivered. This shows the window blinds with which the cars were originally equipped.
Author's collection

This undated card (probably mid 1905) shows steam haulage in its last days at Parsons Green, where an eastbound train arrives. The current rails and cabling are clearly complete, though no sign yet of electric light fittings. Capital Transport collection

One matter that finally received attention was the perverse naming of tracks on the District where all trains heading towards Mansion House from the west were 'down' trains whilst 'up' trains headed west. This defied usual railway practice where 'up' almost always meant towards London and was a hangover from Met railway operation when its own City stations commanded the use of the 'up' designation. With electrification, these labels were finally reversed throughout the whole of the District's system. East of Mansion House, where the tracks were virtually all in the ownership of other companies, the problem did not arise and trains towards Mansion House had always been 'up'. The change resulted in a reversal of naming at the property boundary at the east end of the station (which was also the District's zero point from which mileposts were measured). The American mind found these terms eccentric anyway and for the electric services proceeded to employ the terms 'East to West' (or vice versa) to describe the direction of the trains—later reduced to eastbound and westbound, which terms are used today.

Changes at Hounslow and South Acton

The first new electric service was between Hounslow and South Acton and began on Tuesday 13th June 1905 using the newly-delivered electric cars.

We have already noted that once the Hounslow line came into District ownership in 1903 the potentially better-located station at Hounslow Town was reopened leaving the District operating two branches at the Hounslow end. This was not something that the District was anxious to pursue under electric operation.

An early District electric train at South Acton station. Roy Allen Collection

Fortunately the District owned some spare land in the angle where the branches diverged at Lampton and which had been built up to rail level with muck excavated from Mill Hill Park, the Hammersmith widening works and Piccadilly railway incline. In this space it was just possible to install an exceedingly sharp single-track curve immediately north of Hounslow Town so that trains arriving from the Osterley direction could reverse and proceed to the Barracks, and vice versa. The new curve came into use to coincide with electrification and joined the old route immediately east of the Kingsley Road bridge when the short length of the 'through' route went out of use; although the connections with the old line were lifted there is no indication the intervening track was actually removed. The entire section between Hounslow Town and Hounslow Barracks was single line, but traffic was not heavy.

Hounslow Town terminus in early electric days with a 2-car 1903 stock train from Hounslow Barracks reversing prior to setting off for Mill Hill Park. In electric days the platforms had been shortened. Jim Connor Collection

South Acton was at the end of the new, but hitherto unused, Acton Loop line but when completed in 1901 there was no station at South Acton on the District track and the loop was only single track; indeed no record has been found suggesting this link was ever intended for passenger trains. With the new electric shuttle services that were being introduced on the western branches there was sense in sending some of these onto South Acton to capture some interchange traffic and reduce shunting at Mill Hill Park.

A single wooden platform was hastily constructed alongside the North & South Western Junction Railway (N&SWJR) station together with a shed-like station building incorporating a short platform shelter. The 400ft long platform was at a slightly higher level than the N&SWJR station but the bridge over adjacent Palmerston Road was only just high enough for people to walk underneath. The line was doubled as well as electrified and a crossover north of the station allowed trains from Mill Hill Park to gain access to the platform where they reversed; a small signal box was installed on the platform near the station building.[3] The match-boarded booking hall was accessed from the street by a narrow external stairway and an opening in the east wall made interconnection with the adjacent N&SWJR station. More steps led up to the District platform. The booking office itself probably had only a very short life and a sign soon appeared explaining to passengers that they had to obtain tickets from the porter on the platform (his room had a small window from which he could collect and issue tickets). The external appearance of the station was at best functional and showed the architectural limitations of corrugated iron.

For a few years both District tracks continued northwards to a double junction with the N&SWJR line six chains further on, but no passenger trains ever used it and little or no freight (though the Midland and the LNWR both obtained freight running powers). North of the platforms trap points diverted any runaway District trains into a field, providing a very healthy overrun at the end of the long down gradient. The *Railway & Travel Monthly*[4] suggested occasional main line trains used it to deliver stores to Mill Hill Park works and operating instructions suggest the route was certainly operational for such a purpose until the junction north of South Acton was taken out in 1915. Some of the new District rolling stock came this way. The North & South Western Junction Railway had a 'District Junction' signal box north of the station which was abolished at the same time, though the cabin was not actually removed until 1930.[5]

Electrification Extended

The next electrified service was that between Ealing Broadway and Whitechapel, from Saturday 1st July 1905. The day could have gone better. The first train from Mill Hill Park to South Acton jumped the points at the latter station, blocking it for some hours. Much more seriously, torrential rain in west London during the morning created serious flooding at Hammersmith and the junction at West Kensington where, in both cases, water rose above track level and it was impossible to keep the current on. In turn, this trapped a number of trains, including steam trains sandwiched between the electric ones, and deranged services over the whole line. It was obvious the water was not going to clear very quickly and when the electric trains could be extricated steam took over for the rest of the day. As if that were not bad enough, the Met simultaneously attempted to run its clockwise Inner Circle trains electrically, but this, too, proved disastrous. Along the St James's Park to Sloane Square section the collector shoes kept slipping off the current rails, eventually leading to dislodged or overturned rails. This inevitably caused further huge delays following which steam haulage had to be resumed on the Met's Inner Circle service.

It had been intended to celebrate electric operation with a guests-only special train from Mansion House to Ealing and back, departing at 11.50am and returning at 3pm, probably allowing the guests to inspect some of the facilities. Amongst the chaos the function had to be postponed, which must have been a bitter blow to those who had worked so hard to get everything ready.[6] The flooding happened at a point where track flooding was frequently known and even after electrification still flooded occasionally, despite a strongly worded protest by the District to the LCC (the drainage authority) about the havoc the build up of water had caused.

On 23rd July the Putney to High Street service was converted, followed by Richmond-Whitechapel on 1st August, Whitechapel-East Ham on 20th August and, finally, Putney Bridge-Wimbledon on 27th August, with through electric trains from Wimbledon to Whitechapel. In each case, second-class bookings were withdrawn immediately prior to electric services starting. The LTSR line east of East Ham was not, for the moment, electrified.

The Times **3rd July 1905** Author's collection

DISTRICT RAILWAY ELECTRIFICATION.

The opening of the long-expected electric working on the District Railway was fixed for Saturday, when arrangements were made for four electric trains to run every hour between Ealing and Whitechapel as well as for a complete ten minutes' service, performed by the Metropolitan, on the outer rail of the circle, for the trains running westwards from the Mansion-house. But disappointment awaited the companies concerned. The day's service indeed was begun according to the programme, and worked till between 8 and 9 o'clock; but the heavy fall of rain early in the morning caused flooding of the lines between Hammersmith and Kensington, and the electric trains were brought to a stop by the water. The railway at this point lies very low, and has several times of recent years been rendered impassable by water. The possibility of this happening again was supposed to be obviated by the pumping station lately erected at considerable expense by the London County Council at Lots-road, Chelsea; but either this station has not the capacity to deal with such a downpour as occurred on Saturday morning, or it was not put into operation promptly enough to perform the function for which it was exclusively constructed—viz., to lift flood-water and discharge it into the Thames at times when the height of the river is such as to prevent the free escape of the water by gravitation. At any rate, whatever the precise reason of this failure, the net result was that the inauguration of electric traction was spoiled.

But more misfortunes were to follow. Several small displacements of the conductor rails occurred, but were got over without serious trouble, until at about 9 o'clock a more serious one happened near Sloane-square Station with a Circle train, owing to failure of the conductor rails, presumably through deficiencies of construction, since the train to which the mishap happened, and others like it, had been running satisfactorily over the Metropolitan part of the Circle. Thereupon, in view of the fact that the traffic was already considerably disorganized, the management of the District line deemed it advisable to give up the idea of running any more electric trains that day, and issued instructions for the steam service to be resumed as speedily as possible. It was hoped that the electrical east and west service between Ealing and Whitechapel would be again brought into operation yesterday, and this hope was fulfilled, a large number of people travelling in the trains. Electrical trains on the Metropolitan portion of the Circle were running on Saturday afternoon, though the train service generally was somewhat disorganized.

Ealing Common during 1905, a 4-car train sets off for Whitechapel. This is a very early view of a train in service, apparently before trains were fitted with destination indicators. The new electro-pneumatic signals are in use (the dead posts are perhaps from the old ones). This view shows shutter at rear of signal lamp, the backlight, which showed a small white light when signal was at danger, which proved to staff a signal had returned to danger. *Tramway & Railway World*

This view of the Lillie Bridge area in 1907 shows the Empress Hall in background on right and the exhibition grounds, behind which the old depot and new Piccadilly car sheds are just visible. A new electric train passes along in foreground. Roy Allen Collection

After the conductor rail troubles, Met electric trains were confined to their own tracks between South Kensington and Aldgate and steam services resumed on the full Inner Circle service. Once the rolling stock had been modified, a trial run took place successfully on 11th September 1905 and the Met began substituting electric trains on the Inner Circle from 13th September 1905; by 24th September the whole service was electric.[7] Slow rolling stock delivery meant a few District trains were steam hauled in the rush hours, but these ceased entirely from 5th November, after which, the only remaining steam trains were those of the LNWR to and from Mansion House, electric haulage being substituted from 4th December as described shortly.[8]

There were some early mishaps shortly after electric services began in 1905. Some empty cars ran away down the bank at Mill Hill Park and crashed into the buffers by the bridge near the station. The first two cars were severely damaged. The front (motor) car at left was repaired but the whole end of the all-wooden trailer (in foreground) was destroyed and it was written off. No trace has been found of staff casualties. Roy Allen Collection

A Circular Problem

The Inner Circle trains were at first all composed of six cars and still ran at 10-minute intervals. From 18th March 1907 both Met and District reduced their contribution from six to five cars reflecting relatively low usage (the Met later reduced to four cars). From 2nd April the Inner Circle service was retimed at 50 minutes for the round trip. For many years thereafter the number of cars was frequently altered between four and five cars, the running time was constantly adjusted and the proportion of District trains adjusted from time to time to equalize mileage. The Met also began a 'local' service between South Kensington and Aldgate via the north side of the Circle to improve intervals as 10-minute gaps were thought rather long.[9]

Finding that attempts to operate the Inner Circle reliably proved difficult with different companies providing trains and crews, the operation of the whole train service was given to the Met from 1st January 1908 with an interesting twist. Trains ran at 10-minute intervals from Aldgate (bay road) via Baker Street, Victoria, Aldgate, Baker

For a while the District carried on producing timetable booklets, but adapted the design to suit the modern electric look. This one is for May 1906. Roy Allen Collection

To help promote the enhanced train service to the large Jewish population in the East End, in 1907 the District produced posters for local display in Yiddish. This lists various District destinations and nearby places of interest. Most of the larger stations are listed. *Railway News* 7th September 1907

Street and thence to the bay road at South Kensington. After the train terminated, the same pattern was operated in reverse. The illusion of a continuous circle was thereby preserved and on the Met section between Aldgate and South Kensington trains actually ran at 5-minute intervals as they had done before their local service was absorbed into this new pattern. The great advantage was that, by removing the continuous service, proper terminating points were introduced at the end of each trip. Whether this complied with the letter of the 1879 Act is a moot point but along the District section the 10-minute interval remained unattractive.[10] In any event, from 1st October 1908 the former pattern was resumed with trains operating all the way round, though now at 6-minute intervals during most of the day and ten minutes early and late. This required eighteen trains of which six were Districts, three on each rail.[11] From 1916 to 1920 an additional District train operated on the clockwise service. This general pattern lasted until 1926 when other arrangements were made as will be described.

Early Train Service Development

The timings and intervals of the very first electric trains necessarily echoed the steam services because both types of trains had to inter-run until steam was abolished completely at the end of 1905. There were also huge constraints so long as the existing mechanical signalling controlled the service. The new automatic signalling was not available on a large scale until March 1906 as far as Mansion House and not until later in the year did it reach Bow Road. Nor had all the rolling stock been delivered until the end of 1905. Even after everything was ready, the staff had to learn how to operate a much more intensive service. Because of delays in converting all the trains to electric there was a knock-on effect in getting the automatic signalling commissioned, as it was not felt possible to use it with the steam trains, which also delayed service improvement.

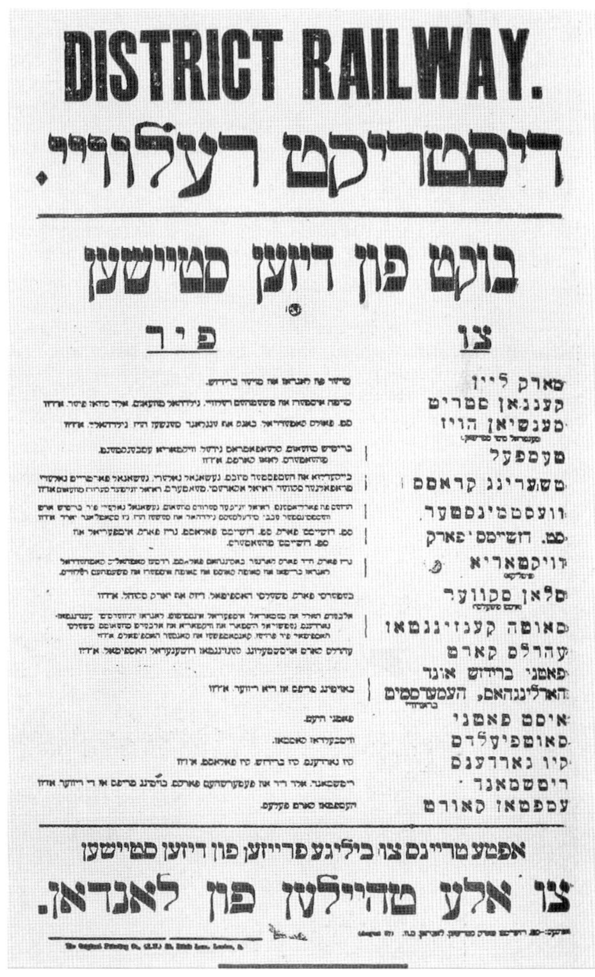

In 1903 the basic steam service through the central area was no more than 18 trains an hour.[12] As the new signalling came into use in stages, starting from the Earls Court end, so train service levels were progressively increased and 26 trains an hour were scheduled from March

1906, including the loco-hauled LNWR trains to Mansion House. Robert Perks (by then deputy chairman) stated in February 1906 that he was hoping to go to 27 trains an hour at the start of March and 30 during March, but this latter was not implemented. Timetables suggest the railway struggled even with 27 and it took many months before 30 trains an hour were offered, from 16th December, the maximum then felt operable. The slack hour service was also increased from 20 to 22 trains an hour from the same date.[13] (The terms busy- and slack-hours were used where today we would use peak and off-peak.)

When steam was eliminated in November 1905 the timetable required 43 electric trains, rising to 47 in January 1906 and 50 in March, coinciding with a 24 trains per hour service through the centre. By 1910 it had further increased to 56 trains; this was only possible because many were shorter than the planned seven cars allowing spare cars to make up extra trains.

The basic weekday slack-hour service in late 1907 was based on a range of overlaid service groups. A 15-minute service operated between Ealing Broadway and East Ham, while 30-minute services operated between Richmond and Mansion House, Wimbledon and Mansion House, Ealing Broadway and Whitechapel and Wimbledon to High Street Kensington. A 15-minute shuttle ran between Putney Bridge and Earls Court, extended alternately to High Street Kensington. A 30-minute LNWR service ran to and from Broad Street and Mansion House via Willesden and Addison Road, and the Inner Circle still operated at 10-minute intervals. In all, 22 trains an hour ran between South Kensington and Mansion House, augmented during the busy hours to 27 trains.

By contrast, the Sunday service was exceedingly thin; just twelve trains in service produced central area intervals of typically ten minutes and even then the service was not quite regular and there were short workings to Mansion House that produced long intervals farther east.

In 1907 the South Harrow service was operated by two shuttle trains, together providing a half-hour service during slack hours and a little more frequently at busy times; both trains comprised just one car. Park Royal station was only open between 8am and 8.15pm but by 1909 some early and late trains called if requested.

Between Hounslow Barracks and Mill Hill Park, intervals were fifteen minutes, with alternate trains projected to South Acton. These trains all had to make a reverse at Hounslow Town. Services were augmented during busy hours, with some through trains to central London. From 9th November 1908 the basic Hounslow service had increased to 10-minutes (using four trains) but alternate trains only went as far west as Hounslow Town.

By June 1910 the slack hours service comprised 26 trains each hour through the central area (sixteen District and ten Inner Circle) and twelve between Hammersmith and Earls Court, presenting a 5-minute service. Of these two came from Richmond, six from Ealing and four started at Hammersmith. Four more trains originated from Wimbledon and joined at Earls Court. Nine operated between Earls Court and High Street, mainly from Putney Bridge. At the east end of the line half the District trains stopped at Mansion House, the rest variously terminating at Bow Road (3), East Ham (2) and Barking (3), though intervals were irregular.

The equivalent busy hours service delivered 34 trains in the busiest hour through the central area (24 District and ten Inner Circle). Of these just two came from Richmond, six from Ealing, four from Hounslow, four from Hammersmith, two from Putney and six from Wimbledon. Of these, eight turned round at Mansion House, two at St Mary's, four at Bow Road and the other ten farther east. Further development depended on infrastructure improvements, covered shortly.

Even in 1912 the Sunday service remained infrequent. From 6th October the Mansion House reversers were instead turned at Charing Cross until 4pm, traffic further east being particularly light. This required fully-signalling the emergency crossover at Charing Cross, controlled from a small mechanical signal cabin. This was the only day that trains normally turned around at Charing Cross and was a feature of District Railway services thereafter. To defray the cost of manning Charing Cross signal box, Mansion House signal box was closed on Sundays.

The Problem of Class

As with other railways, and more particularly the Met, the numbers of Second Class passengers diminished towards the end of the nineteenth century and continued to do so at an accelerating rate at the dawn of the twentieth. The directors noted at the February 1905 shareholders' meeting that the District's attempt to hold onto its traffic by reducing fares probably resulted in some second class ticket holders trading up to first. However the decision had in essence been made to abandon traditional first class travel in the new electric trains as the mark of distinction between classes would be hard to make. Yerkes was influenced by American practice but had also noted the success of the one-class London tube railways with their simple ticket system and had ideas of taking the District in the same direction.

By early 1905 there seems to have been a change of heart and it was now proposed to offer so-called 'special cars' in which, for an extra twopence, passengers might gain extra comfort and (as *The Times* reported the chairman as having said) 'rather better society' that would allow them to travel home 'without coming into contact with the workman and his dirty clothes'. These cars did have more luxurious seating, covered in crimson plush, but there was a certain amount of criticism. The *Morning Leader*, pointing out that nobody knew what the term 'special car' meant and that it caused great confusion. Some newspapers referred to these as 'preferred cars' and the *Railway Magazine* is found calling them 'reserved cars', so confusion in naming seems to have been justified. The *Railway Engineer* was particularly rude about them, referring to them as 'the special, or first class, red "contraptions" which have appeared'. The journal went on: 'Surely Mr. Perks must know that the only difference between the "ordinary" and "special" cars was the label, and now the only difference we can detect is that one class has crimson plush on the seats and the other woven rattan.' In another edition they said: '...every effort was apparently made to get rid of the first-class—the "special" carriages provided as compared with the Metropolitan firsts were (and are) filthy and for a long time identical with the thirds, the short distance first-class fares were and are absurdly high, and no effort was made to reserve the "special cars" for those who paid for them.' At the shareholders' meeting on 6th February 1906 Perks, the vice chairman, was hoping that when the line was in perfect running order much of the former second class traffic that had switched to third would flock to the 'special cars'.[14]

The District complained its first class (special car) ticket sales were reducing but the press suggested that this was because the accommodation was not worth the extra and pointed to the Met where first class traffic was buoyant, perhaps because of the plush accommodation provided. Bowing to pressure, the District quickly re-introduced proper first-class accommodation and began selling first class tickets at the ticket office again. This by no means reduced the criticism and the District was constantly accused of making no effort to keep these cars for first-class ticket holders only (unlike the Met). The always-critical *Railway Engineer* notes:[15]

> We have never been able to discover this 'separate accommodation.' There is certainly on each train a carriage with ' 1 ' painted on the windows, but we have never, except when the cars are on the Metropolitan Rly, seen any attempt made to keep the carriage for the use of those who pay comparatively high fares for the privilege of travelling in it. Another deterrent is that the 'separate accommodation' is equally as dirty as the conglomerate accommodation. The cars with ' 1 ' on them also ride equally badly and make just the same horrible noises as those with ' 3 ' on them do.
>
> During the same period the first-class traffic on the Metropolitan Rly increased, and it is not at all uncommon for passengers, especially ladies to allow a District train to pass and wait for a Metropolitan train, simply because in those cars the carpets and floors are kept clean and the seats dusted—in short, one travels comfortably in a Metropolitan car and with extreme discomfort in a District car, and if Sir Geo. Gibb ever travels in his own 'separate accommodation' he can hardly be surprised that its patrons are rapidly fading away.

So far as can be established the trains when delivered had no first-class areas, just the special cars. The need eventually to provide orthodox first-class accommodation was dealt with in the first instance by simply designating all the special cars first-class. At some point, a partition with integral door was installed near the centre of these cars to create both smoking and non-smoking portions. 62 cars of 1905 stock were designated first-class. All were trailers and were normally allocated to the main portion of the train, which remained in service in the slack hours. Special arrangements had to be made for the very short trains on the local services and some motor cars also received small first-class sections.

After a while it was apparent that this configuration was far from ideal and it would be more convenient to have two first-class sections on long trains, with each section taking up only part of a car. This was at least in part fuelled by complaints from third class passengers that there was insufficient space for them, whilst first-class passengers felt their premium space was being invaded. Beginning in 1914, all the first-class cars and 74 existing third-class trailers were modified to produce composite cars. This appears to have been the result of extensive passenger counts which demonstrated that there was too much first-class accommodation which also made it hard to police.[16] As reconfigured, one end was designated third-class (non-smoking) whilst the rest was divided into two first class compartments, one for smoking and one for non-smoking. These trailers all required two partitions, with integral swing door, to separate the three areas as well as prominent signs. After this each full length train had a composite car towards each end and all short trains had at least one composite. Again, there were some non-standard vehicles that allowed very short trains to have at least a small number of first-class seats.

Doors and Other Problems

Passengers could hardly fail to notice the profound change that was happening as the bright new electric trains arrived with their open saloons and where the doors were not hinged, in the traditional railway fashion, but opened sideways, sliding into the car body. And they were automatic: a nearby member of staff operated the doors by means of compressed air. On each car side, a single sliding door was to be found at each car end and a pair of doors that closed against each other was located at the centre of the cars. Tip up seats were provided on each side of the centre doors and these were available for use on the offside of trains (virtually all platforms were on the nearside).[17] Fuelled by enthusiasm for the arrangement adopted in Boston, the centre doors were reserved for those leaving the train whilst the end doors were designated for those boarding. It was hoped this would reduce the dwell time at stations and encourage passengers to move down inside the cars.[18] Such hopes were immediately found quite unrealistic and virtually impossible to police.

The staff deployed to operate the doors comprised the front and rear conductors and a lesser grade, known officially as gatemen, at the intermediate positions; the total number of staff required (including the driver) was the same as the number of cars—seven staff in the case of a 7-car train. Steam trains had required just four staff so it can be seen that the increase in staffing costs was substantial, even allowing for pay being reduced. At stations the gatemen and conductors stood on the gangways at the ends of the cars where they could operate the door valves of their own and the adjacent car, the valves being on the exterior end panels. The expression 'conductor' was now used consistently for the electric train man in charge of a train, though 'guard' crept back into use in the 1920s.

Staff instructions dated March 1905, and repeated in September, make it clear that on arriving at a station the trainmen were supposed to bawl out an instruction to passengers to leave by the middle doors and to open the middle doors first. As soon as everyone wanting to get out had alighted, the middle doors had to be closed. When everyone had boarded via the end doors the gatemen manipulated a wire that operated a mechanical bell at the forward end, but only if the next bell rearwards had been heard. By this means, news of a train's readiness to depart eventually ended up with a bell ringing in the driver's cab. It was permissible, according to the instructions, for the starting signal to be given before the end doors were actually closed, but doors could then not be reopened.[19]

Most of the equipment and methods used for the District's electrification scheme worked reasonably well but the rolling stock, when it eventually arrived, proved a disappointment in practice. Press reaction to the new cars was at best muted and sometimes hostile, and this was not only because of the apparent unreliability in the early days but also because the cars looked 'American', boarded slowly and were noisy. True to form, the *Railway Engineer* was more outspoken, but its vivid description paints a picture worth recalling.

> We do not remember that it has ever been said that the first cost of these cars was high, the general opinion being that their design is bad and their construction 'cheap and nasty'. ... The bogies might be altered to one of the ordinary pattern, with a view to improve the riding. The variety of noises which attend the cars should be suppressed. At present the cars clatter into the stations like trucks of old iron, and stop with shudders, jerks and squeaks, then the compressed air exhausts are opened, and the rest of the interval is enlivened by the vigorous working of a noisy variety of pump until the train is clanged out by numerous and perfectly useless bells. Then the brass-bound side lights, which have fully developed their rattling powers, commence and continue an excruciating noise until the next stop is made. The middle doors—'gates' we mean—should at least be made draught-tight, as a cold or stiff neck is the result of 'strap-hanging' in the vicinity of them.[20]

Another ungrateful newspaper exclaimed:

> On the electrified District Railway first, second, and third-class has been replaced by special, ordinary, and strap. About 75 per cent of the passengers travel strap.[21]

It was perhaps unfortunate that the Met's new electric trains provided so convenient a comparison and the press was quick to make unfavourable comparisons between the two types of train. The Met trains were regarded as much nicer beasts and were portrayed as better-finished, better-riding, quieter and, most important of all, were all British. Actually the car layouts were not all that different. Build quality came in for criticism and *Electrical Review* commented on the (alleged) excessive maintenance and repair costs: 'this is only what would be expected from the exceedingly poor construction of a very great portion of the District Railway's rolling stock'.[22]

THE DISTRICT RAILWAY.

TO THE EDITOR OF THE TIMES.

Sir,—A sufficient time has now elapsed to have enabled the District Railway to understand its own trains. Overcrowding and strap-hanging may be, at certain times of the day, inevitable, but there is no excuse for the spinal concussion incident on starting and stopping the trains, which is becoming worse and worse day by day. The Metropolitan trains are comfortable and fairly free from dangerous jerking; but the District trains are, I do not hesitate to say, dangerous to the public health as at present stopped and started. It becomes a form of positive suffering to take a long journey in these trains; and I cannot think that the daily experience of the chronic jerking that passengers are subjected to can be free from the risk of subsequent disease.

Your obedient servant,

December 16. A PHYSICIAN.

Letter to *The Times* 23rd December 1905. At about this time numerous letters were being written to the newspapers by outraged passengers purporting to dislike the new methods. Author's collection

The system of air-operated door control proved hopeless. Passengers failed to follow the one way system, either deliberately or because they couldn't understand it, whilst the pneumatic doors proved unreliable and gave rise to some serious incidents. Nor were they very user-friendly, closing with great vigour and without rubber edges to cushion the impact when meeting a passenger who had not got out of the way in time. The press much-derided the whole arrangement and in April 1906 the centre doors were taken out of use, 'ostensibly for fear of accidents' with the intention that the space be used for extra seating, using the tip-up seats on both sides (first class carriages had polished mahogany wooden planks fitted on both sides of the cars, on top of the tip ups, and passengers sat with their backs to the disused doors).[23]

Trials were made to find a way of persisting with and improving the automatic doors, but these showed little promise. The Board of Trade then became interested and in May 1906 the UERL chairman and chief engineer explained the nature of the difficulties which had resulted in the middle doors being taken out of use altogether and only the end doors used—these were easy for the gatemen to supervise. One issue was that the door controllers were located such that the gatemen could not look along the platform when the valves were operated (or see the middle doors from inside when it was busy). A subsequent memo dated 11th July suggested the answer might lie in the controls being operated by station staff (although they were on the external ends of the cars they would need moving nearer to the platform edge so they would be in reach) and that they hoped to have an experimental train available within a week, but unfortunately the file goes silent at this point. The *Electrical Review* refers to an experiment during August 1906 whereby a train operated by a front and rear guard only had been arranged so that these two staff could somehow operate all the doors along the train but again the result of this experiment has not be found.[24]

From 1907 the doors were progressively altered to operation by hand and middle doors brought back into use, handles being fixed to the door leaves that actuated a lock, though there was nothing to stop anyone opening a door at any time. Passengers were trusted to open the doors at stations as well as station staff, while the latter attempted to get them shut when the train had loaded. This enabled staff on trains to be much reduced to just a front and rear conductor, flag signals being given by the rear conductor to the front when the train was ready to go, and the front conductor then giving the starting bell. The shareholders were told on 10th February 1909 that virtually the whole of the stock had been altered to hand-door operation, effecting a useful reduction in staff and 'improved safety'. It was a feature of travel on the District for many years that in hot weather some of the doors (including doors on the offside) would be opened by passengers to improve ventilation and people would happily travel next to an open door. This appears to have been tolerated without any undue concern.

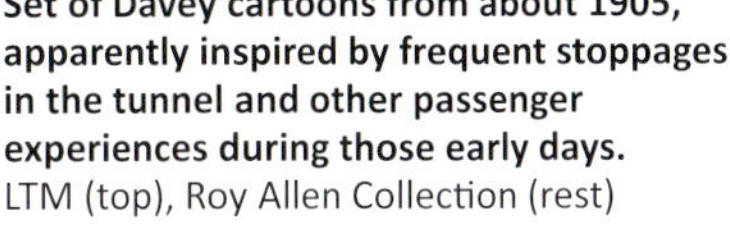

Set of Davey cartoons from about 1905, apparently inspired by frequent stoppages in the tunnel and other passenger experiences during those early days.
LTM (top), Roy Allen Collection (rest)

The scarlet paintwork did not wear well, so reports suggest at the time, and early in 1907 it was decided that in future cars would be painted a dark green colour which also had the advantage of making them look 'less American' (it was also £3 per car cheaper).[25] It was suggested the fireproofing process resulted in some absorption by the wood of salts that was found to react with the paint, and was not completely resolved until steel-bodied cars were later introduced, but since it was mostly the metal panelling that was painted we cannot attach much weight to this.[26] About half the fleet had been repainted by the time [in 1909] when the dark green was also felt unsatisfactory and repainting in red then resumed, perhaps with some adjustment to make it wear better.

A more serious shortcoming was the bogie design where cracking frames on the original cast steel motor and trailer bogies soon required expensive repair and the purchase of additional spares. Within a few years the UERL had designed and built new riveted plate bogies with a longer wheelbase and replaced 180 or the original kind. Most of the new bogies were trailer bogies but a number of replacement motor bogies were also built. In both cases the same wheels were used.

An even more worrying problem was the number of broken axles that soon occurred. A broken axle is a very serious matter that usually involves derailment, which can have disastrous consequences. The railway inspectorate was asked to investigate the circumstances where nine failures had occurred between September 1904 and March 1906 (five of which happened during February and March 1906). All the failures were on the trailing bogies of the motor cars and most of the axles failed near the point where they joined the wheel. Two broke near the centre and were precipitated by electrical burns. The axles were all made by Krupps of Essen and used particularly hard steel. In all cases the failure was preceded by a gradually enlarging crack. There was a puzzle that no axles on trailer cars were affected, though more numerous and of identical type. Further investigation suggested the stresses and greater braking pressures used on motor cars were probably responsible. The conclusion of the inquiry was that the axles were too light for the job. All 400 axles of this type were replaced by new ones from Monkbridge Works of Leeds, of larger section and less brittle steel. The press made a great meal of all this but actually it was easy to fix and it solved the problem.

Almost as worrying were several electrical fires, each of these highly newsworthy and providing more ammunition for the anti-American commentary being fostered. In no case did the fire spread and the fire-resistant treatment given to the wood was found most satisfactory. In April and May 1906 there were fires associated with the end carriages, in both cases causing only minor damage. There was a more serious case at Sloane Square on 8th January 1908 which was caused by arcing in a junction box under the car floor of one of the end motor cars, No 34; the arcing was cut off when traction current was discharged. The cause was an insulation failure in the lighting circuit, thought to have been caused by damp, the resulting arcing vaporising some bitumen whose vapour then exploded, but the arcing continued. The guard used the air valve to open the centre doors and escorted the eight occupants off the train. Above floor level damage was confined to smoke damage to some glazing and blistering of wood around the windows (though the wood had not actually burnt). Once certain possible causes of fire had been identified and rectified, the problem more or less disappeared.

Virtually every stoppage, derangement or incident was covered very fully in the press. There was some sober reporting but the daily newspapers and the specialist railway and electrical magazines took every opportunity to highlight the difficulties and knock the use of foreign equipment or materials (irrespective of whether the incident being covered was caused by something foreign or not). By May 1906 Sir George Gibb was getting very fed up with this and in a long letter to the *Railway News* complained that the District was giving a good service and that the relatively small number of incidents were grossly exaggerated in the importance attributed to them and often incorrectly described. He then gave examples of several things that had happened (all by then fixed) which were nothing to do with the foreignness of the equipment. He particularly slated the anonymous authors of several articles castigating the District whose writings had drawn quite wrong conclusions and wondered if they would care to identify themselves.

Gibb freely admitted that bringing so much new equipment into use at the same time had been difficult and for a while the service was disappointing. On the whole, things were working much better now and some credit might be given to those who had made all the improvements with the minimum of disruption.[27]

Electrification and the Staff

The role of the station staff was not greatly altered by electrification, but this could not be said of the train staff where the changes were profound. The existing on-train establishment comprised a driver and fireman (who were part of the locomotive department) and two guards. The District proposed to run its electric trains with a single driver and on a 7-car train six other staff would be needed, as explained earlier. At least one of these staff would be trained to drive trains in an emergency if the driver became incapacitated. This meant bringing all the train staff together in one department. Following American practice the driver was known as a 'motorman' thus differentiating him beyond doubt from the steam driver. The District expected the motorman's job to be very much less arduous than the steam driver's job and desired to pay motormen less than drivers to reflect this, as well as attempting to save money which was still in scarce supply. A reduction of up to 16 shillings a week was mooted by the District, which sought some sort of equivalence with electric tramway drivers. This was a substantial reduction of the weekly wage, perhaps representing as much as a third.

This shows the motorman's training school set up in a building adjacent to the car sheds at Mill Hill Park. A skeleton car was located here which carried all the electrical equipment of a normal car so motormen could see how it all functioned. Author's collection

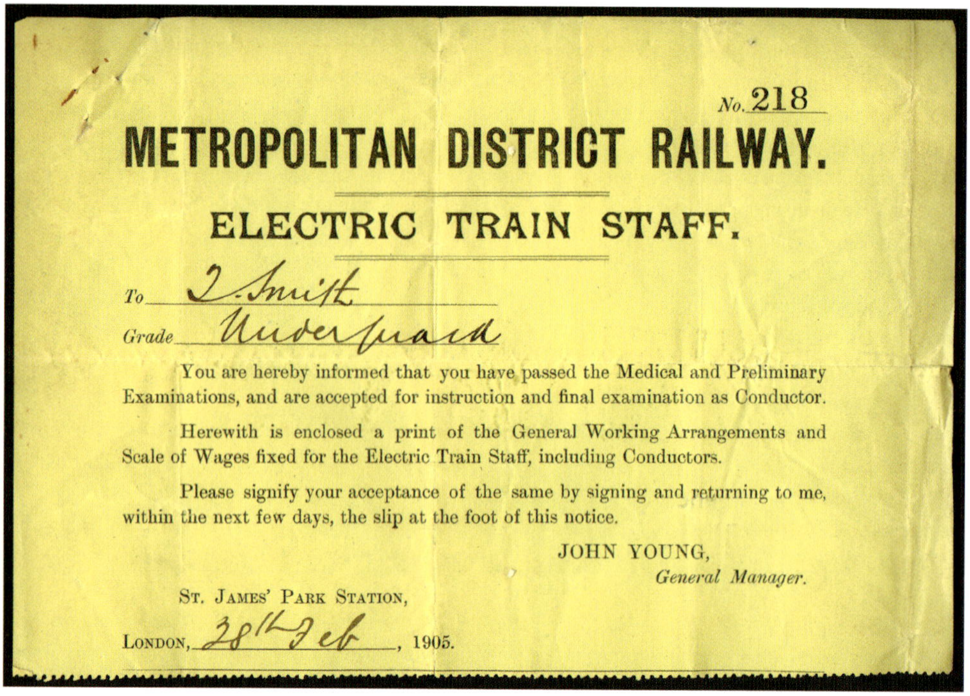

No. 218

METROPOLITAN DISTRICT RAILWAY.

ELECTRIC TRAIN STAFF.

To J. Smith

Grade Underguard

You are hereby informed that you have passed the Medical and Preliminary Examinations, and are accepted for instruction and final examination as Conductor.

Herewith is enclosed a print of the General Working Arrangements and Scale of Wages fixed for the Electric Train Staff, including Conductors.

Please signify your acceptance of the same by signing and returning to me, within the next few days, the slip at the foot of this notice.

JOHN YOUNG,
General Manager.

St. James' Park Station,

London, 28th Feb, 1905.

Certificate of acceptance for electric train staff having completed medical and preliminary examinations. LTM

Predictably, the men's representatives disagreed on various important points and claimed that having only one person in the cab would be dangerous and that the wage reduction would be a very serious loss to the men, though the reduction would be less severe the longer service the drivers had.

A settlement was reached at the beginning of April 1905 to the effect:

1. that all existing drivers would be given the opportunity to retrain as motormen;
2. that all drivers would be found work if at all possible and if suitably retrained would be given preference over newcomers;
3. existing staff who requalified would be paid approximately the same as before, but new staff coming in would be paid less;
4. work would be found for the displaced firemen who would continue to receive like pay.

The men were uneasy about 'one-manning' the cabs and pointed out that in fogs, which were very common in those days, conditions were often so bad that firemen had to leave the cab and climb the signal in order to determine its indication. The railway felt that there were technical solutions to this and with the safety equipment that would be provided on the new trains, having two men in the cab could not possibly be justified.[28] It was found that while some firemen qualified as motormen, most were used to fill the vacancies for conductors and gatemen. An attempt to get improved pay for Sunday work was not conceded. These issues clearly rumbled on for a while and an MP referred to the long hours and 'want of a second man in the cab' of District men in a parliamentary question about accidents in March 1906, the response being that the men had not complained to the Board of Trade about these matters and that it was not seen that a second man would be more likely to prevent accidents. We must remember that until the new automatic signalling was brought into operation during 1906 the motorman of an electric train drove it to the old mechanical block signalling with no trainstop devices and no second man to assist keeping a lookout.[29] The men's case for having a second person in the cab was not helped by the two trades unions involved having diametrically opposing views on the matter.[30]

The job of training all the staff required for electric working whilst maintaining steam services was intricate and time consuming. The job was not helped by the long delay between the training of the first staff and introduction of electric trains, which risked trained drivers forgetting some of what they had been taught.

Training initially took place on the E&SHR using the 1903 cars. Since only some of the cars were actually in daily use others were available in the shed for teaching prospective drivers about all the equipment. Having reached a certain level of proficiency they could then be given driving turns on service trains, under supervision. Such was the level of training required that virtually the whole of the E&SHR operation became a training ground and from 9th August 1904 the whole of the working and control of the staff along that line was taken over by the UERL which worked it on behalf of the District at a net rental of £4000, the UERL undertaking all maintenance and keeping local traffic receipts.[31]

District's training school after removal from Mill Hill Park to West Brompton, but showing original fully-equipped panel used to train the drivers. There was no room for the chassis here and correct motor operation was shown by illuminated lamps. No plans have been found of either training location, but the only space at West Brompton was under the station building, which is consistent with the visible brickwork. Author's collection

Later on a motorman's school was established at Mill Hill Park, the centrepiece being a new underframe based on one of the 1905 cars to which all the correct equipment was attached together with complete driving cab equipment. By operating the cab controls, staff could see exactly how the equipment responded including operation of the motors and wheels (the bogies were jacked up to keep the affair static). The school was in an outbuilding of the works but appears already to have been in use by February 1905.[32]

By the time electrification was being launched the following process was adopted. The staff selected for training as motormen (initially these were mainly loco drivers) were first subjected to hearing and vision tests, including a test for colour blindness. Further tests included reading (by making candidates read part of the rule book) and writing (which took the form of a brief report about something). Those successfully passing the tests were then medically examined. It is of interest that these tests were felt necessary for existing train staff converting to electric operation and begs the question about what the standards had been hitherto, particularly with regard to colour blindness on a railway where often coloured lights had been the only guidance.

Those getting this far were then presented with a copy of the new Electric Train rule book, which was supplementary to the existing Railway Clearing House rule book and included the necessary rules to deal with electrified operation. The candidates then received between ten and fifteen days training on the South Harrow line and in the new instruction school at Mill Hill Park. After passing an examination, the successful candidates were passed for probationary service on a regular train: not all candidates were expected to prove satisfactory. In addition to the regular drivers a number of instructors were specially trained and these staff were expected to spend much time 'on the road' to assist and instruct motormen.

It was expected that two conductors would be required on a full length train and it was decided at the start that this grade should also receive train driver training in case, in some emergency, the motorman was unable to drive the train. These staff were selected mainly from guards and firemen and the training was similar to that of the motormen. For gatemen the training was necessarily much more basic than for driving staff and because so many gatemen were required the opportunity arose to recruit from promising station staff. It was accepted that for the future staff would be recruited as gatemen (or perhaps promoted to the grade) and then progress via conductor to motorman.[33]

The subsequent shortening of trains to match traffic resulted in some train staff being discharged, 60 being reported as having gone by the end of May 1906.[34] Later, the filling of train staff jobs by station staff on promotion caused some apprehension amongst the trades unions as locomotive men had previously been in a different union to other grades and now the staff were being mixed up. Whilst this was tolerated, it led to some inter-union rivalry that still persists today. There was some grumbling about the shareholders and passengers benefiting from electrification whilst the men were expected to work for lower pay. There was not very much that they could do about that.[35]

Eclipse of the Outer Circle Service and Purchase of Electric Locomotives

The circuitous Outer Circle service had long been operated by the LNWR between Broad Street and Mansion House via Willesden Junction and Earls Court but had always been hauled throughout by LNWR locomotives. With looming electrification, these arrangements were reviewed. The LNWR obtained a beneficial clause in the District's 1901 Act requiring the District to pay for converting LNWR stock for electric traction if the District insisted these trains had to be electrically operated.[36] In the end the District agreed to haul the existing trains east of Earls Court by means of its own electric

Above: **Earls Court looking east around 1908. A LNWR train waits in the down platform on the outer circle route during the loco change (a steam loco lurks in the covered way). The new electro-pneumatic signals are particularly prominent.** LTM

Below: **Outer Circle Loco after being equipped at Ealing Common. Perhaps most obvious are the buffing and coupling gear, designed to allow the locos to couple with main line trains. The locos were fitted with Vacuum as well as Westinghouse brakes as the LNWR used the former system.** Author's collection

The inside of one of the District locomotives. On the left is the control gear and starting resistances and on the right are the air compressor and exhauster for the braking equipment. Author's collection

locomotives. The service had been weekday-only but a Sunday shuttle service from Willesden was introduced as far as Addison Road in April 1891 and extended to Earls Court from 5th February 1905 and, from 6th May 1906, to Mansion House.[37]

Ten electric locomotives were acquired from the Metropolitan Amalgamated Railway Carriage & Wagon Co. These had the same profile as the new electric carriages but were rather shorter, at about 25ft. Power was transmitted by two motor bogies (four motors in all), each bogie having its own set of equipment, with both operating simultaneously from the multiple unit control line. Each loco weighed 38 tons. The locomotive bodies had a cab-like space at both ends but driver's controls were fitted at only one end (the other end was available to receive control equipment too, and some later were). These locomotives usually worked in pairs, back to back, with the driver's controls at the outer ends. Two locomotives working in tandem like this could deliver about the same amount of power as a normal electric train. These electric locomotives were unfortunately still not ready when the District had completed its own electric conversion in November 1905 and LNWR steam haulage east of Earls Court continued a month longer, until 4th December.

Soon after electrification the District needed the Outer Circle train paths for its own trains and the less heavily used LNWR service was cut back from 1st January 1909 to Earls Court where passengers could make cross-platform connections. The LNWR trains (still steam hauled) turned round in the siding east of the station and the electric locos were redeployed. From 1912 alterations in the service pattern of trains from Broad Street resulted in the Broad Street–Earls Court paths being switched to Kew Bridge and an LNWR steam shuttle service was introduced between Earls Court and Willesden Junction where it made connections with trains to Broad Street. This echoed what was already done on Sundays, although the Sunday service ceased from the beginning of 1917. This weekday shuttle operated until bombing of the West London Railway in 1940 put paid to it. The shuttle was worked by LNWR steam rail motor trains with the locomotive always at the south end. This greatly simplified the work at Earls Court as it was no longer necessary for locomotives to be changed there, or even run round their trains.[38]

The relatively new, but now redundant, District electric locomotives were available to be redeployed, though three bodies were scrapped in 1911, the traction equipment being recovered for use elsewhere. For a while some 4-car Inner Circle trains were operated using four trailers with a loco at (usually) the leading end, but other developments were in hand that gave these still relatively new locos a new lease of life, and we will cover this shortly.

Improvements on the Tilbury Line

When the District electrification programme began, the LTSR east of Campbell Road had been a double track, mixed traffic railway with a large number of junctions with other connecting railways that were used mainly by goods trains. With train services comprising a mix of fast, stopping and goods services the track capacity had been approaching its limit even before the W&BR was mooted. The extra trains the new line would bring seemed likely to increase congestion beyond tolerable limits and led to a programme to quadruple this section of track.

Little work was done before the W&BR connection opened in 1902, by which time it was becoming obvious that with the District committed to electrification some of the LTSR lines would also need to be electrified. As a precaution, the LTSR's 1902 Act authorized electrification of the whole (or any part) of the LTSR and construction of a power station at Little Ilford, north of the LTSR on the banks of the River Roding. It was not immediately intended to electrify the whole of the LTSR, but obtaining these wide powers left all options open until the optimal plan could be devised. In the end, electrification in the first instance to East Ham was decided. Although Barking had been entertained briefly as the better termination point, the engineering complications were felt too great. With electrification work taking place more or less at the same time as quadrupling the plan was refined to electrify only the local lines (as they would become) and serve those stations mainly with trains to and from the District. The new (non-electric) fast lines would carry LTSR services to Fenchurch Street, running mainly non-stop between East Ham and Burdett Road.

The LTSR investigated the best means of electrifying its tracks and finally decided to appoint the UERL to do the work, for which the LTSR would pay (this came to £42,827). For some reason the LTSR had been reluctant to obtain its electricity from the UERL and at first opened discussions with the Charing Cross & Strand Electricity Supply Co (which generated at Bow) and then Poplar Borough Council, which also had a generating station in the area. Terms could not be agreed with the former and the latter did not think it had the statutory powers. With little other choice, the decision was taken in July 1904 to take a supply from Lots Road and substations were constructed at Campbell Road and East Ham. A Lots Road supply for the LTSR was found by using two spare feeders that had been earmarked for a supply to the ELR but had not been used (the LTSR later purchased these cables from the UERL).

The widening between Campbell Road and East Ham began at the latter point in February 1902 and was introduced piecemeal between April 1903 and August 1905. The track formation was widened on one side or the other (or both) and resulted in four platforms being provided at all stations. In each case this comprised side platforms on the outer roads and an island between the centre (up slow / down fast) roads, except at West Ham which, being built new with widening already in mind, had two islands. Standard LTSR semaphore signalling was installed on all four tracks. From 1st March 1905 a temporary bay road at Bromley became available as part of the stage works and the 28 or so District trains that had previously turned short at Bow Road were extended to Bromley.[39]

With 4-tracking not quite complete when electric trains began operating on the main part of the District it was not felt practical to extend electric trains east of Whitechapel. At first, from 1st July 1905, only the Ealing trains were electric and these were truncated at Whitechapel, connecting with a steam shuttle to and from East Ham. The Richmond and Wimbledon trains (which were still steam hauled) continued to run straight through to East Ham until 1st August when the Richmond service was converted to electric, and as 4-tracking between Bromley and Plaistow had still not been completed these trains, too, had to terminate at Whitechapel and make connections. It was finally possible to bring the electric local lines into use throughout from 20th August 1905, though a few District steam trains still ran at certain times until all the electric rolling stock had been delivered. Between 1st and 20th August the District steam trains that had been turning short at Bromley were extended to East Ham to help out. With electric tracks only as far as East Ham, it was not possible to continue the through District trains to Upminster, and these ceased from 1st October 1905.

When District trains were first extended to East Ham a small depot was erected on the west side of the River Roding north of the LTSR main line, in the large triangle of railway land. Though provided by the LTSR it was used (for a charge) by the District and was available from 31st May 1902. It consisted of just three sidings and locomotive coaling and watering facilities, all accessible only at the west end. Timetables indicate that the three LTSR-maintained joint stock trains were serviced here overnight. Upon electrification, additions were made to the existing sidings including electrification of them all and the use of two temporary sidings that could be converted into running lines when quadrupling was extended to Barking. The new facilities were available from 20th August 1905 although some steam services continued to run for a while. Trains terminating at East Ham generally ran forward into these sidings to turn round.

When the District was electrified the company bought the whole of the new rolling stock required, including that needed for the foreign railways over which the District operated. Many British railways operated over the systems of other companies and well-tested arrangements existed to handle the accounting. Methods varied and were usually governed by specific agreements but, typically, the company owning the track and stations would treat any 'foreign' train as its own whilst it was on its tracks and pay the supplying company an agreed allowance for its provision on a train-mileage basis, to include operating and crew costs. This was what was envisaged when District electric trains began operating to East Ham and Barking.

After a while the two companies concluded that it would be more satisfactory if the supply cables and rolling stock were vested in the LTSR which would place the capital where it was actually used and reduce the amount of cross-accounting. The outcome was that the LTSR purchased 37 motor and 37 trailer cars of new District electric stock, for which the District was paid £130,000; these cars were always pooled with the rest of the District's stock for operating and day-to-day maintenance purposes but these costs were off-charged.[40] The number of cars purchased approximately represented the cars required to operate services east of Bow Road and when services later increased additional cars were added to the LTSR fleet.

This shows one of the new cars sporting the words L. T. S. Railway along the 'letter-board'. Also visible are the pantograph style protective barriers between the cars. Author's collection

Barking, rather than East Ham, had always been the preferred objective for the District trains but complex junctions, unsuitable and congested track layout and already overly-busy level crossings ruled it out at first. Increasing operating challenges, together with pressure from the local district council, finally persuaded the LTSR to embark on reconstruction of the station, rearrangement of the track layout and removal of two level crossings, the latter requiring a huge road bridge upon which it was possible to move the station.

Enlargement work began in January 1906 and was very substantial, requiring the acquisition of more than 130 properties. The transformation converted what had been a double-track railway with four platforms into a 6-track railway with eight platforms, two of which were reserved for reversing electric trains (with three sidings beyond). District electric trains were extended from East Ham to Barking as soon as the stage-works allowed it on 1st April 1908, the trackwork alterations being possible only after the Tanner Street level crossing had been closed in September 1907. Reconstruction work was largely completed in July 1908. Coinciding with the extension of electric trains to Barking the District's sidings east of East Ham were further enlarged, resulting in a 4-road shed and seven (later nine) outside sidings all of which were now accessible from either end.[41]

The electrification and intensification of train services, with through trains to the District, made the use of stations between Bromley and Barking much more attractive than hitherto and sparked a huge growth in traffic. The District naturally welcomed the balancing loads now coming to and from the east, especially as traffic growth elsewhere was lower than hoped as competition from omnibuses and the new tube railways proved fierce. It proved a mixed blessing, though, as the newly-stimulated traffic began overwhelming the train services that could be run.

Chapter Five

MONEY AND MANAGERS

The Challenge

Many readers will know already that prior to 1933 the 'Underground' (the public face of the UERL) ran much of London's transport system—buses, trams and most of the deep tube lines as well as the District. There is some evidence that when Yerkes arrived in London in 1900 he felt there was an opportunity to monopolize the transport scene and that would be very lucrative. The first task was to build the authorized, but unbuilt, tube lines and electrify the District. Whether, when all this was done, he would have sold it on at a profit immediately, or whether he intended to retain ongoing control, we cannot be sure. Either way he was keen to have as much of the central London traffic as he could get and run the railways as one concern, the core being the District.[1] At first, the management of the District and the three tube railways remained quite separate and they retained their individual legal identities throughout Yerkes' time.

This chapter describes the organization and financing of the UERL's modernization programme, the financial misfortune out of which the various railways were brought together perhaps faster than expected and the way the UERL had to evolve very quickly after District electrification from a finance and construction company into an integrated transport operating business that soon found itself operating trams and buses too. In turn this was the first stage of transforming the District from an independent railway into an integrated part of a larger transport business, and consequential erosion of its former individuality.

The District Board

Once Forbes was dethroned in 1901 it is interesting how little of the directors' time was taken up with business connected with modernization, all of which was left in the hands of the Yerkes team. On 19th June 1902, Perks (the chairman) told the directors that a request had been made 'by shareholders holding a large interest' that the board needed strengthening. Arthur Lewis Stride and Charles Ainsworth Spofford were proposed and appointed, which can only have been a consequence of some behind-the-scenes activity initiated by the Yerkes team. Stride was the managing director of the LTSR and became a very active District director, often being given a remit to sort out matters that arose without reference back to the board and

Lord George Hamilton, shortly before joining the District. Author's collection

apparently able to take on complicated District matters in addition to his LTSR duties. He was probably one of the most effective directors the District had ever had. Spofford was an American with railroad, business and electrical engineering experience and was given a seat on the UERL board at the same time. In December 1902, James Clifton Robinson of the London United Tramways joined the board, the UERL having just acquired that concern. He was another very positive asset and had greatly helped Yerkes earlier in the year resulting in the UERL taking over the LUT in September.[2] Robinson was a great supporter of through fares between different transport modes and realized that with trams banned in central London, yet serving areas off the railway network, there was an opportunity to promote longer journeys jointly to the benefit of everyone. He was awarded a knighthood in 1905.

During 1903 the District Board comprised: Perks (chairman), Isaacs (deputy chairman), Dalrymple, Law, Griffith, Stride, Spofford and Robinson. In 1905 Yerkes himself became chairman of the District with Perks stepping back to deputy chairman and Isaacs retiring. In 1904 Baron Herbert de Stern joined the board. He has been described as a banker, businessman and philanthropist and headed the firm of Herbert Stern & Co. The barony he inherited from his father and represents the Portuguese nobility. He was created a British baronet in 1905 but later during the year became an English baron, entitled 1st Baron Michelham of Hellingly.

In 1905 William Henry Brown and Rt Hon Lord George Hamilton MP JP also joined the board. Brown was a partner in the firm of Speyer Bros and was presumably installed in order to look after that firm's interests. Lord George Hamilton had a more eventful career including at various times as an officer in the Coldstream Guards, First Lord of the Admiralty and Secretary of State for India. At the time of joining the board (he also joined the UERL board) he was Member of Parliament for Ealing. The 'Lord' was honorary, as a younger son of a duke (his father was Duke of Abercorn) though he was also a knight, being a Knight Grand Commander of the Order of the Star of India. He found time to be a justice of the peace for Middlesex, was Captain of Deal Castle and later found himself President of the Royal Statistical Society. The board was now occupied by a group of very capable and influential individuals compared with the Forbes days.

John Young. LTM from original in *Illustrated London News*

Managers and Engineers

The District Railway

The day-to-day business of the District had to continue despite the disruption caused by the electrification works and with the added challenge of training and reorganizing the staff. This task fell to the District's general manager (this title was sometimes styled simply 'manager').

We have already noted that Mr John Young was appointed towards the end of 1904, having been tempted down from Glasgow. He had been the well-respected manager of the Glasgow Corporation tramways, and that city mourned Young's loss. He had neither been seeking a new post, nor had he been expecting to move down south, but it seems that Yerkes had sought him out and made an offer he could not refuse, a move that appears to have been fully justified.

Young had the unenviable job of managing the operational aspects of the conversion to electric working and introducing the new train services. He also acted as a general assistant to Yerkes for the whole of group's construction activities. As is so often the way, he needed experienced people he could trust to help him and soon recruited J.B. MacKinnon, W.A. Agnew and C.A. King, all from the Glasgow tramways.[3] Agnew became the District's rolling stock superintendent and staff instructor and in 1927 he was the mechanical engineer for all of the UERL lines. Charles A. King arrived in 1905 to become chief engineer of the District and replaced the respected George Estall on his retirement. He stayed until 1908 but was thereafter retained as consulting engineer, a position he still held in 1911. J.B. MacKinnon's position is not clear but he is found with London United Tramways in 1913.

Working for the District during the difficult period of electrification showed off Young's great ability and he joined the board on 1st May 1906, resigning the post of manager to do so. He was replaced by Arthur Collinson, who was paid a great deal less than Young had been but did not endure and was only in post for a year.

W.A. Agnew. LTM

J.P. Thomas. The badge he is wearing is that of a commandant in the Metropolitan Special Constabulary (Thomas was later a senior manager of the London General Omnibus Company which, during the Great War, sponsored a police division). LTM

The Underground Electric Railways

A few words should be said about the Yerkes team which was undertaking the modernization work in parallel with other developments on the District

The Yerkes team was directed by James Russell Chapman, Yerkes' chief engineer and general manager. A Kansas City man, Chapman was engineer to the Union Traction Company in Chicago. He is credited with constructing and equipping most of the surface electric lines on the North and West sides as well as the North Western and Union Elevated roads. He remained with the UERL until 1910 when he returned to the USA. He died in Santa Barbara in 1934, aged 82.[4]

With Chapman came Frank D. Ward, Master Mechanic, who became responsible for the rolling stock and the great car sheds at Mill Hill Park. Prior to coming to London he was general master mechanic of the Lake Street and Northwestern Elevated Railroad Companies.[5]

Zachariah Ellis Knapp became the team's Chief Draughtsman. Originally from North Carolina, Knapp came to London in 1901 bringing with him a reputation for building power houses in Chicago. Unusually for members of the team he remained in London after the great works were completed. In 1910 he was appointed general manager of the London United Tramways, returning to the UERL in 1913 as chief engineer of all the railways. In 1915 he became manager for maintenance and construction, and in 1921 he was director of construction. For a while, before becoming a director, he was also commercial manager. He died in 1926 at the early age of 59.[6]

Samuel B. Fortenbaugh was seconded from the General Electric Company, Schenectady, and was noted as a scientist and mathematician. He was heavily involved in the earlier stages of the modernization work but later returned to General Electric where he was involved in schemes around the World. He died in 1943.[7] Others who came over were Jim Thompson, responsible for Lighting, Telephones and Drainage and W.E. Hanson, from Kansas City, who was responsible for track, tunnels and other civil engineering.

The engineer John Pattinson Thomas, English, and of whom more will be said later, worked closely with the Yerkes team and shortly before his death in 1973 wrote some brief observations about their methods:[8]

On most railways, District included, personal metal passes were issued to senior managers and directors. Usually referred to as medallion passes, these were very often issued to directors of other companies too, including rivals, to reflect their status. Silver passes were usually issued to senior managers and gold reserved for directors and perhaps general managers. These images show a District silver pass and a later gold pass issued for all the UERL lines (the gold one was issued to Felix Pole, a GWR director). Metal passes continued to be issued by British Railways and London Transport until about 1990. LTM

> These astonishing engineers and scientists from the Chicago Elevated Railway and street railways and other organizations who accompanied Yerkes arrived in London in 1900 and gathered around them a skilled group of engineers of several nationalities. There were Germans, Italians, Swedes, French, all having affirmed qualification. The qualities required were experience and efficiency—and relentless efficiency at that. Nothing mattered but completed work of the highest standard and speed. Their staff were very well paid: no 'sit down delaying strikes' in that organization. The whole environment was that of goodwill and the highest quality of such work.
>
> The technical generating features of Lots Road Power Station and the motor generating system of the 34 substations and distribution of energy were acclaimed exemplary throughout the profession. All of these men had contempt for office work, and forms of any kind were anathema. They had no physical office except a hut in the depot or room in a house and a male shorthand typist whom they called 'the boy'. When Hanson was asked where his office was he said 'In my bowler hat'—the seven all wore bowlers.
>
> Correspondence of technical or legal kind was centralised in the Chief Draughtsman at Hamilton House, who acted as clearing house and liaison, reporting to Chapman, who held the pulse of the whole system and seemed to make light of it all, which is the way of genius. None of these men was ever seen with a brief case: Hanson was quite right—they carried their offices in their hats, and were by no means beyond removing their coats and working in shirt-sleeves alongside their men and showing them how. Yet these ingenious fellows got through hundreds of thousands of pounds worth of invaluable work.

The Hamilton House referred to was a then new building along Victoria Embankment with its front door almost above the District tunnel; the building still stands today. Named by its owners after Lord Claud Hamilton, it was occupied by several firms and Robert Perks had his solicitor's office here when the MDETC moved in. The building provided sufficient office accommodation during the UERL's construction period, after which the remaining staff moved to St James's Park.

Fares Troubles

The District's money virtually all came from passengers dutifully paying their fares and since the District's outgoings were usually reduced to meet the money available, the company was especially alive to the need to maximize fares yield.

Fare setting is a peculiar art. The intention is that all revenue covers all costs and leaves a margin for profit, but 'all revenue' comprises millions of individual journeys each one charged separately according to some scheme that appears fair and reasonable. The easiest way of setting fares is (for each class of passenger) to charge a particular rate for a particular distance, and this is often the basis of fare setting arrangements. Such a system fails to recognize the reality that passengers have choice where there are competing services and, in any case, railways knew that low fares stimulate traffic whilst high fares tend to discourage it. There is also an expectation that on very long journeys some kind of 'discount' will be provided. These factors cannot be ignored and are often allowed to distort the so-much-per-mile scale, with varying success. District shareholders' meetings usually attracted some comment about the fares from the floor where vent was given to divergent and often quite impractical opinions which were usually (though not always) tactfully deflected by the chairman.

District railway fares had been reasonably stable for many years but as traffic declined a debate began about whether fares should go up to cover the losses or down to stimulate traffic, in the hope that fares from the extra people would generate more revenue than it cost to carry them.

The District announced in April 1901 that fare reductions were to be made in order to try and stem the falling volume of traffic, the new fares coming into force on 1st May. The minimum rate of one penny would continue to be charged for up to the first mile but beyond that the usual graduated rates would apply, though somewhat reduced compared with prevailing rates, and also slightly targeting the areas where there was most competition. In addition, for the first time, third-class season tickets would be introduced and existing season ticket rates would be reduced. The District also introduced what it called a system of instalments, but what this actually meant was that 3-month seasons would be introduced at a quarter of the annual rate. Other changes introduced from the same date included extending the time workman's tickets could be obtained until 7.30 in the morning (it was previously 6.30) and in the case of ordinary return tickets making the return halves additionally available the following day (or Saturday to Monday).[9]

The 1901 fares changes proved to be a mixed blessing. By the February 1902 shareholder's meeting Perks was firmly installed in the chair and, though he had not been there long, shows evidence of energy and insight that were unfamiliar to the company's proprietors. Perks had to explain that since the 1901 fares adjustments, fares revenue was down over 6 per cent, profits were down 19 per cent and passengers carried up only 0.3 per cent. Major contributory reasons he ascribed to the opening of the Central London Railway (CLR) and introduction of electric trams to Acton, Kew and Hounslow.

In addition there were many more workmen, attracted in part by the later availability of workmen's tickets. Perks estimated that the transfer of workmen who had previously been content to pay for third-class tickets, but who were now buying workmen's tickets, had cost £3344 for the half year and allowed no reduction in working expenses. He was pleased with the increase in sales of seasons but wondered if more could be done by not requiring 3-months payment in advance which was a deterrent.

Perks was critical of the old regime. 'We did not intelligently prepare for this competition', he admitted. He thought the existing fares reduction had probably arrested decline in West End traffic but that more needed to be done for the western suburbs. He gave the example of a first class fare from Ealing to Mansion House, which cost 1s 8d return, whilst a tram to Shepherds Bush and Central London Railway to Bank, and back, cost just 8d, saving that passenger a shilling a day.

This thinking resulted in a further fares decrease. An announcement on 31st May 1902 stated that fares, particularly those to Mansion House from Ealing, Acton and Hounslow would now match the new competition so that would cost no more to travel by District than the tram and tube (8d). In addition the Mansion House fare was to be extended to Aldgate, offering an advantage over the CLR. The new fares were to come into effect on 1st June 1902 (coinciding with opening of Whitechapel & Bow Railway). There were to be some further adjustments on 1st July, together with some increase in scheduled speed.[10]

The loss of traffic on the District in 1903 was so disastrous that the District felt compelled to reduce fares further to arrest the losses; the average fare became 1.6d compared with 1.8d or 1.9d along comparable lines. This move was a partial success and the report for the second half of 1903 stated that passenger journeys had risen to 24,390,966, an increase of 1,738,583, which in the circumstances was commendable. The chairman remarked it was the highest traffic ever carried. Although this resulted in slightly more income, working expenses had gone up significantly in consequence and the profit for the year was therefore down, again. As usual, this meant no dividend on most classes of share and the payment of only 1½ per cent on the 4% guaranteed stock.

Yerkes was convinced that a greatly simplified fares structure would boost traffic on the District, if experience on the new tube railways was anything to go by. Though having the aspiration to charge 2d for any distance on the District and joint lines, the economics made this impossible given the District's prevailing financial position. In October 1905 he told the press he was now considering a system of zone fares, 2d covering journeys between stations Hammersmith to the City or High Street and Aldgate; this was expected to cover about half of all ticket sales. Fourpence would cover any distance. This system could only be brought in after the new electric services had been introduced.

Zone fares had been authorized by the District's 1904 Act and allowed the District, should it choose, to introduce five fares zones with boundaries east of Hammersmith, South Kensington, Aldgate East and Whitechapel, though with some overlapping at the east end. The minimum fare was to be 2d, usually with a penny for every extra zone (or two zones at east end). The requirement to provide accommodation for first- and second-class passengers was removed, but if continued the zone fares were to be charged plus a fee not exceeding 3d. The introduction of zone fares was hugely complicated by many through fares agreements with other railways, but Yerkes still felt the scheme was worth pursuing.[11]

The District recognized that even if economic conditions improved it was impractical to introduce zone fares in one go. A few tentative moves were made, though, and on 1st December 1905 fares between Earls Court, High Street and Aldgate East were modified so that third-class fares did not exceed 2d and first-class 4d and annoying short distance fares were withdrawn. For the full journey between these points this represented a reduction from 3d and 6d respectively and was as near as the District got to implementing the complete zone fare scheme.[12]

Once the new electric services were introduced, the awful truth dawned that costs had gone up more than the revenue and that the extra traffic electrification was supposed to stimulate was not happening as rapidly as had been hoped. Under these circumstances, the idea of pursuing zone fares (with its attendant risk) was halted and the question again arose about what to do.

Nothing much had changed about the actual ticket system and the ticket markings insisting which way around the inner circle one should travel or the decorative lettering codes describing destination station. The vast majority of journeys were still made using single journey tickets purchased at the start, often requiring queueing. Seasons could still only be obtained from the Mansion House season ticket office. This was to change, but only very slowly.

Raising the Cash

Before embarking on an explanation of the difficulty in which the UERL found itself it might be helpful to summarize the position as it was when electric trains began operating in 1905. Yerkes was intending to build and operate the power house, thereafter selling electricity to the District and other railways. The costs for this (though somewhat over budget) were comfortably met by the marketing of the UERL's own shares. As stated earlier, the UERL was authorized to create £5 million stock in the form of 500,000 £10 shares. All the shares were placed without difficulty, mainly to well-established financial interests in the US (over half), Amsterdam, Frankfurt and Paris, though there were a few English buyers. As the money was not all required at once, the initial calls were for only half this amount, raising just £2,500,000.

Electrification of the District (including rolling stock) was expected to cost no more than £1,400,000.[13] To pay for this work, the scheme devised by Speyer and Yerkes was for the District to transfer to the UERL free of charge a proportion of its unissued stock totalling almost £1,200,000. This mainly comprised unissued preference shares and debentures that were less likely to fall in price and were transferred to the UERL in tranches as the electrification work progressed. There were batches of ordinary shares included in these transfers, though, and the value of the capital transferred sat on the District's books. The UERL was free to sell the stock at any time, converting it into cash in order to pay the subcontractors. Since the value of the different types of District stock varied, the UERL thought it could sell the more robust stock quickly in order to meet immediate cash needs. It would hold back the volatile and low-value ordinary stock until electrification was completed, in the hope that the transformation of the railway would create the confidence needed for a substantial price rise, so generating a useful profit.

One problem in all this was that most of the stock the UERL was interested in was already being traded on the market at values other than the face value, and market prices were unpredictable. To get around this, purchase prices for District shares were agreed in advance and it was hoped that these prices did not change adversely before the UERL sold the stock. The basis for this was set out in agreements of 18th July 1901 with the traction company (and carried across to the UERL) and of 23rd April 1903. Both were recited in the District's Acts of those years.[14] By 1908 the nominal value of stock transferred to the UERL was about £3.3 million but because £1.8 million was ordinary stock representing a very low cash value the actual value of the whole of the transferred stock more or less balanced the electrification costs.[15]

It was recognized that it was entirely possible that construction costs would outstrip immediate cash and that it might not be prudent (or even possible) to unload the shares being held. In this instance the UERL would have to raise more money itself by making further calls on the existing shares or borrowing. Both had to be done and it was very, very expensive. It is here that the seeds of a future problem were sown.

The financial mechanism just described relied upon the value of the various railway shares held by the UERL rising in value, the price increase thus captured had to pay for all the financial costs involved and it was hoped a large increase in value would also deliver a reasonable profit. If the shares did not increase in value the UERL would make a loss that would be troublesome to make good, and if the shares fell in price it would be disastrous. It is worth a look why these outcomes were thought unlikely.

Perks, in the *Railway Times*, was predicting that passenger journeys on the District would double after electrification and plans were being made to run 40 trains an hour instead of 18 being run by steam locomotives. Stephen Sellon, an independent consultant, was brought in to forecast likely usage of the new tube railways: 145 million a year across all three tubes was the answer, presented with surprising certainty. Naturally, such optimism produced little immediate cause for concern.

Borrow, Borrow, Borrow

Although the electrification of the District initially progressed as planned, the tube lines became a problem for the UERL. The tube lines were expensive and when the authorized shares of the Piccadilly were made available in January 1903 there was reluctance to buy them, prejudicing the building of that railway and acting as a warning about trying to place the other tube shares. As cash was now needed urgently, Yerkes and Speyer Brothers devised a form of loan note, secured on the unissued shares, bearing 5 per cent interest, sold at a discount of 96 and redeemable on 1st June 1908. £7 million of notes were created, bringing in £6,620,000 cash.

There was no difficulty placing these notes, even though they were secured only by share certificates nobody wanted and there were at first few real assets. Confidence in the UERL, backed by Speyer Brothers, was evidently sufficient. The unissued railway shares held by the UERL were valued at over £10 million, which some felt was unfeasibly high.

Included in the bundle were shares in the District and LUT, which did have assets, but these amounted to only £2.3 million. An attractive feature of these notes was a promise that when the supporting tube shares were actually sold then the note-holders would be entitled to half the profits of sale above 95. If the tubes came to be successful then potentially this could be a lot of money.

The notes were made available in June 1903 and the purchasers appeared to have got a bargain. The majority of notes, valued at £5 million, went to existing shareholders to whom they were made available first, and the remaining £2 million were marketed by Speyer Brothers and Old Colony Trust, the last being disposed of in February 1905.[16] The interest (or coupon) was payable in London or New York and all the notes were made out 'to bearer' and could be freely transferred and traded.* Once the notes had been marketed, the total cash raised by the UERL reached £9,120,000 (allowing for discounts and the heavy banking costs of 1902); in addition there existed the facility for calling in the remaining £2,500,000 from the UERL shares when the time came. This was nevertheless not going to be anything like enough and as the difficult-to-shift shares in the District and tubes were required as security for the notes they could not be sold even had there been a market for them.

In October 1904, UERL shareholders were told additional cash was required. By this time there were some tangible assets, notably the power house where the construction of the building was in hand, though as an operational entity it was perhaps only a quarter finished, if that. It was proposed to raise up to £850,000 on the strength of its security and shareholder agreement was obtained. It was found possible to market £1000 debentures to the value of £700,000 (increased later £775,000) and these promised a 'coupon' of 4½ per cent.

As yet more money was urgently required in early 1905 Speyer brothers succeeded in creating yet more 4% debentures supported by the part-constructed tube lines and raised a further £2,500,000. By this time the total cash raised was £12,395,000 which, with the final call possible on the original UERL shares, meant that almost £15 million was in theory available (project cost comparisons, though fraught, suggest that in today's value this is equivalent to £6-7 billion, which is indicative of the size of the job Yerkes had taken on).

Position at	**30th June 1905**	**30th June 1906**
500,000 £10 ordinary shares part paid	£2,500,000	£2,500,000
5% secured profit sharing notes	£7,000,000	£7,000,000
4½% power house debentures issued	£700,000	£775,000
Amounts received for construction contracts	£2,583,329	£3,633,664
Other	£868,025	£2,058,608
Total	£13,651,354	£15,967,272
Total less discounts on the notes	£13,371,354	£15,687,272

* At that time a half per cent stamp duty was charged on the transfer of railway stocks and shares, but this did not apply to debentures made out to 'bearer'. Most early UERL loan notes and debentures were so made out. The UERL unexpectedly found itself owing stamp duty on the transfer of the operating company shares from the MDETC to the UERL and lost its case after appealing to the House of Lords. After this expensive mistake the UERL appears to have resolved not to pay stamp duty ever again if it could be avoided.

Early in 1907 even more money was needed and there was a new bond issue secured by the power house, called second power house debentures, of which £600,000 were authorized and, by June, £300,000 issued. These differed slightly from the first issue in that the security did not entitle anyone benefiting through default to include shutting down the source of electricity supply. The annual cost to the UERL of servicing the loan notes was £350,000 a year and the repayment date in 1908 really was not very far away.

Yerkes' Death

Whether the stress of the final two years of Yerkes' life materially contributed to his death at the relatively early age of 67 is unclear. His works in London were extensive and complicated but most of it was in the hands of his very competent engineers (though Yerkes did get involved in some detail). Yerkes' talents had been focused on obtaining money on a vast scale at the cheapest rate possible under difficult conditions. We will see shortly that the problem of paying for the debts due on these lavish works was a problem for another day that he would deal with when the time came. That he was so certain the London system would ultimately be profitable was sufficient to convince him that these problems could somehow be overcome.

Such faith would have served him better had it not been undermined by the failure in April 1903 of the Chicago Union Traction Group which had guaranteed the bonds of another traction company that was in difficulty. Yerkes was now exposed to criticism for having set up the arrangement where debt levels were really too heavy. In addition, much of his own wealth was conditional on the integrity of this guarantee, which must have been a worry. The details of this American problem do not concern the District except that there were those in London who felt the UERL was also heading for an over-heavy debt burden supported by guarantees of an insubstantial nature and the ever-critical LCC wanted people to know about it. The Chicago problem was clearly something of a distraction.

At about the same time his health began to deteriorate leaving him increasingly fatigued, though he stoically carried on, spending much time in London. It was not until mid-1905 that the illness became seriously debilitating, though after much rest he was able to chair a shareholders' meeting in October. After that his health went downhill quickly and he returned to New York suspecting it was going to be a one-way trip.

Yerkes died in New York on 29th December 1905 and left behind him a bit of a problem. Yet more money was needed by the UERL, the tubes were taking their time to come on stream and, very worryingly, the new electric services on the District were bringing in nothing like the additional traffic that had been hoped for and it was difficult to see how the massive debts were going to be paid for. Perks reported to shareholders:

> Permit me, on behalf of the proprietors, to say how deeply we regret the unexpected death of the late chairman of this undertaking, Mr. Charles Yerkes whom we, unfortunately, had not in our midst last July, but whose illness we did not expect to take the fatal turn which at the last moment it did. Mr. Yerkes, the last time I saw him, expressed his complete confidence in the future of the District Railway, and he did not seem to be disheartened or disturbed by the temporary difficulties with which we were then, and have still been, confronted. We have already sent to Mr. Yerkes' representatives in America an expression, on your behalf, of your sympathy with his family in their loss.

The British press had often been a bit cautious about Yerkes, whilst acknowledging that he was doing what no British financier was prepared to do. Most British reports of his death reflected on the huge task he had set himself in London in raising cash, electrifying the District and building three tube railways, the first opening less than three months later and from most points of view were found to be a resounding success. His friends, colleagues and staff spoke highly of him. Press caution in part resulted from rumours about 'shady' dealings in America, but perhaps all American business methods were regarded with suspicion in Britain, if only because the truth was hard to get at and the context not understood over 3000 miles away. Although there were a few who wondered if Yerkes was not extending himself too far, it is hard to find any meaningful suggestions that in Britain Yerkes acted improperly or as less than a perfect gentleman. Moreover, it is very difficult to imagine that Speyer, who had the highest reputation, would have been prepared to associate himself with anyone who seemed untrustworthy.

Reports of his time in America suggest that staff close to him had a great respect for him too and when he left Chicago his immediate staff were very sorry to see him go. It was his business rivals and those who (in his view) got in his way who had mixed feelings. There is no doubt that Yerkes was crafty and in his zeal to get things done was capable of playing rough and against the rules. There is no doubt he had been a bit of a chancer (some used the word gambler) but risk taking is a characteristic of the entrepreneur. The stakes were high. The circumstances in turn-of-the-century Chicago, then one of the most corrupt of American cities, promoted this kind of behaviour, in him, in his rivals, in the City officials and even in the law officers. For better or worse this was the climate in which Yerkes attempted to improve the City's transit system. Most people were happy to accept that the transit systems he was involved with were built or improved as a result of his activity. His vision and ability were rarely questioned, but his methods were divisive, at least in the US.

Yerkes was interested in the way British and American management techniques diverged and makes some interesting observations in a long (but undated) letter sent to the magazine *Traction & Transmission* during Autumn 1901. He was rather critical of British management which appeared content to be led into foolish decision-making by engineers (he had in mind the Met's, in his opinion, naïve acceptance of the Ganz proposals):

> I had been told that the alternating system had been recommended to the companies by two engineers, but, unfortunately, I did not know the customs of English corporations, neither did I know the great importance which was placed on the recommendation of engineers. In our country, notwithstanding that it is acknowledged that the American engineers are in no way inferior to any others, their opinions are subservient to the managers of the company, for the reason that the managers of American companies understand their business thoroughly, and merely use the engineers as they would any other of their very important employees. The idea of using a system which had never been tried to any extent seemed eminently unpractical. ... The idea of adopting such a plan in a crowded place like the Metropolitan Road was such deliberate recklessness that it did not seem to me possible that business men could suggest such a thing.

This was nothing to the genuine surprise he evinces about the extraordinary lack of action of the Met, though his comments would have been substantially as valid about the District, which his syndicate had just purchased:

> I was more perplexed than ever. Here was a lot of men, who called themselves business men, in charge of railroad property, sitting by and seeing the Central London Road being built, which operation had taken about five years; then seeing it in operation after it was built, and the natural consequence affecting the Metropolitan, namely, the loss of business, said business going to the Central, and never raising a finger to protect themselves. ... They must certainly have seen the handwriting on the wall,

> wherein it was distinctly told that another and formidable rival was rising up; also that the day of steam for such work was done; also that the miserable tunnel—made so by the operating of steam locomotives—was a thing of the past, long gone by; and also that this new competitor which was coming into life would certainly take their dividends. And still they sat idly by, and saw this condition going on before them, without moving a hand. Then, after their Act was passed, they simply did nothing but sat and looked. When the Central London really opened, and their trade began to fall away, they did not even move then, but sat and looked further, and have continued to do the same thing ever since.

And so we see an insight into Yerkes' character, genuine puzzlement based upon his experience of American business methods, where he could simply not fathom why sensible business people didn't just get on and do what had to be done. With this in mind we can see why he brought an entire team of American engineers across the Atlantic to deliver what had to be done in London whilst he took management decisions based on his own knowledge and experience. The British press was inclined to regard his desire simply to get on with the job in hand, and to do whatever was necessary to deliver it, as impatience! This seems to have been the worst fault levelled at him on this side of the Atlantic.

On his death the American press was harsher than in Britain, partly, no doubt, because his apparent successes in London were too remote to be appreciated, partly because some of the more finely-balanced deals in the US had come unstuck, and partly because his lifestyle on the US side of the pond seemed fair game to those who had nothing better to do than criticize his morals—his young and equally colourful mistress got fed up with this moralizing and after Yerkes' death moved to the UK; she acquired both a London home and a country cottage at West Drayton, and died as recently as 1964. She left her Elizabethan cottage to the National Trust but the jewellery given by many lovers was auctioned.

In speaking of the personal traits of Mr. Yerkes, John M. Roach, general manager of the Union Traction Co. of Chicago, pays him the following tribute:

> He was always kind, courteous and considerate to his employees. He was generous and charitable, but never paraded the fact. There was nothing in Mr. Yerkes but good. Anything else was forced from him by conditions. Mr. Yerkes was not ambitious to be a millionaire, but he was ambitious to be known as the foremost traction man in the country, and I think he was.[17]

One thing is for sure, without him London's Edwardian transport system would have stalled and the precarious District might have come to the abrupt end its shareholders had feared, though no doubt the railway assets would have carried on in some form.

The Yerkes estate was less fortunate. Everybody thought that Yerkes was a multi-millionaire and his will made extensive provisions. $700,000 was left to family but his home and extensive contents was to be left to New York as an art gallery with an endowment of $750,000 and a sufficient amount of the rest of his estate was to be used to build a hospital for those with inadequate means to pay for treatment. It was rumoured his whole estate might be worth as much as $22,000,000.

In fact his 'wealth' was discovered to be largely in the form of financial instruments, many of which were of questionable value, and his sources of income had been so complex it took several years to unravel. He had in fact been short of ready cash and had borrowed heavily to support his lifestyle. We do not know what would have happened had he lived longer and kept the edifice firmly propped up and if the Underground securities had come good. What we do know is that far from leaving a fortune he left extensive debts with lenders all wanting their money. New York got neither an art gallery nor hospital but an auction of the effects (itself a spectacular event) raised over $2,000,000. With the subsequent sale of the house in 1910 the estate showed a small surplus after his wife had received a bequest but it was not finally settled until 1912.[18]

Calls for the residue of the part-paid UERL shares were made in July 1906 and January 1907. Yerkes himself had continued to own a large block of shares and the unpaid calls came to £160,000. As might be imagined from the condition of his estate the UERL had great difficulty obtaining the extra £5 cash due on each of them from the executors, the matter ending up in court and resulted in his estate having to sell part of his art collection. The matter was not finally settled until 1910 when the outstanding amount plus interest at 5 per cent was paid off.

At his death, Yerkes must have known the results of the District Railway electrification were very disappointing, but as none of the new tubes had opened there was still room to have some faith in their success. Their early failure to live up to financial expectations was disastrous. With such low levels of traffic, share prices could not possibly soar as had been hoped and without that happening there was no possibility that £7 million in cash could be found by 1st June 1908 to pay off the profit-sharing notes. Without some further wizardry, the UERL would be bankrupt on 1st June 1908. What Yerkes would have done about this had he lived we will never know, but he would not have seen all this effort get so far without making it a success somehow.

The Baker Street & Waterloo Railway (known almost immediately as the Bakerloo tube) opened in March 1906, and the Piccadilly tube in December. The results from each disappointed and during 1907 became a matter of increasing concern. Nor were matters subsequently helped by an international financial crisis, partly resulting in October 1907 from the San Francisco earthquake. By this time it was quite impossible to contemplate placing many of the tube shares at all, let alone at a profit, and as a result the value of the other stocks collapsed, rendering them hopeless security for the UERL loan notes and greatly agitating their holders.

A New Top Team

Towards the end of 1905 it became increasingly obvious to friends and colleagues that Yerkes was dying. With the emerging financial difficulties, it was also clear that a successor was required as soon as possible. The problem of replacing Yerkes was a formidable one and fell largely upon Speyer, who had the largest interest. It would be difficult to replace Yerkes' single-minded determination to complete the works quickly, but to the highest standard. It would be equally challenging to find someone who inspired financial confidence. Yerkes' reputation was still high and it was not yet apparent that there were elements of his high-risk plan that were slightly misjudged. Speyer himself decided to chair the UERL and take direct control of its financial affairs but he needed a competent managing director who knew how to develop the new electric services and inspire confidence.

The choice of Sir George Stegmann Gibb, general manager of the North Eastern Railway, came about by accident when a meeting was arranged by colleague George Paish with Speyer to discuss financing some project in which they had an interest.* It was at that meeting that Gibb was quietly sounded out when Speyer asked him if he could

---

* Paish was a noted economist and statistician who had written about railway economics and edited *The Statist*.

George Gibb. LTM

Frank Pick. Author's collection

recommend a man to take charge of the London electric lines and the District Railway, which led to him being made an offer. The salary of £8000 a year was very generous (he had only £5000 at the North Eastern), but on discovering that Gibb would forfeit his pension, Speyer arranged for Gibb to be awarded a £10,000 lump sum as compensation.[19]

One can see that Speyer was very keen to get Gibb involved and it could rightly be thought Gibb was the right man in the right place. Although he had been brought up as a lawyer he succeeded to the general managership of the huge North Eastern Railway in 1891. He was an innovator and sought to bring new thinking into railway management by using statistical methods to ascertain what was going on and how to differentiate between profitable and unprofitable methods, with some success. This culminated in 1902 with the separation of the operating and commercial departments which is the invariable practice now but was unheard of at the time. The North Eastern was one of the earliest railways in the country to adopt (limited) electric working, partly in response to fierce competition from tramways and partly because a large power supply company established itself in Newcastle and could offer favourable terms. It meant Gibb understood many of the issues around electrifying existing railway lines and dealing with competition. Moreover he had served on the Royal Commission on London Traffic, which met between February 1903 and June 1905 and conducted an exhaustive inquiry into London's traffic and transport conditions, so he was familiar with the problems in London. Gibb was appointed deputy chairman and managing director of the UERL and chairman and managing director of the District (Perks remained as vice chairman until he resigned in June 1907 because of pressure of his other interests).

It is little surprise that Gibb felt comfortable with the professionals he had worked with on the North Eastern. In April 1906, Arthur Collinson was the first to arrive. As mentioned earlier he was needed to replace Young upon his elevation and he took over as general manager of the District, though he was paid rather less than Young had received. The next was Frank Pick, who had pioneered some of the statistical analysis on the North

Eastern and whom Gibb felt could help identify what needed to be done on the District (Pick was Gibb's personal assistant and had a wider role, but at this stage the District needed the most urgent attention). It was Pick's work in London that helped identify that the 1904 fare reductions had gone too far and resulted in uplifted fare scales from 1st September 1906. The arrival of a young man called Walter Gott, again in 1906, was a valuable result. He was not from the North Eastern, but he was a Yorkshireman, from Bradford, who had become advertising manager for the Great Northern Railway by the age of 25. He was appointed at the age of 26 as passenger agent of the Piccadilly tube, but as Gibb fused the separate railways together found himself responsible for the advertising and publicity of most of the UERL's work and was regarded at the time as quite successful. He moved to the Partington Advertising Company in 1909.

Crisis

The new management team quickly found the financial difficulties converting into a crisis. Fresh money was still needed as late as 1907 as the works were still incomplete (the Hampstead tube was not finished until June and Lots Road was still being fully-equipped). With the final calls on the UERL shares of £2,500,000 at last being made, by June 1907 these shares had raised a total of £4,834,125 (the Yerkes estate debt accounted for most of the shortfall). The total raised by the UERL for electrifying the District and constructing the tubes was now about £17½ million of which, at that time, operating company shares to the value of only £3,723,291 had been marketed by the UERL. The difference in value between the £8½ million raised by the UERL shares and the money actually spent was represented mainly by the expensive loan notes. This would have been bad enough, but there was now only a year to go before the loan notes were due for payment and there was no money for this. Worse still, the options for raising more cash (including cash for repayment of the notes) were exhausted. The UERL began to look a bit shaky.

The situation would have been manageable had the revolution in travel happened as forecast, allowing the value of UERL and its railway companies to soar. As it was, nothing at all was soaring. The people did not come. When electric services on the District had settled down in 1906, it was found to be carrying ten per cent more traffic than in the last days of steam, not 'double'. This was insufficient to pay either for the UERL investment or to get the District out of its own financial mess. All hopes were now pinned on the new tubes to generate much needed cash. They didn't either. In their first full year of operation the tubes generated just 71.5 million journeys, just half that predicted. Whilst in a very real sense this was creditable, it made them barely able to cover their costs, let alone produce any profit.

The failure to generate the required traffic has been partly explained already and boils down to not having appreciated what technical developments would be available in the wider world and how the competition would respond. It is to be questioned how the forecasts were arrived at, since they were either wrong or misinterpreted. Some of this is down to Yerkes himself, as his thinking was entirely conditioned by his experience in America. It seems not to have occurred to him that London might respond differently to Chicago and there was not then the experience in Britain about how people would actually react to improved transport services on a large scale. The forecasts for the tube services put together by an independent expert were simply fanciful. Nothing obvious from the records suggests it occurred to anyone to ask over what period of time these traffic increases would take place, for surely they would not happen overnight? Eventually traffic reached and exceeded the predicted levels, but not until after the Great War and a great deal of hard work.

The Speyer Solution

With no obvious cash to repay the loan notes and the securing shares much depleted in value the UERL now faced bankruptcy. The job of trying to save the UERL after Yerkes' death fell to Edgar Speyer, who after becoming chairman in January 1906 remained one of the main creditors. His task was becoming more difficult by the arrival on London's roads of large numbers of motor buses, which seriously threatened to diminish further the takings on the various railways, especially for short distance traffic. We shall see shortly exactly what the UERL did to counter this assault and generate much-needed traffic for itself, but suffice to say that by the middle of 1908 the UERL felt that there was some room for optimism in the longer term if the immediate financial hiatus could be averted.

In the meantime, the financial results had been extraordinarily poor and the District itself was plunging into crisis. Early in 1906 District shareholders were told that post-electrification earnings were up just £6000 or so for the previous half year whilst working expenses had risen by about £30,000. After interest payments had been made, and the District's proportion of the loss of the City Lines paid (of £10,000), it was found the company had made a loss over the half year of £36,000. The situation continued to deteriorate and over the whole of 1906 the District was showing a loss of £100,000. This was unsustainable and the railway press was talking of inevitable bankruptcy. During 1907 the shares fell further, never even commanding 20, and hit an all-time low of 7¼ at the very time when to market them to raise much needed cash they needed to be at an all-time high (the UERL had paid £25 a share for the ordinaries so this represented a terrific loss). For a while the UERL also had to loan the District money in order to keep it functioning as a business (repaid in 1908). Indicative of the despair being shown, District shares also fell below 10 in 1908.

The District was forced to borrow, yet again. The MDR Act of 1908 authorized the company to raise £750,000 4% prior lien stock. Since this ranked reasonably highly in the pecking order, the District hurriedly marketed £550,000 of it, successfully placing the stock by October 1908. This would inevitably increase fixed outgoings (even more) but shareholders were told the move was required in order to cover the mounting losses of the company which was also unable to pay all its fixed charges. The promoters of the bill explained to the select committee examining it that owing to increasing traffic it was expected that after 1909 the revenue would be sufficient to meet the company's prior charges. In the meantime it was no longer possible to borrow money on assets because everything that could be mortgaged already was, but this stock would be secured by the income from surplus estates. Without the benefit of the new stock, or some similar scheme, the money owed to the debenture holders would go into arrears and enable them to appoint a receiver.

Meanwhile the UERL's troubles were getting worse. By the end of 1907 the holders of the profit sharing loan notes that had been so attractive when issued were beginning to panic. Not only was there no apparent means of repaying them but the security upon which the holders relied was—whilst by no means worthless—manifestly insufficient to cover the debt. Some note-holders were already vocal in querying how secure these notes really were. The notes were tradeable and it is indicative of the worry they were causing that in November 1907 the £100 notes were being traded at just £35 and everyone knew this represented a loss of confidence that the notes would be redeemed on time, or at all.

By now the UERL was running out of liquid cash and could not afford to pay the December interest, amounting to £175,000. Speyer brothers paid this themselves, together with a further £300,000 owed to various creditors in order to avoid bankruptcy and necessary to maintain note-holder confidence, and it was found necessary to issue £1 million prior lien 5% bonds (repayable on 1st November 1920) to repay Speyer and provide much needed working capital; the practical effect of this was to increase interest payments by another £50,000 a year from income insufficient to meet it.

By the middle of 1908, slowly rising traffic hinted at evidence of a turnaround in fortunes just sufficient to persuade the various parties in London, New York and Amsterdam not to insist on the profit-sharing notes immediately being redeemed in cash. The cash was not there and neither was the security, but there was reason to have hope. It appeared that with sufficient time capital could be repaid and that good security could be offered by the companies' real assets.

The following table clearly shows the struggle the District had been having and that the 1908 figures showed reason for optimism.

District Railway Passenger Numbers 1900 - 1908

Year	*1st class*	*2nd class*	*3rd class*	*Season trips*	*Total*
1900	2,641,330	5,535,539	31,298,385	4,366,457	43,841,711
1901	2,610,487	5,300,483	30,208,106	4,149,087	42,268,173
1902	2,975,187	6,169,261	33,144,257	4,725,826	47,014,531
1903	2,924,823	6,425,485	35,631,288	5,057,975	50,039,571
1904	3,127,747	6,322,527	37,126,208	4,591,310	51,167,792
1905	3,634,145	3,195,937	41,805,694	2,912,641	51,548,417
1906	3,363,920	-	48,683,292	3,015,212	55,062,424
1907	2,528,997	-	45,038,715	3,457,845	51,235,557
1908	2,413,371	-	53,008,642	6,598,669	61,130,308

District Railway passenger revenue and working expenses

	Pass Revenue	*Wkg expenses*
1900	£392,102	
1901	£356,813	£233,674
1902	£371,094	£227,096
1903	£370,323	£239,619
1904	£366,392	£242,020
1905	£373,135	£262,916
1906	£403,315	£327,024
1907	£406,981	£305,219
1908	£472,649	£314,170

The UERL board was sufficiently concerned that creditors might press their claims for payment that bankruptcy was a real possibility. Although the operating companies were immediately protected, the power house was directly owned by the UERL and it was impossible to tell what might be done with it if it ended up in the hands of a liquidator. The board therefore decided to get the protection of the court by asking for a receiver to be appointed until such time as the interested parties could be induced to accept the proposal to restructure the finances. The surreal position arose of Speyer Brothers, acting for themselves and the noteholders and other claimants, bringing an action in the chancery division against the UERL whose chairman was Sir Edgar Speyer himself. The action was heard on 15th April 1908 and George Gibb, the UERL vice-chairman, was appointed receiver of the assets and manager of the UERL.[20]

The deal that was finally accepted was put together in London and Amsterdam (New York took some persuasion and had their own ideas) and was that for every £100 of 1908 profit sharing notes there would be issued £40 worth of 4½% fixed interest bonds due on

1st January 1933 with interest guaranteed until January 1912, and £70 worth of 6% fixed interest bonds due on 1st January 1948 that were not guaranteed but were payable as a kind of preference share with voting rights (unlike the notes). Interest would be paid only if profits permitted and anything owed could not be carried forward. By offering a blend of the two types of bond their holders would be assured of getting something (1.64% minimum) with a reasonable chance of high rewards if business continued to pick up. It will be seen the pain was further lessened by replacing £100 of the existing bonds by £110 of the blend of the new ones.

There was a complicated system of providing assurance that the full amount of interest would actually be paid on the proportion of 4½% bonds. If four successive coupons were not paid then creditors could require the trustees of the shares held as security to redeem those shares to create the necessary cash. In the meantime Speyer brothers and certain other finance houses had signed an agreement on 7th April requiring them to buy sufficient bonds each half year, at a pre-agreed rate, to provide cash to make up, with whatever the company could contribute, the amount required to be disbursed so that all 4½% bondholders received the full amount. This guarantee was conditional on noteholders accepting the revised scheme in full.

The proposal was well thought out and there had clearly been some important consultation. It is little surprise that 96 per cent of note-holders felt this to be a good deal (compared with the alternatives). In fact, interest was not paid on the 6% bonds until the end of the half-year June 1910 though it rose quickly to 6% by December 1912. A meeting of the noteholders was held on 30th June 1908 and the proposal was accepted on a show of hands. Separate meetings of other classes of stockholders came to a similar conclusion. Once the deal was formally agreed it was put to the court on 16th July for its approval. It was clear it was overwhelmingly supported but such dissent as there was related to the amount that Speyer Brothers might possibly make from bond purchases necessary to guarantee the interest. The judge considered that this was necessarily a money transaction, for which reward was expected, and that in the circumstances he was not disposed to interfere. The court was eventually satisfied that there was practical approval by everyone that a proper solution had been found and the court's protection was set aside on 21st July 1908.[21]

This dealt with (or at least postponed) the pain of having to repay a large amount of borrowing but it did not bring in extra money. As part of the package £1 million of 5% prior lien bonds were also created (redeemable 1920) which were guaranteed for payment ahead of most other instruments and were made available at a discounted price of £93 per £100 of stock and were available only to existing shareholders and noteholders (again conditional on the restructuring going ahead). These instruments were made available in instalments almost as soon as the court accepted the restructuring and some of the money raised was used to repay the debts to Speyer. Payment was acceptable in pounds, dollars, marks or Dutch florins as these denominations reflected the locations where it was thought the holders of the bonds would find convenient. These were secured by large numbers of unsold District and tube shares including £1.8 million of District ordinary shares and £90,000 preference shares.[22] (All the instruments referred to were made out to bearer and therefore there was no register of holders. This was to be an interesting feature of the work required when London Transport was eventually set up as it was not known who owned much of the stock.)

It must be appreciated that these returns, particularly those on the 6% interest bonds, were quite generous. Such was the size of this obligation that the UERL had insufficient money to pay any dividend on its ordinary shares. In turn it made it impossible to market any new ordinary shares and meant that any future borrowing would have to be by means of bonds of some kind, which would inevitably be more expensive. Unwittingly the UERL had created for itself the same financial burden that had been crippling the District.

American Backup

In November 1906, Gibb and Speyer felt that it would be more efficient if the three tube railways were amalgamated, enabling efficiencies to be made and the three lines to be put on the same statutory basis. A bill was prepared but not submitted to the 1906-7 Session. The proposal made the already-twitchy American bankers nervous as they felt (with or without justification) that the move would depress rather than improve the value of the tube shares when marketed. This led to lengthy discussions about the best course of action in the context of the UERL's wider financial challenges and Gibb was persuaded this was not the time to risk affecting the tube share values.

By the end of 1906 Gibb (probably under American pressure) was looking for a general manager to act for the UERL and all the railways and in February 1907 placed a young man who was by repute the choice of the Old Colony Trust, who wanted someone in the organization it could rely on to look after its interests in those financially turbulent times. This was a successful but rather young tramways expert, who was appointed by the UERL board as general manager from 1st April 1907. He was 32 year old Albert Stanley (British by birth) who at the time of his appointment was general manager of the Public Service Corporation of New Jersey. In addition to his UERL duties, Stanley replaced Collinson as general manager of the District on 26th September 1907 and was appointed to the UERL board from 1908. The short-lived Collinson returned to the North Eastern as District Superintendent Middlesbrough (Pick's biographer described Collinson as 'a sad disappointment'[23]).

It is convenient to mention here that Gibb made known his resignation from the District in May 1910 to become head of the government's Roads Board. This caused a flurry of

Albert Stanley. LTM

W. E. Manderlick. LTM

activity and it was quickly announced that Albert Stanley, the general manager, had so quickly proved his worth that he was to be appointed to the board as managing director. In fact Stanley had been approaching the end of his existing 3-year contract and had shown great interest in the managing director's job perhaps encouraging Gibbs' departure. He was appointed for four years in his new role.[24] Joseph Carter relinquished his post as secretary to become Stanley's assistant with William Edward Mandelick, secretary to the UERL, taking on the District role as well (Mandelick, an American, had been involved with Yerkes since he came to London and was initially assistant secretary to the MDETC; he retired through failing health and died in Berlin in 1921.[25]). District deputy chairman, Lord George Hamilton, stepped up to chairman. Speyer (Sir Edgar from 1906) remained as chairman of the UERL and upon Gibb's departure in 1910 Hamilton became deputy chairman of the UERL.

Selling the Service

Despite electrification, the District management did not readily change many of its promotional methods. Not only did it carry on with its old-fashioned large-format maps but it introduced a new version too, covering Greater London. First seen in 1902, shown adjacent is a 1908 edition that really does not shout 'new' and 'electric', indeed the word electric does not appear. Of some interest, the District is shown running through all the way to Uxbridge, which it did not actually achieve for a couple more years. These are not hallmarks of cutting edge promotional material, and radically new methods were required. The new directors and management team were transformational compared with the best-do-nothing attitude of the Forbes era but Gibb, in particular, rapidly brought to bear the power of statistics to identify areas to put right. Even at his first shareholders' meeting, when he had scarcely had time to take stock, he is found quoting statistics to make some point or other and it is doubtful if shareholders were accustomed to being acquainted with detailed management information.

Gibb lamented the amount of workman's traffic being carried as it was a legal requirement to do so but the cheap prices charged meant this traffic was totally unremunerative. It had grown from 5 million a year to 16 million in only ten years and required levels of train service expensive to provide. By the end of 1906, some 8½ million workmen had been carried at an average fare of only 0.65d and that was quite unsustainable. It amounted to nearly a third of the whole of the traffic being carried at a loss. Increases would somehow have to be made, he said.

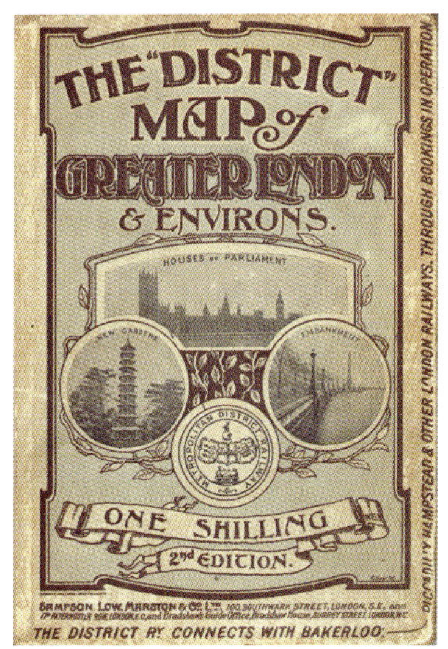

Furthermore, some simple statistical analysis of ordinary fares revenue was very concerning. Since 1899 the number of passengers had increased by 42 per cent but the revenue this produced had gone down by 3.2 per cent. It appeared to Gibb that 9½ million extra passengers were effectively being carried for nothing! The average fare paid had been 2.19d in 1899 but had now dropped to 1.49d. Whatever the merits of stimulating traffic might have been the reality was that it had pushed up costs but not done anything for income and he felt the previous fares reductions had gone too far and needed revisiting. There were some other things to note. When second-class was abolished it was hoped many who previously travelled that way

Ealing and Mansion House (Distance 10.9 miles).

	Single.			Return.		
	1st.	2nd.	3rd.	1st.	2nd.	3rd.
	s. d.	s. d.	d.	s. d.	s. d.	s. d.
On 30th April, 1901......	1 5	1 0	8½	2 2	1 6	1 3
From 1st May, 1901......	1 1	0 9	7	1 8	1 1	0 11
From 1st June, 1902......	0 8	0 6	5	1 0	0 9	0 8
From 1st Sept., 1906* ...	0 7	—	4½	1 2	—	0 9

* In this case the single journey fares are decreased.

Hammersmith and Mansion House (Distance 6.575 miles).

	Single.			Return.		
	1st.	2nd.	3rd.	1st.	2nd.	3rd.
	d.	d.	d.	s. d.	d.	d.
On 30th April, 1901......	8	6	5	1 0	9	8
From 1st May, 1901......	7	5	3½	0 11	7	6
From 1st July, 1902......	6	4	3	0 9	6	5
From 28th March, 1904	6	4	3	0 7	5	4
From 1st Sept., 1906* ...	5	—	3	0 10	—	6

* In this case the 1st class single journey fare is decreased.

Putney Bridge and Mansion House (Distance 7.15 miles).

	Single.			Return.		
	1st.	2nd.	3rd.	1st.	2nd.	3rd.
	d.	d.	d.	s. d.	d.	d.
On 30th April, 1901......	9	7	5	1 2	10	8
From 1st May, 1901......	8½	6½	4½	1 1	9	8
From 1st July, 1902......	8	5	4	1 0	8	7
From 1st Sept., 1906* ..	6	—	3½	1 0	—	7

* In this case the single journey fares are decreased.

George Gibb wrote to the *Railway News* in 1906 explaining the District's fares policy and in which he offered the examples in this image. *Railway News* Vol 86 1906

would trade up to first-class, but in fact nearly all had traded down to third, representing a further area of loss.

A proposed new fares scheme was put forward in August 1906 for implementation on 1st September, amidst some adverse carping in the press. In fact many single fares were more or less unchanged (and some longer journeys went down); the thrust was to remove the substantial discount that had been introduced for return tickets, restoring them to the earlier arrangement where they were double the single fare. Gibb was quick to point out that though some fares had gone up, they were still cheaper than they had been in 1899. At the shareholders' meeting in February 1907 Gibb was pleased to report that the new fares had generated an extra £10,000 in only four months and were doing what had been expected.[26]

There was some insight into Gibb's statistical methods in his report of 1907 when income appeared to remain stubbornly flat and further change was demanded. Gibb explained he and his staff had gone minutely into everything and concluded that the revised fares of 1906 had succeeded in generating an extra £24,000 a year, as predicted. This was offset by a loss of £22,000 a year in traffic along the District route to Temple diverting to the new Piccadilly route to Holborn. This illustrated that just looking at totals could be very misleading and traffic flows had always to be looked at in detail if correct inferences were to be drawn.

Through fares were much expanded from 1907 as the main line railways and UERL lines recognized that requiring passengers to rebook at interchange stations was irksome and discouraged travel. Through fares to and from Great Eastern Railway suburban stations was introduced on 3rd October 1907 and with the South Eastern & Chatham Railway system shortly afterwards (the SER and LCDR by this time operated their railways jointly under the name South Eastern & Chatham Railway, or SECR).

Once the fares had been adjusted in 1906 there were no further material changes although the issues were often discussed. By 1910 it was felt that the fares were probably best left alone as motor bus competition would make it hard to justify an increase and rising traffic (especially suburban traffic) was producing useful extra income anyway. In February 1909 Gibb was keen to recommend shareholders read Sir Herbert Jekyll's observations in the annual report of the Board of Trade's London Traffic branch where after careful study he concluded that cheap fares tended to increase the price of land,

Examples of generic District seasons from instruction book, showing class distinction and rear view. This style was in use by 1911. *District Railway Instruction Book* (Author's collection)

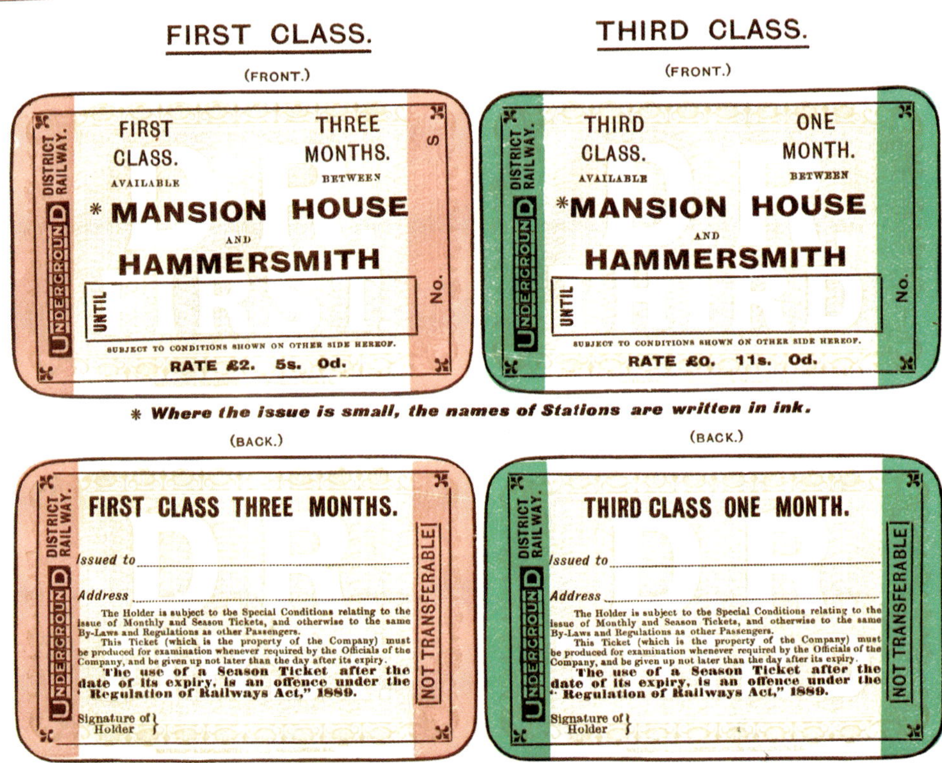

A 1908 quad-royal poster map of the central part of the District Railway and also showing the various UERL tube lines and other connecting services. LTM

leading to higher rents. By this means the passenger would be no better off but money the railway ought to have had was transferred to private landlords. An observation perhaps equally valid today?

Like many other railways, the District had long offered season tickets. Although these were always marked with an expiry date the District was pre-occupied with collecting them immediately upon expiry and charged a deposit, an irksome arrangement that was not abolished until 1st January 1911.

Just after electrification the District seriously considered getting rid of season tickets altogether and early in 1906 restricted issues to monthly tickets as a preliminary. This was quickly reconsidered (longer issued tickets were restored from 1st September 1906) and they were continued 'as a convenience' on the basis of charging for 11 journeys a week with some slight further reduction for 3-monthly tickets. After complaints about the rates charged for through tickets to LSWR stations Gibb was minded to agree and after discussion with the LSWR some reductions were made to the through season ticket rates on 1st December 1906, these rates having not been changed with the ordinary fares in September. The new rates were designed to stimulate new traffic but season rates were often adjusted slightly to fine-tune demand; for example on 1st January 1914 rates

The Underground was quick to use the power of the poster. The problem on the outlying branches was that few people lived there to advertise to. The only way to make money was to encourage people in crowded inner London to visit these vast open spaces. The illustrator Mabel Lucie Atwell drew the artwork for this poster in 1913, but the image also appeared in smaller formats such as booklets. Roy Allen collection

In an attempt to encourage leisure traffic, even the reverse sides of tickets were pressed into use. Author's collection

This splendid card was produced to promote carriage of pleasure parties. The scenic views through the windows would have been visible in only a very few places along the South Harrow route. LTM

The panoramic carriage postcard appeared in a small booklet produced to promote pleasure outings with covers by Violet Holdsworth. The booklet appears first to have been issued in 1915 but at least one later version, dated 1922, has been noted. Capital Transport collection

were reduced on Wimbledon and Richmond lines to stimulate traffic.[27] It was a source of friction that third class travellers often sat in the first class coach and paid the excess if it were asked for, but retaining their seat, to the annoyance of first-class ticket holders who had to stand.[28]

Although the District (and to a lesser extent the tubes) had finally identified a more or less scientific method for arriving at an optimal level of fares, Gibb recognized very quickly that costs had to be lowered, the railways needed to be promoted far more aggressively to gain more passengers and the wasteful competition had to be reduced. While the electrification work had been in hand the motor omnibus had begun to appear and so had the electric tram and they were causing heavy inroads. This was in addition to the competing electric tubes which had already inflicted much damage.

Since the problems to some extent resonated with other railways, Sir George Gibb promoted the idea of a traffic conference to coordinate their activities and a meeting was arranged in May 1907. Those present included Gibb, from the UERL, Clifton Robinson from London United Trams, A.C. Ellis from the Met, Granville Cuningham from the Central London, Thomas Jenkin from the City & South London and R.P. Brousson from the Great Northern & City. An early result was the Met and CLR agreeing to revise their fares. Since the major bus companies were also struggling with costs they soon joined in. Pointedly the LCC refused to take part. In July 1907 the conference was placed on a 'standing' basis. Each participating company was to have one vote but no company was compelled to abide by a decision if it dissented.[29]

Above: **This suggests the District met with some success with its drive to increase leisure traffic. This is The Ballot Box at Horsenden Hill one summer and probably on a Sunday. A District Railway direction sign is prominent. This pub is no more, though there is one with the same name 400 yards further north along Horsenden Lane.** Roy Allen collection

Below: **This is one of the earliest all-line maps where each of Gibb's traffic conference lines was shown in a distinct colour under the common 'UndergrounD' brand. From this point the Underground began to be promoted as a system and, very gradually, the District began to lose its separate identity.** Author's collection

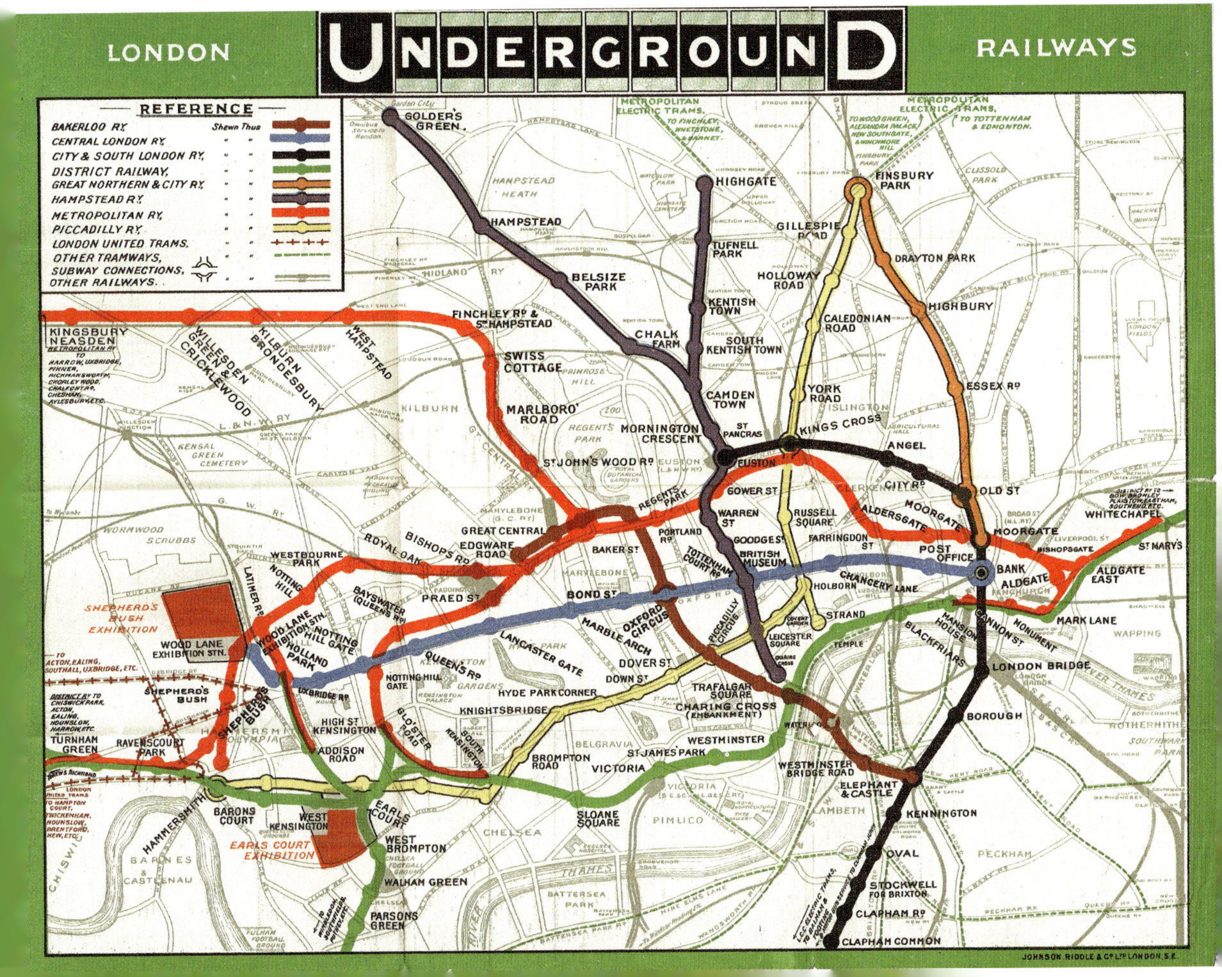

1908 leaflet promoting the improved District services, miniature map on rear. An early use of the new logotype with enlarged end letters. LTM

1908 poster promoting District electric services. This is one of the few colour images which hints at the bright red colouring of the trains and the darker (wooden) doors. Author's collection

By coordinating fares, the railways made some progress in raising revenue to the benefit of all, and Gibb's background statistical analysis was persuasive. Today such activity would be regarded as illegal, as constituting a cartel. In those days it was actually felt to be in the public interest, and traffic went up. It is interesting how fashions change. The bus companies came in briefly but had their own problems. The main bus competition was against the Central London which eventually came to terms with the more prominent operators.

The railway and tramway conference members continued to meet and in 1908, irked by growing bus competition, the railway members all agreed that they would promote their services using the name 'Underground'. The name would be used in a stylized form so as to be an obvious trademark, the name being prominently shown outside stations and on jointly-produced publicity, particularly a new style of system map with each railway shown in a different colour. The system would be marketed as one coherent whole. This idea of 'one-ness' was accentuated by successive introductions of through fares so that between the conference lines there would be a more or less complete system of through booking. Traffic responded accordingly.

District annual passengers carried and net revenue generated (revenue less costs)

1906	1907	1908	1909	1910
55.0m	51.2m	61.1m	66.9m	72.7m
£116,770	£146,866	£203,595	£256,083	£311,191

Although the District began experimenting with new forms of publicity, for a while it persisted with the old materials, including its various maps. The District miniature map was also produced in other languages (probably for foreign guide books of London) and this shows two of the rear panels for a French variant of 1907. Author's collection

LES GARES TERMINUS DE LONDRES, Etc.

LE DISTRICT RAILWAY

(CHEMIN DE FER DU DISTRICT)

DESSERT PAR SES LIGNES ET EMBRANCHEMENTS

TOUTES LES

ATTRACTIONS de LONDRES

ET SES ENVIRONS.

Il dessert également toutes les GARES TERMINUS de LONDRES, il est le plus rapide moyen de communication entre le

EAST END, CITÉ, WEST END,

ET TOUS LES QUARTIERS DE LONDRES.

Les Wagons sont très confortables et éclairés par la lumière électrique.

La Compagnie délivre des billets de correspondance pour toutes les Stations sur Piccadilly Tube et du Bakerloo Tube et pour celles faisant partie des Faubourgs. Ouest desservis par la Compagnie "THE LONDON UNITED ELECTRIC TRAMWAYS."

Prendre les billets pour Charing Cross Station, de là tourner à droite de la gare Villiers Street pour le (Tube) d'Hampstead.

Des billets d'abonnements sont délivrés pour la durée de 1, 3, 6, 9 et 12 mois.

Position sur le

CHEMIN DE FER DU DISTRICT.

JOURS DE SEMAINE.	TRAINS ÉLECTRIQUES DE ET POUR:	DIMANCHES.
Chaque 15 minutes.	EAST HAM, Upton Park, Plaistow et West Ham, Bromley *(8 à 15 Trains par heure, matins et soirs pendant la semaine).*	Chaque 15 minutes.
Chaque 10 minutes.	Bow Road, Mile End et Stepney Green *(8 à 15 Trains par heure, matins et soirs pendant la semaine).*	
Chaque 10 minutes.	NEW CROSS, Deptford Road, Rotherhithe, Wapping et Shadwell *(Changer à Whitechapel).*	
Chaque 10 minutes.	Whitechapel, St. Mary's et Aldgate East *(12 Trains par heure matins et soirs pendant la semaine).*	
4 ou 5	Mark Lane, Monument et Cannon Street	Chaque 5 ou 6 minutes.
2 ou 3	MANSION HOUSE, Blackfriars, Temple, Charing Cross, Westminster, St. James Park, Victoria, Sloane Street, South Kensington et Gloucester Road.	
10	High Street, Notting Hill Gate, Bayswater, Praed Street, Edgware Road, Baker Street, King's Cross et autres Gares comprises dans le réseau de petite ceinture.	Chaque 15 minutes.
3 ou 4	EARLS COURT.	Chaque 7 ou 8 minutes
7 ou 8	West Brompton, Walham Green, Parsons Green, Putney Bridge et Hurlingham *(Trains supplémentaires matins et soirs pendant la semaine).*	15
15	East Putney, Southfields, Wimbledon Park et Wimbledon.	30
6 ou 7	West Kensington, Baron's Court, Hammersmith *(Trains supplémentaires matins et soirs pendant la semaine).*	15
6 ou 8	Ravenscourt Park et Turnham Green.	
30	Gunnersbury, Kew et Richmond.	30
10	Chiswick Park et Acton Green, Mill Hill Park (Acton Town), Ealing Common et Ealing Broadway *(Trains supplémentaires les soirs en semaine).*	
15	South Acton, South Ealing, Boston Road, Osterley, Hounslow Town, Heston-Hounslow et Hounslow Barracks (casernes) *(6 Trains par heure, matins et soirs pour Hounslow pendant la semaine).* [illegible]	
30	North Ealing, Park Royal et Twyford Abbey, Perivale-Alperton, Sudbury Town, Sudbury Hill et South Harrow *(3 Trains par heure).*	
30	Addison Road, Uxbridge Road, St. Quintin Park, Willesden et gare de Broad Street.	

ST. JAMES'S PARK STATION, S.W.
9660 (8.07).

This is a July 1908 cover for the English version of the halfpenny miniature map, still called the District Railway Miniature Map but also branded **UNDERGROUND.** Capital Transport collection

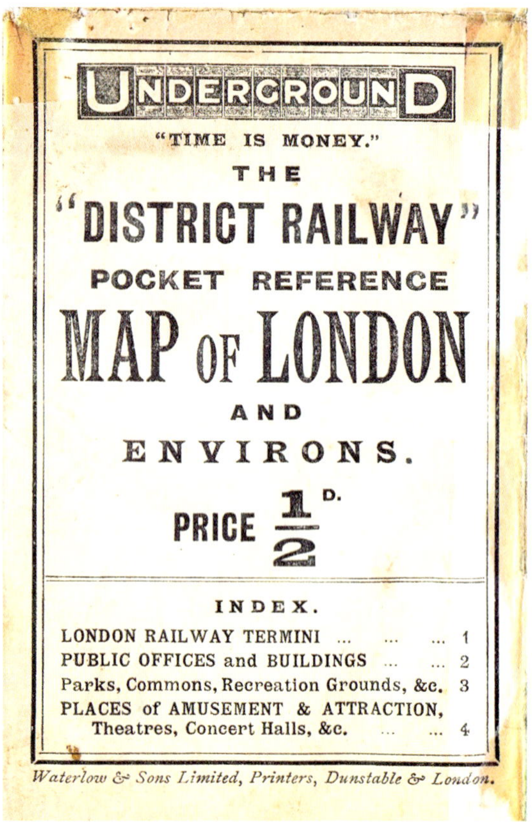

In conjunction with this the UERL and its subsidiaries (particularly the District) began a heavy advertising campaign to promote the various services, emphasising the speed and convenience for ordinary travel, the connectional facilities, the cheap fares and new places people could visit by train they might not otherwise have thought about. The posters were heavily promoted at the stations and supported by leaflet and informative maps. Again, this awareness campaign began to produce results. There had been no single department responsible for developing and promoting the services until the end of April 1909 when Stanley created one and put Frank Pick in charge, Pick having involved himself in this area off his own bat for over a year and shown some aptitude for the task. His work was very much part of the successful transformation of the various UERL railways during 1908 and began showing how useful high quality poster advertising could be in promoting the services.

Not quite all the money came from fares. For many years the District differed little from other railways in trying to generate additional revenue from unused space by installing kiosks and displaying commercial advertising, the advertising 'privilege' being managed for many years by the Partington Advertising Company who made light work of the task of covering walls and any other flat surfaces with posters. In addition there was a great deal of other clutter, including vending and weighing machines to contend with. The revenue from these activities was significant, the more so for the District which was always short of money. It was further augmented by renting out property and other space that had to be retained but was not in immediate railway use. We will see shortly that this included exploitation of air rights over stations.

The District's new electric cars were advertisement-free zones, at least for a while. It was reported in August 1907 that the District began advertising in its electric carriages. The shareholders were invited to think that, when the advertisements did appear, the displays had been done tastefully, and were likely to bring in about £5000 a year upwards. The displays appeared very much like the car cards on today's underground trains. We find that responsibility for third party income like this was the responsibility of the secretary, at that time Joseph Carter, who also managed rental income from property and other like matters; a quarter increase in commercial revenue was expected that year.

An Underground Brand

Questions had been asked by the Board of Trade during 1895 about how conspicuous station name signs were at all British railway stations and the District explained that on its system the station names were prominently displayed in large white letters on blue enamelled ground in three places on each platform, besides having the names conspicuously printed on the platform lamps and painted on the backs of the platform seats. In addition, the advertising contractor was directed to keep a clear space round the station name-boards to the extent of 2ft, at the same time limiting the advertisements adjoining that distance to the use of 4-inch letters. We have no way of knowing how successful this was.

Notwithstanding the alleged problem of identifying station names, the chaotic arrangement of revenue-generating activity looked increasingly out of place in the new electric era. It was also apparent that it could be quite difficult to identify the station name and direction signs *quickly*, which was not conducive to speeding passengers on their way. As part of the general clean up, the commercial advertising was completely rearranged and confined to approved sites. The Victorian fear that any unoccupied space represented a loss of money was found to be completely false. Advertisers wanted their adverts to be seen, and neatly arranged adverts clearly displayed and properly maintained enabled them to command premium prices, a philosophy that still applies today.

The belief that the District's station names were not very clear attracted the attention of Stanley who felt the existing white on blue signs could be improved. After some

Example of how the new bar and disk signs stood out reasonably well against the mass of surrounding advertising (which itself has been cleaned up). LTM

This view of Ealing Broadway shows a typical application of the new station name-boards. Also visible is the impressive train shed roof. The view today is not all that different. Capital Transport collection

investigation, he felt that the Parisian idea of greater separation between the name-board and surrounding advertising would make the names much more prominent. Trials were made at St James's Park during 1908, placing the name-sign on a much larger white sheet completely clear of surrounding material. By incremental stages, the idea emerged of a shape to draw in the eye and which might become some kind of trade mark. After further tests, the preferred solution was to place bright red shapes above and below the sign, giving the appearance the station name was superimposed upon a solid red circular target, and this idea was adopted. As implemented, the new signs were presented on large white enamelled iron panels with the name target in the centre, advertising spaces for the company's advertisements below, and space for directional signing above. The new signs went up on most of the busy District stations from 1909. Similar signs went up on the tube lines, although there was less clutter down below, and this also contributed to the portrayal of the network as a single system. The old signs were generally changed only as necessary and the design using the solid circle may be seen even now at Ealing Broadway.

Station entrances also gained consistent name-signs and near each entrance was an illuminated map and information poster carrying the slogan 'Underground to Everywhere – Quickest Way, Cheapest Fare'. As mentioned earlier the traffic conference decided to share the brand name 'Underground' which was integrated with the new external signs. To give a distinctive look, the name appeared as UndergrounD, with larger initial and final letters and could appear in both a horizontal or vertical format. A large number of substantial signs of this type were fitted at District stations in 1908-9, intended to be visible from some distance away. At about the same time many stations received a characteristic iron and glass shelter over the main entrance bearing the name of the station. A year or so later the use of this symbol was made more characteristic by inserting

Above: **This view of Chiswick Park shows the early exterior treatment using the word 'Underground' with its characteristic dashes. In later years (visible in some of the later photos) a bullseye type sign was often used.** Capital Transport collection

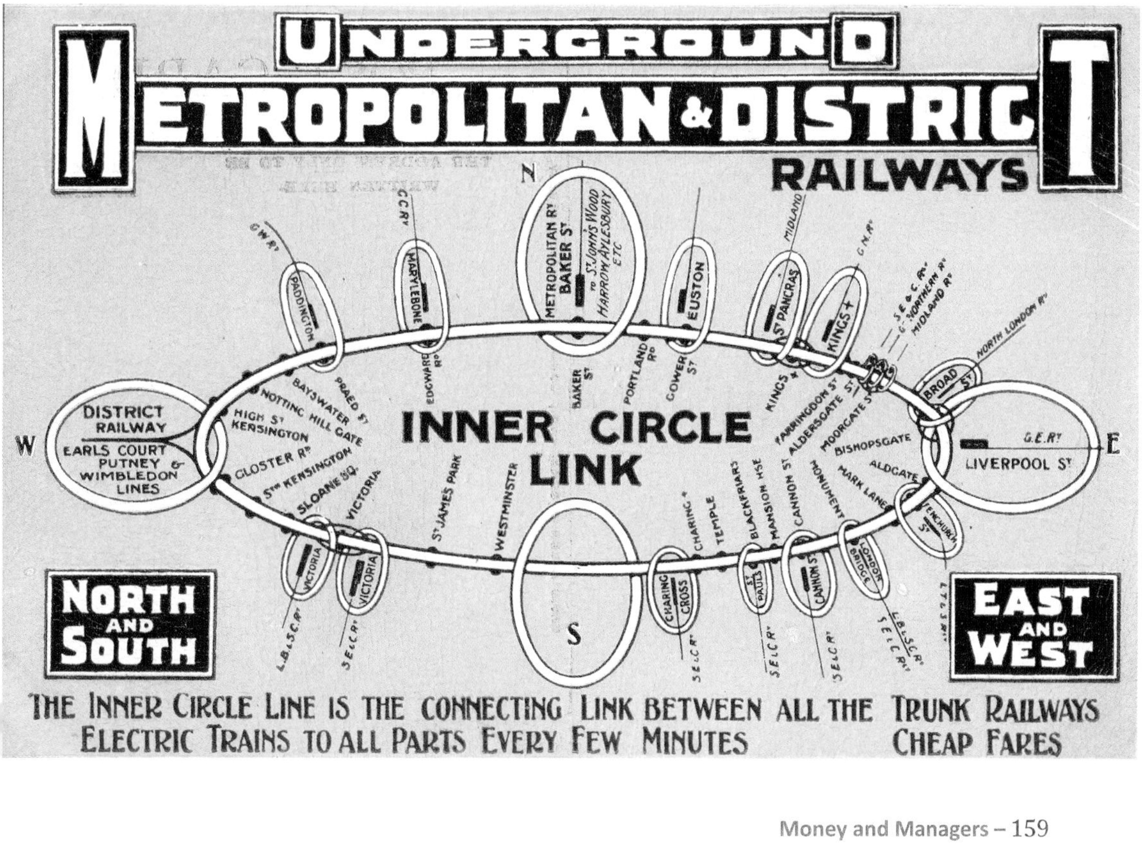

Below: **Whilst the District was energetically selling its services even the Inner Circle was promoted, highlighting its facility to link most of the main line termini.** Roy Allen collection

dashes above and below all the smaller capitals. Following the success of the platform signs, where space permitted, the UndergrounD symbol was superimposed on a solid red disk on a square white ground and prominently displayed at stations to announce it was an Underground station.

In 1916 the typographer Edward Johnston presented his first version of the famous Johnston lettering for use on the publicity of the UERL's system, though it could not be regarded as the UERL's standard typeface for signs and posters for many more years. Frank Pick is often credited with trying to improve the nameboards further by using a red ring rather than a solid red target. To obtain a satisfactory design, Johnston was employed to devise the necessary proportions and to incorporate his new lettering, designs being registered in 1917 and deployed from the early 1920s. The new signs took the form of a blue bar superimposed upon a red ring on a white ground and this pattern is still used (with many variations) today. He also redesigned the UndergrounD symbol to incorporate his new lettering and altered the dashes to include stylish notched ends. The proportions were carefully devised and the result could be used as a horizontal bar or superimposed on a red ring (which was the more common version). Single-colour variants were available for use as headers on publicity. During this transformation, which took over a decade, the name 'Underground' dominated and the use of the name 'District Railway' was much diminished, being primarily used after entering the system to differentiate the District train service from that of the other associated companies.

Underground Group gets Bigger

By 1912 London's largest bus operator was the London General Omnibus Company (LGOC). Ever since the 1908 traffic conference the UERL had been keen to co-ordinate its railway and tramway services with bus operators to reduce wasteful competition and encourage bus operators to provide feeder services to railheads for the benefit of both parties. Discussions rumbled on but aggressive competition between bus operators and the threat of increased competition between buses and rail once reliable motor buses became available changed the dynamics of all this. In 1911, circumstances favoured the UERL taking over the LGOC and its horse-bus dominated board. The hope was to use the new motor buses to generate revenue quickly for both bus and rail by expanding services and reducing competitive routes—buses were profitable and could be redeployed very quickly. The takeover took effect from early January (backdated to first of that month) and a new board was in place from 26th April.[30] There is no space here to enlarge upon this complicated takeover by the UERL beyond stating that it set the scene for the District and the LGOC working more closely together in the wider interest of what was now being referred to as 'The Combine'.

Evidence of co-ordination was quick. Enterprise especially beckoned at Hounslow Barracks where there was virtually no habitation apart from the barracks itself. In July 1912 a Sunday bus service began that operated between Hounslow Barracks, Staines and Windsor. Hourly bus departures were co-ordinated to meet the trains and through tickets were available from District stations. This arrangement proved so popular that the service was almost immediately increased to half-hourly, and later to every 15 minutes; even that was insufficient and it finally settled down to every ten minutes, requiring augmentation of the train service (which remained at 2-cars and still required people to change at Acton Town for through services to and from London). Through fares were 2/- return. The service was later extended to run on weekdays, though not so frequently. Part of the success was the very heavy promotion the services received as the District got to grips with the art of effective poster advertising.

From September 1912 additional bus and rail services were introduced, some designed to appeal to those wanting somewhere interesting to visit and others extending the usefulness of the existing termini by making onward travel easier.

The main new services were: [31]

Railhead	**Destination**
Hounslow Barracks	Staines; Windsor and (on Sundays) Burnham Beeches and Virginia Water (though only briefly)
Ealing Broadway	Northfields, Kew Bridge and (soon) Richmond
Hammersmith	Richmond via Barnes
Richmond	Isleworth
Putney Bridge	Roehampton and (on Sundays) Kingston
Barking	Barkingside; North Woolwich
Bow Road	Romford

Through road-rail bookings (both by bus and tram) became a long-standing feature of travel by the District and lasted well into London Transport days. Additional services were run on Sundays aimed entirely at pleasure seekers and became a feature for many years.

A new motor bus at Hounslow Barracks on 14th July 1912 on a new Windsor service, a facility designed to attract more traffic onto the District. *Railway Magazine* October 1912

On 1st January 1913 two independent underground railways joined the group. Both had been technically successful but the problems of competition had not receded, even with a measure of co-operation with the UERL. Moreover, both these small companies found it even more difficult to raise investment capital than the UERL. The latter, on the other hand, was firmly of the opinion that reducing competition through takeovers was a good thing and after making offers that were hard to refuse saw both the Central London and City & South London Railways join the fold. Over the next few years they were firmly welded into what was rapidly becoming an integrated London transport system.

Nor did integration stop there. With most buses and most underground railways now part of the combine the remaining tramways had to be brought in, though there was no prospect of taking over the LCC tramways with their annoyingly low fares. The largest independent tramway system was the Metropolitan Electric Tramways which was owned by British Electric Traction (BET) and, curiously, also ran buses. The method here was to establish the London & Suburban Traction Company in which the UERL and BET had substantial shareholdings and into which the Metropolitan Electric and London United Tramways would be transferred from 1st January 1913 (South Metropolitan Tramways also became a part from May 1913). Although the UERL did not obtain a controlling interest until the 1920s, when BET pulled out, the tram network fell under the UERL's administrative control from 1915 and was promoted as part of the UERL's system and enjoyed the benefits of joint marketing and fares schemes.

With the substantial expansion of the UERL to include buses a significant management move was made by the appointment of a single commercial manager to function across the whole of the bus and rail businesses. This role was given early in 1912 to Frank Pick, who had shown aptitude in this area.

During this decade we have seen electrification and new railways, a transformation of the management, the employment of proper business methods and the tentative beginnings of a London-wide transportation system that hugely improved travelling conditions in London. Because of its size the District was a crucial part of all this, though it did mean the beginning of the slow process of, to an extent, losing its own identity and being part of a larger network.

Chapter Six

INFRASTRUCTURE IMPROVEMENTS

Station Improvements Electrification to the Great War

During electrification, Yerkes had been fully aware of the concerns about fire risk and whilst arranging to lay power ducts beneath the various platforms found it convenient to replace the timber surface and substructure at the tunnel stations with concrete, the work largely being finished before electric services began. Platform nosing stones of Doulton's grooved vitreous pattern were installed at the same time. The work was difficult because the stations were in use during the day when access was very restricted and most of it had to be done at night. New concrete surfaces were not necessarily dry by the time stations were opened each day and keeping passengers away from the wet concrete was a problem not always solved successfully. At some stations, it was also possible to extend the platforms at the same time, to make it easier to run longer trains. In later years the wooden platforms at most of the open-air stations were also upgraded to concrete and stone.

The District tunnels were filthy when steam was withdrawn and this device helped to clean them up. According to the description, the arm had a wide and versatile reach and the bristles rotated at great speed under the driving force of compressed air. Author's collection

With all this work in hand the opportunity was taken to install electric lighting at all the tunnel stations. Once Lots Road was up and running this was achieved by means of a 220 volt 3-phase lighting main running throughout the tunnel section and fed from lighting transformers at each substation. The lighting main was broken about half way between substations to reduce the effect of faults spreading but the mains could be coupled up if a substation were shut down for any reason. At the tunnel stations, electric lighting was completed and available throughout from October 1905 and once it was operational the gas fittings were progressively removed.[1]

Once steam haulage had been abandoned the District's tunnel stations were all deep cleaned. The District did a thorough job of cleaning and repainting the stations and in removing the accumulated sooty crud from within the tunnels. During October work was in hand using a cleaning wagon with a brush attached that could reach the tunnel crown but although a demonstration had been made by the British Vacuum Cleaning Company to remove soot from tunnels it has not been possible to establish whether they assisted.[2]

Now ventilation was less of an issue, over the succeeding thirty years many of the difficult-to-maintain arched glass and iron platform roofs were removed and some or all of the airspace covered over by lucrative property developments. The District then embarked on a programme of station modernization.

Putney Bridge

Following electrification, some operational features soon proved unsatisfactory. Putney Bridge was the southern limit of District ownership and most of the High Street service turned round there by running south of the 2-track station to reverse on the running line, sometimes delaying the Wimbledon service. The District responded by building an additional track around the back of the 'down' (towards Wimbledon) platform and

Putney Bridge station immediately after electrification. Obvious here is the metal gantry supporting the platform. The signal box is newly-provided for power frame (the original box was at end of right hand platform). Capital Transport collection

Putney Bridge shortly after track alterations. This view, looking south, shows the widened platform on left with new track run round the extra face and extra waiting area. The centre road is now a bay road. The diverted track required moving the signal cabin (which is probably where photographer was located). LTM

converted the former 'down' platform into a bay road, with hydraulic buffers at the south end. This was no easy job with the railway on a viaduct and the new westbound track was carried on a massive steel framework attached to the east side of the viaduct. Because of constraints at both end of the station the space was restricted and the bay road could never handle trains longer than six cars—though this was adequate for the High Street shuttles. The new arrangements came into use in July 1910 (and lasted until 2016 when the little-used bay was removed and the pre-1910 layout put back, allowing platforms to be extended).

Walham Green

The original station at Walham Green had been a 2-storey block-like structure with the usual narrow arched windows on the ground floor and more modern rectangular sash windows (with a slightly arched top) on the first floor. The entrance was rather a surprise and took the form of a massive, ornamented stone block with a heavy balustrade around the top taking the height up to the top of the building. The block was pierced by two huge arches that would have suited a large museum or town hall. The District evidently felt it did not match its own expectations or make the best use of the site and a completely new station building was erected on the same site to a design by Harry Ford (the District's architect) and completed in 1910.[3]

The upper part looked rather like a Queen Anne style town house, with five vast windows and suitable decoration and mouldings above which was a large, slightly projecting, flat roof with ornamentation. On top of that was a panel bearing the station

The street scene at Walham Green station shortly before station reconstruction. Capital Transport collection

name in a large tablet. The exterior finish was in glazed terra cotta. The ground floor was more railway-like with a huge central entrance and shops either side; the building was large enough to include within an arcade of shops between the entrance and the booking hall. A large dedicated exit was provided to the south of the building, looking a little like an afterthought, but this was almost certainly not in use when traffic was light (at the time it was stated that the scale of the works here was to ensure it could handle the football crowds for Stamford Bridge).

Walham Green station shortly after reconstruction. The new station stands in marked contrast to its predecessor which looked old fashioned even when new. Capital Transport collection

Northfields

A new station between South Ealing and Boston Road opened on 16th April 1908 when the area showed signs of development. The station was initially called Northfield Halt [Ealing]. The new station was located on the west side of what was then Northfield Lane, the eastbound platform backing onto the Ealing District Steam Laundry, which had been for some years the only building in the area, though development was appearing rapidly, particularly to the north. A tiny booking office, very much in the garden shed style, was erected on the railway overbridge with steps to the London-bound platform and separate steps at the south end of the bridge to the Hounslow platform. The platforms had no awnings and only rudimentary shelters.

This modest halt quickly achieved its purpose of stimulating development. The hut was soon replaced by a proper station building in brick that extended right across the bridge, the work costing £3600; this appears to have been co-ordinated with the widening and 'suburbanizing' of the road outside, which was renamed Northfield Avenue at about the same time. Either side of the central, canopied entrance there were shop units. Inside, the booking hall was quite deep and had a 3-windowed booking office along one side and toilets and bookstall along the other. At the far end, a new footbridge gave access to the stairs down to the platforms. Both platforms were equipped with substantial pitched awnings that extended along about a third of their length. On 11th December 1911, when the work was finished, the station was renamed Northfields & Little Ealing, while Boston Road became Boston Manor on the same day.[4]

New station at Northfield Halt on the Northfield Lane bridge about 1910. The structure is on the London side but steps to the Hounslow platform may be seen on left (the platforms were connected only via the road bridge). LTM

Above: **This shows the new platforms at Northfield Halt in June 1908 and the precarious rear of the ticket office, constructed partly of corrugated iron. An uninviting waiting room, also of corrugated iron, is visible at left. A short train of 1903 cars departs, marker lights having been fitted to unrebuilt end and some Americana removed.** LTM

Below: **Permanent station at Northfields once some traffic had developed. The name 'Northfields & Little Ealing Station' lurks above the canopy, which partly obscures it.** LTM

Ealing Broadway

Ealing Broadway station was not only of the same style as Walham Green but shared a similar fate. Looking old-fashioned and inefficient, it was rebuilt in 1911 in rather the same way. Although finished in stone, the upper parts also looked rather like a posh town house. Ten rectangular windows with segmental arched pediments were spread across the upper storey, which had a flat, slightly overhanging roof with edge decoration. The whole of the central section was adorned with decorative pilasters and stood forward a few inches to give prominence. At street level, there were five bays. The central one formed the station entrance with canopy above and the flanking bays were for shop units. A large stone tablet on the front of the roof prominently displayed the station name. Inside the building a broad arcade included shop windows for the flanking shops, a newspaper stall and the 3-windowed booking office with polished wooden façade above a tiled wall.

Ealing Broadway was also a source of train service delay, bearing in mind cars were added and detached there and it handled some trains entering or leaving service from Mill Hill Park depot (which quickly became known as Ealing Common depot). The answer was a third platform. This was constructed by lengthening the southern District platform and installing a new face on the south side, creating a very long bay that stopped just short of the train shed; it came into use from April 1913 but lacked much in the way of any sheltering. At that time the District and Great Western stations were entirely separate facilities with an expanse of waste land between them, so adding the new track was not a problem. Interchange between the stations involved a walk along the street until, from 1920, the Ealing & Shepherds Bush station opened. This occupied the intervening space between the two stations (where the Central Line platforms are now) and as part of the works a massive bridge serving all platforms was opened about half way along the station.

Station building at Ealing Broadway after reconstruction. LTM

Above: **Ealing Broadway at platform level in 1921 showing the 1913-installed additional platform (on the right with the long train in it). The 1879 signal box is visible at far end of platforms and the array of signals, required because of the number of sidings here. Most cars are of the 1905 wooden type and the open offside door of nearest car suggests a warm day.** LTM

Below: **A view near Lampton Junction looking south-west in 1909. In the foreground is a new signal box (to work the crossover) and a little beyond are the new (unfinished) platforms for Hounslow Town on the old direct line, about to come back into use. Electrification and signalling await completion. The original Hounslow Town branch is out of view on the left.** LTM

Hounslow Branch

The need to reverse Hounslow Barracks trains at Hounslow Town was highly inconvenient and constrained the train service, with some busy-hour trains terminating at Hounslow Town when the single line was already occupied. From 2nd May 1909 (a Sunday) the spur and the connecting curve were permanently closed and the old direct line was reopened. A new station (also called Hounslow Town) was opened on the direct line just east of the Kingsley Road bridge; at the same time the old line between Lampton Junction and a point just short of Heston-Hounslow was doubled. Site conditions meant that the westbound platform had to be built across the route of the curve from the old station (it intersected the platform near its west end); the transition from one station to another seems to have been done without any gap in service, advantage being taken of the extra time available on a Saturday night to tackle the job.

The replacement station was rather basic compared with the substantial building that was being abandoned. Curiously, the new station building was near the top of the embankment slope so one walked up a flight of steps into the building's basement, to discover a wooden ticket office, and then proceeded up a flight of internal stairs to arrive at platform level where one found a small cottage-style waiting room covered by an overhanging pitched roof; there was another small shelter further along. There was a separate set of steps from street to the westbound platform which had virtually no facilities at all and no connection with the ticket office. Trams and buses would in any case have been a better option than the thin train service for anyone needing to go west from here.

This scene along the Hounslow branch after the double track section was extended to just west of Heston-Hounslow. This shows the point where the remaining single track section began; a District train (1905 car at rear) has just left the single line. Housing development is notable by its absence. Author's collection

After the alterations, the District was very proud of the way this branch was worked. A 10-minute train service was operated over a 1¼-mile section of single track that included an intermediate station requiring a call in both directions. Trains had a bare minimum of turn-round time at Hounslow Barracks and there was scarcely any leeway at Hounslow Town where a new train for the single line would be arriving more or less when the branch train was departing. The whole section was controlled by track circuiting and there was no requirement for a train staff, which would have caused delays.

Maps suggest that for some years after the new station opened track along the old route, and the old station, were just left in place, except Lampton Junction itself which was removed. The actual station was on viaduct and it was eventually demolished and the land used to build Hounslow bus garage, which opened in 1913. The loss of this site for the Underground was regrettable given its excellent position in the town, but with the need to serve Hounslow Barracks as well there was very little option.

Heston-Hounslow's single track station partly on a bridge presented a problem when in 1912 it was desired to extend the double track section a quarter mile westwards to increase capacity. The only way around this was to construct an entirely new station on the east side of the bridge, very unusually employing an island platform. A pleasing, brick cottage-style booking hall was built at street level on the south side of the line and a short subway and steps led up to the platform which had a waiting room and awnings along about half its length. The double track became single immediately west of the bridge and the single line to Hounslow Barracks (and the 1884 station) had to wait until after the war before improvements were finally made.

This is the replacement station for Hounslow Town, opened in 1909. Departing may be seen one of the 1903 experimental cars. It is a middle motor car (still with right hand driving position) and was probably all there was of the train. This view also shows an early treatment of the station name coupled to the new red 'bullseye'. Author's collection

Hounslow Town (new) station on Kingsley Road looking at entrance on the London (up) side. The ticket hall is at the top of the steps, with further steps leading to platform. A notable feature here is the 'DR' monogram fixed above the poster frames (a number of District stations had these). Another stairway serves 'down' platform. LTM

Mill Hill Park (Acton Town)

At Mill Hill Park the track arrangements became a serious source of delay. This was not surprising given the convergence of branches, the need to reverse shuttle services from the west, and the nearby depot requiring trains to come in and out of service. The District decided to build a flyover west of the station so that the westbound Ealing line could cross the Hounslow branch without conflicting. This was relatively easy as the Hounslow line was already at a much lower level than the surrounding area at this point.

The station was more of a problem. At track level the existing station consisted of two side platforms in a slight cutting and the desire was to increase the number of tracks to three and install island platforms between them. This involved a certain amount of stage working and a reconstructed station building. The existing London-bound platform was more or less retained, with an additional track around the north-east side. When that had been done the existing westbound track and platform were swapped so as to form a second island, one side facing what was now the middle road (with a platform each side) and the other face serving the westbound line along the south west side. The effect was to produce a station a little like Golders Green still appears today, the local trains that reversed using the middle track. Additional sidings were also installed east of the station alongside the eastbound lines and adjacent to Bollo Lane, occupying land still in Underground ownership today. The work was completed in February 1910 and the station was renamed Acton Town from 1st March.

The existing single storey station building, with station master's house adjacent, faced Bollo Lane across its large forecourt with one entrance in Bollo Lane and the other in Gunnersbury Avenue. The new track layout meant the only practical arrangement was for a new station on the bridge with two staircases down from the rear, one to each island platform. In response to this, a substantial single-storey building with pitched roof was erected on the bridge in Portland stone; this had a central entrance with an arched top and an arched pediment above that proclaiming its new name 'Acton Town'. The old station building was demolished and a new station master's house built along the south side of the station—this looked more like something one would find along a suburban street than in connection with a railway.

The *Railway Magazine* made a great fuss over the new name, explaining that Mill Hill Park had been the name of a mere estate and that the traditional name for this spot was Bollo Bridge, where the Bollo Brook passed underneath Gunnersbury Lane into the area now occupied by the railway depot. Given nobody would know where either of these places were, it should have been called Acton Town (or similar) from the start as it was the nearest station, the magazine averred, to the town centre, being just under half a mile. The problem was felt originally to have been that the station was located about 25 yards outside the Acton boundary, in Brentford. As part of the process of making sure that everybody knew Acton Town was the station for Acton, from the same date 'West Acton' was dropped from the name of Ealing Common and 'Acton Green' was dropped as the suffix of Chiswick Park.

Acton Town platforms after reconstruction as a 3-track station. This view looks towards the new station building on the bridge. LTM

It was quite unusual for the District to suspend a train service, even during major engineering work. At Mill Hill Park major track alterations were required during the reconstruction and to facilitate what had to be done it was apparently felt that starting the South Acton service late one Sunday was the preferred solution. LTM

New station building on the road bridge at Acton Town, opening coinciding with name change from Mill Hill Park (this image 1916). It was here that the booking office was broken into in the early hours of 11th February 1920 and in making his getaway the thief shot newly-married police constable Kelly (T Division) who died of his injuries. 1000 police officers attended the funeral at Westminster Cathedral. LTM

Hammersmith Broadway probably early 1906 showing the new joint station for District and Piccadilly Railways, apparently before Piccadilly opened. Brian Hardy collection

Hammersmith

Major changes at Hammersmith were required to accommodate the Piccadilly tube. The District's station had comprised an island platform on the west side, both faces serving westbound trains, a central island platform with the west face serving eastbound trains, then there were two bay roads and a single platform on the eastern edge of the site (so there were five platforms in all). The bay roads were not heavily used and so the District agreed to give them up so that a new Piccadilly station could be provided in the space released. Two tracks were installed with a central island platform between (for boarding passengers) and flanking side platforms (for those alighting) and the platforms were all rather narrow.* The ticket hall was entirely rebuilt, although the access and booking arrangements for the two railways were at first kept separate. The frontage comprised a 2-storey structure designed by the District's architect, Harry Ford. The new frontage took the form of five huge arches dividing the ground floor into five bays with the arched tops serving as windows for the upper floor. The central bay was the joint District and Piccadilly entrance and the other four were let for commercial use or as exits. A flat roof was fronted by a low wall with a balustrade central section and the whole frontage was faced by faience tiles.

After the Piccadilly opened in 1906 it slowly became apparent that its passengers found the interchange at Hammersmith very useful and wanted to continue their journeys on the District. Unfortunately, the narrow platforms on both District and Piccadilly sides of the station meant narrow staircases as well and these soon became congested as those trying to interchange fought their way through the crowds entering and leaving the station.

* The station cutting today is the same width as it was in Victorian times and today contains four platforms. One can imagine how cramped it was when there were seven platforms.

In 1910 an additional entrance was brought into use serving Fulham Palace Road and Great Church Lane. This required a new footbridge at the south-east end of the platforms, also greatly assisting those wishing to change between the Piccadilly and District lines. The footbridge was connected to a compact new ticket hall in Great Church Lane, to the west of the railway. It was here that the Albert Stanley Institute, a club run by District Railway staff, was opened on 14th May 1914 and was much extended in 1923 (opening on 4th December). The club was built over part of the new Hammersmith motor-bus garage of the LGOC, an early example of benefits to be obtained from both companies being part of the UERL.

Barons Court

To the west of Gliddon Road bridge a new station called Barons Court was opened on 9th October 1905 to serve District trains and ready to serve the Piccadilly when it opened. This had two rather narrow concrete islands, both 360ft long, one serving each railway; the platforms were almost entirely protected by umbrella-type awnings made by the St Pancras Ironworks. The glass in the awnings was protected with wire mesh from the inevitable consequences of young boys throwing stones, probably reflecting bitter experience elsewhere and the existence of a parallel road that would make a good launching point. The single-storey station building on the bridge was faced in pale brown terra cotta with the station name emblazoned on the tiled pediment and the name District Railway beneath. The flat roof was edged with a decorative stone parapet and the effect was rather elegant. Inside the station building a 14ft wide booking hall formed a corridor

A scene at Earls Court, probably about 1910, looking west. One of the District's new battery locomotives is seen at head of an engineering train servicing the concreting of the platform surface, though the station appears open. The tunnel platforms were concreted first but open stations were subsequently converted. Also visible in background is the west end exit for the exhibitions, and the prominent sign advertising Sunday afternoons in the fresh air. LTM

Earls Court Road showing the old station not long before it was reconstructed to support the modernized District and new Piccadilly services. Capital Transport collection

between two independent booking offices, the District office on the south side and the Piccadilly office (not yet open) on the north; the finishings were in Doulton's tilework in three shades of green. Steps to the platforms were located at the west end. Electric lighting was installed, using lamps in groups of five taking current from the conductor rails. The station name was taken from Barons Court Road (opposite station).

Earls Court

Earls Court station on the west side of Earls Court Road had been a (mainly) single-storey brick building set back slightly from the building line. Although the District station did not require modification for electrification, it did need to accommodate the Piccadilly tube. The outcome was reconstruction of the station to the design of Harry Ford, as a two storey structure. The Piccadilly tracks were below the District on the north side and access had to be provided by lifts rising up to ticket hall level. Four lifts were provided, requiring two shafts, and the top landings were on the north side of the station. The lift entrances were in the area between the two shafts and exits took passengers to an exit along the north side of the property leading direct to the street (which also served as a direct exit from the District platforms). The enlarged station building frontage was rather similar to Hammersmith and also included the 5-arch formula with central entrance; only some small detailing differed. Biscuit coloured faience cladding was installed on the outside of the structure and the station name, and names of the two railways, was set out in tiled letters at the top. The flat roof was protected at its front edge by a stone balustrade with a solid, arched central section carrying the words City and West End Railways.

These alterations left the Warwick Road entrance untouched except for signs encouraging Piccadilly passengers to come in that way and walk the length of the District platforms.

The new frontage at Earls Court was designed to draw attention to the building and its new railway facilities, as well as providing plenty of space for retail. Capital Transport collection

High Street Kensington

This was one of several stations little-altered since opening in 1868 and one that had a frontage on one of London's more affluent shopping streets. The wish to provide modern facilities and an improved street presence provided an opportunity to make use of the valuable air space over the station. This was done by roofing over the platforms at the north end and creating a new booking hall at the end of the new deck via a high-quality shopping arcade. An entirely new frontage was created in red brick and portland stone

The new frontage at High Street Kensington was a profound change from that originally provided. The entrance leads through a shopping arcade with booking hall at far end, built over the tracks. The arrangement better suited this affluent area as well as bringing in welcome income. Alan A Jackson collection

much improving its attractiveness. The shopping arcade (designed by George Sherrin) also provided direct access to some of the more important adjacent shops, some of which had been enlarged by expanding onto the new raft over the platforms. At platform level the layout was left unchanged except for the loss of the all-over glass roof and provision of standard awnings at the south end. No attempt was made to replace the old way in and way out galleries that imposed a one-way flow and, instead, wide stairways were installed (though that to the physically separate Platform 4 was necessarily quite narrow). The work was mainly undertaken between 1904 and 1907.

Gloucester Road

As electrification approached, the need arose to remove the all-over glass roof at Gloucester Road and at the same time construct a footbridge at the west end of the station to improve interchange between Inner Circle trains and westbound District (reducing pressure on the stairs at the east end). Again, the original booking office arrangements were now a hindrance but, uniquely, the existing two-storey station building was retained. The old arrival and departure galleries were swept away and a new basement-level booking hall built on a raft immediately west of the old building with a single stairway to each platform. Access to the new booking hall was gained from stairs at either end that emerged in the existing wings either side of the main station at street level, allowing the interior of the old building to be converted to commercial use. Each railway insisted in having its own booking office in the new and rather narrow booking hall, these being placed at either end with signage at each street level entrance signifying which one was intended for which railway's passengers (though at booking hall level it was a single common area). The District street-level entrance also served as an entrance to the new street-level Piccadilly station next door.

South Kensington

The joint station at South Kensington had not much altered since 1871 when the widening works were complete, although some small changes were necessary when the Exhibition Road subway was built and the difficult-to-maintain glazed double roof over the platforms was removed around 1903 with ordinary awnings installed instead.

Significant changes here were precipitated by the need to accommodate the new Piccadilly tube station next door and a suitable interchange connection. The work consisted in replacing the standard street level building with a new booking hall created at a lower level over the west end of the platforms, with new stairways replacing the old galleries. A huge semi-circular booking office was placed in the centre of the booking hall against the west wall. The station design was placed in the hands of George Sherrin.[5]

From the below-ground booking hall, two stairways rose to street level, the top of the stairs emerging within a new shopping arcade connecting Pelham Street and Alfred Place West, now Thurloe Street. At each end there was an imposing stone entrance with the name of the railways spelt out in a large decorative ironwork grille over the entrance. Connecting stairs led from the joint booking hall to the new Piccadilly one at street level in Pelham Street. There was no other connection between these lines. Work was completed in 1907.

Victoria

Somehow Victoria station survived in essentially original form until after electrification, after which provision of extra capacity was very urgent. To provide this, plans were drawn up by the architect George Sherrin for a handsome stone surface building that would be a good advertisement for the railway and make some commercial use of the air space, the old arched glass roof being now hidden behind the rows of small shops that had appeared in Victoria Street and Terminus Place. The actual ticket hall was shifted into an enlarged area at basement level, though still immediately over the tracks near the centre of the station. A novel feature was that the whole booking hall was to be hung from the main station girders rather than supported on a set of its own.

Sherrin unfortunately died in 1909, whilst this was in hand, and the designs were completed by the District's architect Harry Ford, largely in accordance with Sherrin's plans. The single story building provided Terminus Place with a façade comprising what appears to be a single-storey Portland stone structure of seventeen adjacent arches, mainly occupied by individual shops though actually the top semi-circular windows comprise a compact second storey. The west-most arch is in a small block that follows the turn of the road towards the main line station. Near the eastern end an attractive arcade was formed, linking Terminus Place and Victoria Street; several small shops were placed here, together with one of several new station entrances. The work took place between 1909 and 1911 and the new ticket hall connected into the existing long subway to the main line station as well as new connections to and from the platforms. No alterations were made along Victoria Street except for the four arches of the arcade and the station entrance on the site of the old building. A major factor affecting the completion of the project was the forthcoming coronation which threatened to bring enormous crowds into the area.

Victoria in 1916 when the arcade had been built but not the superstructure. The poster on left is promoting the use of season tickets instead of daily tickets in order to help reduce imports of wood pulp. LTM

St James's Park and General Offices

For forty years only minor changes were made at St James's Park station where the old-fashioned booking office (located opposite what, today, is Queen Anne's Gate) served the station by means of the usual stairs to galleries over the track and further stairs to platform level. Meanwhile the District was finding its existing offices at Parliament Mansions too small and expensive and looked at constructing a premises on its own land.

In 1897 the District commissioned the architect Mr. Florence, of the firm of Florence and Isaacs, to prepare plans and estimates for general offices to be built over the east end of St James's Park station. The tender of Messrs Cubitts was accepted and the work was put in hand on 10th January 1898 and completed shortly before the end of that year at a cost of slightly over £20,000, including considerable alterations to the station. This included the removal of five of the fifteen 22ft roof bays at the east end of the roof and rafting over the space above the platforms. The opportunity was taken to replace the original booking hall by a new one incorporated in the new building (at some point a direct entrance was installed into the St Ermin's Hotel, the back of which was adjacent). The company moved in on 20th and 21st December 1898. Expansion was soon required to accommodate staff for the UERL and its other subsidiaries and it was decided to extend the newly-built accommodation by means of adjacent new blocks working west along York Street, and these were available from 1905 and again in 1909. The new blocks soon acquired the name Electric Railway House. The work also included covering over the former open space at the extreme east end of the site and installing rows of shops and other business premises that filled up the gap to the St James', a public house that had already been built on District land over the tunnel mouth and which faced down Tothill Street.

While this activity was in hand, a second entrance was installed at the west end of the station in 1910, with a small booking hall facing Palmer Street. This was designed to serve the important shops in Victoria Street more easily. The work was all carried out on railway land, mainly above the railway tracks, and involved the loss of two more of the roofing bays and decking over what had been a short open space. The new steps down to the platforms meant moving the emergency signal box from the eastbound platform into the tunnel on the westbound side and into the space vacated by the engine spur line.

Westminster

A number of alterations at Westminster were made in steam days, already described, but electrification triggering more alterations, substantially because of rising traffic levels. In 1909 it was necessary to improve the existing entrance in Bridge Street, which was doubled in width by appropriating the space occupied by a shop unit. This also provided sufficient space within which to install a ticket office that was quite close to the entrance, releasing space in the old station building. The space over the tracks, previously occupied by the ticket office, was converted into a refreshment room occupied by J. Lyons & Co who took the opportunity to add a second storey to much-increase the dining area.

Charing Cross

Electrification did not call for much change at Charing Cross although there was some disturbance caused by the building of the underground substation and the long interchange passage between the District and the new Bakerloo tube. The station soon became very busy, though, and enlargement was then called for. The impetus for creating something better was extension of the Hampstead tube in 1914.

The station was virtually reconstructed. The Hampstead tube's loop platform was installed, with escalator access, together with escalators to the Bakerloo platforms. The

Charing Cross station in 1909, little changed from the day it opened. The forthcoming rebuilding will see the roof removed and a much-enlarged booking hall built above the platforms. Author's collection

1914 Poster advertising the rebuilt station at Charing Cross. A 'Now Open' sticker has been over-posted and it probably said 'Opening Soon' underneath, or something similar. LTM

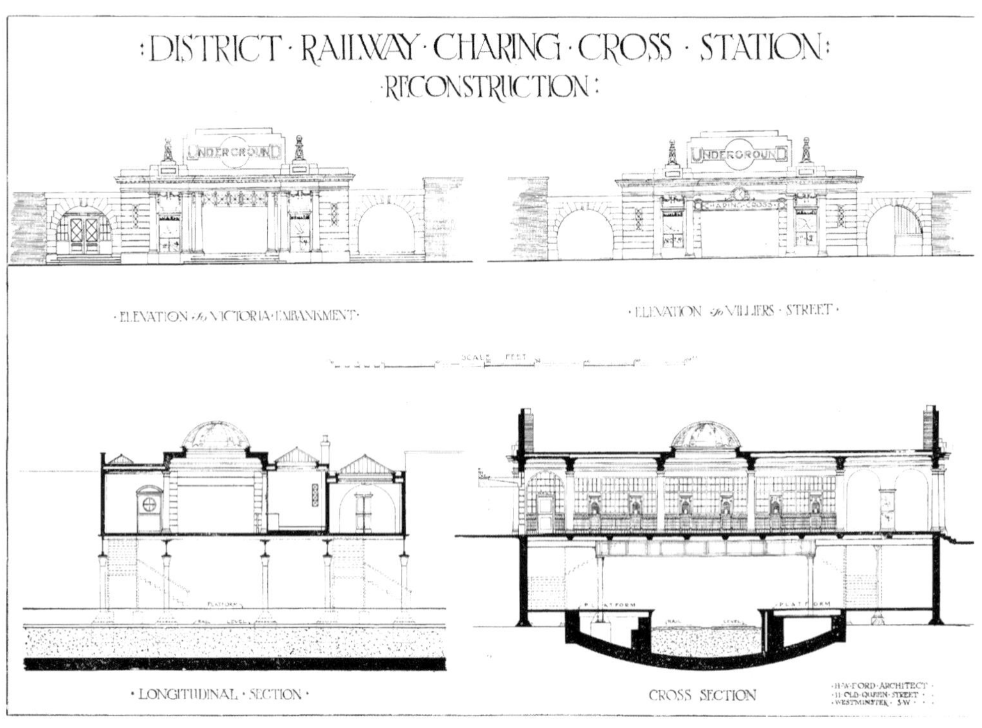

Above: **Section through the station site and proposed elevations at Charing Cross showing the new station building over the tracks.** Author's collection

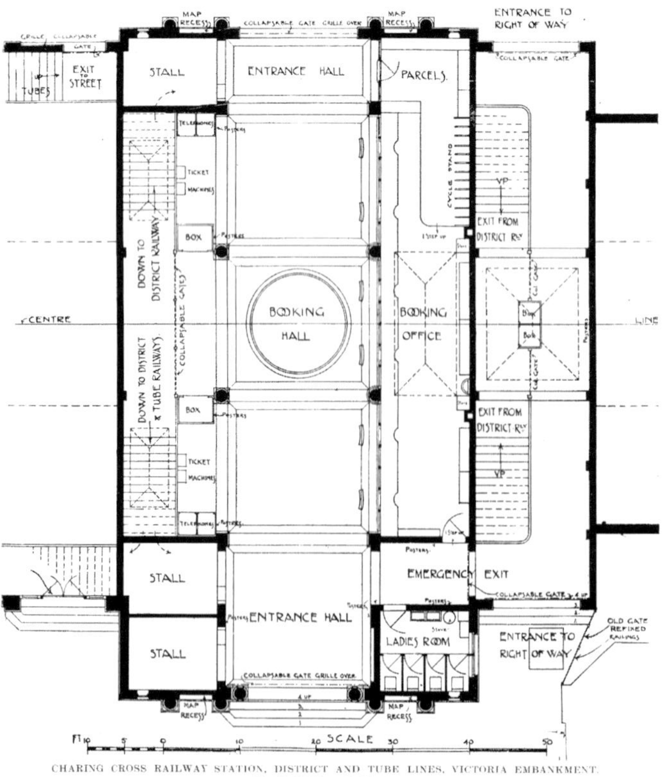

Left: **Plan of the new ticket hall at Charing Cross showing the new station building over the tracks and the right of way connecting Villiers Street and Victoria Embankment.** Author's collection

alterations involved removal of the District's overall roof and 1870 station building and expanding the existing street-level raft. The new building comprised an entrance from both the embankment and Villiers Street, each consisting of a single story structure with a large central entrance in portland stone and flanked by Doric pillars; at the centre of the building a glazed dome topped the structure. A notable feature was the booking office frontage that ran the whole length of the eastern end of the structure, the frontage being beautifully finished woodwork above a decorative tilework plinth. Flanking the main building were smaller arches used as exits to the street. Wide new stairways led down to the platforms with further stairs down to a concourse underneath the platforms from which the new Bakerloo tube escalators dropped down to meet the existing Bakerloo platforms (replacing an awkward and lengthy inclined subway at first provided in 1906). On being completed, the new station was extravagantly described as 'The Finest Interchange Station in the World'.[6]

Temple

Temple station had been little-altered since it opened, apart from a modest platform extension at the west end and closure of the steam engines at the pump house when electricity became available. After electrification, the mean station building struggled to handle growing traffic and failed to present the modern attractive image the new order required. Nor was the air-space used to good effect. The result was that in 1912 a new station building was erected next door, occupying the corner site on the Victoria Embankment and extending into the old station area when it had been vacated.

The new frontage took up the whole western edge of the passageway between The Approach and Victoria Embankment with the station entrance in the centre and flanking shops. The frontage curved around the corner where there was a second entrance onto the embankment. The exterior was finished in Portland stone blocks.

At the same time, the central open section over the platforms was roofed over and a long, low building in the same style as the station was constructed over the whole of the site, nearly to the western end of the station, incorporating the building already erected on the north side. The embankment frontage presented seventeen bays divided by barely-projecting pilasters, nearly all enclosing semi-circular arched windows in the stone panels except where there entrances to the building or the station. Owing to the restrictive clauses in the 1864 Act, a new Act was required to make the alterations and powers were granted in 1910; this authorized the new building over the tracks and preserved the obligation for the much-enlarged roof terrace to be open to the public (as it still is). As before, the whole arrangement barely rose above the level of The Approach. The Partington Advertising Company occupied the whole of the enlarged over-platforms building for many years.*

The new station building was much larger and better-arranged than previously. Internally, both way in and adjacent exit stairs led to the westbound platform whilst there were way in stairs only to the eastbound and a quite separate way out route that led directly outside the station (in exactly the position where they had been in the old station). These were probably only used during rush hours as a separate ticket collector would have been required.

* Partington's poster business thrived until 1966 when it became part of the London & Provincial Group, later acquired by Reed. In turn this poster business became part of London and Continental in 1985 and Mills and Allen in 1987. The goodwill now vests with Messrs JC Decaux.

Blackfriars

Blackfriars station had been little altered since opening in 1870 although some changes were made at about the time steam was eliminated, described earlier. After electrification, congested parts needed attention, causing work to be carried out during 1913. The District station then consisted of a street level ticket hall on the approach to the bridge and behind this, to the east, was a great deal of ugly bridge-work where the LCDR tracks crossed the District platforms, though there had not actually been a main line station here until 1886 when St Pauls station was opened.* St Pauls was connected via a tortuous passageway to the District's Blackfriars station, immediately underneath, and this had opened on 13th November 1886.

By 1913 it was found necessary to make some improvements. On the westbound platform there was only one set of stairs, which were inconveniently located and restricted the platform width where it was particularly busy. These led up to a bridge (to the ticket hall) and it was possible to rearrange this so separate ascending and descending stairs came down to the platform, each set back to provide more space, and the old stairs were taken away. An opening was then made in the wall at the head of the stairs at the south end of the passage and a new subway installed leading to the existing connection with the LCDR station (a small ticket office being put in at the same time for interchange traffic).

Mansion House

The layout inherited from the 1884 rebuilding at Mansion House was thoroughly objectionable, with the bay roads either side of the through roads (so that any reversing move interrupted through services in at least one direction) and there was much redundant pointwork following withdrawal of steam operation. When the LNWR service was cut back (to Earls Court) at the end of 1908 the District reconstructed the entire south side of the station by removing the south siding and bay and widening the island platform considerably to fill part of the vacated space. The westbound line was rerouted around the southern face of the new island and the track alongside the northern face became a bay road, which, being between the running lines, avoided fouling movements. A metal gantry-type footbridge was added at the west end of the platforms to assist eastbound passengers arriving in the centre bay to cross over to the eastbound platform. The track rearrangement was completed on 15th January 1911 and most of the rest of the work in May.[7]

The rebuilding of the platform and rerouting of the westbound line made it impossible to retain the original gallery and passenger access, which had to be moved somewhat to the west where the platform was widest. The only way to connect access steps to the ticket hall was by means of a huge bridge crossing the intervening tracks on the skew and connecting with the existing route to the ticket hall at the top of the steps to the eastbound platform. The bridge had a span of 90ft, was 13ft wide and of plate girder construction. In turn this involved replacing a long length of standard umbrella roofing with an entirely new roof 15ft high. As if this was not complex enough at this congested site, another complication was the need to disturb some columns supporting the substation, built across the route of the altered westbound tracks at the east end and which involved the provision of new columns and girders without disturbing any of the substation equipment.

* St Pauls (LCDR) station was not renamed Blackfriars until 1937.

There were also alterations to the station entrance. In 1910 the City of London Corporation was concerned about the number of street accidents near Mansion House station and concluded that it should build a system of subways under the roadway, a matter of great difficulty owing to the mass of gas, water, electric and telegraph cables and sewers already occupying the space. Nevertheless they pressed ahead and the network of tiled subways with steel-troughed roofs was formally opened by the Lord Mayor on 2nd December 1913. In June 1912, the District agreed to create a new and enlarged booking hall below the existing one into which the new subways would link. The new ticket hall extended beyond the old property line and under the Great Trinity Lane, increasing the width available, and made a seamless connection with the existing station passages passing beneath Great Trinity Lane. The work was completed during 1913 and the street level space vacated was used as an extension to Messrs Spiers and Pond's restaurant. At the same time a tearoom and a relief exit to the south side of the station were built, both linked to the long overbridge serving the westbound platform.[8]

City Lines stations

The City Lines stations also required attention between 1909 and 1914, despite being more recent than many of the District ones. Again the need was for a more efficient layout and exploitation of the commercial potential. Cannon Street already had a ticket hall below road level, under the main line station forecourt, but the steps down from the street had been installed in a rather ugly block-like building between the two stairways

Station reconstruction at Monument resulted in a smaller entrance from King William Street comprising a stairway to a low level ticket hall. A tearoom uses the remaining part of old entrance and ground floor. This image 1916 (there is a small notice right of entrance about air raids). LTM

Mark Lane station was rebuilt, by Sherrin, on more spacious lines which allowed for lucrative over-station development at a prominent location. Most of the superstructure work was completed in 1911. The building (further extended) still stands. Capital Transport collection

to the main line station; there was a much smaller entrance round the side in Dowgate Hill. The solution here was to provide a much wider stairway entrance to the below-ground booking hall, with entrance canopy above, and rearrange the rest of the frontage to form flanking shops.

At Monument the usual formula was applied by installing a basement-level booking hall located near the old one. The entrance from King William Street was modified to incorporate stairs down in one half and a shop in the other; the Fish Street Hill entrance was unchanged apart from the internal passages.

Mark Lane station was poorly laid out and commanded a valuable site so an entirely new station building was designed. Stage one comprised a single storey corner block in Portland stone with rows of arched windows along the two street frontages. A station entrance was installed in one of the bays along the Great Tower Street frontage* and (unusually) the ticket office was installed at ground floor level. Wide stairways led down to the basement level from which stairs led directly to the eastbound platform and two footbridges leading to the stairs to the westbound platform. The new station was designed by George Sherrin.[9] Stage two comprised a five-storey commercial office block by Delissa Joseph that seamlessly incorporated the existing work but added entrances to the superstructure at each end.† Most of this building was in use in 1911 but it was extended at the rear in 1922.

* This section of the Great Tower Street spur was renamed Byward Street in 1910.

† This building still stands and still looks perfectly in keeping with the area. The station itself was resited in 1967. The main entrance to the superstructure had the name Mark Lane Station Buildings prominently incised into the mock stone arch over the entrance, but in recent years this had been removed.

On closure of the District station entrance at Whitechapel to effect economies, all traffic was handled via the interconnected ELR station entrance next door. Signage is heavily influenced by Underground practice but the other railways entitled to use Whitechapel promoted their own services on poster space. LTM

The station at Aldgate East was rebuilt and enlarged in 1913/4 and was another to receive a two-storeyed faience front with the names of the more important destinations appearing in raised letters in the tilework near the flat top with further names on the outside of the solid roof balustrade. The building was designed by the District's architect, Harry Ford, and was erected around a steel frame. The frontage was arranged in three bays with large windows on the upper floor; one lower bay formed the station entrance, the other two were retail with the central bay including access to the upper storey. The name 'Metropolitan and District Railways' was to have been ornately arranged in an arched tablet mounted in the centre of the roof but when the tablet was installed it had only the word 'Underground' following the curve of the arch and 'M&DR' in the centre.[10]

Beautifying the Scenery

A feature that came to typify open air sections of the Underground was begun by the District in 1909. This was the deliberate planting by permanent way staff of shrubs and bushes along the banks of cuttings, making them more interesting to the casual viewer looking out of the carriage windows. The main reason for this type of planting was to strengthen the slopes and prevent erosion, a job these plants did well. This was followed in 1918 by the controlled planting of small fruit trees, which added further interest. As this initiative was useful and required managing, a nursery was started in 1919, based on cuttings from existing plants, and this provided stocks of plants for future expansion (the planting of shrubs was later extended to the open parts of tube lines).[11]

At about the same time as official planting of trees and shrubs was taken in hand, the District began encouraging the staff at its outdoor stations to create and maintain station gardens in approved locations to make them more attractive. This was promoted by an annual station gardens competition in which stations that were nominated for a prize were visited by a number of senior managers (often with their wives) and prizes were awarded for the best ones, the prizes being sufficient to engage further interest (in 1913 some £37 prize money was made available, the highest single prizes being £5). Staff were given assistance to start a garden, five shillings being made available for seeds and the like with the company providing things like stone edging. From the extensive photographic records taken at these events it is clear that many hours must have been spent attending gardens, some of them quite large and ornate. Some staff were most innovative and found spaces even in central London stations where shafts of sunlight could support some kind of flower bed (Mansion House and St James's Park enjoyed small flower beds where track had been removed). The awards were made not necessarily for the best gardens, but the best given the site conditions. Staff could also cultivate gardens of the kitchen garden type (and then make their own use of the produce) but vegetables were frowned on. This initiative did much to brighten up the atmosphere at stations and gave them a welcoming appearance.[12]

Changes at Lillie Bridge

When the District's shifted its rolling stock maintenance from Lillie Bridge to Mill Hill Park because of electrification it released space at the former sufficient for a tube depot for the new Piccadilly tube. Agreement was reached for the land to be leased to the Piccadilly and the UERL constructed a quarter-mile long 6-road car shed along the eastern edge, each road stabling up to four trains. At the south end of the shed was a small workshop to facilitate running repairs, but it was always expected that heavy work and repainting would be done at Mill Hill Park. Although the shed was only to be used by tube stock it was built to District gauge. The shed was only just ready when the Piccadilly tube opened on 12th December 1906 and a temporary shed had to be thrown up at South Harrow to store the new cars as they arrived that autumn as there was not room to store them at Mill Hill Park depot where they were being fitted out.

This arrangement meant that when the Piccadilly opened a large number of empty train movements had to be made by Piccadilly trains between West Kensington and Barons Court; these were not very convenient but were arranged to minimize delays to District services. The Piccadilly trains entering service had to negotiate a single-line connection between the depot and the east end of West Kensington station then run through the station on the eastbound line before they could gain access to connection with the Piccadilly's transfer sidings at the west end—all highly inconvenient, and only a little less so when stabling trains came the other way.

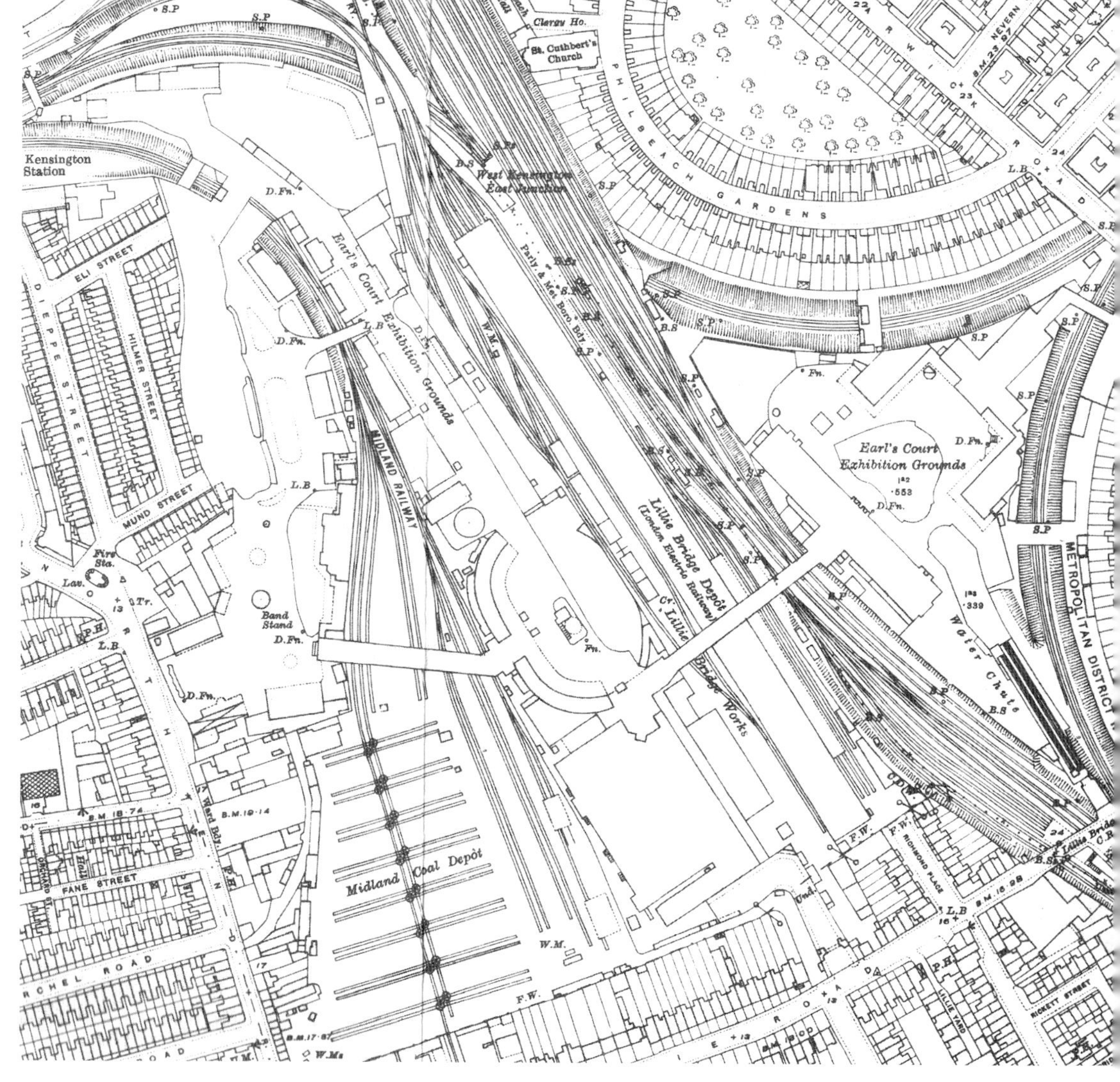

This map shows the area around Lillie Bridge before the Great War. The remains of the Exhibition grounds are obvious in the triangular area and to the west of Lillie Bridge works. The Midland goods yard occupies much land to the west. Lillie Bridge works is now a small engineering depot for the District Railway and much of the old District land is occupied by the Piccadilly's massive car shed. Author's collection

The remainder of the site at Lillie Bridge was retained by the District and converted into engineering workshops, mainly for track and signalling maintenance and ballast trains usually began and finished their overnight journeys here. To support the operation of ballast trains, and for shunting in the yard, the District retained six of its steam locomotives, but only two were still serviceable in 1909. One of these, No 33, was scrapped in 1925 and replaced by a similar locomotive purchased from the Metropolitan Railway.* District loco No 34 was fitted with a cab in 1927 and survived, with the former Met loco, until 1932. For some years six of the steam carriages were retained as stores vehicles and also kept at Lillie Bridge, occasionally venturing out in the charge of a steam locomotive to make deliveries to stations and depots.

* This had been Met loco No 22, but was numbered 35 in the District fleet. 34 and 35 became L34 and L35 in 1931. The other locomotives initially retained but soon scrapped were Nos 27, 35, 36 and 39.

Changes at Lots Road

In 1910, once the financial hiatus had settled down, another attempt was made to fuse the three UERL tube lines into a single company to reduce administration and harmonize the statutory obligations. This time the proposal received the blessing of the various interested parties and was authorized by the London Electric Railway Act 1910. The mechanism was to vest the Hampstead tube and Bakerloo tube in the Piccadilly tube and rename it the London Electric Railway. It made little difference at a practical level but for the purposes of this book the new company will be referred to as the LER and the three components will be called the Hampstead Line, Bakerloo Line and Piccadilly Line, which is how they were portrayed to the public.

The new arrangement acquired early importance because the LER (with the District) soon became more intimately involved with the supply of power. The UERL was immensely proud of its Lots Road power house. Costing about £1,500,000 it was one of the finest in the country, at least when the replacement Parsons turbines were all installed. Output had risen to about 157MWh a year but ultimate capacity was 500MWh and the equipment now worked most satisfactorily.

During 1911, power house ownership and control was re-arranged. The change was ostensibly made because the UERL, which owned the power house, was not a statutory company and in theory could dispose of part or all of its interest in a very valuable site, leaving the operating companies unable to obtain electricity (this eventuality was not considered likely, but there were circumstances that could arise where the power station might become vulnerable). In addition there were business reasons why the rearrangement was thought advantageous. The UERL explained to shareholders that in view of the financial pressure on the company the power station was more useful if converted to liquid assets (ie cash) in order to relieve the financial burden upon it. Giving the operating companies more direct control also seemed likely to assist them so the sale would therefore be beneficial to all parties.[13] What was proposed was a statutory joint committee of the District and London Electric Railway with the object of buying the power station from the UERL and then leasing it to the two railways jointly for 999 years for a rent.[14]

Upon the bill receiving the Royal Assent the joint committee was established and authorized to issue a perpetual stock called the Met District and LER joint power house rent charge stock, of which £2.2m was issued with perpetual interest of 4 per cent. The sum raised created a surplus over the cost of Lots Road which was intended to redeem the whole £1 million of first power house debentures secured by the generating station. What was left was used to redeem some of the 4½% 1993 bonds, reducing them from £2,800,000 to £1,600,000.[15]

When the District's bill was originally submitted to the 1911 Session Lots Road had much greater capacity than was required at that time and the District sought powers to supply electricity in bulk to any electrical distribution company needing a supply. London had a large number of very small power stations at that time and many of them were quite inefficient and supplied only small areas. There was already a move for local electricity suppliers to buy supplies in bulk from larger and more efficient stations to top up or replace existing small generating plant. The London electricity generators were horrified by the thought that railway companies should muscle in on their business and sell them cheap electricity and furious opposition was mustered from which the District had to retreat.

Nevertheless the District (on behalf of its associated companies) had a legitimate reason to involve itself with the North Metropolitan Electric Power Supply Company which generated power to operate the Metropolitan Electric Tramways and already had powers to distribute electricity in a number of districts and to sell electricity in bulk to distribution companies, which it came to do on a very large scale. The power supply company was owned by the Metropolitan Electric Tramways to which it also supplied all the traction power, but further expansion offered the possibility of Lots Road providing assistance. Accordingly, powers to supply electricity in bulk to the power supply company were sought in both the District's and LER's bills for the 1912 Session but the provision was again not authorized. In the same bill authority was sought, this time successfully, to supply electricity in bulk to the Richmond (Surrey) Electric Light and Power Company and a high-voltage supply was quickly provided (the electric lighting company had it in mind to close its own power station in due course).[16]

By 1911 Lots Road usage was also approaching its installed maximum capacity, which made it difficult to enhance train services. The war provided a brief respite, but as time progressed services were placed under great stress and making extra power available had to be part of the solution.

So far as the equipment was concerned, the eighth and last of the 6kW Parsons turbines actually came into service only in 1911.[17] Another turbine by Parsons, this time of 15MW, was installed in 1915. A little later it was hoped to install another one but the company had great difficulty here owing to wartime restrictions. A 'priority certificate' for the extra set was sought from the Ministry of Munitions in March 1917 but this was refused and only finally obtained in December 1918. The machine was being manufactured in mid-1919 and expected to be installed later that year but the circumstances at the end of the war were very difficult and the generator (described as Parsons-Metropolitan Vickers) was not in fact ready till 1921. It was similar in power to the earlier one but operated at 2000rpm, double the speed of all the earlier machines. To support this extra capacity the number of boilers was increased to 68.

When new tube works were authorized under the government-supported scheme in 1922 a third 15MW set was obtained, though it was not commissioned until 1925. When these additions were finished, the total capacity of the station had increased to 93MW, though each of the 15MW generators could safely deliver 18MW on overload if required to do so for brief periods. In 1924 (before the third 15MW set was available) the railways explained that on a normal day the maximum load was 61MW and this was produced by the two large sets which ran most of the time, together with between two and five of the older 6MW sets as required. At night, when no trains were running, only one of the old sets was employed.[18]

During the 1921 coal strike 16 boilers were converted to oil burning using the Scarab system which avoided rebuilding, but they were converted back after the emergency.[19] It was during this coal strike that the remaining coal fired boilers were obliged to make use of inferior coal, which was all that could be obtained. During the evening of 18th June the poor steaming gave rise to a shortage of steam which caused the whole station to shut down at 6.25pm stranding many trains in tunnels. Fortunately it was possible to resume supplies after just half an hour.[20]

Dedicated Track to Turnham Green

Between Turnham Green and Ravenscourt Park the District's electric trains still operated over manually-signalled LSWR tracks that carried main line trains between Richmond and the WLR and GWR trains between Richmond and Ladbroke Grove (the GWR had taken this service over from the Met when the Hammersmith & City was electrified); these trains, all steam-hauled, became a real source of delay to the District and required action of the kind deferred in 1903. The District's traffic manager observed that flat junctions existed at both Studland Road and Turnham Green and whilst the timetables were carefully devised to avoid conflicts irregular running of both District and LSWR trains meant that in practice delays were inevitable and where trains arrived at converging junctions simultaneously one of them could be delayed by up to five minutes. In practice the District could not work more than ten trains an hour.

With demand increasing, the only way forward was to duplicate the lines in order to give the District a clear route of its own upon which automatic signalling could be used without the complication of a mixed train service. During 1909 a widening scheme was devised that dealt with the problem of getting the LSWR tracks, which were on the north side at Studland Road, onto the south side of the District's Ealing lines before reaching Chiswick. Because of the availability of land, the only place where this could be done was west of Turnham Green where the LSWR lines towards Richmond were on a descending gradient and by raising the Ealing line embankment it would be possible to pass the LSWR tracks beneath it.

The consulting engineer concluded that the stage-works required to keep the railway functioning throughout, and other areas of uncertainty, would make it very difficult to get realistic tenders and the conclusion was that the LSWR should carry out the work itself. The District obtained the necessary powers in its 1910 Act whilst the LSWR acquired the land and constructed the works at its own cost, estimated at £286,377. The District continued to pay for its agreed running rights and, in addition, a sum equivalent to 4 per cent of the actual construction cost. When the works were completed, the District had the exclusive use of the southern (electrified) pair of tracks between Studland Road and Turnham Green.

At Ravenscourt Park and Turnham Green, the stations were entirely reconstructed in several stages, the existing wooden side platforms becoming concrete-clad islands with new canopies, entrances and exits. The existing alignments were retained through the platforms and the opportunity was taken to replace the double-line bridges at each end. Space was obtained for new tracks to be run round the outer sides of the islands and these all required extra single-line bridges to be installed. Between stations it was more convenient to widen on one side or the other (and more land was acquired on the south side because it was cheaper). Between stations new double line bridges were added on the widened side. An interesting situation arose at The Avenue, Ravenscourt Park, where there had been an iron bridge where the trains created a lot of noise; the widening work provided the opportunity to deal with the problem (which was causing a park ranger living next to it many sleepless nights). A steel bridge was looked at for the new lines but finally it was agreed that a large elliptically-arched brick bridge carrying all four lines would be the best solution as it was practically noiseless, Hammersmith Council agreeing to the reduced headroom. At Prebend Gardens there was already an elliptically-arched brick bridge and this was widened along each side in similar style.

The District desired a new station at Goldhawk Road and it was convenient to buy the whole of the extra land along the south side of the old viaduct to the west of that road, a smart red-brick station building being constructed of similar proportions to the semi-detached villas along this section. At viaduct level a new island platform was installed virtually identical to the others. The station was called Stamford Brook when opened and though LSWR freehold was always staffed by the District. The other two stations, in much modified form, remained staffed by the LSWR and the single booking offices sold tickets for all the companies using the stations.

The works east of the bridge over the old Hammersmith and Chiswick railway yard were entirely on viaduct, the widened sections having to be pinned to the old parts. In the

Above: **Work taking place on the LSWR widening west of Fishers Lane bridge where work is in hand to construct a temporary ramp from the Richmond tracks (right) onto the existing District formation on left. View looks towards Turnham Green (station footbridge just visible).** Capital Transport collection

Below: **Looking towards Chiswick this shows the Fishers Lane bridge in foreground and temporary rerouting of District towards Ealing climbing up side of embankment so work could take place installing bridges further east. Line to Gunnersbury dead ahead. Note temporary signal box.** Author's collection

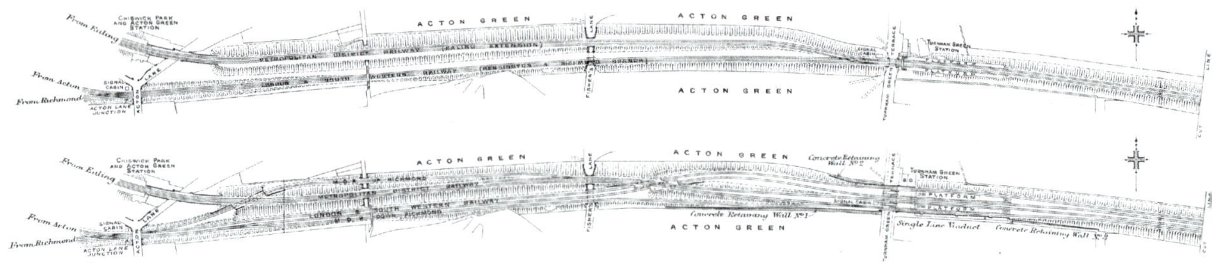

Diagram showing Chiswick-Hammersmith widening scheme WESTERN END. Author's collection

Studland Road area, matters were complicated by the crowded road arrangements there and the opportunity was again taken to replace some existing bridges. This required Studland Road Junction to be replaced by a temporary junction close by and the moving by 18 inches of the signal box to the north to obtain the required clearances; this was tricky and required the disconnection of all the rodding, supporting the box and jacking it to the new position, then connecting everything up in the new position. The object was to finish the civil engineering required and move the two tracks in use, in stages, to the new position on the north side and then lay in so far as possible the two extra tracks on the south side to await commissioning.

At the west end, the whole of the line was on embankment and though some extra land was obtained for widening there were other places where stout retaining walls were required with the space behind backfilled to obtain the wider width at track level. At Turnham Green it was felt the foundations of the new platforms could not be supported by the embankment and very deep footings were installed dropping into the original ground below. The work was difficult and required stage-working with the existing tracks at various times re-routed around both of the formative islands.

The old junction west of Turnham Green was not conveniently located for the various stage-works needed (nineteen track layout alterations were required in all) and it was impossible to raise the height of the District's embankment with trains running. The junction was therefore shifted west, to a point just beyond Fisher's Lane bridge and a ramp inserted into the side of the District's embankment which

Poster advertising the train service improvements following the widening of lines between Hammersmith and Turnham Green, 1911. This view looks west with the District's electrified tracks on left. LTM

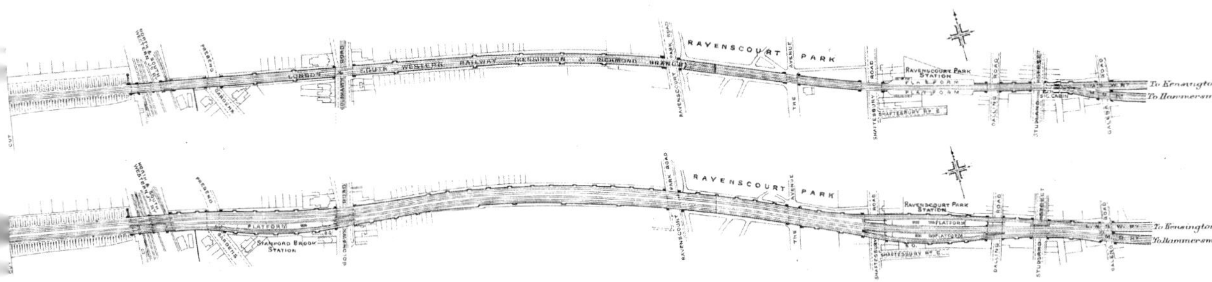

Diagram showing Chiswick-Hammersmith widening scheme EASTERN END. Author's collection

rose at 1:45 until it reached the top where District tracks were slewed south to make the end on connection. With the section to the east now cleared of trains as far as Turnham Green Terrace the embankment was raised to the point where the new bridge over the LSWR was required and then dropped down again to its original level near the road bridge. Meanwhile all traffic was diverted by what had become the new southern island and west of the northern island a new embankment was built dropping down to about 10ft above ground level with the new trackbed installed underneath the new District bridge. The new alignment met the old just east of Fishers Lane, but was not yet brought into use. Farther west the plan was for the up District trains to divert from the old route near Acton Lane and plunge through the Ealing viaduct rising up to make a flying junction with the up line from Ealing. This was difficult work given it was done with no interruption to the service and that the tracks on the Ealing line had to be supported while an arched subway was built beneath on a skew.

Bringing the new lines into use presented challenges as it was desired to achieve the linking-up overnight, without disturbing scheduled train services. At the east end the temporary Studland Road junction had to come out and the existing signal box (which was now in the way) had to be demolished before the District line, emerging up the incline, could be joined up to the new lines. The work at the west end was much more difficult. On the night of the changeover, the temporary incline went out of use and it was necessary to deposit several hundred yards of filling to bring the embankment level up to the new work. This was done by bringing in train loads of ashes as soon as the last Ealing train had passed. This having been done, new track was laid to link up the existing tracks to the west with the new embankment and flyover to the east where track and signalling had already been installed. All was completed before the first train was due.[21]

The new tracks came into use on 3rd December 1911 and the new station at Stamford Brook on 1st February 1912. Although only the southern pair of tracks were electrified and used by the District all four tracks remained LSWR property. New automatic signalling was brought into use on the electric tracks as far as Turnham Green (the Ealing branch beyond was already automatic). The new junctions between the District's Ealing and Richmond lines were controlled from an electro-pneumatic power frame operated by District signalmen but the points and signals along the whole of the LSWR lines was all mechanical. The dedicated LSWR line west of Turnham Green was double track all the way to Acton Lane and what became the down District line towards Richmond ran parallel west of Fishers Lane along the south side, only making a junction near Acton Lane. This provided a lengthy section of lay-by where a District could wait out of the way if an LSWR Richmond train was already signalled. The completion of this work allowed District services more or less to be doubled overnight.

This view is from Fishers Lane bridge after widening complete. Ahead is Turnham Green station looking along the old route to Richmond (now 'down' District). The rerouted LSWR tracks pass underneath the flyover where the raised District route to Ealing passes across, District train in view. Author's collection

Turnham Green 'down' junction after widening complete. On right are rerouted LSWR lines diving under the newly-raised District embankment on the Ealing route. The old (now District only) route towards Gunnersbury is on left. Author's collection

At Acton Lane can be seen the new 'up' District track piercing the old District embankment to form a junction for westbound trains from Richmond. The old LSWR route from Richmond is dead ahead. The two unelectrified tracks dive under the District further east, the electrified line on right carries District trains to Richmond. Author's collection

Above: **This view of Turnham Green station shows the old station, with its characteristic footbridge, before widening work was undertaken.** Author's collection

Below: **This image is taken from a similar viewpoint to the earlier image but after widening was completed. Visible is the northern new flanking bridge, requiring the abutments to be much widened. The new platforms are obvious, together with the large running-in board. The station building is (for the moment) little altered.** Capital Transport collection

London & South Western Electrification

In 1913 the LSWR decided to electrify some of its London inner suburban lines. The system adopted was influenced by the existing inter-running with the District's system but the LSWR decided on a 3-rail system with running rail return. This nevertheless required the positive rail to be located in the same position as the District if problems were not to arise where trains inter-ran.

The section of LSWR between East Putney and Wimbledon was already electrified to District standards with two conductor rails embodying an insulated return. In order for LSWR trains to work along this section the running rails had to be bonded to the negative return rail, which was thereby brought to earth potential. In turn this meant that this section of line had to be separated from the District's main electrification system since it was not desired generally to earth the negative rails. Moreover the systems had to be separated in a way where no train could bridge these two different systems. The most convenient place to do this was across the Thames bridge at Putney where a length of conductor rail on each track slightly longer than a whole train was disconnected, the idea being that a train would coast over this neutral section. Arrangements had to be made to feed the dead section from the section ahead if a train did manage to stall on the neutral

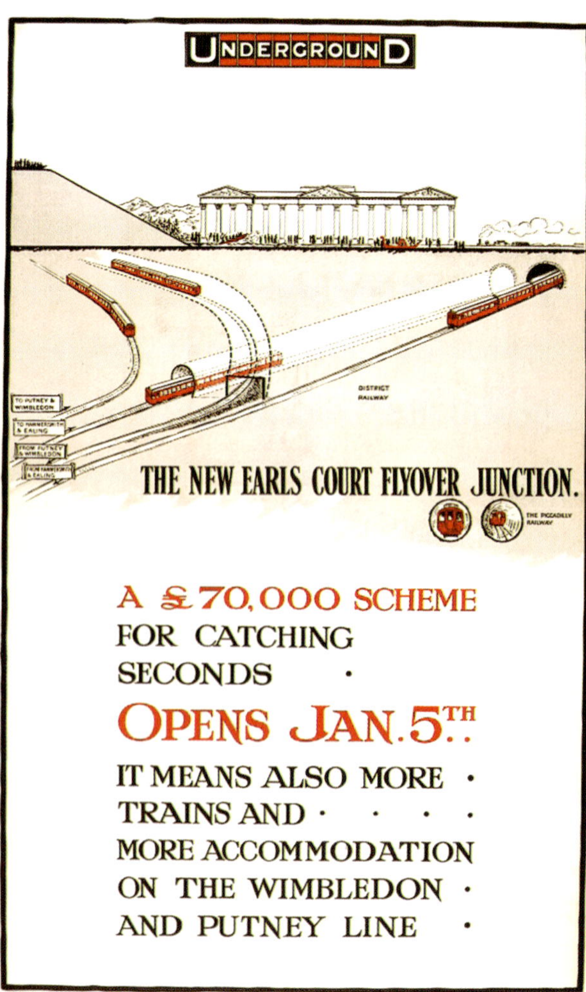

The District was very proud of its new flyover west of Earls Court and was keen to explain how it would improve services, as this poster shows. Author's collection

section. This change also required division of the supplies in Putney Bridge substation to avoid the main section of the District becoming earthed. The first LSWR electric train operated in service via East Putney on 25th October 1915.[22] The same problem fortunately did not arise on the Gunnersbury-Richmond line where LSWR electric trains were not expected to operate.

Improvements at Earls Court

At the west end of Earls Court the westbound Hammersmith and eastbound Putney lines crossed on the level, which was a source of delay. As there was plenty of room, and the District owned the land, a flying junction was installed. The conflicting routes were shifted west and the eastbound line from Putney carried over the westbound to Hammersmith. The double track formations on the old routes were retained to provide

The new flyover arrangement west of Earls Court involved the Westbound line to Hammersmith diving underneath a new eastbound line from Putney. This construction image, near the point of intersection, shows the large elliptical brick-built tunnel required to accommodate the District trains. *Railway Magazine* December 1913

a loop for westbound trains on the Putney line, while the eastbound line from Addison Road was carried to a point just outside Earls Court before it joined the line from Hammersmith (this arrangement endures today).

The new westbound line was actually constructed in a large elliptical brick tunnel about 1300ft long and broken only at the point where it was crossed by the new eastbound line, which was at that time all in the open air. The new works were introduced in stages, the last of which was commissioned in January 1914.

At Earls Court the tracks through the two eastbound platforms converged immediately east of the station before throwing off the connection to the siding. This became a source of significant congestion and from 1914 a direct connection was put in between the local platform and the siding to allow a train to enter the siding without delaying a service train on the eastbound main; this mainly assisted reversing LNWR trains and more or less coincided with the LNWR trains becoming electrically operated, covered shortly.

East London Railway Electrification

It was in July 1905 when the through East London trains from District destinations to New Cross ceased. The joint committee had not been prepared to fund electrification as the extra traffic seemed unlikely to pay for it (it was hoped most through passengers would change trains at Whitechapel, even if they grumbled). From 1906, therefore, the East London train service was operated on behalf of the committee by the LBSCR. GER trains operated to and from Liverpool Street to New Cross (LBSCR) and until 30th June 1911 some of these went to New Croydon. LBSCR trains operated to New Cross (and, until 1st December 1909, Peckham Rye) and SECR trains operated between Whitechapel and New Cross (SE) station.

It may come as no surprise that when the through trains to and from the ELR were withdrawn, many passengers avoided the awkward change at Whitechapel and the traffic on the ELR fell even more rapidly. The efficient and frequent electric trains serving the District station only served to highlight the unfavourable conditions downstairs where only infrequent steam trains were offered. These relatively poor travelling conditions encouraged the transfer of some traffic to the new motor buses and electric trams and it was reported that ELR traffic had more than halved by 1912.

The joint committee realized that electrification was essential, whatever the cost, but there was a new factor now since the LBSCR (one of the lessees) had embarked on its own scheme of electrification, which began operation in December 1909. The LBSCR used an overhead system at 6600 volts single-phase alternating current. The question now arose whether it would be better to use the same system on the ELR, opening up the possibility of running through electric trains to and from the LBSCR system. However the technology was entirely incompatible with the District and Met system using conductor rails. Even as early as the end of 1908 the committee was being told that the LBSCR system had exceeded expected costs and installation time and it was not yet possible to say whether it would cost more or less than the equivalent steam service. This provided further opportunity for the ELR to delay doing anything, the substantial losses having to be made good equally by the lessees. It was eventually conceded that there was not the headroom to install a suitable design of catenary for the overhead system.[23]

The joint committee finally accepted that immediate electrification was vital if losses were not going to get even worse. Work was put in hand in 1911, the GER agreeing to provide the funding, the Met agreeing to find and operate the trains and the District agreeing to provide the power, from Lots Road. The cost of electrification was £77,591 and the GER charged 4% interest on this to the committee.

Electrified operation began 30th March 1913, but only between Shoreditch and both of the stations at New Cross (this became known as the local service). In addition, the Met re-instated through trains from the northern side of the Inner Circle, initially from the terminal platform at South Kensington but from 9th February 1914 it was instead the practice that about half of the Hammersmith & City trains ran between Hammersmith and New Cross. The through service was useful for District passengers who could change between District and Met trains at Aldgate East or St Mary's, where they served the same platforms, rather than at Whitechapel where it involved a trek via the ticket hall. It also maintained a through service from Liverpool Street following the cutting back to Shoreditch of the old route, which was never a very useful place to turn round the trains (the GER had no capacity at Liverpool Street to entertain more than the previous moth-eaten service). Train services varied but typically through trains operated every 15 minutes, alternately to what from 9th July 1923 had become New Cross and New Cross Gate stations, supplemented by local trains at 5- or 10-minute intervals to give a combined 5-minute service along the core section of the line.

For this to be possible it was necessary to install automatic signalling with track circuiting, and the McKenzie & Holland all-electric system recently installed on the Met was deployed here as well, the existing signal boxes being retained and adapted to operate the signals where there were junctions and crossovers. Semaphore signals (some converted to electric operation) were retained along the open air sections but two-aspect colour light signals were installed in the tunnels. All the points remained mechanically operated. A new substation was constructed by the District at Surrey Docks (as Deptford Road had become) and a pair of high tension feeder cables connected this with the existing substation at Whitechapel.

Another useful piece of investment was the introduction of electric lifts at Wapping, which had rather deep platforms. Even so, the lifts could only be brought down to a landing immediately above the tracks and the historic lower flight of stairs had still to be negotiated by those entering and leaving. In 1921 the joint committee ceded day to day responsibility for running the line entirely to the Met, which ran it on the committee's behalf. In 1925, the government accepted that the East London fell into the Southern Railway's sphere of influence following the Railways Act amalgamation scheme and supported transfer of the East London Railway Company to the Southern under its 1925 Act. This made no practical difference to day-to-day operations as the joint committee had a perpetual lease. The District's interest therefore remained until transferred to London Transport in 1933, so the ELR usually appeared on District publicity even though direct trains did not operate.

Chapter Seven

TRAIN SERVICE DEVELOPMENT

Train Frequencies

The train services were operating at a maximum rate of 34 trains an hour through the central area by 1910, but further increases were then constrained by infrastructure shortcomings, including constraints beyond the District's borders. One of these was eased from 1st January 1911, from which day the GWR withdrew its paths between the Hammersmith & City Railway and Richmond along the LSWR 2-track section west of Studland Road. These paths were quickly taken up by the District, enabling it to improve its own services through the central area to 38 trains an hour. When additional cars had been delivered, and the Hammersmith-Chiswick widening had been completed from 3rd December 1911, the general superintendent, the enterprising Mr Blake, arranged for a much enhanced timetable to come into use from 11th December. At last, a 40 trains an hour service came into use between South Kensington and Mansion House.[1]

The two extra tracks, together with automatic signalling, also enabled much heavier services to operate west of Hammersmith and the following service enhancements were announced by the press just before the new services began:

Route	Existing trains/day	Revised trains/day
Ealing	119	198
Hounslow	121	135
South Harrow	68	92
Richmond	68	70
Turnham Green	200	270

The main beneficiary was clearly the busy Ealing Broadway service (with enhanced connecting trains on the branches) but Richmond scarcely benefited as it remained entirely in the hands of the LSWR and its mechanical signalling and shared line capacity with steam-hauled North London trains. In addition to the increased frequencies, run times were also improved.[2]

Train Length

Peak hour electric trains on the main part of the District were at first seven cars long, but from January 1906 these were gradually reduced to six cars, both formations operating until December 1907 when 6-car trains were the longest operated.[3] There then followed a period when the District aggressively sought to match demand against the capacity of individual trains, running no more cars than was necessary and successfully reducing car mileage whilst passenger numbers were going up. This resulted in trains of widely varying length appearing.

The District was very proud to explain that between the end of 1905 and the end of 1906 train mileage had increased from 1,031,103 miles to 1,179,495 (up 14.3%) whilst car mileage had dropped from 5,836,474 miles to 5,195,487 (down 10.9%); this was achieved

W.E. Blake. LTM

by reducing average train length by about a quarter. This increased earning per car mile from 5.25d to 6.84d. The District really was trying hard to improve efficiency.[4]

In December 1907, the busy hours main line trains were nearly all of six cars, with the exception of a few 5-car sets operating trains running partly non-stop at the western end of the line and described later. In the slack hours, the service was provided almost entirely by 3-car trains. By April 1908 busy hour trains were mainly 6-car with several 5-car sets and the odd 3-car set; these must have been rather inconvenient in a long, crowded platform and were eliminated in September. The slack hours service continued to be provided by 3-car trains. On Sunday evenings, 6-car trains were operated but earlier in the day many trains were just 3-car sets.[5]

Unless trains actually entered service as 3-car sets, the short trains were all formed by uncoupling three cars from the east end of the train at East Ham, Whitechapel, Parsons Green, Hammersmith and Ealing Broadway; the uncoupled portions were stored locally in sidings. A small number of trains coupled or uncoupled in Cromwell Depot. The 3-car portions remaining in service had a motor car at each end whilst the stabling portion had a motor car at only the outer end.

By January 1909, the slack hours main line service was operated almost entirely by 4-car sets. During the busy hours, most trains were 6-cars but some 7-car workings had reappeared and there were also a few 4-car trains; the few 5-car trains that had been running had been lengthened to six. After the busy hours, the detached portions to be stabled were of only two cars.

After various experiments, eight cars was identified as the maximum length west of Whitechapel and a few trains this long began operating from 1st October 1910, coinciding with service increases (one train this length operated from 1 June 1910).[6] By 1915 these were used on nearly all of the busiest trains. The operation of 8-car trains was a mixed blessing as platforms (while of varying length) could rarely accommodate more than seven cars west of Whitechapel. At first it was determined that, if the driver stopped accurately, only the first and rearmost set of double doors would be outside platform limits and passengers would get used to it. Certain stations (particularly in the open air) lent themselves to platform extension; at tunnel stations extension was sometimes possible but at first trains ran with the end doors locked. In due course narrow catwalks, about a half-car long, were installed into the tunnels at each end of the platforms and staff had to check they were clear of any passengers before trains moved off. These catwalks remained in everyday use until the late 1970s.

This shows a station where platforms have been extended into the tunnels in form of a catwalk (note the small nameplates in tunnel). These particular catwalks are quite short but at certain stations they might extend up to half a car. Author's collection

A Nine Car Train is Tried

In the June 1914 timetable another innovation was introduced to try and mitigate the effects of overcrowding. The 8.50am from Ealing Broadway was given a ninth car (a composite) which was dedicated solely to those travelling to Mansion House. Most platforms could not accommodate the ninth car, which remained in tunnel at the inner London stations, the occupants enjoying an undisturbed trip. At Mansion House the train stopped forward of its usual position so those in the rear car could alight, this car then ran empty. Meanwhile those in the front were warned the car would not 'stop' at Mansion House, but if anyone did want to get out staff ushered them into the next car via the communicating door.[7] The extra car had its own member of staff to supervise the operation and only picked up at Ealing Broadway, Acton Town, Turnham Green and Hammersmith. This innovation was not long lived as when war broke out it was not feasible to find the extra staff required. A proposal to extend the platform at Charing Cross so the train might call there as well was also shelved until after the war.[8]

Control Trailer Working

Ordinary service trains could be reduced in length either by detaching cars and stabling them or by dividing a train and leaving both portions in service. In all cases portions remaining in service, at first, had to have a motor car at each end as that was where the driving cab was situated. Portions stabling had to have at least one motor car to enable movement to or from a siding. These constraints quickly proved wasteful and inflexible and made the operation of very short trains awkward, although the middle motors could be used as single-car trains.

To improve flexibility, between 1906 and 1910 some 32 trailers of the 1905 stock (and all eight of the 1903 cars) were fitted with driving positions: designated 'control trailers' these could lead in a 2- or 3-car train where only one motor car was needed. This was easy to do as it only required installing master controllers and brake handles at car ends and connecting them up to the train wires and pipes already installed. The control equipment could be locked away when not in use so that there was minimal interference with passenger access and when not required as a driving vehicle a control trailer could be used as an ordinary trailer. At first these cars facilitated short train operation on the western branches. Of the converted cars, 21 had driving equipment at both ends and the balance had it at one end only. This provided considerable flexibility in possible train lengths with at some point every variation between a single car and eleven cars being operated.

It may be puzzling today the effort made after electrification to balance train lengths to prevailing demand. This affectation was pursued at first to keep costs at an absolute minimum but later because it postponed the need to buy additional cars. So-called 'control trailer working' was a complicated contribution to all this and arose because certain trains were particularly heavily loaded. Shortly after control trailers had become available, it was felt that these could be attached to busy trains for one or two trips then taken off again. Since these cars were unpowered, and could not move independently, this process was not straightforward.

'Control trailer working' began early in 1908 and the April 1908 timetable is illustrative. Three control trailers were involved and these were all allocated to Ealing Broadway. 'A' was attached at Ealing at about 10.30am when the 3-car east end portion was uncoupled and stabled (this portion was probably used to shunt the control trailer). The resulting 4-car train proceeded to Bow Road and back to Hammersmith, where the control trailer was uncoupled, the (now) 3-car train carried on to Richmond, departing 12.16pm. The control trailer was now attached to the following train and returned to Ealing, the extra car being at the front. This was shunted somewhere out of the way at Ealing by the service train during its 9-minute turnround. Car 'B' did something similar during the morning but was parked at Parsons Green at 12.24pm and used to strengthen a mid-evening train before stabling at Ealing. Car 'C' more or less replicated the movements of car 'A', but a few minutes later.

This is one of the 1903 stock cars after conversion to control trailer, a half-cab for the driver having been installed. Author's collection

As if this was not complicated enough, by January 1909 there were five control trailer cars meandering around, three based on Ealing and two from Hammersmith. The reintroduction of a few 7-car trains offered new creative opportunities. One early morning train came from Mill Hill Park depot as 6-cars and, on reaching Ealing Broadway, a standby motor car was added in the middle of the train so it left as a 7-car set. At 6.11pm this extra car was detached (from the middle) at Ealing and stabled there overnight to await the next day; the remaining 6-car train remained in service and stabled at East Ham. Another train added a middle motor and trailer pair at Ealing at 4.56pm as well as a control trailer to make up a 7-car set from what had been four cars. These came off at East Ham at 7.59. This complex working left three spent control trailers at Hammersmith which were added to a passing westbound 6-car train to be drawn back to Ealing in a 9-car formation with the added cars empty. How they were disposed of at Ealing is not explained.[9] The 1910 timetable shows 13 control trailers in operation and three middle motors and this method of operation had by now spread to Saturday operations.

Naturally this timetabling finesse was chaotic when the service was deranged and with a general lengthening of trains to meet continually rising traffic this form of working had been abandoned by 1914.

1903 Cars Modernized

When the 1903 trailers were converted to single-ended control trailers from 1906, a driving position was erected on the platform at one end of the cars, on the left hand side, and at the same time a small enclosed half-cab was installed to give the driver some weather protection. As with the new stock, this area could be used by passengers when not required by the driver. A number of other changes were also made to make them more compatible with the 1905 fleet. Improvements included replacement of the van Dorn couplers by the standard Ward coupler so the cars could couple with the main fleet if required; the air hoses were moved into the standard position at the same time. The shoegear, originally mounted at the outer end of the bogies, was reinstalled half way between the wheels and the end shoe-beams removed. The car bodies were also reinforced by aluminium sheeting that obscured the original matchboard finish.

1903 motor car after driving cab reconfigured and luggage compartment replaced by small first-class section.
Capital Transport collection

In February 1910 the District board resolved to equip all six of the 1903 motor cars with a small section containing eight first class seats, as it had not previously been possible to provide this accommodation on short trains, resulting in complaints and confusion.[10] Whilst this work was being done, the luggage compartments were removed from the end motor cars and the existing cab fronts were removed and a something similar to the 1905 cars was built up; the opportunity was taken to shift the driving controls to the left hand side at the same time. In 1911 the two 1903 middle motors were partitioned, presumably to offer smoking and non-smoking accommodation.[11] The middle motor driving positions were also moved to the left hand sides.

The Local Services

Perhaps conditioned by practice during steam days, from the beginning of electric operation the Hounslow, South Harrow and High Street Kensington to Putney (or Wimbledon) services were treated as self-contained shuttles known as 'local' trains (as opposed to the 'main line' service through central London).

In 1907 the South Harrow shuttle was being worked by two single-car trains providing a half-hour service. The Hounslow service was operated by three 2-car trains providing a 15-minute service but at busy times two more 2-car trains were available as well as a small number of through trains of normal length. The High Street shuttle service was operated by 6-car trains in the morning busy period then 2-car sets in the midday period (with some 3-car trains) and a mixture into the evening settling down to 2-car trains again.

A 1905 middle-motor car (No 203) working the Acton-Uxbridge local service around 1911. Obvious are the 'Entrance' signs over the end gangways, which were available to passengers except where the driver was making use of his half-cab. The train stands at Sudbury Town. Roy Allen collection

This 1909 poster was an early post-electrification attempt to promote traffic along the Hounslow branch but even after electrification the service was infrequent and often required a change at Acton Town. LTM

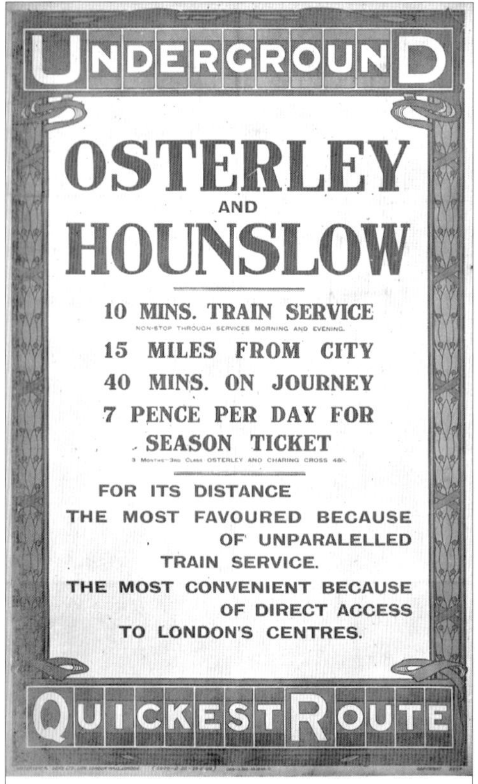

In 1909 the High Street service was 2-car during slack hours and 4-car at busy times (though odd trains were of other lengths). The South Harrow service was improved by reducing intervals to 20-minutes during what passed as the busy hours, with the odd return trip made up with a 2-car train. The Hounslow service also continued with two cars and some through trains. On both Hounslow and South Harrow services many trains only called at intermediate stations by request.

By about 1912 the District standardized on 6-car or 8-car trains for main line service in the busy hours whilst the local trains could be any length between one and six cars depending on which branch and at what time of day they were being used. In the slack hours the usual train length through central London was four cars.

Non Stop Trains (Barking Line)

The term non-stop became a feature of electric operation, though it was a bit misleading as most non-stop trains only missed a few stations. However, the non-stopping pattern became ferociously complicated making communication of the calling pattern quite challenging.

The practice of missing out certain stations appears first to have occurred on the LTSR and W&BR sections, east of Whitechapel, where trains missed out a number of stations in the morning rush hour. The April 1907 timetable shows various stations omitted either singly or in combination with others. West Ham, Bromley, Bow Road and Mile End were favoured for treatment but several others appear sparingly as well.

Between 7am and 8am, the majority of trains in the London direction departed East Ham with most trains omitting some sequence of stations. This had little practical impact on the running times and was probably done to manage loadings. East of Whitechapel there were soon at least twelve different non-stopping patterns and virtually all trains missed out at least one station. The simplest was the omission of a single station, such as Mile End or West Ham, and the most complicated the omission of eight stations. By doing this it was possible for trains to depart from the most easterly stations regularly and gather together in bunches by Aldgate East, as the fastest caught up the slowest; this left a slight gap into which an Inner Circle train could slip from Aldgate, or a Met from the East London could scuttle through on its way to Liverpool Street.

In the reverse direction fewer trains non-stopped anywhere and they were much more spread out, though were equally varied. No attempt was made to replicate this in the evening peak, but on Saturdays there was some afternoon non-stopping in the eastbound direction. This slightly haphazard system of operation was to endure for some years.

Non-Stop Trains (Western End)

Further west, on the District's own territory, non-stopping was introduced cautiously at first with rare examples detected in timetables as early as April 1907. By slow increments, some consistency of practice developed on the approach to key junctions, particularly in the evenings to smooth out workings. By judicious non-stopping west of South Kensington, gaps left by Inner Circles turning off could be closed up, and services on the western branches evened out. Equally, where a Wimbledon train peeled off at Earls Court, so a gap would be left in the Ealing/Richmond service into which a non-stop train could be allowed to proceed without being delayed by a train in front.[12]

At first, non-stop services were confined to the Wimbledon and Ealing services, but from 1st October 1909 Richmond trains were included in the scheme with four departures from Mansion House timed to depart three minutes later and omit stations between Sloane Square and Hammersmith (with trains accelerated to pass between Mansion House and Hammersmith in 20 minutes).[13] Such complexity (with accompanying passenger confusion) is unlikely to have delivered the full theoretical benefits but clearly worked to an extent since from the 1920s non-stopping patterns were simplified and in that form carried on until as late as 1964.

The most common pattern was to omit either South Kensington and Gloucester Road, or West Kensington and Barons Court, or West Brompton, Walham Green and Parsons Green. Although non-stopping also took place eastbound it was complicated by the track layout at Earls Court as the tracks converged east of the station onto a single eastbound line for a quarter mile, making parallel eastbound movements impossible. A few stations

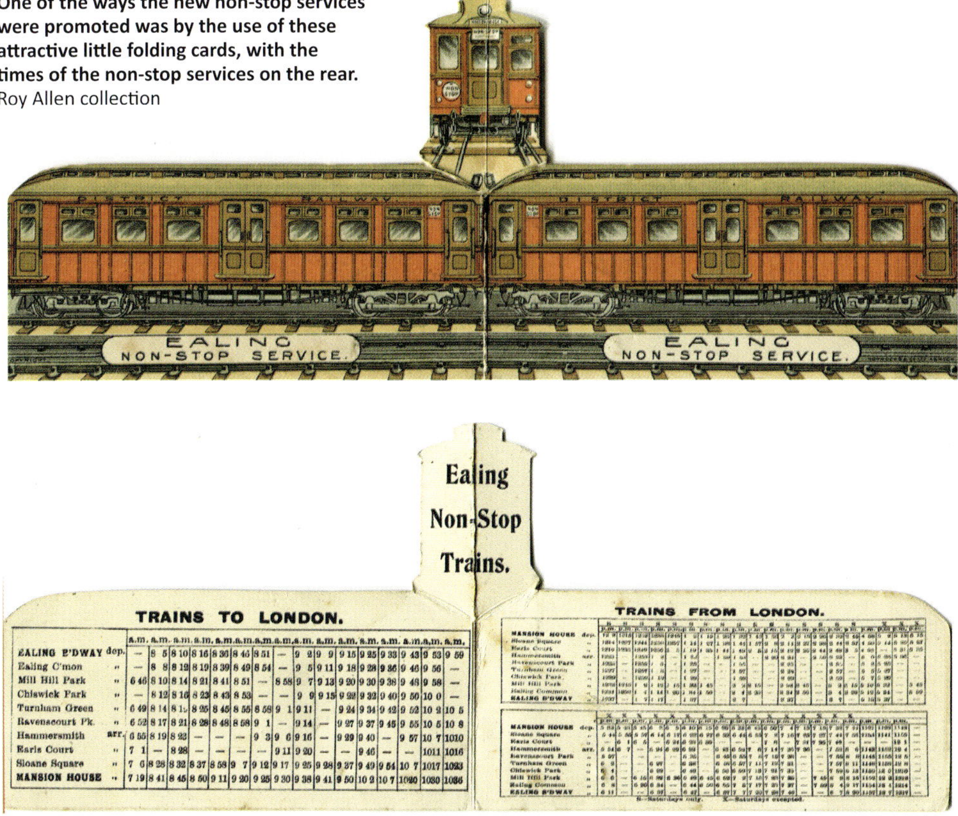

TRAINS TO LONDON.

	a.m.	a.m.	a.m.	a.m.	a.m.	a.m.	a.m.	a.m.	a.m.	a.m.	a.m.	a.m.	a.m.	a.m.	a.m.	a.m.
EALING B'DWAY dep.	—	8 5	8 10	8 16	8 36	8 46	8 51	—	9 2	9 9	9 15	9 25	9 33	9 43	9 53	9 59
Ealing C'mon "	—	8 8	8 12	8 19	8 39	8 49	8 54	—	9 5	9 11	9 18	9 28	9 36	9 46	9 56	—
Mill Hill Park "	6 46	8 10	8 14	8 21	8 41	8 51	—	8 58	9 7	9 13	9 20	9 30	9 38	9 48	9 58	—
Chiswick Park "	—	8 12	8 16	8 23	8 43	8 53	—	—	9 9	9 15	9 22	9 32	9 40	9 50	10 0	—
Turnham Green "	6 49	8 14	8 1[illegible]	8 25	8 45	8 55	8 58	9 1	9 11	—	9 24	9 34	9 42	9 52	10 2	10 5
Ravenscourt Pk. "	6 52	8 17	8 21	8 28	8 48	8 58	9 1	—	9 14	—	9 27	9 37	9 45	9 55	10 5	10 8
Hammersmith arr.	6 55	8 19	8 23	—	—	—	9 3	9 6	9 16	—	9 29	9 40	—	9 57	10 7	1010
Earls Court "	7 1	—	8 28	—	—	—	—	9 11	9 20	—	—	9 46	—	—	1011	1016
Sloane Square "	7 6	8 28	8 32	8 37	8 58	9 7	9 12	9 17	9 25	9 28	9 37	9 49	9 54	10 7	1017	1023
MANSION HOUSE "	7 19	8 41	8 45	8 50	9 11	9 20	9 25	9 30	9 38	9 41	9 50	10 2	10 7	1020	1030	1036

One of the ways the new non-stop services were promoted was by the use of these attractive little folding cards, with the times of the non-stop services on the rear.
Roy Allen collection

Poster produced in 1909 to advertise non-stop trains along the Hounslow branch. LTM

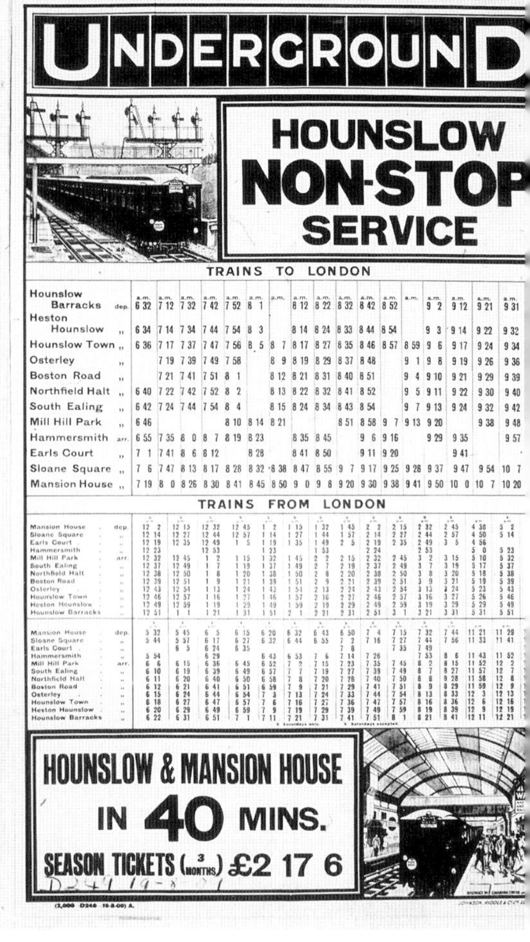

Ealing Broadway about 1913; the train bears an early variety of 'non-stop' sign on the front. Author's collection

1905 stock first-class trailer shown in immaculate condition after fitting with non-stop boards by far entrance. By this time the cars were fitted with continuous footboards (just visible). The whole car was still first-class only but divided into smoking and non smoking. Capital Transport collection

Shown here is one of the non stop display boards with train destination sign at top. Stations liable to be non -stopped were displayed in order on the small rotating slats; before each trip, staff had to rotate the slats required to display the particular stations where that train would not call. The boards were at first placed at diagonally opposite ends of the cars but were later placed by the middle doors (latterly only on trailers). LTM had so little traffic that trains did not always call, but Park Royal was a station with such low numbers that many trains did not call and for some years was a request stop.

In addition to operating non-stop trains for operational purposes some trains were clearly run 'express' as a feature to manage passenger loadings and give a pleasing illusion of speed. For example, in October 1907, the 8.20am train from Hounslow ran non-stop between South Ealing and Hammersmith, saving about four minutes. Two years later this train was still running and there was an earlier one, also non-stopping several stations. Once the tracks between Turnham Green and Hammersmith had been widened, the operation of additional non-stop services was possible.[14] The District was proud of its 9.9am fast train from Ealing Broadway which called only at Ealing Common, Acton Town and Chiswick Park thence all stations from South Kensington. This was timed at 30 minutes to Mansion House and was known to achieve this in practice, on a good day. This was an 8-car train and was described as 'very full train' after Chiswick Park.[15] The train was still running in 1914 but further accelerated to do the journey in 28 minutes; retimed to depart a minute later, the train called only at Ealing Common, Hammersmith and Sloane Square, thence all stations.[16]

The train service in the evening was arranged differently but was also subject to some non-stopping. In January 1921 an 8-car evening westbound train was put on departing Mansion House and non-stopping all the way between Sloane Square and Acton Town. This was accompanied by a scurrilous rumour it had been put on to improve the journey home of a timetable clerk who lived out that way.

Non Stop Markings

At first, the trains designated non-stop carried a red disk on the front (marked Non Stop) but from the end of 1912 arrangements were made for all trains to carry a special plate, underneath the regular destination plate, reading NON STOP or ALL STATIONS and this was swivelled to whatever position was required. The new displays required shifting the front destination plate from the rather awkward location above the cab door to a new position under the nearside cab window, the bracket having provision for this plate as well as the non-stop plate below.[17]

At around the same time boards were also fitted to the sides of cars listing the specific stations missed out. These consisted of panels attached to the exteriors at number of doorway positions and were headed 'Not Stopping At', below which were mounted small swivelling plates, stacked vertically, each with the name of one station on one side and blank on the other. A destination plate was also carried in a bracket at the top. Needless to say, changing all this paraphernalia at the end of each journey consumed much staff time; the fact the regulations needed to remind staff not to make the changes while the train was moving suggests short-cuts were not unknown.[18]

That all doors were hand-operated greatly eased the problem of changing the indicators on the off side at terminal stations, but correct door operation relied heavily on passenger conformance that was not always forthcoming. There was nothing to stop passengers pulling open doors on an accelerating train in order to leap on as a train started away, let alone to shut the door afterwards. Indeed in warm weather passengers would partly (or even fully) open doors to improve ventilation between stations. At Barking, some years later, terminating trains stopped at an adjacent track to the through trains and (rather than embarking on the tedious route over the bridge) it was quite common for passengers to wait until a through train stopped, open the offside doors of each train and simply step from one to the other. In a desperate attempt to stop this dangerous practice, instructions were issued that through trains had to stop so that the doors did not line up.

At stations where there were train indicators on the platforms it was felt some clue was required to warn passengers that an approaching train would not call everywhere. This was a significant technical challenge and the only simple way to meet it was to rearrange the destinations to show non-stop trains. These were made more prominent by reversing out the displays (red lettering on white enamel) and necessarily required removing the lesser-used destinations. That it was of dubious benefit simply to display (say) 'Ealing Non Stop', without disclosing which stations were to be omitted, failed to produce any better method of informing passengers than the customary bawling of the information by staff.

Although the marker light displays on the front of trains was never used to indicate non-stop trains it might be noted that from the end of 1911 they were altered so that instead of covering them up with a cap when not needed as part of a headcode, swivelling shutters were installed that could be operated from within the cab, avoiding the need for the driver to perform unnecessary gymnastics when changing a code. Altering the central top light was impossible because of the roof dome and the central lamp was shifted to the top of the offside window, an arrangement that was followed on new trains until the late 1920s.[19]

Composite Trains

From December 1907, four westbound trains were scheduled to uncouple in service at Acton Town during the evening peak (midday peak on Saturdays).[20] These all ran as express trains not stopping between Earls Court and Mill Hill Park, then splitting into a Hounslow and a South Harrow portion. As with the morning non-stop running, only three minutes or so was saved. This practice continued for many years and with numerous variations, though four trains was a typical number. Generally the longer train portion worked the busier Hounslow route and departed first. These trains started service (unusually) as 5-car sets and stabled after the morning busy period until they uncoupled on their outward trips in the evening. These were soon officially described as 'composite trains'. By 1909 they had been lengthened to 6-car trains uncoupling into 4-car and 2-car portions. Exact operation varied over the years; by 1914, for example, one of the portions sometimes worked to Ealing Broadway.

From October 1910 it is reported that an up train from Wimbledon in the morning busy hour was uncoupled at Putney Bridge, the front portion running to the City non-stopping several stations whilst the rear portion (presumably two cars) continued all-stations to High Street.[21] The use of paths this way is ingenious when considering that the semaphore signalling south of Putney Bridge had restricted train capacity, but this particular solution was probably made redundant when the new bay road at Putney came into use.

The Harrovian

Composite working was harder to arrange in the eastbound direction as there was far more opportunity for something to go wrong, but it was tried out from 1st December 1909 when the 8.13am shuttle from South Harrow (two cars) was extended to Hammersmith, non-stop, and coupled up to the train in front. The front portion was the 8.12 from Hounslow Barracks, due to arrive a couple of minutes before, having also run non-stop; this was a 4-car train though prior to December it had run with six cars. The coupled train then ran forward normally as a 6-car train. This marks the first occasion that a through working to London operated directly from the Harrow branch.

Coupling up this way was always more of a challenge than uncoupling portions as the sets to be coupled at Hammersmith had to arrive on time, in the right order and one

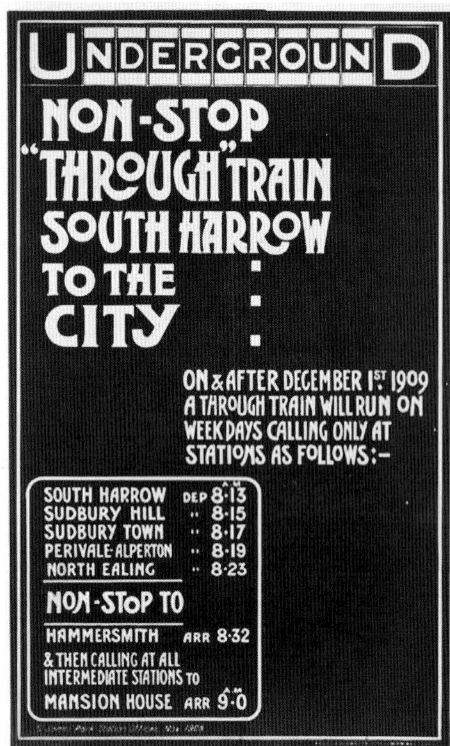

This is a representation of the poster used to announce the launch of a through City train from South Harrow. LTM

behind the other. Even so, this 'composite' operation carried on until 1914 by which time both portions were 4-car sets coupling at Hammersmith to form an 8-car train. So far as it has been possible to establish no further attempt was made to couple up two passenger trains in service.

From 1st January 1915[22] the coupling up process at Hammersmith was cancelled and the Hounslow portion was increased to six cars to meet demand (it would have been impossible to run a 10-car train east of Hammersmith). The South Harrow portion continued as a 4-car train but was further accelerated to non-stop eleven stations* and was accorded the honour of being named '*The Harrovian*'. In theory, it completed the South Harrow to Victoria journey in only 31 minutes. This train was the District's only named train and operated only in the morning; the name was used in public timetables but the train does not appear to have carried a headboard or other markings. The train became popular and was subsequently increased to six and later eight cars. Composite train operation in the westbound direction endured until the Piccadilly Line extensions of the 1930s rendered it unnecessary.

Uxbridge At Last

The District reached South Harrow in 1903 but the trains went no further. The rails (owned by the Metropolitan) carried on to Rayners Lane junction where they met the Metropolitan's 1904 Uxbridge branch from Harrow-on-the-Hill, the whole branch being electrified from 1st January 1905. At first the only stations were at Ruislip and at Uxbridge, though halts appeared at Ickenham (25th September 1905), Eastcote and Rayners Lane (both 26th May 1906) and Ruislip Manor (5th August 1912). The District's shareholder reports make frequent reference to how slowly the Metropolitan was making progress in building the line and how much traffic it was losing in consequence. Nevertheless, when the Harrow & Uxbridge finally opened in 1904 the District made no attempt to run trains and gave notice to the Met that it would not exercise running rights for the foreseeable future.[23] There was some excuse whilst the Met's new branch was steam worked, but this wasn't for very long and once electrified the District evidently felt it was not worth the bother of sending trains into this very thinly populated area when it had the headache of electrification to worry about.

* The omitted stations were Park Royal, Acton Town, Turnham Green, Stamford Brook, Ravenscourt Park, Barons Court, West Kensington, Earls Court, Gloucester Road and South Kensington.

The South Harrow to Rayners Lane link did serve some purpose though. The Met had installed current rails when the rest of the branch was electrified and was looking for somewhere to test trains and train staff for its own new electric service. By agreement with the District, a supply of electricity was obtained from the South Harrow end in March 1904 in order to supply current between South Harrow and a point short of Rayners Lane to allow the first of the Met's new electric cars to be tested.[24] This was done merely by connecting together the respective current rails and drawing a supply from Alperton (and tolerating the large voltage drop owing to the distance).

The first occasion the line was used by a passenger train was during the summer of 1909 when a pleasure party was conveyed from the District system to Ruislip by District train (which presumably made a return trip), the train being hand-signalled along the unopened section to and from Rayners Lane and a Met pilot driver provided.[25]

After some criticism in the press, the District condescended to introduce a service to Uxbridge and exercised its running powers from 1st March 1910. At the same time the basic service along the South Harrow line was improved to 20-minutes, with one train an hour extended to Uxbridge. From 20th March 1912 some trains operating the South Harrow service started or terminated at Ealing Common where there were convenient connections with Ealing Broadway trains, the shuttles reversing via the depot. Short trains were all that were required, whether turning round at Ealing Common, Acton Town or South Acton. To try and bolster traffic, cheap tickets were issued to South Harrow and Uxbridge line stations from most District stations on Sundays and some leisure traffic was stimulated.[26]

Catering for Demand

A novel feature in the evenings was a succession of trains for theatre goers and the 1909 arrangements appear typical. The most suitable station for theatres was Charing Cross where three trains for Ealing and one for Wimbledon departed between 11.26pm and 11.48pm omitting calls at a number of stations to help speed the journey home.

'The Paddocks' comprised 30 acres of pleasure grounds on what had been Grove Farm. Situated in Northolt Road, it was only half a mile from South Harrow station, enabling large parties of children to be delivered by train, providing useful income for the District. The facilities included a model railway, donkey rides and the promise of a large tea. This image shows a party from the direction of the station arriving for their day out. Roy Allen collection

When regular trains began using the Uxbridge line, late theatre trains were operated on Wednesdays and Fridays. These were sufficiently popular to be converted into daily trains from January 1911.

The District laid on extra trains when traffic demanded it. Amongst the many special services operated, the company was exceedingly proud of the way it handled very heavy football traffic for a Chelsea match during the 1911 season. Between 1.52pm and 3.28pm some 63 down trains were handled through Earls Court, equivalent to 40 trains an hour at a time when the flat junctions west of the station were still in place and a few trains terminated there.[27]

The press was always interested in covering railway improvements, no doubt thinking it 'news' useful to its various readers. The *Middlesex Times* was expansive about the improvements flowing from the Chiswick widening in 1911, announcing '200 Ealing Trains Each Way', and giving considerable detail about train timings and non-stop operation. In the same item was noted that the service to South Acton had been improved to quarter-hourly and it was felt worthwhile introducing through tickets between the District's westerly branches and the North London and LNWR lines via Willesden Junction.[28] A wait of up to 15-minutes was regarded as acceptable in those days, especially as the South Acton trains would usually serve Hounslow or Uxbridge (or at least South Harrow), and changing at Acton Town was easy. Even the larger circulation papers often mentioned improvements even if the detail was minimal.

Service Control

In steam days, the timetable was king and the operation of the service was almost entirely entrusted to the dozens of local signalmen who endeavoured to run the operation punctually with little knowledge of the general state of the service. On the whole a very good job was done, with only limited means of communication. The telephone was not yet prevalent and messages were sent by train or by the telegraph using the Morse code. A chief inspector at Earls Court was responsible for the general state of the service and was kept informed of matters deserving his attention, but it was only the more serious incidents he could influence.

The Americans already knew from experience that in running a more intense and less forgiving level of service some means of co-ordination was essential, and for this excellent communications were required. A traffic control office was established at Earls Court together with private telephone lines to the main termini which could call, or be called up, as required. There was an 'omnibus' circuit to the other principal stations where in case of urgency the person in charge could be summoned to the phone by means of the existing telegraph system. By this means the signalmen and station staff could immediately advise the traffic controller of delays, late running, unusual or heavy traffic, or serious incidents and the traffic controller could coordinate activity, despatch emergency staff and give whatever instructions were necessary to get the scheduled service back in order. The system was interconnected with the circuits between the power station and the various substations. These slightly primitive communications arrangements were much improved in 1912 when a complete telephone system and telephone exchange was installed to supersede the telegraph, the traffic controller having priority access to any of the telephone lines and retaining direct lines to the key operating points. Another important role was that, in case of breakdown, arrangements existed with other railways for mutual assistance so that passengers could use alternative railways (not just other railways in the group) with their existing tickets via any reasonable route. Requests for assistance either way were channelled through the traffic controllers and the same kind of mutual aid arrangement is still in use today.

Station staff (which included the signalmen) were expected to deal themselves with most incidents that arose, including many that affected train running. However, a small number of head office inspectors were appointed to maintain train and station staff discipline and act as the eyes and ears of the senior managers; a head office inspector would be available to investigate incidents and disruption and if necessary attend very serious incidents. It is a testament to the forward thinking of these electric train service pioneers that the roles of traffic controller and head office inspector survived with very little change for more than eighty years.

With rapidly increasing services, improvements in service control were necessary. By January 1908 the superintendent of the line had a train recorder installed in his office. This was a device carrying a circular cardboard dial which rotated once each day and on the face of which was marked the hours. As it rotated, inked markings could be impressed on the dial by electrically actuated stamps controlled by treadles on each road at St James's Park station, below his office. The marks around the periphery of the dial provided a permanent record of the train running on each track, the dial being sufficiently large to enable the exact time of each train to be ascertained. It was obvious from looking at the dial whether the service was running erratically, inviting enquiry.[29] The traffic controller also had similar equipment available.

The working of trains in fog has always been problematic and as much of the District was in the open air, and the signals were semaphore, fog was a major problem as the trains ran slower. At first 'fogmen' were appointed to assist driver's read signals that they might not be able to see in fog, but this was hugely labour-intensive and not without danger as it involved staff on the track in conditions of low visibility. This resulted in the District installing Clayton's patent apparatus from 1909 and much extended in 1912. A Clayton's machine was placed some distance ahead of a signal and automatically placed a detonator on the line if the signal were at danger (warning the driver) and removed it if the signal cleared. The clever bit was the ability to insert a live detonator from the reservoir into the operating arm if the previous one had actually exploded. When the detonator cartridge had only four or fewer left, the passage of a train also blew an air whistle so that a 'fog-man' knew he had to go and replace it. If it ran out the whistle blew continuously, alerting drivers to the problem too.

More Cars

In Yerkes' early interviews he spoke in terms of the need for 480 cars but even including the 1903 cars only 434 were being built.[30] While the 1905 cars were being delivered, the UERL ordered another 70 cars on the District's behalf. The first order was on 14th December 1905 for 30 cars from Les Ateliers de Construction du Nord de la France and was clearly for motor cars; the second was January 1906 with Brush Electrical Engineering Co for 40 trailers.[31] The District appears to have been slightly bemused by this since it was already clear that (to use their board's words) 'no new cars will be required for some time' and 'electric stock is about 30 per cent in excess of requirements'.[32]

It had been intended these extra cars would be similar to existing cars but all-steel and probably rather more robust than wood. Car-builders had been very active in developing all-steel construction and Brush managed to get the District to host a the display of a sample tube car at Mill Hill Park works in September 1905 where the good and the great inspected it and were told it was lighter, stronger, safer and less expensive than a wooden equivalent.[33] Persuaded extra cars were not then needed, however, the UERL was induced to cancel the order for extra District cars in October 1906, £4000 compensation payable to Brush and what was probably a proportionate amount to the French.[34]

The rolling stock situation had rather changed by 1909 when the daily service was approaching the limits of what could be done with the rolling stock as passenger demand grew. The position had been reached where the number of spare cars was insufficient to meet maintenance and spare train needs. Since train services (and train lengths) would need increasing again quite soon, more trains were clearly needed and three batches of cars were ordered, none very large. The new cars were ordered in numbers sufficient to use the existing stock more efficiently given the train lengths actually being operated and that it had been discovered motor cars needed more maintenance than trailers so a higher 'float' of those was needed.

Nor was everyone happy that the existing cars were helping to make the compelling case for travelling by 'UndergrounD' that was being promoted by Stanley, who wanted people to use the District rather than just talk about it. The *Railway Engineer* expressed its opinion thus:[35]

> Mr. Stanley ought to have lived when the Inquisition was in full swing. It is truly a pleasant prospect to have to choose between being bored to death and riding in those nerve-wracking red jingle boxes which run on the Met. District R., and in which we feel sure no one ever willingly travels. We do not, of course, suggest that he is in any way responsible for either their design or construction, but we suggest, as they are probably the worst railway cars he has ever seen, that their proper place is the scrap-heap, and that his staff, meanwhile, would be better employed in screwing up rattling windows than in talking about 'UndergrounD'. Unnecessary noise is strongly objected to by railway passengers in this country; they do not trouble to complain but avoid travelling on the line as much as possible.

A new Hurst Nelson motor car of 1911. Few opportunities were missed by staff to appear in the early photographs. This view is useful in showing the entry door open but behind which is another door which is part of the paraphernalia that allowed the driver to create a half-cab when he needed to drive. When not needed, the visible interior partition closed back against the front to conceal the driving controls. This view also shows the non-stop board, apparently clipped over the tail light bracket. These cars were delivered from new with the characteristic shuttered type of headlamp (the shutters could be moved from within the cab). Older cars were also modified. Roy Allen collection

One of the 1912 motor cars from Metropolitan Amalgamated. These were virtually indistinguishable from the Hurst Nelson cars. Roy Allen collection

We may perhaps see that in ordering new cars there was scope for some improvement in quality. Reliability was also being challenged. In December 1909, 401,295 train miles were being run and during that month 303 delays occurred creating 1186 delay-minutes. Compared with the tube lines this was ten times the number of delay-minutes for a slightly smaller mileage. 54 of the delays were caused by electrical difficulties on the train, more than double that of the tubes. The District felt that much of the service unreliability occurred on the foreign lines being worked over (a problem that did not exist on the tubes) but this didn't really answer the higher train failure issue.[36] In August 1910 the chairman (Gibb) waxed favourably to shareholders about the excellence of the District's system which was one of the finest underground railways in the world, with the exception of the rolling stock about which (revealingly) he 'would not commit himself'.

When tenders were sought for new cars in March 1910 the District made it known only British car-builders were being sought and the new cars would be sheeted in steel with no visible rivets. This order for car bodies was placed with Hurst Nelson of Motherwell with delivery early in April 1911; the bogies were made by the District at Ealing Common although some were recovered from older vehicles. A trial trip comprising a short train of the new cars operated on 3rd January 1911 between Mansion House and South Harrow, the dignitaries on board being treated to a top speed of 52 mph for a short section on the return journey, after which a hearty lunch at St Ermin's hotel was required.[37]

The car structures were for the first time on the District built of steel throughout but car interiors and window frames included some wood. The cars were finished in the usual bright red paint, but as the doors were now steel they had to be painted rather than just varnished, as previously. Interior roofs were of Bell's asbestos and coated in flat white

Above: **Interior of a Hurst Nelson (1911) steel trailer car (No 189). Effort has been made to provide comfortable seating. Author's collection**

Below: **Plan of one of the 1914 Gloucester cars (with elliptical roof). The plan gives general dimensions of the car and is useful in showing layout of guard's and driver's areas, including the moveable partitioning in the driver's half cab.** *Railway Gazette* 7th August 1914

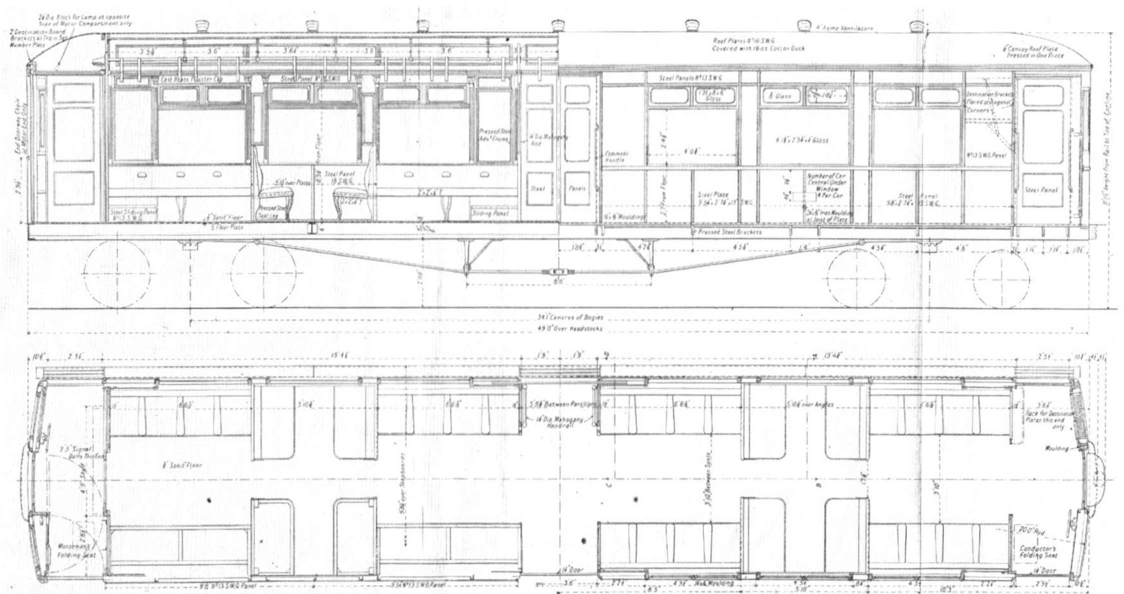

enamel. Twenty 25 candlepower lamps were installed in each car, again in groups of five powered directly by the traction current, and twenty heaters were fitted under the seats. The overall appearance of the new cars was similar to the original cars but cleaned up in appearance.

The interior was made to feel spacious by the use of light-coloured paint whilst the seats were upholstered with red moquette velvet (first class), blue moquette velvet (third class non-smoking) and royal blue faced leather (third class smoking). The existing door arrangement was retained but glazed draught screens were placed either side of the centre doors and at the car ends where they replaced the earlier solid partitions. The doors incorporated a new catch handle that made them easy to use while providing a positive lock when they were closed. These were the first cars to incorporate small grab handles on the tops of the cross seats so passengers could steady themselves when passing down the car.

This is one of the 1914 Gloucester cars at their works, under construction. The usual method of assembly was to construct the underframe first, upside down, and then to invert it and erect the steel structural members. *Railway Gazette* 7th August 1914

1914 type Gloucester steel car upon delivery. From the start these cars had a combined destination and non-stop board mounted beneath the driver's window. The non-stop plate was permanently fitted but could swivel around to show all-stations. *Railway Gazette* 7th August 1914

There were 32 motor cars and 20 trailers and all cars were 49ft 9ins long. The control equipment was similar to that on the original cars, and six sets were recovered from three of the electric locomotives which were withdrawn in 1910 as there was no use for them; a further three sets came from a pair of redundant breakdown vehicles and one motor car that had been written off after an empty train collided with the stops at Ealing Broadway in November 1909. New designs of motor and trailer bogies were employed, learning from the unfortunate experience the District had had previously. Much of the electrical equipment was new but to the existing specification. All of it was fitted at Ealing Common to cars as they were delivered.

It appears clear that the number of new cars ordered was quickly regarded as insufficient and that rather more were going to be required. After tendering in March 1911 another batch, numbering 22 motors and eight trailers, was ordered in April from the Metropolitan Amalgamated Carriage and Wagon Co and arrived in 1912 to a very similar design (the minute book refers to fifteen motors and a similar number of trailers being ordered but this was clearly changed).[38] They employed the same design of motor bogie, and same motors, but yet a further new design of trailer bogie. This and the previous batch largely increased the available trains whilst mopping up the excess of trailer cars the District found itself with. The equipment, too, was similar. The eight trailers and eight of the motor cars were part of the LTSR's contribution.

In fact, growth still appeared likely to outstrip resources and it became obvious even more cars were required and tenders were sought at the end of 1912. This final batch was ordered from the Gloucester Carriage and Wagon Co in January 1913 and was delivered during 1914; it comprised 26 motor cars and just four trailers. The trailer bogies were the same type as previously but yet another new type of motor bogie was devised. The bodywork was broadly similar to the others but an elliptical roof was provided, rather than a clerestory, and this gave the cars a more modern appearance. Interior fittings were of steel, aluminium and polished aluminium alloy. The emphasis on motor cars might be noted. This was partly because they needed more maintenance and partly because the number of 8-car trains had increased and these required extra motor cars as there were four per train.

On earlier cars ventilators had been installed in the risers of the clerestory but as these latest cars did not have one a new means of sourcing fresh air was required and torpedo style ventilators appeared along the roof. These soon proved a little too efficient and they were soon removed.

The traction motors on this batch were of the more powerful BTH type GE212, rated at 250hp. Although the bogies of these cars differed from each other and the older cars they were interchangeable and did move around between batches, an eventuality encouraged by the ongoing bogie problems that dogged the District and required large numbers of replacements to be built.

All the motor cars had driving equipment at one end only, and although passengers were now excluded from the whole of the end gangway when occupied by the driver, passengers could use it when the driving compartment was not in use. A complicated arrangement of doors closed off access to the controls when they were not in use; when the driver needed them a lower door was swung out across the nearside driver's door (leaving the window unobstructed) while the upper door swung and latched right across the central front door. The original cars were later altered to a similar arrangement, making the whole of the end platform available to the driver rather than the area of a cupboard as provided at first.

Train at Turnham Green with Gloucester 1914 type car with elliptical roof trailing, apparently taken in late 1915.
Capital Transport collection

From this period train formations, so far as possible, sought to use an equal number of motor and trailer cars, providing consistency of train performance irrespective of length. The motor cars were nearly all designated third-class whilst the trailers were either thirds or composites, with the first-class areas also subdivided into smoking and non-smoking sections. It was a challenge to get the right mix of vehicles on all trains, especially if trains uncoupled cars or split into two short formations during the slack hours (as the off-peak was still then called).

In 1910 a pair of storage battery locomotives were provided for use at Lillie Bridge depot. These were described as 'switching engines' for use about the yard, which was not electrified. They were used for shunting, use in an emergency and at night for moving ballast trains. Each accumulator weighed about 32 tons, and consisted of a battery of 80 cells containing 21 plates each. The battery had a discharge capacity of 179 amperes for eight hours, and for short periods could discharge as much as 800 amps. The normal potential was from 150 to 155 volts. The control equipment was arranged to take current from the conductor rails where this was available.[39]

The bodies were built by W.E. Renshaw & Co and equipped with BTH control equipment and GE69 motors. They were moved to Ealing Common depot during the war and used for shunting, the batteries later being removed as difficult to maintain and not essential in a depot where current railways were always available.[40] One of the District's existing electric locomotives was also converted to double-ended in 1911 to act as a shunter and stores train locomotive, mainly at Ealing Common depot (three more of the seven survivors were also made double-ended during the 1920s).[41]

LNWR London Lines Electrification

Seeing how successful electrification had been on other railways, the LNWR embarked on a scheme of electrifying its London local services around 1910; some of these lines were electrified before war broke out but most were delayed. The services concerned included the WLR between Willesden and Addison Road, allowing the existing shuttle service to Earls Court to be operated electrically, and this section was electrified first. The scheme also included what is best known as the North London Line, from Richmond and Kew Bridge to Broad Street via Willesden, and the Euston to Watford Junction local service where existing tracks were to be widened, with the new electric lines allowing through running of Bakerloo Line trains. Because all these services would somewhere interwork with District or Bakerloo trains, it was inevitable that the LNWR would have to choose the 4-rail dc system already used by the UERL companies.

The LNWR opted to electrify the WLR section first because it was short, self-contained and was already partly electrified; the section between Uxbridge Road and Addison Road had been equipped when the Hammersmith & City Railway was electrified. The LNWR substations and power station at Stonebridge Park were far from complete in 1914 but by extending the GWR supply northwards to Willesden from its Shepherds Bush substation, and obtaining a District supply for the section south of Addison Road, it was possible to electrify the whole of this section very quickly on a temporary basis. This required electrification by the District (at a cost of £4000) of the link between West Kensington East Junction and the main platforms at Addison Road, which had not been electrified in 1905.[42]

The LNWR purchased for this service twelve cars of saloon stock with sliding passenger doors from the Metropolitan Railway Carriage & Wagon Co, intended to be formed into four 3-car sets. Electrical equipment was provided by Siemens (by which name this stock was often known). Unfortunately these trains were not ready when the

Images of the District trains lent to the LNWR are rare. This rather poor image shows an empty District train approaching Willesden Junction High Level on the Earls Court service, having just reversed in the sidings. A 1905 car leads. Alan A Jackson collection

electrification work had been completed and arrangements were made with the District to borrow several 3-car trains so that the LNWR crews could be trained. As events turned out, further delays meant the District cars were then used to inaugurate the new electric services between Willesden and Earls Court, four 3-car trains being hired for £3 per day per train, with steam superseded from 1st May 1914.[43] As a temporary measure, these trains were stabled at the adjacent Lillie Bridge depot and this meant installing a direct connection into the car sheds from the incline running into the depot from the north, which District trains had at first used as an access in 1871; it also meant electrifying this incline, which had not previously been necessary. When the new LNWR rolling stock arrived later in 1914 the newly-built car sheds at Mitre Bridge were still not ready and these trains, too, were accommodated at Lillie Bridge. By agreement, maintenance and cleaning was undertaken by LER staff in the car sheds, which fortunately had been built to main line gauge. The District trains carried on until 22nd November when the whole of the LNWR's own trains had been delivered. The electric service operated at 15-minute intervals and still reversed via Earls Court east siding.[44]

This vestigial Outer Circle service was maintained by the London Midland & Scottish Railway (LMSR) when it took over the LNWR in 1923 and it continued until 1940 when wartime bombing of the WLR put paid to it. During this time the service was usually maintained by the Siemens trains but sometimes other electric stock from the London electrified lines was used.

Along the Richmond line, the District already operated the power supply system between Gunnersbury and Richmond and very little change was required to allow the North London electric trains to take over the steam services. The LNWR power supply system was divided from that of the District by a long dead section north of Gunnersbury along the line towards South Acton, the District feeding the line to the south (the Underground continued to supply traction current along this section until 1966 when British Rail took over).

Through trains to Southend and LTSR Improvements

The District had for many years recognized the attractions of Southend for day-tripping and worked with the LTSR to promote ticket sales to Southend from District stations. In steam days, a few special trains were worked by the LTSR to Southend from Whitechapel, demonstrating the value of the new link.

It was not until electric days that a tempting commercial opportunity presented itself for long-distance journeys of special trains to Southend via the connection between the District and the LTSR. The first was for the flotilla of battleships assembled just off Southend in July 1909, expected to draw considerable crowds. The District's response was to run an excursion train on 22nd July direct from Ealing to Southend and back for the benefit of sightseers. Although the train was of twelve carriages, and could seat 620 persons, the accommodation was insufficient for those wanting to use it. The carriages were supplied by the LTSR and were the 4-wheeled vehicles initially supplied for use on the W&BR when it opened. They were brought to Whitechapel by LTSR loco the previous evening and then hauled to Ealing using the electric locos. On the day itself, the train departed from Ealing Broadway at 10.16am calling at all stations to Hammersmith then Earls Court and non-stop to Southend except for a loco change near Little Ilford. The train arrived at Southend at 12.10pm. The return journey was virtually the reverse of this, leaving Southend at 8pm and arriving at Ealing at 10.3pm. All concerned thought this was a great success.[45]

Poster from 1915 to promote the new Southend direct trains. LTM

A Southend-bound train at Barking with a pair of District locos hauling the smart through carriages, built for the purpose. The locos are about to be detached and replaced by a steam locomotive. Author's collection

Later the same year the success of this and at least one other direct excursion train to Southend and back suggested the possibility of operating a daily train service. After trial runs in April and May 1910 regular trains were operated from 1st June. The weekday service involved two round trips with one on Sundays. Timings were designed to appeal to different types of traffic, notably day-trippers, London theatre goers and those needing to get to the London markets early. The initial service was operated by a single set of refurbished LTSR 4- and 6-wheelers in 9-carriage formation but its popularity caused longer trains to operate on occasions and this was awkward as they were too long for District platforms. Sometimes relief trains were operated. This operation continued until the summer 1911 timetable when an additional two round trips were added to the mix, one timed to catch rush hour traffic and intended partly to relieve pressure at Fenchurch Street. This required a second train set.

The success of this service suggested some dedicated rolling stock was called for and in 1911 the LTSR ordered two sets of purpose-built rolling stock from the Birmingham Railway Carriage and Wagon Co., Ltd., to the designs of Robert Whitelegg, the LTSR carriage and wagon superintendent. These came into service in January 1912. Unusually the coaches were of the open type, though divided by partitions into two main saloons in the third class coaches and three in the composite coaches. A central gangway led to sliding doors at each end giving access to the end vestibules, the compartment partitions having double sliding doors. The end vestibules were connected to the next carriage by flexible gangways at the coach ends, so passengers could walk through. The vestibules were also the means of entry to and exit from each carriage to the platforms, also via sliding doors.

The trains were intended to be operated in 8-coach sets comprising five 3rd class coaches, one 1st/3rd composite and two 3rd class brakes; capacity was stated as 400 seated. Each coach was 50ft long over its body and 9ft wide at waist height. A complete train had a tare weight of 200 tons. They were described by some in the railway press as 'sumptuous'. The underframes were of steel angle and channel iron but the bodies were wooden, with exterior panelling teak. The floors were packed with felt to reduce noise. Continuous draw-gear and standard buffers were fitted, and also air brakes were fitted, with hand brakes worked from the guard's compartments. The carriages were electrically lighted and heated, employing current generated by axle-driven dynamos. The carriage construction was rendered fireproof.

The first-class compartments were upholstered in tapestry, which was felt to go well with the oak panelling used, and the floor was covered with Turkey felt. The third-class smoking compartments were upholstered in Rexine, and the non-smoking in bluish mohair velvet, the floors throughout being covered with linoleum. The third-class brake coaches at each end of the train included lavatories and luggage compartments.[46] The lavatories, very unusually at that time, had retention tanks but were nevertheless locked out of use west of Barking.

East of Barking the trains were hauled by a single steam locomotive and to the west they were hauled by a back-to-back pair of the District's electric locomotives, released from the Outer Circle workings. The use of two electric locomotives on these long and heavy trains meant that their performance would match the ordinary electric trains and avoid delays. When the Southend service started, the newly-electrified platforms at Barking were both bay roads and it was necessary to change the locomotives just to the west, at Little Ilford No 1 signal box, but during 1911 platforms 2 and 3 were also electrified and this allowed locomotives to be exchanged at the station.

The open coaches and end corridors meant that although the trains were too long for District platforms passengers could walk along to a convenient exit point. Perhaps as importantly it meant no difficulty with the Railway Inspectorate when the District constructed single-bore tunnels at Earls Court for a new flyover (the inspectorate disliked the idea of trains running through close-fitting single bore tunnels unless an escape route was available at the ends; each train carried an escape ladder in the brake compartments and in the forward direction escape was possible via the end doorways in the locomotives).

The summer 1912 timetable shows four return trips in weekdays, two to Shoeburyness and two only to Southend; this includes a new return trip put on only on 1st June. On Sundays there were four return trips and a fifth Southend-bound trip (with a sixth early Southend-bound trip that ran only between 21st July and 8th September).[47]

From 1st October 1914 an additional through train was put on between Upminster and Hammersmith, departing at 7.55am and not calling between Barking and Aldgate East, nor at Monument, Westminster, Sloane Square, South Kensington, Gloucester Road, West Kensington and Barons Court. A return trip started at Hammersmith at 4.50pm (1.42pm Saturdays) missing out slightly fewer stations and connecting at Barking into a Southend train. This ran for several years and was made up of LTSR 4-wheeled stock which must have presented an interesting contrast with the District's saloon stock trains.[48]

The early excursions that kicked off the idea of a Southend service have already been mentioned but there is evidence that the District was amenable to more of them when opportunities presented themselves. On 17th July 1912 a so-called 'half-day excursion' train to Southend was run from Ealing Broadway at 1.20pm and timed at only 90 minutes. It called only at Acton Town, Earls Court, Victoria, Mansion House, Barking and Westcliff-on-Sea. Over seven hours were allowed at Southend before the return trip departed at 10pm (though the return tickets could be used on ordinary trains). Nor were special through trains unknown. On 11th January 1913 a football special train was run from Southend to Walham Green comprising eleven 6-wheeled coaches with capacity of 515, the steam loco being changed for electric at Barking and the run along the District conducted non-stop. There were almost certainly other examples.

In 1915 there were three trains a day each way to and from Ealing Broadway and several on Sundays but times and numbers varied over the years. In the 1920s a third set was required and this was worked with a short train of conventional stock (sometimes, at least, with only one loco).[49]

Train services for pleasure were much reduced during the Great War and its aftermath and by 1918 there were only two daily return trips and only one by 1921. But the service recovered and remained fairly stable. There were three 'up' trains in the morning, two from Thorpe Bay and one from Upminster, and three mid-evening trains, two from Southend and one from Thorpe Bay. These all ran non-stop between Barking and Aldgate East (but called at Mile End), and also missed out a small selection of District stations further west. In the 'down' direction a morning train to Shoeburyness (the only one suitable for day trippers) departed Ealing at 9.32am but the next train (all stations to Pitsea except St Mary's) was not until 3.35. A 4.18 departure to Southend was timed to suit City office workers and was followed by a mid-evening and two late night trains, all to Shoeburyness, timed to suit early evening diners and evening theatre goers. These trains non-stopped various different groups of stations including most of those east of Aldgate East (except Barking) to Laindon or Leigh and some other District stations. Along the District section there was nothing to stop ordinary passengers using the trains for local journeys.[50]

These trains outlived the District Railway by some years but the 1st May 1939 timetable saw the service reduced to one return trip every day, and this was withdrawn on 30th September 1939, shortly after war broke out, and never reintroduced.

The Longest Electric Train in the World

Even after the tracks east of Campbell Road had been quadrupled, line capacity along the LTSR was restricted by the mechanical signalling, operation of goods trains and the number of conflicting moves. Quite quickly the number of train paths available approached the limit and extra capacity could only be achieved in the short term by increasing train lengths. Here, too, operation of ever-longer trains was reaching the practical limit of 8-cars which was all that could be squeezed into District platforms west of Whitechapel. There was a solution though.

On 10th February 1908 a 9-car train was put into operation along the LTSR section, operating the 7.36am from East Ham, primarily to handle the workman's traffic.[51] This train uncoupled at Whitechapel and ran westwards in two portions. When trains were extended to Barking, this working became the 7.33 ex Barking and ran fast to Bow Road, stopping only at Upton Park. On reaching Whitechapel and uncoupling, the front three cars formed an Ealing service (not calling at St Marys) and the rear 6-car train ran all stations, also to Ealing.[52] On 1st June 1908 a second 9-car train was put on, operating the 7.24am service from Barking to a very similar pattern except both portions worked to Hammersmith.[53]

The uncoupling formula appearing to work, the decision was made to try out 10-car trains from 1st October 1908.[54] A timetable issued soon after shows the 7.24am train still operating in 9-car formation but the 7.33 had been extended to 10-cars (in 4-car + 6-car portions) and there was another 10-car train at 7.59 entering service from East

Ham.[55] In all cases many of the stations between East Ham and Whitechapel were non-stopped, suggesting just how heavy the loading must have been at East Ham. The District explained that heavy workman's traffic justified these operations and later timetables actually state that the 7.59am train was the last one upon which workman's tickets were available, which certainly explains the heavy loading of that train.

On 5th January 1911 the operation of a 12-car train took place between East Ham and Whitechapel; the train ran empty but called all-stations to Bromley. It returned to East Ham as two 6-car sets.[56] Although *Railway Magazine* was forecasting 12-car trains,[57] there is no evidence that trains that long ever operated a scheduled working, but from 1st February 1911 the earliest of the three long trains was increased to eleven cars; the timings of all three trains continued to include non-stop sections. By this time many of the ordinary trains had been made up to eight cars and from 2nd October 1911 the 7.33 train was reduced to 8 cars, and no longer uncoupled, and the 7.24 went the same way from 1914. The 7.59am ex East Ham 10-car train continued substantially the same form until 4th May 1925 when it too became normal 8-car train, advantage being taken of the high capacity of the new stock then being available.[58]

The LTSR was a line seriously inconvenienced every time one of London's famous thick fogs descended, as the precautionary measures required meant line capacity was reduced, even though Clayton's famous fog detonating machines were installed in large numbers. The railway rather liked the District's idea of coupling trains together to reduce paths required and encouraged the W&BR to make this easier by extending a platform at Whitechapel so that it could take a double-length train. The LTSR's objective was that during foggy weather a number of District trains would couple up and run as long trains to release capacity, with the District uncoupling them at Whitechapel—the long platform would reduce the inconvenience all round.

This shows what the District was pleased to describe as the longest electric train in the world, a 10-car set at Whitechapel. The train is uncoupling to run forward as two ordinary length trains. Author's collection

THE "DISTRICT" MONSTER.

The longest electric train in the world, hauled by motors developing 2,000 h.p.

Whitechapel platforms were already quite long but is was found possible to extend the westbound loop platform eastwards beyond the ELR bridge to a total length of 550ft, long enough for double-length District trains, though the extension was quite narrow. The resulting track layout would also have allowed a loco-hauled LTSR train to use the long platform together with a loco run-round allowing a main line train to turn here, but no evidence has been found this was ever done. The arrangement came into use in May 1910 and survived well into London Transport days. The extra-long platform was handy for dealing with the ordinary double length trains being deployed and could comfortably handle eleven cars.

After 1910 special District fog schedules were available for the morning rush hour with slightly thinned down services, cancellation of non-stopping and the use of longer trains, but not double-length; it is to be doubted whether coupling trains together during fog was actually done. By the October 1916 timetable fog working was no longer necessary and it was not reintroduced. After 1925 the extra length of the platform was seldom needed.[59]

On 30th May 1914 certain District trains were timed to connect at Barking with the 'Belle' boat trains that went on to Tilbury Pier to service the 'Belle' steamers that took people to and from East Coast resort towns.* The arrangement was that third-class passengers bought tickets from District stations to Tilbury Pier and on presenting them at the steamer's booking office obtained a discount. The discount equalled or exceeded the difference in cost of boarding at London Bridge, where the steamers started, the benefit being the substantial time saving in the London Bridge to Tilbury section of the journey. The timing was dreadful as the service was obliged to stop when the war broke out and the ships were requisitioned as minesweepers.

With the LTSR line west of Barking becoming more congested it was desirable to bring to life a bay road at Plaistow, on the north side of the down local platform early in 1912. This was already in position but had been too short to be useful and had hitherto been unelectrified; it was now made long enough to accommodate District trains. It was reported at the time that this allowed five extra trains to be run along the Barking line, the bay being used almost exclusively by the Districts.[60]

At Whitechapel the northern platform was a bay road and when through services to the ELR were withdrawn in 1905 it was used to reverse diverted District and Met trains. Through Met services to the ELR resumed in 1913 when that railway was electrified and the northern bay was then less heavily used and it was converted into a loop road by extending the track eastwards, bridging the ELR, and connecting into a siding that rejoined the main line; this substantial work came into use at the end of 1914 and allowed certain non-stopping trains to overtake trains calling at Whitechapel.

---

* Belle operated paddle steamers between London Bridge and Great Yarmouth but served several intermediate East Anglian resorts. The full journey took 11 hours.

Chapter Eight

THE GREAT WAR AND ITS AFTERMATH

Government Control

Upon the outbreak of war with Germany, most of the railways in Britain came under government control. This was to ensure that wartime effort was co-ordinated, with priority given to essential services, particularly ammunition and troop movements. The military will was directed through a Railway Executive Committee, comprising ten of the railway general managers, and a secretary provided by the industry. This was notionally chaired by the president of the Board of Trade, though actually the deputy chairman, the LSWR's general manager, Herbert Walker, took the chair. Formal notice was given by the government on 4th August 1914 that the District, W&BR and ELR had been taken over (together with the main lines and the Met). The tube lines and other paraphernalia of the UERL were of little interest to the government and were not taken over, creating a substantial administrative headache. In fact the District was not called upon to do a great deal by comparison with most other railways, but one can see that with its large number of connections government control was a sensible precaution.*

The financial arrangements had not been settled when war broke out. The legislation required the controlled railways to be compensated but explained neither how nor when this should happen. It was eventually agreed that the net revenue† would be ascertained for the year 1913 and with some minor provisos the railways would be compensated in subsequent years for any shortfall compared with the 1913 figure, and such was the arrangement with the District. Railways would in turn undertake government transport and other work free, on the basis that the formula would adequately deal with compensation for any extra outlay incurred.[1]

The government authorized the controlled railways to increase fares by a half in January 1917 to try and constrain travel. The District obliged immediately but the uncontrolled tube lines introduced a more modest increase later.

Because so many men were called up (the UERL's railways released over 3000) it became impossible to fill all the jobs, even with unskilled labour. Matters got so bad that by 1915 women were being recruited to fill posts. On the District, women became porters, ticket collectors and carriage cleaners, amongst other jobs. Another example of the difficulty of maintaining the system arose when successive calls arrived for skilled platelayers to go to France to repair the French railways, which were crucial to the war effort. Many railways supplied these skilled and hard-to-replace staff, including a number from the District. Although financial compensation was provided, the District was so short of critical staff it was not able to catch up with the maintenance that was required. After the war £60m was available to deal with arrears of maintenance and the like but it took years to get maintenance back to normal as new staff had to be recruited and trained.

---

* Authority for the government to take control was by Section 16 of the Regulation of the Forces Act, 1871.

† Net revenue being the difference between total actual revenue received each year and total allowable costs.

Woman porters at an unknown District station during the Great War. These views show the type of door handles used on the earliest electric cars (one appears to have been fitted with different handles with integral latch). The small notice on the first-class door reads 'To open slide sideways'. The prominent cap badge bears a large number. LTM

The war affected the District indirectly, as we shall see, but the direct effects, for example from air-raids by either enemy aeroplanes or airships, caused occasional upset. The first one that appears to have affected District services was on 13th June 1917 when bombs were dropped at Minories Junction, without significant damage. More serious was a large raid on 29th September when outlying District services were suspended 'during gun-fire' (this also affected LNWR and Met services). Overall, though, air raids on District property had only a minor impact, although the LTSR lines in East London were badly affected by frequent air raids, which affected District services on the Barking line.

Nor was the District affected (much) by the surges of shelterers who from July 1917 flocked to the deep tube stations which were considered fairly safe from air raids; the District stations were still then all wholly or partly open to the sky. Some inconvenience was caused by the introduction of a blackout at the beginning of the war and enhanced in April 1915. Inessential lighting had to be switched off and the remainder somehow shaded. Trains had to run with blinds down (where fitted), but the arrangements were not as draconian as in the 1939-45 war. The effect of the blackout was magnified during heavy fog. On the evening of 31st January 1918, conditions were so bad that eighteen passengers fell off District platforms, two of them were hit by trains, one being killed and the other seriously injured. Some stations had to be closed completely.[2]

The District was one of 27 British railway companies that helped the war effort by contributing to the challenge of munitions manufacture and this work was carried out at both Ealing Common and Lillie Bridge, diverting some effort from ordinary maintenance and repair. The work was varied and included machining lorry parts, heavy machining of 18-pounder shell cases and the forging of 6-inch howitzers.[3] On 1st January 1916 train heating was discontinued to save coal. This was rather uncomfortable as it was a cold

Female porters at West Kensington station near the entrance to Lillie Bridge depot. Conveniently In view are two standard district electro-pneumatic signals: the stop and repeater arms to the right and the shunting signal arm partly obscured by the woman on the left. LTM

winter; passengers on 28th March suffered during a heavy blizzard that delayed and disorganized trains and blew down hoardings and telegraph wires.

The impact of war, particularly the war production effort, resulted in a huge increase in traffic at the very time many buses were taken off the road, being requisitioned for service in France. The UERL lines found themselves towards the end of the war carrying two thirds as many people again as it had at the start, putting the system under enormous strain. Shortage of maintenance staff, who had volunteered or been called up, and a doubling of costs over the same period took its toll as well. On the District 40 cars of 544 notionally available were temporarily withdrawn because it was not possible or economic to repair them. This inevitably affected services.

The War Bonus

It was a problem that each of the UERL transport subsidiaries, except the LGOC, was a statutory company with objectives, privileges and restrictions set by Parliament. The UERL wanted to weld them together so they could function as a single body, but there were practical difficulties, including the need for parliamentary authority that could not be taken for granted.

Little was done before war broke out. As we have seen, the District was brought under government control, together with its interests in the joint companies, but control did not extend to the tube lines or the LGOC. This was an administrative inconvenience in its own right, but became more serious when the government agreed to pay a war bonus to the controlled railways to reflect the extra effort provided by railway staff to help the prosecution of the war and, more practically, the rapidly increasing cost of living. The bonus was first introduced in February 1915 and was initially paid at the rate of 3 shillings a week to men earning less than 30 shillings, and 2 shillings a week to those earning more. The bonus was at first entirely provided by the government, initially only to operating staff but after much angry debate it was increased and much-extended (eventually including women). By the end of the war the standard bonus had reached 21 shillings a week and had become indispensable.[4]

Because of the way the bonus developed it was applied very unequally and hugely distorted the relative rates paid to various staff. During the war the cost of living had roughly doubled but some poorly-paid staff had received much less than this via the bonus system while other staff effectively received much more than double their pre-war earnings. This tension contributed to the post-war railway strike, which also included the District's staff and is covered later.

Returning to the situation in 1915, the UERL quickly concluded that as District and tube lines staff did substantially the same job, and as it was desired that the staff be treated as one body, the unequal distribution of war bonus was a problem and it was expected that the staff who did not get it would not accept this without adverse reaction. One solution was to bring the other subsidiary companies under government control as well, a possibility about which Lord Kitchener* personally objected as it was not necessary from a military point of view.

Albert Stanley, the managing director, then tackled the Board of Trade which had some sympathy with the dilemma. Stanley quickly put to the President of the Board, Walter Runciman, a proposal for a net revenue pool of the main subsidiaries, by which device it was intended that the benefit received by the District would flow through the pool to the benefit of all the subsidiaries. Runciman agreed and on that basis the war bonus was paid to all eligible staff. Parliamentary authority was obtained in the London Electric Railway Act 1915, receiving the Royal Assent on 29th July 1915. In the meantime, from August 1915, the railways were required to fund a quarter of the bonus from their own resources.

The Common Fund

The funding pool just described became known as the common fund, into which the net receipts of the four railways and the LGOC were paid. The net receipts included all revenue less working expenses, interest and dividends on 'prior charge' stocks. The

* Lord Horatio Herbert Kitchener was then Secretary of State for War.

latter were usually guaranteed or preference shares and in the District's case included its first preference stock, but not its second (though this was later included). The pooled receipts were then apportioned among the various railways according to a formula, the District's apportionment being 12 per cent. The common fund came into existence on 21st December 1915 but was retrospective to 1st January, so it may reasonably be said that a substantial co-ordination of transport in London took place in 1915.

There were significant advantages of the common fund. The main one was the ability to jettison the complex and tedious cross-accounting that had previously been necessary to reconcile all transactions between the companies: the incentive was now to do whatever was expedient to increase the size of the whole Underground 'pot' as all the companies would benefit. This quickly simplified management and accounting structures and facilitated decisions being made faster.

When the common fund came into being, an interesting problem arose. Since accurate cross-accounting between the UERL's subsidiaries was abandoned, it was no longer possible to ascertain accurate net revenue for the District alone. Runciman therefore agreed that the District's net revenue, uniquely amongst the controlled railways, would be ascertained by reference to the gross revenue in 1913, less current costs (which could be measured more accurately). There was a disagreeable sequel to this. Actual costs and revenues both increased hugely during the war but by fixing the reference point for revenue in 1913 and then deducting the mounting actual costs the compensation due grew enormous whilst the actual income benefited the District as well. In 1917 the compensation was of the order of £200,000 and by 1919 the compensation was so huge that it exceeded the whole of the net revenue earned in 1913. Because of the common fund, much of this largess flowed to the various tube lines with the District keeping only its percentage (and the extra revenue).

Naturally the District was pleased to accept very large amounts of unexpected compensation as well as the benefits of all the extra traffic that was flowing through the system, and it did rather well out of it. When this unintended consequence was discovered it caused uproar in Parliament where Runciman's abilities were questioned along with Stanley's morals, for there were some who thought he had perpetrated a trick. In the event it was accepted that the arrangement had been urgent and was carried out by a busy and under-staffed department and the outcome could not have been foreseen. Whether this was an accident, or whether it was Ashfield's guile, we may never know.[5]

Because the war bonus had become an essential part of the wage packet, the railway unions feared it would stop abruptly when hostilities ended, leaving railwaymen facing hardship in the face of the huge price increases that had not been matched by increases in the basic wage. In consequence, Runciman felt obliged to state in 1916 that the wartime control (and therefore war bonus) would continue for two years after war finished. When the District's excessive compensation was discovered by the public in 1920 (when it seemed likely to hit £1 million), Runciman had a quiet word with Stanley and the latter agreed that the position was unacceptable and should stop. Officials found legal impediments to achieving this and the practical solution was to release the District from government control as quickly as possible after which the compensation ceased automatically. The last day of control was 25th September 1920, so only three-quarters of that year's compensation was payable.[6]

From this point the District was so closely associated with the other UERL lines that it will be convenient to refer to the 'Underground' rather than the 'UERL lines' and the term includes the District unless otherwise stated.

Senior Staff Changes

From 25th January 1915 (and anticipating consent to the common fund) various changes were made to the senior staff that brought the District and the tube lines closer together for the purposes of management. Mr W.E. Mandelick had been secretary to all the railways and was now appointed business manager as well. Z.E. Knapp became manager for maintenance and construction (all lines), Mr H.E. Blain became operating manager (all lines), having previously been operating manager LGOC (which function he also retained). Mr W.E. Blake had been superintendent of the line to the District, but the role was expanded across all lines (replacing J.P. Thomas who moved to the London General Omnibus Co).

Blake had joined the District in 1887 as a junior clerk in the outside traffic department aged 14. He showed great flair and after being put in charge of one of the stations, he was transferred to the general offices, first as staff and then as time-table clerk working his way up to superintendent of the line during the electrification period, a very challenging time. This job allowed him to be most innovative in making enhancements to the train service.

Blain had previously been with West Ham Tramways and joined the Underground in 1913 as purchasing agent but showed such flair he was soon appointed operating manager buses before taking on the railways as well.[7]

Perhaps more prominent amongst the changes to the management was the loss for the duration of the managing director, Albert Stanley (now Sir Albert, since he was knighted in the 1914 birthday honours at the age of only 39). Sir Albert volunteered himself for government service early in the war but it was not until 1916 when his offer was accepted and he was appointed director-general of mechanical transport at the Ministry of Munitions, though retaining his Underground responsibilities. When Lloyd George formed a new coalition government in December 1916 Stanley was chosen (perhaps unexpectedly) as the president of the Board of Trade, Stanley being one of several specialist outsiders brought in. This was a political post and a seat had to be found for him. Max Aitken MP held Ashton-under-Lyne and was prevailed to go to the Lords as Lord Beaverbrook (he had hoped for the president's job himself) and Stanley was elected unopposed. His Underground duties were taken over by William Corwin Burton (also a District director). As president of the Board of Trade Ashfield immediately found himself de facto chairman of the Railway Executive Committee, the wartime body exercising control of most of Britain's railways including the District, though in practice a member of the committee chaired all usual business.

H.E. Blain. LTM

Sir Albert had a difficult time as president. His organizational skills in rearranging the Board to better suit it to wartime conditions was never in doubt.

Unfortunately wartime conditions created a great deal of underlying industrial stress which as the war came to its conclusion released itself in unrest and demands for improvements that (whether or not were justified) could only in part be met. The miners and the railwaymen were particularly difficult to control and Stanley's negotiating skills were not found sufficient. This made him ill and he made it known during the spring of 1919 he wished to resign owing to ill health. His position was taken by Auckland Geddes on 26th May. After recovery, he returned to the Underground though remaining an MP until the government saw fit to elevate him to the peerage as Baron Ashfield of Southwell in the 1920 New Year's honours (at which point he ceased to be an MP).

It is perhaps not so surprising that shortly after taking over at the Board of Trade Stanley needed someone to fulfil a particular role in the mines department and he prevailed upon Frank Pick to take up those duties, presumably regarding him already as a trustworthy pair of hands. The miners presented particularly tricky issues that had to be managed. His main challenge had been to manage coal rationing and the equitable and efficient distribution of vast numbers of small domestic deliveries, a task done better than had been expected. Pick also returned to the Underground in 1919.*

Staff and the War

The prosecution of the Great War famously required vast numbers of men to be at first encouraged and later conscripted to join the colours. Since one of the country's largest employers were the railways the effect was to create a shortfall of staff as it was very difficult to fill the vacancies and harder to replace the skills.

Towards the end of 1915 figures issued by the Railway Executive Committee showed that the percentage of men who enlisted from the District was considerably higher than any other of the controlled railways. At the commencement of the war the total number of men employed on the District was 2499. Up to 31st August of that year the number of men enlisted had reached 769, no less than 30 per cent, of the staff employed.[8] By the end of the war the proportion of enlisted staff on the District and tubes had increased to nearly half and was a higher proportion than on any other British railway (except one very small company which had only four staff).[9] This created an enormous problem through inability to maintain and renew equipment properly and even to run the day-to-day services.

Because there was not full employment before the war the problem took a little while to manifest itself, but soon it was obvious something drastic would have to be done and the obvious answer of employing women had to be considered against against a background of management reticence and trades union suspicion. The latter were reassured that the jobs thus filled would all be temporary and rates of pay would match those of the men. It was not until the summer of 1915 that real jobs on the Underground were actually occupied by women.[10] Not all jobs were made available but station staff, guards and routine work in workshops and so on were filled by quite large numbers of women. The first woman porter on the District was employed on 14th November 1916.

In 1918, District staff had the use of the Albert Stanley Institute at Hammersmith which in addition to messing facilities had a concert hall and billiard rooms. Female traffic staff (resulting from the war) had a mess-room created at Brompton Road above the Piccadilly station, but an easy journey from the District. Again there was a hall for concerts and a canteen for the purchase of light refreshments.

* In February 1919 *The Times* described his role as Assistant to the Coal Controller, but in March he was being referred to as in charge of the Fuel and Lighting Branch of the Coal Control department. He also served on the Civil Aviation Transport Committee which reported in December 1918.

The District's wartime women's dining and recreation rooms at Earls Court, converted from an adjacent shop and dwelling house. LTM

The needs of female administrative staff were a more permanent requirement and early in 1917 a luncheon and social club was opened at Earls Court by Albert Stanley shortly before he moved to the Board of Trade. The club was located in an old 5-storey building next to the station at 218 Earls Court Road. This backed onto the railway with access at the rear direct from Earls Court station. The basement incorporated the kitchen and offices. The club was expected to produce over 200 meals a day using the four 'Tricity' ovens with which the kitchen was provided.[11]

There was a dining room in the basement and two more on the ground floor with serving lift from the kitchen. The alterations to the building were designed 'in house' and electricity was supplied from the District's Earls Court substation. The club was intended for use by large numbers of female staff including ticket sorters and administrative staff from St James's Park offices.[12]

A touching wartime development was the foundation of the Train-Omnibus-Tram Mutual Aid Fund, designed to provide some kind of support to households of the whole of the UERL's staff where the breadwinner had been called to the colours. This was founded in the first month of the war and all employees, from top to bottom, contributed what they could afford each week, the money raised being matched by a similar contribution from the companies. Over £250,000 was raised for the dependent families in need in addition to Christmas entertainments and country outings for the wives and children.[13]

Men on Strike

In the first years of the twentieth century railway staff became increasingly resentful about the difficulty they were having voicing their concerns to their bosses; at that time the railway unions were weak and several were not even recognized by the companies. The government had some sympathy with this and brokered a 'conciliation' process, involving staff councils in each company representing particular skills in the railway industry and upon which sat both management and staff representatives. The idea of these appealed to railway companies who saw it as a means of avoiding union recognition. They also appealed to the men as it was better than what they had, but neither side was very enthusiastic. Lloyd George took the credit when the schemes were introduced at the end of 1907, but they had actually been drafted by one of the railway general managers. Curiously, the District (and one of the northern railways) did already recognize one of the trades unions still seeking recognition by everyone else but went along with the process. Unfortunately, at a national level, the schemes did not work very well.

Mounting tension in 1910-11 arose from the feeling that the conciliation schemes were not helping the men's continuing grievances being heard or resolved. The tension was heightened because of lack of recognition of the railway trades unions and evidence of sharp practice by the managers of certain railways, which added further fuel. This culminated in large numbers of railwaymen striking between 14th and 19th August 1911, more of a problem in the north of the country but obtaining some support from Underground and Met staff. The government was at first unsympathetic and deployed armed troops and special constables conspicuously and in large numbers, though it is hard to see how in practice such arms might have been used against civilians. In London there were some reductions in services in support of the main line railwaymen. Met services were badly hit, and one or two tube railways, but the District was able to offer a fairly good service throughout.

The issues bubbling up in 1911 had been superficially buried during the war but were ready to erupt as soon as it had ended. One of the main complaints was the length of the rostered working day given the nature of the work. The railway trades unions had been pressing for an 8-hour day commensurate with many other industries but did not want to see average pay reduced, though pay was another minefield along the course of events.

Since railways remained under government control, matters proceeded more smoothly than they might otherwise have done and the 8-hour day was conceded in 1919. Somehow, an issue arose with Underground staff where they had expected the rostered half-hour meal-break to be included within the eight hours but during January 1919 it became evident this was not what the management side was planning. Matters were not helped by draft rosters having been produced reflecting the views of the motormen's union, only to be withdrawn and replaced by ones not including a paid meal-break. The National Union of Railwaymen (the 'NUR', representing guards and station staff) were inclined to discuss the matter but motormen on the tube lines (members of the Associated Society of Locomotive Enginemen and Firemen, or ASLEF) took unilateral action and closed down the five tube lines from 3rd February 1919. The suspicion was that the government, not wanting to pay the bill for the paid meal-break, had effectively gone back on its promise whilst the trainstaff explained that meal-breaks had previously been included within the paid shifts.

District motormen were in the same position but whilst not having joined in on the first day did join in on the following day, bringing much of London to a halt as the buses and trams were quite unable to cope. Matters then escalated rapidly bringing out the motormen on the LSWR and LBSCR with power station workers in London and other

UNDERGROUND

"CARRY ON."

Daily Notes for the Voluntary and Loyal Staff.

No. 1. Saturday, 4th October, 1919.

WHAT **YOU** HAVE HELPED TO DO.

The Crisis and the Call.

First Steps in Reorganisation.

On FRIDAY, September 26th, at midnight, the great National Railway Strike commenced.

On SATURDAY, plans for carrying on Underground services were in active preparation at headquarters. Volunteers' names were already being registered.

On SUNDAY, special dispatch riders at 1 p.m. carried the call to the first group of volunteers. At 3 p.m., they began to report for service. At midnight, the Power House at Lots Road was manned by a competent staff.

The Diary of Public Duty.

What this great volunteer railway force has enabled the Management to do for the public.

MONDAY.

Active training for working trains on the District and Hampstead lines.

TUESDAY.

District Railway opened between Hammersmith and Mansion House; Hampstead Tube between Charing Cross and Hampstead, and later Golder's Green. Public amazed, incredulous, delighted. No such happy journeying by UndergrounD since 1914.

Total number of volunteers enrolled 1,500.

WEDNESDAY.

Central London Railway opened between Shepherd's Bush and Liverpool Street, and later to Wood Lane. Much public relief and gratitude. Volunteers most popular men in London. Recruits offering is steady stream.

Total number enrolled 3,000.

THURSDAY.

Piccadilly tube opened between Hammersmith and Finsbury Park. District Railway extended to Aldgate East. Number of passengers greatly increasing. Patient and pleasant queues at times of greatest pressure. Notice issued to Press, no more volunteers required at the moment.

Total number of volunteers 3,700.

FRIDAY.

District Railway extended to Ealing Broadway.

Total number of volunteers 4,300.

In the never-ceasing reverberation of traffic by road and rail, you hear the beating of London's heart. Its strengthening or its weakening signalise prosperity or misery. Complete stoppage would mean ruin and starvation.

SATURDAY.

Highgate Tube opened between Highgate and Charing Cross. Bakerloo Tube opened between Elephant and Castle and Paddington. Underground staff never so popular. Papers full of praise.

Total number of volunteers 4,500.

Sunday Service.

Careful consideration was given to the running of trains on Sunday, having regard to the comparative absence of business necessities for the service. Important reasons with reference to the

In the face of the railway strike of 1919 one of the tools used by the Underground was what might have been a series of newsletters. In fact the strike was so short only a first and final edition appeared. This is the first, the final had a useful chronology of what was done to overcome the difficulties. Author's collection

industries threatening to join them based on their quite separate grievances. The intervention of Lord Ashfield (still at the Board of Trade) and a promise to go into all this and come to a firm joint agreement was found acceptable and train services were resumed, with some difficulty, late on 8th February.[14] There were several repercussions from this stoppage including that motor lorries had been used as emergency buses and the drivers later discovered they were being paid much less than bus drivers, and so on. Altogether, the industrial situation was very tense.

The matter of railway pay across the whole of Britain's railways was an issue that would explode if not dealt with. The near-doubling in retail prices during the war had been addressed only temporarily by the war bonus whose future was uncertain. The piecemeal wartime adjustments to hundreds of grades had also produced a great deal of unfairness, about which all parties agreed. Government formulated a policy to appease the train drivers (who were viewed as 'difficult') on the basis that if they could be kept happy they would not support the larger body of other railway staff who were less vital in the event of a strike, should agreement not be reached. In the summer, the ASLEF union discovered that the war bonus would be consolidated in full and so far as the considerable number of anomalies were concerned they would either be dealt with or rounded up to match the highest rates being paid by any of the companies. The deal was unprecedented, unexpected and at any other time unaffordable. ASLEF went away with an exceptionally good pay settlement, their 8-hour day and generous overtime for shifts unavoidably longer than eight hours.

Naturally, the NUR expected the same treatment, but didn't get it. The offer was ineptly put and whilst it would do a certain amount to secure an appropriate post-war level of pay, it left too many grades earning less than that required to run a household, did not deal with some long running areas of unfairness and was conspicuously worse than the drivers had got. Members were not inclined to be manipulated this way and called an immediate strike from 26th September. Quite unexpectedly the drivers saw the injustice and felt the NUR should be supported and came out as well, more or less closing the national rail network and with it the Met (which tended to echo main line conditions). Underground staff, although in a slightly different position, also had concerns and decided to support the NUR. Moreover, the staff at Lots Road also supported a strike, and that inevitably threatened a total stoppage.

In those days a railway strike was such a serious matter that it could not be left and the defence forces were brought in and the government called for large numbers of volunteers. The Underground managed to enrol 5000 volunteers, who, with managers, got Lots Road Power House going and managed to get some trains running on 30th, more coming into use in the following days after rudimentary training had been given. Emergency hostels and canteens were somehow provided and by 6th October some services were running on all lines though only on a very limited basis.

On the District, services were completely stopped on 27th September and a call for volunteers was made on the Sunday. On the Monday, training took place for volunteer drivers and on Tuesday a limited service was in operation between Hammersmith and Mansion House (the Underground as a whole having by then accepted 1500 volunteers). On Thursday, District services were extended to Aldgate East and on Friday to Ealing. Services across all the lines were very thin, though. By the end, only 100 volunteer drivers had been accepted across all lines, all trained and qualified within five days, an average of twenty a day, all of whom were required to pass the ordinary written test.

Meanwhile the strike was threatening to spill over into other awkward areas of industry and the cabinet agreed during a lengthy meeting on Sunday 5th October to withdraw the mischievous 'final proposal' that had been made and sort out something acceptable with immediate effect, leading to a consensual agreement shortly afterwards. With that regarded as satisfactory, the strike was called off and staff asked to return to work from the following day.

District and tube staff were encouraged to join the London bus and tram strike at the end of March 1924 but it was settled before the railways joined in. During the strike, traffic on the Underground more than doubled and services were so busy they approached breaking point. At Victoria, for example, the automatic machines usually sold about 7000 tickets daily but during the strike were selling 25,000 tickets daily. On one day alone the weight of copper coinage taken amounted to half a ton. The strike was settled, and men started to return to work, on the evening of 31st March, three days after the King proclaimed a state of emergency (revoked on 1st April).

The 1926 General Strike began in the coal mines following an enforced pay cut. It quickly spread to other industries as unions showed support for the miners, whether or not they had any disagreement with their own industries. By this time the staff of the Underground had fairly harmonious relations with their employers but they were nevertheless called out from 4th May 1926 by the national railway unions which were close to the miners. To mitigate the impact, the pattern of 1919 was followed but on a larger scale, with 9610 volunteers being recruited by the Underground to do all the various jobs normally done by the 39,000 usually employed across the railway, bus and tram systems who went on strike. Allowing for the fact training was needed and some volunteers were only part time, the numbers are consistent with eventually being able to get about a third of the Underground's trains working. To make life easier a flat fare of 3d was introduced for the duration; this also discouraged unhelpful short distance traffic.

The staff at Lots Road were a particular problem. These were part of the electrical trades unions and came out in their entirety, with the prospect of no trains running at all.

Several newspapers covered the struggle to keep the country going during the general strike. The *Illustrated London News* selected an image of the boiler house at Lots Road where volunteers and naval ratings were able to keep the power house running. Author's collection

EXPERTS IN LOTS ROAD POWER STATION, SUPPLYING THE UNDERGROUND RAILWAYS WITH ELECTRICITY : SAILORS HANDLING THE BOILERS.

A press bureau photo purporting to show a volunteer guard seeing away his train during the 1926 general strike. Although (some) training was given it is interesting that he bears no indication of his role and is not using any of the train despatch equipment, not even a flag. Capital Transport collection

Large numbers of volunteers were quickly deployed with teams of naval ratings supplied by the government to train and assist volunteers to operate the equipment and stoke the boilers. Power was thus available very quickly.

With some staff trained, a few District trains operated briefly on 5th May in the early evening, but only between Mansion House and Hammersmith, calling at only at four intermediate stations. A similar service resumed at 9am the following morning. On 7th May an additional train ran between Putney Bridge and Earls Court. By 13th May a 15-minute service had been extended east to Whitechapel.

The dynamics of the general strike are quite complex and it was increasingly clear that a nationwide sympathetic strike could not possibly endure, particularly with the government making extensive use of emergency powers. The railwaymen agreed to go back to work on 14th May but there were difficulties. Those who had worked throughout found themselves resented by those who went out. Those going back early were readily accepted by management but those returning later were taken back slowly and reluctantly on the basis that they had broken their contracts because they had withdrawn labour summarily when there was no dispute (the real reason on the main lines was that the coal miners argument carried on and traffic was hugely reduced). It was all pretty ugly. Underground services were not back at full strength until Monday 17th May.

Chapter Nine

THE ROARING 'TWENTIES

London

When the District was committing to electrification in 1901 the population of Greater London had reached 6.6 million.[1] Of this number the vast majority—four fifths—lived within the County of London (today's Inner London) whilst the remaining fifth lived in the vast outer ring. Even in this outer ring, the population largely clustered in the larger centres such as West Ham and Acton and the rest of this outer area was fairly empty. A combination of factors resulted in the population of Inner London declining and industrial activities moving further out where there was more space. In parallel, the population in the outer areas increased rapidly, developing areas congregating where good transport facilities were already in place. Between 1901 and 1921 the population of Greater London increased by nearly 900,000, but nearly all of this was in the outer London areas. In District territory, there were already clusters of population in the small towns of Ealing, Harrow and Hounslow, with almost nothing in between. As a general rule, the early twentieth century suburbs developed outwards from the County of London border (and the three towns just mentioned), slowly filling up the intermediate space.

By 1920 nearly all the land between Hammersmith and Ealing had been built up, but there was almost nothing along the South Harrow line or beyond. Housing development around Ealing had spread southwards to include the area around South Ealing and Northfields but the land towards Hounslow was still barren; Hounslow itself had not grown much and there was still no development at Hounslow Barracks. Within a decade, development was in full swing in Osterley and Hounslow but it was not until the early 1930s that development along the South Harrow and Uxbridge lines began to explode.

The table below gives a flavour and it can be seen the outer areas have increased significantly, though the Wimbledon line population has reduced whilst Richmond is moderately low. It was obvious where services needed major strengthening.

Population change in districts bordering west end of the District*

Local gov't areas	*1921*	*1931*	*Increase*	*Increase*
Wembley	16,187	48,561	32,374	200%
Heston & Isleworth	46,664	75,460	28,796	62%
Harrow	19,637	26,380	6743	34%
Ealing	90,433	117,707	27,274	30%
Acton	61,299	70,510	9211	15%
Richmond	35,639	37,797	2158	6%
Hammersmith	130,295	135,523	5228	4%
Wimbledon	61,418	59,524	-1894	-3%
Fulham	157,938	150,928	-7010	-4%
Total	619,510	722,390	102,880	17%

* There was no formal area called Greater London in 1901, but the area referred to here is approximately similar to the area of London today.

T-O-T

While the London population was moving into the suburbs, the transport system had to respond with better and properly co-ordinated services. The process of producing one organization from a number of diverse constituent parts did start before the common fund and we have already seen the widespread use from 1908 of the word 'Underground' used as a trademark across London's various underground railways. This was not without complication as the word was applied equally across railways that were nothing to do with the UERL, whilst the latter also came to operate buses and trams. To deal with this, from 17th May 1913, the publicity department of the Underground companies began the fortnightly publication of 'T.O.T' (Train, Omnibus, Tram), a leaflet for general distribution 'to give news of what is new, to recall to the memory what is old, in the way of traffic facilities.' This was a four-page bulletin containing data of the company's traffic and its facilities, descriptions of places worth visiting whether open-air resorts or buildings, lists of events, changes in service and so on. There were 33 issues between this first one and the outbreak of the Great War and they were available at all stations as well as on buses and trams.[2]

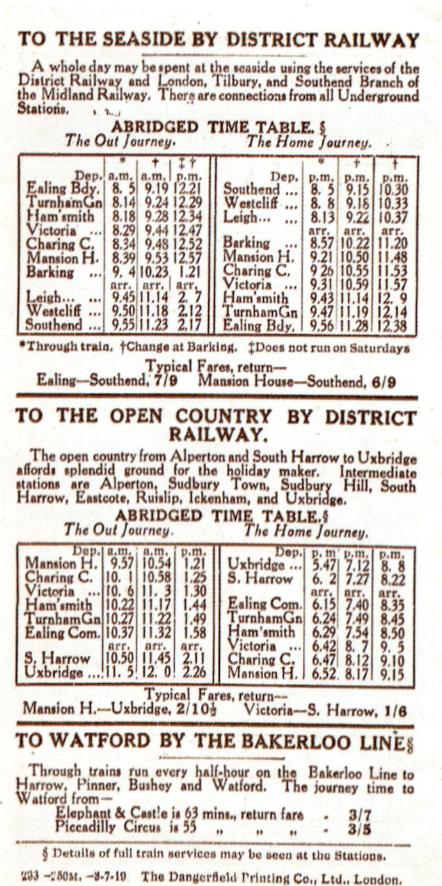

TO THE SEASIDE BY DISTRICT RAILWAY

A whole day may be spent at the seaside using the services of the District Railway and London, Tilbury, and Southend Branch of the Midland Railway. There are connections from all Underground Stations.

ABRIDGED TIME TABLE. §

The Out Journey. *The Home Journey.*

	*	†	‡†		*	†	†
Dep.	a.m.	a.m.	p.m.	Dep.	p.m.	p.m.	p.m.
Ealing Bdy.	8. 5	9.19	12.21	Southend ...	8. 5	9.15	10.30
TurnhamGn	8.14	9.24	12.29	Westcliff ...	8. 8	9.18	10.33
Ham'smith	8.18	9.28	12.34	Leigh... ...	8.13	9.22	10.37
Victoria ...	8.29	9.44	12.47		arr.	arr.	arr.
Charing C.	8.34	9.48	12.52	Barking ...	8.57	10.22	11.20
Mansion H.	8.39	9.53	12.57	Mansion H.	9.21	10.50	11.48
Barking ...	9. 4	10.23	1.21	Charing C.	9 26	10.55	11.53
	arr.	arr.	arr.	Victoria ...	9.31	10.59	11.57
Leigh... ...	9.45	11.14	2. 7	Ham'smith	9.43	11.14	12. 9
Westcliff ...	9.50	11.18	2.12	TurnhamGn	9.47	11.19	12.14
Southend ...	9.55	11.23	2.17	Ealing Bdy.	9.56	11.28	12.38

*Through train. †Change at Barking. ‡Does not run on Saturdays

Typical Fares, return—
Ealing—Southend, 7/9 Mansion House—Southend, 6/9

TO THE OPEN COUNTRY BY DISTRICT RAILWAY.

The open country from Alperton and South Harrow to Uxbridge affords splendid ground for the holiday maker. Intermediate stations are Alperton, Sudbury Town, Sudbury Hill, South Harrow, Eastcote, Ruislip, Ickenham, and Uxbridge.

ABRIDGED TIME TABLE.§

The Out Journey. *The Home Journey.*

Dep.	a.m.	a.m.	p.m.	Dep.	p.m	p.m.	p.m.
Mansion H.	9.57	10.54	1.21	Uxbridge ...	5.47	7.12	8. 8
Charing C.	10. 1	10.58	1.25	S. Harrow	6. 2	7.27	8.22
Victoria ...	10. 6	11. 3	1.30		arr.	arr.	arr.
Ham'smith	10.22	11.17	1.44	Ealing Com.	6.15	7.40	8.35
TurnhamGn	10.27	11.22	1.49	TurnhamGn	6.24	7.49	8.45
Ealing Com.	10.37	11.32	1.58	Ham'smith	6.29	7.54	8.50
	arr.	arr.	arr.	Victoria ...	6.42	8. 7	9. 5
S. Harrow	10.50	11.45	2.11	Charing C.	6.47	8.12	9.10
Uxbridge	11. 5	12. 0	2.26	Mansion H.	6.52	8.17	9.15

Typical Fares, return—
Mansion H.—Uxbridge, 2/10½ Victoria—S. Harrow, 1/6

TO WATFORD BY THE BAKERLOO LINE§

Through trains run every half-hour on the Bakerloo Line to Harrow, Pinner, Bushey and Watford. The journey time to Watford from—
Elephant & Castle is 63 mins., return fare - 3/7
Piccadilly Circus is 55 " " " - 3/5

§ Details of full train services may be seen at the Stations.

233 —250M. —8-7-19 The Dangerfield Printing Co., Ltd., London.

Photo] [F. P. Kodak
THE SEASIDE—SOUTHEND (by District Railway).

SEA, FOREST AND MEADOWLAND

BY

T. O. T

The Companies cannot be responsible for the exact adherence to the times of the buses or trams, nor can they guarantee the running of the services to be as stated, though every effort will be made to maintain them. The Conductor should be asked for time of last bus or tram, in case of alteration.

Photo] EPPING FOREST (by Motor-bus). [F. P. Kodak

One of many T-O-T leaflets designed to help promote travel. This one, from 1919, has eight panels, many devoted to promoting travel by the various country bus services and longer distance trams that connected with the Underground (many of which were District stations). The rear panel is promoting, in equal measure, the Southend service and trains to South Harrow and Uxbridge, still considered remote country. Author's collection

The leaflets were considered moderately successful and the T.O.T. theme gained traction with through-fares and tickets and (later) in the name of the staff magazine and the staff benevolent fund (and noted earlier was the T.O.T. Mutual Aid Society). It all seems a bit clumsy today but the UERL had at first projected the 'Underground' theme and this became less appropriate when buses and trams were being promoted as part of the same integrated system, so T.O.T. it was. The public may not have embraced the theme with much enthusiasm and the brand was later split between 'Underground', 'General' and 'Tramways', but T.O.T. endured internally to promote the idea of a staff family. Against this onslaught, the District 'brand' rather withered.

An important move towards the single family of staff was to extend the validity in May 1914 of staff free passes for any one line across all of the Underground lines, and this helped promote the feeling of one-ness. Stanley made the announcement himself at the first annual meeting of the combined operating staff from all lines, such meetings being designed to exchange ideas and promote good practice.[3]

The wartime measures and the common fund had the combined effect of welding the District and the Tubes more closely together and, to a slightly lesser extent, the buses and trams. At the end of the war, London was rather short of buses as about 1000 of them (a third of the fleet) had been sent to the European front line as troop carriers, ambulances and other transport vehicles. There were stopgap measures to fill the shortage but in the end new vehicles were acquired which resulted in a comparatively modern fleet of motor buses. These did a good job serving the growing suburban areas and bringing people to and from the outer Underground stations, a matter in which the District greatly benefited. The trams were a rather less versatile mode but thanks to the early association with the LUT made good connections at Hammersmith, Ealing and Wimbledon.

We have already seen how keen Clifton Robinson had been to have through tickets between the District and LUT. From 1st February 1914 the Underground extended the T.O.T. idea (Train, Omnibus Tram) to promote seamless travel. T.O.T. publicity promoted through travel whilst a range of through single and return tickets were made available where the remote end of the journey could be made to one or more bus or tram stops via a suitable interchange station. The tickets were redesigned in 1917 and included a prominent letter B or T on the left hand portion, representing Bus or Tram.

From 1st June 1923 through season tickets were introduced between the District and LGOC buses to Barnes and East Sheen via Hammersmith, monthlies being available from ten stations and quarterlies from the season ticket office at Mansion House. This scheme was rapidly extended during the rest of 1923 and much of 1924 to cover buses or tram journeys via Ealing Broadway, Putney Bridge, Northfields, Boston Manor, Ealing Common and Sudbury Town and the tickets became very popular as they represented a discount on ordinary bookings and avoided the need for change for the bus or tram. The facility was extended to trolleybuses when they eventually replaced the trams.

Wimbledon & Sutton Railway

On 9th February 1910, shareholders were told that the District had been approached by the Wimbledon & Sutton Railway (W&SR), which wanted to make its line across largely open countryside between those two towns. The W&SR wanted the District involved in its construction and operation and this offered the possibility of District trains to Wimbledon being projected south another 5½ miles to Sutton at low cost. The District agreed to support the proposal but not put any money into it.

The W&SR has a curious history. It was entirely conceived by landowners and developers irritated by existing railway companies which shunned the area, thereby

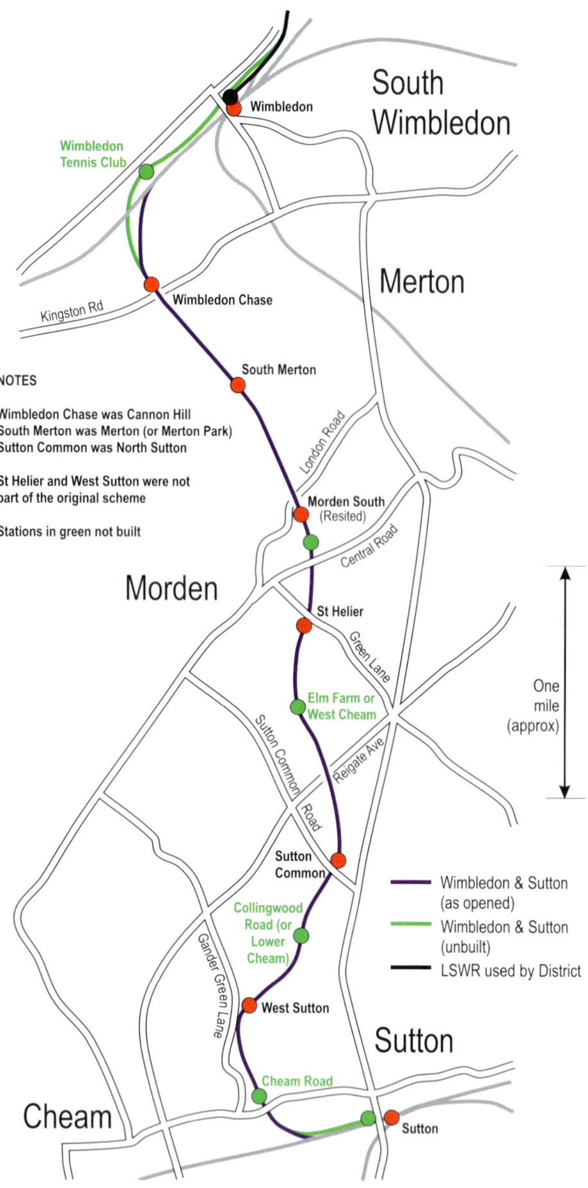

Map showing line of route of the Wimbledon & Sutton Railway, as built and as proposed. MACH

denying local landowners the rewards from rising land values as housebuilding responded to greater accessibility. The land was said to be 'ripe for development'. Interested parties met in October 1908 and after investigating the practicalities, notice was given that a bill was to be submitted in the 1910 Session of Parliament.[4] The promoters were prepared to subscribe to some (but not all) of the capital and received encouragement from the Merton Park Estate Company, desperate for improved transport in the area. Significantly, District director, Major Isaacs, was directly involved.[5] One local landowner who was not supportive was thoroughly against the line because it 'would develop a certain class of residents who were not desirable'.

The line was to include ten stations in all; of these, it was suggested seven would be remunerative immediately whilst three were speculative. The railway included sixteen bridges and a short cutting at Wimbledon, south of which the line was to pass under the LSWR. The highest bank was to be 21ft and some of the line required major earthworks through difficult ground—the widened cutting at Sutton, for example, was expected to require 500,000 tons of earth removing. Some of the curves were sharp and gradients steep, making it suitable only for electrical working. The bill provided for the District to have running powers and for the Underground to supply power from Lots Road. The capital was set at £350,000 (with usual additional borrowing powers) and the engineer's estimate for construction was £311,554.[6]

It was hoped to run the line as an extension of the District Railway, and even the residents of Sutton would find this useful as the existing LBSCR train service was felt unsatisfactory. A running junction with the LBSCR at Sutton was considered but the LBSCR wanted nothing to do with one. A junction with the LSWR slow tracks was allowed for at Wimbledon.[7] The Act received the Royal Assent in July 1910.

The planned route began at a junction with the Putney line north of Wimbledon station and a widening of the existing 2-platform station would provide additional platforms. South of the road bridge, the existing railway cutting would be widened to make room for the new tracks as far as Courthope Villas. Here, the new tracks would swing out to the west on a falling gradient and turn directly south, crossing beneath the LSWR main line before heading south towards Sutton. The proposed station here was on the Cheam Road, near St James's Road, but was later moved much nearer the LBSCR station. The exact track arrangement at Wimbledon does not appear to have been settled. Between Wimbledon station and the underpass beneath the LSWR there was to have been a station serving the Wimbledon All-England Tennis Club off Worple Road (the club only moving to its present location in 1922). It was hoped this station would attract a lot of traffic during matches.[8]

Trying to raise the money proved hard work and very unrewarding and attempts to arouse interest from either the Underground or the LSWR failed to produce anything useful. The promoters realized that the existing railways were simply not prepared to risk bearing the potential losses on a line which at that time would pass through quite a thinly populated area; after further discussion with Albert Stanley a proposal was made in October 1911 for the District to build the line if the promoters would guarantee £6000 per year for 10 years (at first the hopeless amount of £20,000 was suggested). If the income failed to cover 4½ per cent of capital (perhaps £15,000 a year) then the District would bear the loss. On that basis, in December 1912, the W&SR board was replaced by Underground nominees and for practical purposes the railway became an Underground subsidiary. The move was not entirely philanthropic as the District wanted to protect its own interests and there seemed a reasonable chance that housing development would eventually yield a return. In 1913 a further Act was obtained increasing the share capital to £550,000, but only £5350 worth of capital was actually raised. No further progress was made during wartime.[9]

On taking control of the W&SR, the Underground reviewed the task and found the case for two of the stations weak. In addition it was decided that not all trains from London would run through to Sutton and part of the service would reverse at Merton Park where there would be a siding. Additional stabling would be provided at Morden South. Before war broke out the venture was felt comparable with Hounslow and Harrow lines and could with care be profitable.[10]

North of Wimbledon the District felt it could not provide a good service to Sutton if it had to share tracks south of Putney with the LSWR: the situation was similar to west of Studland Road which had just been improved by quadrupling the line and giving the District use of its own independent tracks and that is what was wanted south of East Putney. Authority was obtained in the MDR Act 1912 with the District agreeing to pay interest on the capital raised by the LSWR, which was to carry out the work. Widening was to be along the west side of the line at the Wimbledon end, and the east side at the Putney end. Of the four tracks, the pair on the west side (referred to as the western lines) would be used exclusively by the District.

North of Putney Bridge there had also been concerns about W&SR trains overloading the facilities and in 1913 the District acquired powers for widening part of the route along its Fulham branch. Four-tracking the whole way through District territory was not justified but non-stop services to serve the Sutton extension would be greatly aided by installation of additional running lines between the south end of Walham Green station and the viaduct section south of the Parsons Green sidings (at Munster Road). Much of the land was already in District ownership. Parsons Green station was to have been rebuilt with four platforms, but in wartime conditions nothing was done.

After the Great War it was found that circumstances had changed. The pressure was on for a southward extension of the CSLR towards Mitcham and meanwhile the District had become so overcrowded that there was concern about adding W&SR loadings onto the Wimbledon line. The Underground determined that it would be better to extend the

CSLR through Morden and connect with the W&SR there: the W&SR would be built as part of a CSLR extension at the same time, rather than as part of the District. Meanwhile, prices for constructing the line had increased enormously and now seemed in the order of £1,300,000, including rolling stock.

During 1920, the government decided to 'group' the main line railways into four groups, or regional monopolies, whilst leaving them as private companies. The new Southern group included both the LSWR and LBSCR and took the view that both the unbuilt W&SR and connecting CSLR extension invaded its newly-defined territory, and so became hostile to both. After some difficult horse-trading with the Underground about this and other proposals, it was agreed that the new Southern Railway would take over the W&SR powers and build the line, and that the CSLR extension would be chopped off at Morden. The W&SR powers were formally transferred to the Southern in 1924, the separate company being dissolved. The W&SR finally opened in 1929-30 as part of the main line railway system but financially it was always a disappointment.

When opened there were just six intermediate stations, two of which (Morden South and West Sutton) were slightly relocated. Stations at the Tennis Club, Elm Farm and Cheam Road were not constructed but an additional station was built at St Helier to serve a new housing estate.

At Wimbledon, some preparatory work was done before war broke out and interrupted matters. In 1912-3 the platform on the north side of the station was widened to form an island, with an additional track installed to its north. The new platform was used exclusively by District trains whilst the original pair was shared with LSWR trains. The third platform was probably required on traffic grounds alone but reports at the time suggested that it was in contemplation of the W&SR which would use the island before the tracks disappeared south into a short tunnel.[11] At about the same time some of the land acquired elsewhere along the route was fenced.

Between 1926 and 1928 Wimbledon station was entirely reconstructed by the Southern Railway and the north station integrated within the development. The north station's central siding was removed in 1926 and the two platforms lengthened and widened to form two islands with four platform faces, virtually exclusively for District trains. A connecting concourse was installed at the south end with wide steps up to the main station overbridge. No provision was made for any future southwards extension.

Ticket Issuing Improvements

Electrification had no direct impact on ticket issuing technology, where the vast bulk of tickets were sold from ticket offices. Separate ticket stocks had to be kept for nearly every journey for which there was a demand, including variants by class of travel and many other factors. The accounting required was formidable and, of course, all transactions were by cash, especially copper. From about 1910 there was some simplification by grouping several journeys onto just one ticket where the ticket type and fare were the same, slightly reducing the stocks having to be held. Even so, these tickets did not cover journeys requiring completion by a non-Underground company and it was not until the late 1920s that a more aggressive approach was adopted to reduce the stocks having to be held; such a move was encouraged by the widening use of passenger-operated machines which could not handle the complexity of the existing system. The resulting tickets could be rather cluttered as they had to list all the stations to which they were available and this could take up so much space the list had sometimes to be continued on the back.

The ability to purchase season tickets at any station was in evidence by 1912 for certain journeys but the process was not complete until 1st July 1928 when the Mansion

Mile End ticket hall in 1927. This shows one of the Underground's standard ticket booths installed to improve flows although the rest of the station had not altered much since opening in 1902. These booths were installed in large numbers in the late 1920s. LTM

House season ticket office closed. Making it easier to buy seasons helped promote sales and reduced daily queueing but the need to keep season ticket records at stations of issue was restrictive and time consuming where a season was demanded or renewed.[12]

It is perhaps surprising to note that the shortest period (or season) ticket was for a month and it was not until 21st September 1925 that the District experimented with weekly tickets following tests on other lines. These were available on demand on the basis of eleven journeys charged for whilst at least twelve were expected. They were technically available Sunday to Saturday but could be purchased (and used) from midday Saturday. They were at first only available from stations Osterley–Hounslow Barracks but were so successful they were quickly made generally available and included T.O.T. through journeys.[13]

There was some investigation into the use of passenger-operated machines; these had long been available but had been mechanically-operated and inflexible and not really much help in the busy environment of a bustling District ticket hall. The practice developed from 1908 of installing electrically-driven machines at the busiest stations that issued tickets at only one fare upon insertion of the correct money. Machines were installed, increasingly in banks, for the most heavily used fares and this arrangement allowed tickets to be sold very quickly to those knowing exactly what they wanted and who had the right money, relieving pressure on ticket offices. These early machines did not give change and issued pre-printed tickets, which were an accounting headache. It was not until 1928 when tickets were actually printed on demand by automatic machines onto blank ticket rolls and 1930 when change giving, very gradually, became practical as reliable change-giving mechanisms were devised.

1927 poster explaining that weekly tickets were now available at this station on demand. LTM

A monthly season from 1920 (not printed very straight on its card). At this time most tickets like this were issued from the District's season ticket office at Mansion House. Author's collection

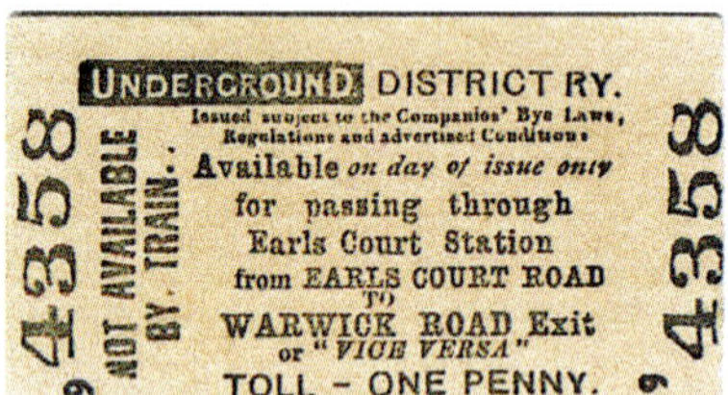

Toll tickets were at one time available at both West Kensington and Earls Court for transit through the respective stations, primarily for those going to and from the exhibition grounds. The Earls Court facility was useful for residents and lasted until the present century, a return version was also available. This ticket was issued 1st October 1921. Author's collection

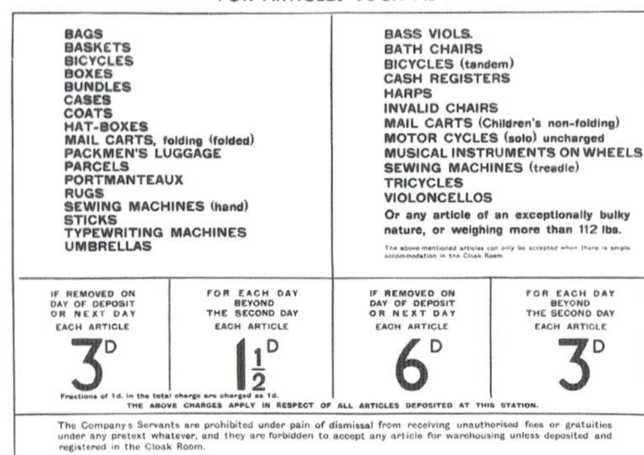

Left luggage Offices (cloakrooms) remained a feature of District stations throughout. A 1931 poster sets out the conditions. LTM

No. B 58148 28 JUL 1933

DISTRICT RAILWAY, ______ 193

Hammersmith Station Cloak Room.

Description of Article.	Amount Paid covering day of deposit and following day.	Issued By
Case	3d	N

Additional charge for each day or part of a day beyond the second day ... ... 1½d.

Sundays not counted unless the article be either deposited or taken out on that day.

(Fractions of one penny in the total amount payable are charged as One Penny.)

This Ticket **MUST BE SURRENDERED** before the Article referred to hereon can be released.

Released by ______

ISSUED SUBJECT TO THE COMPANY'S CONDITIONS AND REGULATIONS.

SEE BACK

A typical District cloakroom ticket. The ability to leave bags, coats and luggage at stations was considered an important duty of many railway companies. Author's collection

At Victoria in 1914 a machine was tested that could print any of five different kinds of tickets and could deal with up to ten kinds if required. It was operated by depressing levers and power was transmitted through a chain drive from a 200 volt dc motor, apparently obtained from a 550 volt supply (perhaps the traction supply) through resistances.[14] This is not the only example of a multi-fare machine that was tried, but the Underground found single-fare machines far more effective and stuck with the principle until the 1980s.

Another measure to improve flows was the substitution of small ticket booths in ticket halls to interact better with passenger flows, thereby speeding up traffic. Typically these free-standing booths (often called passimeters) had a window on each side, one always open and the other opened at busy times. Sometimes the old wall offices were kept in use to sell season tickets or assist at busy times.

The 1920s also saw a great deal of automation inside ticket offices with machines like the 'Rolltic' or the power-operated 'automaticket', which could cut and issue tickets from pre-printed rolls. Several of these could issue the most popular fares faster than a clerk having to withdraw tickets from a rack and they were also less prone to fraud. Then there were the big beasts such as the automatic printer that could issue any of fifteen different types at the push of a button by the ticket clerk, the tickets printed from blank rolls upon issue and were very fast. Combinations of this new technology could be installed in many of the busier offices and could also be installed in the passimeter booths. The deployment of change-giving machines inside ticket offices meant the chore of giving change was also speeded up and made more accurate.

Very much related to the fare collection process was the collection of money at the end of journeys. For all sorts of reasons large numbers of passengers on arrival at their destination station either had the wrong ticket, or no ticket, and ticket collectors had to ascertain what was owed and collect the difference as cash. No ticket was issued as passengers were completing their journey and although receipts were supposed to be given this was time consuming and delayed passengers behind. Understandably, passengers did not wait for any receipt, even had they been aware they existed, and staff found themselves at the end of their shift with an appreciable amount of money which they were required to pay into the ticket office where (for the first time) there was a process for accounting for it. Needless to say, tests revealed that there was an appreciable difference between the money collected and that which was paid in.

Attempts were periodically made to minimize the leakage of money collected this way. Following the reconstruction of Blackfriars station in 1914, the ticket collectors there were provided with cash registers to record excess fares. These were quite large and expensive pieces of equipment but could ring up a fare visibly (so that passengers could see it tally with the cash paid) and the transaction was recorded immediately and so had to reconcile with the cash paid in. The cash registers were provided by the National Cash Register Co and also allocated to Mansion House, Charing Cross, Sloane Square, Walham Green, Chiswick Park and Ealing Broadway.[15] We do not know how long they lasted, but they did not endure and in later years pre-printed receipts were attempted as a means of encouraging passengers to take receipts. This was almost equally hopeless a solution as passengers could not be bothered to wait and it was impossible to reconcile the few receipts issued with particular transactions.

District stations no longer accepted unaccompanied parcels but retained left luggage offices and facilities to weight passenger's luggage and other accoutrements where charges might be necessary. As before, left luggage offices were usually attached to the ticket office where items left were secure and properly accounted for.

Station Development after the Great War

Developments at stations came in two categories. The first included the actions taken by the District primarily to exploit property rights, either by using air space or by moving stations into basement level and using the space released at street level for commercial purposes. The second was a combination of initiatives to improve flows through stations and to speed up the process of issuing tickets (already referred to), often requiring significant changes to station layouts. These activities inevitably overlapped.

Mansion House station in 1924, showing a busy westbound train. This view captures the scene at many District stations, particularly the Smiths bookstall, Finlay's kiosk, chocolate machine and the typical train indicator. A very similar scene would have been found possible until the 1960s. LTM

Many of the District stations were improved internally during the 1920s, usually to improve flows. On the whole, station exteriors were not greatly altered although some effort was put into tidying up the exteriors so that station names (usually on canopy signs) were clear and a small number of maps and poster frames were correctly displayed. The early box-like illuminated Undergound signs of 1909 were eventually replaced by more modern signs usually incorporating the red and blue bar and ring device which was by now regarded as the Underground's trade mark. More extensive work took place at the stations set out below.

Mansion House

The comprehensive changes at Mansion House before the war served the station well but in the 1920s further piecemeal improvements were required. These were announced in January 1928 and were substantially completed by October, though further remodelling of the booking hall was still in hand. The ticket hall was entirely redecorated and new equipment installed. The main station entrance was also faced with Portland stone, after the fashion of the new station on the Underground's Morden extension.[16] The entrance was floodlit at night.

A Mansion House curiosity was a small collection of stuffed animals displayed for some years in glass cases at the west end of the eastbound platform. These had some tenuous association with the railway. The caption of the otter, for example, indicated it was caught at Acton Town on 4th April 1911, but did not explain why. There were also some owls. The cases were there by 1925 but were shifted to the new low-level concourse at Charing Cross in 1929. The Underground publicity people playfully referred to the display as 'The Zoo'.[17]

Blackfriars

As traffic increased after the war, it was found that further changes were needed at Blackfriars where the basic design still harked back to 1870 and in August 1925 it was announced the station was to be rebuilt. The works were associated with a network of subways which a thoughtful City of London Corporation built in 1910. These connected the Embankment, Queen Victoria Street and New Bridge Street, one exit of which was close to the station entrance.

The plan, hatched in 1923, was to build a much more efficient ticket hall at a lower level and plug it into the subway network, thereby linking the station with both Victoria Embankment and New Bridge Street.[18] This involved creating a short passage from the new ticket hall, through the basement of the station restaurant to meet the subway. The old ticket hall and access stairways had to be swept away and a large new intermediate landing created where passimeter-type ticket booths could be installed. New stairs had to connect this new space both with each platform as well as with the Southern's station above. The new passimeters came into use on 2nd February 1927, together with up-to-date ticket printing equipment. The huge reconstruction work was declared complete later that month though the *Railway Times* complained about dirty water dripping from the old LCDR bridge onto District passengers below.

Charing Cross

The extension of the Hampstead Line to Kennington (opened in 1926) required additional escalators and considerable expansion of the interchange concourse area under the District where four additional escalators and new stairways had to be accommodated. The opportunity was taken to enlarge the ticket hall (again) by expanding to the west of the main entrances, under the main line viaduct, and installing the usual passimeter ticket booths. In turn this enabled the existing ticket office to be removed and a number of shops to be introduced into what looked like a small shopping arcade. The extra space allowed direct stairs to be installed between the ticket hall and the interchange concourse.

Although the new lower-level escalators were available for the opening of the extended Hampstead tube link the work of reconstruction carried on for some time, with a second phase seeing escalators connecting the ticket hall with the interchange concourse, these opening on 4th December 1928.

This was one of the Underground's busiest stations and when finished was designed to accommodate 50 million passengers a year. Guides in distinctive uniforms had been appointed in 1928 to help direct passengers to the correct platforms and the following year a scheme of coloured lights was installed to give directions using small coloured route signs placed at intervals in the ceilings. For example, someone arriving from a tube platform and wanting Victoria would follow a succession of illuminated green signs every 15-20ft to the westbound platform. Other destinations used red lights, or blue, and so on. Though the number of colours available was limited, the lights were reckoned to cover more than two thirds of the journeys required by people unacquainted with the station.[19] The updated concourse was equipped with several novel floor signs made of large aluminium letters sunk into the floor but, though quite conspicuous, the idea wasn't used elsewhere.[20]

Ticket hall at Charing Cross (now Embankment) in June 1931. The Underground persistently sought the best way of automating ticket issue and this arrangement was about as convenient as it could get and was clearly arranged as the main points of ticket sale. The ticket office was retained for issue of more complicated tickets.
LTM

Auxiliary exit at Westminster station onto Victoria Embankment as it was in 1916. This was accessed by steps from east end of platform. The exit was not open all the time. This image shows well the early use of the 'bullseye' device as a trademark; for some years this was used alongside the early 'Underground' devices until during the 1920s the new bar-and-circle symbol began to predominate. LTM

Westminster

The 1909 changes at Westminster unfortunately proved to be only a stop-gap remedy and by the early 1920s the station again demanded enlargement, the work taking place between January and October 1923. The main entrance in Bridge Street was further widened and the 1909 booking office, at street level, was done away with. In the space occupied by a large restaurant (by the ticket barriers) a large new circulating area was installed, with modern passimeters and automatic machines which came into use on 20th October. A new and wider staircase to this area was made from the street and the stairs to the westbound platform were improved, making more space at platform level.[21] The following year the District was pleased to observe traffic here rise by half a million a year, largely attributed to the better facilities.

An unexpected addition was a pair of lunette paintings, representing Hampstead Heath, produced by the Westminster School of Art and offered to the London County Council for display at their new County Hall headquarters but, ungraciously, declined. These were gratefully accepted by the Underground for display in the new ticket hall at Westminster.*

In April 1925 it was announced that the embankment entrance would be improved, with a passimeter replacing the existing hole-in-the-wall ticket office. This secondary access

* A lunette painting is on a semi-circular background, redolent of a half-moon, usually with the flat portion at the base. Their fate is unknown, but *Survey of London* suggests they were returned to the school before WW2, the school not re-opening after the war.

This shows St James's Park station where the roof is being removed preparatory to erecting offices over the platforms. A protective crash deck has been installed whilst work is in progress. The photo appears to have been taken from the rear of Electric Railway House looking towards St Ermin's Hotel. Author's collection

has been described as a 'temporary' timber exit opened in 1898* from a point near the east end of the platforms onto Victoria Embankment right next to St Stephens House.[22] It appears to have been improved in 1906 when on 15th December a small ticket office was installed and this facilitated interchange between the District and the new electric LCC trams that began operation along the embankment.[23] Further improvements, in 1911, were designed to address the heavy traffic expected during the Coronation.[24]

The 1925 reconstruction was undertaken by the architect Charles Holden who devised a portland stone entrance and remodelled, tiled ticket hall with a small passimeter type ticket office. This was Holden's first work for any of the Underground railways.

St James's Park

In 1922 the Underground had a space problem: the organization was growing anyway but more urgently the lease on former LGOC offices in Grosvenor Road were shortly to expire. It was now desired to consolidate the whole of the companies' management at St James's Park, but the existing office space, inherited from the District, was hopelessly too small.[25] Wishing also to get rid of the large all-over glass and iron station roof, the decision was made to take off the roof and floor over the platforms in order to build a long, thin office block that followed the line of the railway, the offices connected to the existing offices at the eastern end. This arrangement was not without complication as the station could not be closed except at night and the new building had to rest on 22 girders, together weighing 550 tons and needing to be supported on ferro-concrete piers sunk far

* This was possibly in connection with the arrangements for Gladstone's funeral where very large numbers of spectators were expected.

below platform level. Work began in August 1922 and it was ready for occupation in 1924 under the name 55 Broadway, attempts to find a more interesting name by means of a competition with a five pound prize proving fruitless.

In January 1927 the Underground made it known it wished to build large new offices at the east end of the over-station offices where the main station booking hall and some miscellaneous buildings lay. The offices were to be large enough to accommodate staff in rented outlying offices, with room to spare for letting. Work was quickly put in hand to clear the site and the main work began in July; by October, pile driving was already in progress—a lengthy process as there were to be 700 of them. On Sunday 11th December 1927 a crane collapsed over the tunnel whilst attempting to lift a 30 ton girder in place, the line being blocked till 9.50am.

The result was a 'skyscraper' building, capped with a tower and flagpole, and occupying a site partly over the railway at the junction of Broadway and Tothill Street. There were nine principal floors above ground level, all designed as open spaces that would be partitioned into individual offices as required; the top of the ninth floor was 113ft above the street. The large first floor followed the ground floor plan but, above that, the block was of cruciform plan with each 48ft wide wing stepped back at seventh and ninth floor levels. The lifts continued to a tenth floor landing in the base of the tower but this space was only about the size of the entrance hall. The directors and principal officers were accommodated on the seventh floor which was lavishly panelled in wood.

The station entrance was subsumed within the reconstruction and occupied the Petty France entrance, more or less directly above the tracks. Additional entrances were available in Broadway and opposite Tothill Street. The new ticket hall benefited from the sumptuous architecture of the main building though there was little done at platform level where finishes were already quite modern. The resulting head office complex (which incorporated the linked 1905-9 and 1924 buildings) was large enough for expected future expansion and at first only four of the nine floors in the new block were actually occupied by Underground staff with the rest of the space let out. The formal opening ceremony was held on 1st December 1929.

Victoria

The pre-war works at Victoria had been started with the intention by the District to locate a 'high-class' hotel over the platforms, to showcase how a good site could be exploited. Before his death, George Sherrin had actually designed the superstructure for the hotel building but the plans were turned down by the London County Council and the project stalled, not being pursued until after the war.

The substantial foundations for the new station building anticipated a large superstructure being added later. The existing station was supported on a concrete raft 3ft 6ins thick and extending 29ft below road level. To carry the expected future loads, the new foundations were much deeper, addressing the poor ground above the clay level 42ft down, above which sat a 12ft layer that was waterlogged (the area having once been part of the Westbourne River).[26] In addition, the whole of the platform area was covered over by a reinforced concrete raft.

After the war a more modest office block was designed by Trehearne and Norman (office design specialists); this included a large restaurant area, operated by Callard, Stewart & Watt, a small London chain. This work was confined to the area over the ticket hall and was complete by about 1925 and included the name Victoria Station House in tilework near the top of the Terminus Place façade. The block was seven storeys high, exclusive of the two-storey street level building and arcade already built; it had an

Terminus Place at Victoria in about 1924 showing Victoria Station House being constructed above Sherrin's pre-war station arcade. Capital Transport collection

Victoria station platforms in May 1924, perhaps a tad dingy because of the relatively low overhead structures. Just visible at top left is the wire for the train starting device (this type required the guard to pull down slightly on the lower wire using his flag). LTM

entrance on the Victoria Street frontage to the west of the arcade, with the restaurant entrance at the west end.[27]

Whilst work on the superstructure was in hand, other improvements were also carried out. Traffic levels had risen from 16 million in 1914 to 22 million in 1923 and it had become necessary to improve flows through the station. During 1924 two new staircases were constructed.[28] One of these led to the east end of the westbound platform and succeeded in getting passengers to spread out more, reducing congestion.

Victoria had already made use of numerous banks of ticket machines to ease the pressure at the ticket office and it was reported in August 1923 that a new bank of twelve ticket machines were doing well and that four were issuing at rate of 2½ million tickets a year. In 1926 it was decided to reorganize the ticket hall, replacing the existing clutter with passimeter booths and automatic machines, stairways being illuminated by flood lighting. An area of 4000 square feet was made available for the reworked ticket hall. At the same time work was in hand to construct a proper bus terminal on ground between the District and main line station, further increasing Victoria's usefulness as a transport interchange.

Sloane Square

Sloane Square station reached the 1920s little-changed from the day it opened in 1868, though two shops extending forward to the square obscured much of the station frontage. The problem here was felt to be the great depth of the platforms (owing to the need to pass under the River Westbourne) and hence the very lengthy and irksome steps. In January 1927 the railway announced a scheme to rebuild the station in, by-now, fashionable Portland stone and at the same time install an up escalator from the westbound platform to an intermediate gallery, and another up escalator from there to the remodelled ticket hall; those ascending from the eastbound direction would be able to use the upper flight too.[29] Owing to other commitments this modest scheme was not pursued for another decade and the most modern feature at the station was the special illumination of a 22ft by 11ft sign above the station entrance by a projector lamp 25ft away, installed in 1921 to replace the old box-type sign with 30 lamps in it. More plans were drawn up during the interim, including a proposal for a circular below street ticket hall in 1930, connected to the outside world by subways, but this was no more affordable. The station was used throughout the electric period as a crew relief point enabling train staff to have a meal break there (a mess-room was provided on the premises and a staff waiting area was provided on the platforms).

South Kensington

It was at South Kensington that smart dining rooms were created for the Underground's administrative staff above the District's substation, with an entrance in Pelham Street. Two floors were available, one mainly for functions and the other as a restaurant with adjacent kitchens. The pleasant frontage was improved with large oriel windows overlooking the street. The dining rooms replaced facilities at St James Park, but were only a 5-minute train journey away. They were formally opened by Lord Ashfield on 7th November 1922 and handed over to the staff to operate themselves as the Underground Electric Railways Dining Club.[30] The station itself was not further altered until the 1950s.

South Kensington station booking hall in February 1928 showing semi-circular ticket office (on right) between the entrance stairways and access to platforms on left. The basic arrangements here had not altered since 1906 reconstruction. LTM

The Warwick Road entrance to Earls Court had changed little since its opening to serve the exhibition grounds. Signage has attempted to improve the appearance, including the District's scripted initials, which have survived the relentless UNDERGROUND branding in this October 1927 view. LTM

Earls Court

Earls Court had seen very little change since the arrival of the new Earls Court Road building in 1906, apart from the 1911 escalator interchange with the Piccadilly Line, which did not affect access to the District parts of the station (though it allowed two of the four lifts to be removed).

In June 1928 the District announced that it proposed to redevelop the Exhibition site west of the station as an exhibition hall for hosting large public and trade exhibitions; this would be the largest building of its kind to be erected in London. It was hoped to complete this within next two years.[31] In the event endless delays meant that the new exhibition building was not even started until 1936, but the District began to design a new station building, walkway and stairs in 1932 though the work was not completed until after the District ceased to exist.

West Kensington

West Kensington received some updating. It had survived quite well with its original station configuration but it was proving quite unsuited to prevailing conditions. The whole of the internal arrangements at street level were swept away and a spacious new ticket hall produced with a small ticket-issuing booth set into the barrier line. The old-fashioned frontage was refaced by a modern-looking Portland stone façade with wider entrances, completed by February 1928.

Above: **Earls Court Warwick Road entrance in 1928 looking towards platforms, showing corrugated-iron roof of the old walkway and a new-ish ticket booth.** LTM

Below: **This view of Ealing Broadway in early 1920s shows off the vast recently-built bridge that connected the platforms together (at that time each of the three stations was operated separately). In the foreground is French 1905 trailer 518 with unidentified motor car of similar date leading.** Alan A Jackson collection

Hounslow Line station improvements

The doubling of tracks in stages towards Hounslow Barracks before the Great War allowed service improvements to be made, matching population growth in the area. Even so, the still-remote Hounslow Barracks station was not itself privileged to be on the double track railway until 1926, and when it did the existing Victorian station building was felt adequate. At platform level the original single platform was retained, nestling against the cutting along the south side. In the space to the north once occupied by a siding and engine run-round a new island platform was installed, giving three platform faces in all. All platforms had waiting facilities and awnings, extending about a quarter of their length. Even at this stage, development in this area was very slow and barely extended west of the station at all.

By this time the station names had been simplified, Hounslow Barracks became Hounslow West, Heston-Hounslow became Hounslow Central and Hounslow Town became Hounslow East, the changes being made from 1st December 1925.

Goods and Freight

The District might have developed a sizeable freight business by allowing other companies to use its lines but, through inertia, allowed the matter to drop with the exception of the Midland's trains to the Kensington freight yards which dated back to the 1870s. The idea of developing freight was discussed quite often, but not much was actually done.

In 1899 both the Midland and LNWR made overtures to the District about providing access to possible new depots but (according to those companies) 'no reasonable arrangement could be come to' and the matter dropped. With Forbes gone the District attempted to revive discussions in 1902 but with electrification looming the matter again dropped.

In 1908, the District revived discussions and after three years of procrastination an agreement was entered into in 1911. There was now some activity but no attempt was made to construct any yards, blame being placed firstly on the Great War and then on the diversion of effort required to implement the Railways Act 1921, which resulted in the creation of the LMSR which now took the matter up, but not until 1926. After further desultory discussions with the District, even this barely perceptible momentum was lost and the idea was allowed to die of natural causes.

The early planning work had identified five sites for freight yards. The smallest was at Hounslow on the made ground north of the LGOC garage where the Hounslow Town triangle had once been. The next was at Acton Town on former siding land alongside the South Acton branch where the District planned to break down long freight trains arriving from Willesden into shorter trains for the District yards, and make up longer trains for the departing trips. There was then to be a yard near North Ealing on the east side on land in District ownership. Another yard was planned at South Harrow, south of the station where the old car sheds had been for the 1903 experimental electrification. Finally, a huge yard was planned at Northfields on ten acres of land purchased for the purpose by the District for £12,390 and rented out for allotments.

The LMSR believed the 1911 agreement actually obliged the District to build these depots, though by 1926 only the Northfields one really appealed, and then in part only to deny the facility to competitors. The LMSR even identified six traders who might occupy the depot. The moment had, however, passed.[32]

Technology

The signalling installed in 1905-6 worked well enough but some of the outlying sections had been left with mechanical signalling which was unsuited to the intensity of services now being run. Between 1905 and 1908 fourteen Westinghouse miniature frames had been installed and thirteen mechanical frames had been adapted, including an emergency frame at St James's Park. Mechanical frames at Hounslow West, Osterley and North Ealing were quickly found redundant and the frame at Chiswick Park went out of use after the upgraded station at Acton Town was completed.

Additional signal boxes were required from time to time. Mechanical frames were introduced at Charing Cross (1906, enlarged 1912) and Northfields (1919), in both cases to operate new crossovers that were unlikely to be heavily used. A new signal box was required at Turnham Green to handle District traffic on the rearranged tracks in 1911 and this was a new miniature electro-pneumatic frame with enough spare lever spaces to cope with considerable expansion if ever required.

On the Hounslow branch, signalling was upgraded in 1926 when the last section of single line was removed, the new track layout at Hounslow West being operated from a new brick-built signal box with power frame.

The mechanical signalling at Ealing Common, controlling the station and depot entrance, was replaced during 1925 by a new electro-pneumatic frame in the same signal box. Later in the year the mechanical signalling at Hanger Lane junction was abolished with control of points and signals shifted to the Ealing Common power frame where space had been left. Some mechanical frames remained but with the exception of South Harrow and Ealing Broadway these were now all emergency boxes not normally staffed.

Ealing Common signal cabin before and after power frame installed in 1925.

Not all signal boxes were open throughout the traffic day and over the years arrangements for handling closed signal boxes evolved. Some of the technical details about how this was managed is given in Appendix 3. In broad terms, when a signal box was closed the signals on the through lines were arranged to operate automatically. In its final form, from the mid-1920s the signals affected were provided with an illuminated sign (displaying a letter 'A') when they were working automatically. Station staff were usually trained to open a box in an emergency if trains had unexpectedly to be turned or stabled.

Several boxes were routinely closed where staff could be saved. The closure of Mansion House on Sundays (when Charing Cross was opened instead) has already been mentioned. Another example is the box at Earls Court West in 1921. When the LNWR trains were not running, on Sundays for example, the cabin could be switched out and all trains at the west end of the station worked automatically; this required the signalman at the east end to put them into the correct platforms. When the box was closed arrangements were made for the electrical train descriptions to be passed forward automatically to the next box as there was no signalman to do it.

Between signal boxes the signalling was entirely automatic, using Brown's relays, direct-current track circuits and pneumatic signals of either semaphore or the rising spectacle type. In addition to starting and home signals there was at first an intermediate signal between stations, or perhaps more than one in the longer sections, and this alone much-increased the line capacity compared with steam days, allowing more frequent services to run. Over time, further signals were added where found necessary. Continual improvements to improve train running in the light of experience also involved repositioning of some signals and the reduction of some of the section lengths where this could be done safely.

It was then found expedient to add extra home signals to reduce delays at busy stations where stopping times were unduly long. To achieve the timetable, the standard station stop time had not to exceed 20 seconds but this was quite impossible at many central stations—two and, later, three home signals were found necessary to maintain intervals at many of the busier stations. In order to run a 90-second service, it was necessary at the few exceptionally busy stations, during which a train might be stationary in the platform for 30 seconds or more, to have four home signals, successively clearing right in front of a train following behind one just pulling away. The idea was to minimise the possibility of a train having to stop in the tunnel behind a train in the platform if it had actually started to move.

The need to couple up trains in service required the introduction of calling-on signals to allow a train into an occupied section. The District had not at first thought these signals necessary, as virtually all coupling portions came out sidings, but this was not always convenient where cars had to be added at the east end which quickly became the standard arrangement. Calling-on signals of this type were first installed at Hammersmith and Parsons Green in 1913, in both cases to allow passenger trains to couple up to portions already in the platform.[33] These were not strictly the first calling on signals at there had been a short-lived one outside Earls Court in 1911 to allow trains from Putney to creep up close to the junction, but the new flyover there made it redundant.

Train dispatch was at first a complicated process, not helped by the lack of any positive indication that all the doors were closed and with the possibility that in hot weather passengers would insist on having some doors open throughout the journey. Nevertheless the staff were strongly encouraged to try and get all the doors shut before a train departed and to discourage people from attempting to board trains after they had started, not always successfully. Electric trains, after the early abandonment of air-worked doors, were worked with a guard on both the front and the rear cars. The rear guard used a flag when he considered all was ready for a train to depart. The front guard would observe the flag and when he, too, felt all was well he operated a bell that sounded in the driver's cab, upon hearing which the driver would drive away the train. Of the various weak points in this process, the ability of the front guard seeing the rear guard's flag signal was one.

To assist staff, the District installed an experimental train starting device at St James's Park (westbound) on 20th June 1921. This consisted of two 'pleasant toned' bells operated by a pull wire near the rear guard's position. When the rear guard considered it was safe to depart he operated the pull wire. When the front guard heard the bells he confirmed it was safe at his end of the train and then gave the driver the starting signal. This simple arrangement worked well enough and it was soon found that regular passengers reacted to the bells and got on or stood away knowing the train was about to move. Between 1922 and 1924 the system was extended to all platforms between Blackfriars and Sloane Square.[34]

On 8th May 1927 a modified kind of train starting device was introduced at Barons Court (westbound), after experiments at Earls Court and South Kensington.[35] With this device the pull-wire was replaced by a pair of bare wires attached by insulators to brackets suspended from the canopy or a column. This required the guard to press the metal ferrule on his flag stick against both wires to complete a circuit, which caused the starting bells to ring. At stations where the platform was on the offside (as at Barons Court) there was an illuminated indicator bearing the letter 'S', but this was only illuminated where the guard had actuated the bells and the starting signal was clear. The driver may or may not have heard the bells at a noisy station, but would have seen the indicator. This refinement was not considered necessary where platforms were on the nearside as drivers could look back along the train to see the guard's flag, either by opening the side window or using the rear view mirrors with which District driving cabs were fitted. The new style starting devices were fitted at all busy stations not already having one of the older devices during 1927 and 1928. By this time the number of train staff on most District trains had been reduced to a driver and one guard (at the rear), a change made during 1925. On 8-car trains a front guard was retained and continued to give the starting signal when the train starting device was operated. To provide an additional pair of eyes at the front of the trains, additional platform staff were provided. These devices were not fitted on foreign lines over which the District ran.

Another feature, introduced on 5th June 1921, was tested at Victoria when a warning device sounded a prescribed interval after each train arrived. This warning was in the form of a siren and indicated to passengers and staff alike when the train was expected to depart; it was operated by a clockwork mechanism initiated when the train stopped but only sounded if the starting signal were clear. This contraption appears to have followed an earlier experiment at Victoria when a member of staff was placed in an observation post armed with a stop watch and siren which (if the starting signal was clear) he would operate after the prescribed time. The system was used between 8 and 10am on the up line and 5 and 7pm on the down line. Extra station staff were deployed to hustle stragglers onto trains the moment the siren rang and it was stated that train stopping time had been reduced to 22¾ seconds.[36] It was reported that the siren system had proved so useful that it was also to be introduced at Charing Cross.[37]

Train recording clocks had been in use by the various railway traffic controllers for many years and proved very useful in monitoring the service, identifying gaps and producing a permanent record of performance. In late 1927 a bank of these recording clocks, one for each line, was installed in the foyer of the general offices at St James's Park (Electric Railway House), enabling senior managers to see at a glance what they were in for when they arrived and perhaps to remind other staff that they were dealing with a real time transport business (these were relocated to the foyer of the 1929 office block at 55 Broadway when it had been completed). A similar bank of clocks was installed near the entrance at Westminster station in the summer of 1928, perhaps to impress Members of Parliament with the efficiency of London's transport system.[38]

Keeping the trains clean was a necessary but very staff-intensive activity and in 1927 an automatic car washing plant was installed at Ealing Common depot. It was designed and built entirely by Underground staff, but the design was inspired by one on the Paris Metro. The machine comprised a succession of sprays that drenched the outside of the cars, which were driven slowly through the equipment whilst, at the same time, rotating leather strips were flung gently against the car sides to ease off the dirt. A final set of water sprays rinsed the sides before the train emerged from the departure end. The machine was about a car-length long and it was undesirable to carry the conductor rails through it so the sets to be washed needed to include several cars to avoid the risk of stalling off current. It was hoped to pass the entire fleet through the machine every four to six days, though some less-frequent manual external cleaning was needed to remove embedded grime.[39]

During the 1920s District service enhancements and taking on the CLR supply from Wood Lane was taking up the last of the spare capacity at Lots Road. In the meantime some of the equipment was by then quite old and not particularly efficient by modern standards. Looming extensions were going to need at least some extra power. The station was modernized between 1928 and 1932 when the original boilers and Parsons turbo-generators were replaced by seven new 15 MW turbo-alternator sets and 32 larger boilers (leaving eight older boilers in service). This resulted in three old and seven new 15MW generators installed although two of the older sets were replaced during the late 1930s by the later type. The maximum station capacity was 150MW continuous with extended operation at 25 per cent overload, with some loss of efficiency.[40]

When the decision was made in the mid-1920s to shut down the Central London Railway's power station at Wood Lane it was necessary to provide new current supplies from Lots Road. As part of this, the District's Mansion House substation was upgraded and feeder cables to Bank (CLR) installed in August 1926.

The traffic hustler at Victoria in his rather home-made observation point. LTM

THE COLLISION OF DISTRICT ELECTRIC TRAINS AT WIMBLEDON: THE FRONT PART OF AN OUTGOING TRAIN TELESCOPED BY THE FIRST COACH OF AN INCOMING TRAIN CONTAINING PASSENGERS FOR THE LAWN-TENNIS TOURNAMENT.

Seen here at Wimbledon is the result of a serious head on collision on 27th June 1927 after irregular departure. The car behind (No 447) telescoped into the leading car and was damaged beyond repair. *Illustrated London News* 2nd July 1927

This shows the recovery of outgoing leading car car 185 which was fortunately at road level where access was straightforward. London Underground Railway Society collection

Mishaps

The District was comparatively free of serious accidents although there were inevitable bumps and derailments, most of which were of a minor nature, together with some major shutdowns because of external events, including a number of serious floodings.

An unusual event occurred on 19th February 1919 when fusing took place on a train's overhead line receptacle box (where power is obtained in depots) and this caused heavy stray currents to flow through the track at Osterley, which got into the gas main causing the gas meter house to explode. Three days later a GER goods train on ELR derailed sending high currents onto the District tracks burning out relays and seriously delaying the start of service. An interesting failure occurred on 6th August 1919 when a pickup shoe got wedged between positive and running rails at St Mary's; there was no obvious damage locally but by bringing the whole of the District track to traction potential, negative fusing broke out at weak points at Sudbury Town and Heston-Hounslow (seventeen miles away) causing trains there to be delayed. Sudbury also came to note the following month when a bullock was electrocuted at Sudbury Hill at 6.28pm causing 27 minutes delay. We know not how it was removed. On 5th September 1919 there was an awkward derailment at Westminster following a broken axle at 9.35am. The initial incident was dealt with quite quickly but the train derailed twice more before it could be got out of the way at Mansion House at 6.53pm.

A much more serious incident took place at Wimbledon at 10.53am on 14th October 1920 when a 4-car District train collided with the buffers and mounted the concourse, killing one woman and injuring seven bystanders on the concourse and injuring three people on the train. The buffers were demolished and the leading car significantly damaged. The subsequent investigation found nothing wrong with the equipment but some evidence of slight skidding as wheels locked at the last moment when the emergency brake was applied. The investigating officer found the driver had been travelling faster than usual (there were no speedometers in those days) and did not have his train under proper control. The officer was critical that the usual twin main-line type spring buffers were provided by the LSWR, which owned the station, while the train had a central buffer and this contributed to the demolition which thereby occurred and the train mounting the concourse. He wondered if there was a technical solution to slowing a train down at terminal stations.

Wimbledon was also the scene of the next serious accident when a District train arriving at Wimbledon at 12.13pm collided virtually head on with a train departing from an adjacent platform. The point of collision was about 100ft north of the platform ends and resulted in eight passengers and four staff being injured, seriously in the case of four passengers and one member of staff. There was moderate damage to a number of cars but telescoping took place between the first two cars of the outgoing train and the second car, a wooden trailer, was so badly damaged it had to be written off. The facts were disputed but it was eventually determined that on the outbound train neither the driver nor the guard giving the 'right away' had actually checked the starting signal was lowered and as the LSWR did not install trainstops on their railway there was nothing to stop a train proceeding irregularly. The enquiry observed that there had been other similar instances at Wimbledon of trains starting against a signal and further noted that whilst the District rules required the guard to check the starting signal before waving his flag the LSWR rules (which applied on this section) did not. The inspecting officer thought the LSWR should alter the height to make the signals visible from the rear of the train.[41]

Finance

Early in February 1921 the Press was bemused to be told that the directors had declared a 1 per cent dividend on the ordinary shares of the District, the first dividend since 1882 when it was just 0.18 per cent. At last, the appreciable levels of traffic were beginning to overcome the dead weight of the expenditure in those early years, though the existence of the common fund was just as much the cause as there was some cross-subsidy. In subsequent years a modest dividend continued to be paid. In 1921 the District results included £705,347 war compensation (now stopped). The results might have been better had there not been the coal strike between April and June and the subsequent depression.

The operation of the common fund means the published results of the District are more a reflection of the Underground as a whole. To that extent the District was for the first time in its life reasonably successful and between 1928 and 1930 was paying no less than 5 per cent on its ordinary shares, though these fell back slightly as the serious depression of the early 1930s reduced demand.

In 1931, by way of example, traffic receipts after the operation of the common fund came to £1,470,865 with costs of £976,342. Allowing for miscellaneous income and costs, and sums put aside as reserves for renewals, the balance was £423,275. This was sufficient to pay the full amount of £275,930 for the fixed charges, guaranteed and preference shares with £145,575 to pay 4½ per cent on ordinary shares with a small amount carried forward. This was a fair performance.

Meanwhile the UERL's finances also improved as income (the profits from the companies it controlled) slowly rose. Until the mid-1920s no dividend had ever been paid on the ordinary shares as the dead weight of the 6% income bonds hoovered money out of the company. The situation was made more difficult by the bonds being paid tax free (the UERL, in effect, paid the tax) and the interest being payable in several currencies and locations. The adverse exchange rate with America, in particular, had become a huge problem and resulted in the bondholders, if they could, demanding to be paid in New York and costing the UERL tens of thousands of pounds a year in high exchange rates. The problem was that a fixed rate of exchange had been agreed in 1908 that now bore no relation to the prevailing rate. Fortunately, at least for the UERL, in 1925 Britain returned to the gold standard and this reduced the problem. Nevertheless the UERL was very keen to reduce the burden of these 6% bonds. With the enterprise now bordering on the profitable, the time had come to address the issue.

The UERL shares were a different problem. Apart from the five million £10 ordinary shares issued in 1902 the purchase of the LGOC involved issuing nearly £1.2 million one shilling 'A' shares and it was now desired to combine them taking into account their market value and expectation of imminent dividends. Both shares were swapped: the old UERL shares were exchanged on the basis of 7.1 new £1 shares for each old £10 share and the 'A' shares on basis of eleven new £1 shares for ten old one shilling 'A' shares. The outcome was virtually the same capital but divided into 5,068,878 £1 shares (this also included shares exchanged for certain 'contingent certificates' held by the holders of the old shares). The expected profits were delivered, at last. 1½ per cent was paid in 1926, rising to 8 per cent in 1929 and 1930 before dropping back a little during the recession. Allowing for the share swap, an 8 per cent rate of interest was equivalent to over 5½ per cent on the original value, which was reasonable for the 3850 investors who had held them for a quarter century without seeing a penny. They also began trading at a premium, showing confidence.[42]

The income bond problem was addressed during 1927 with the UERL explaining that the present arrangement was too generous and the tax concession meant bondholders were receiving the equivalent of 7½ per cent. Whilst the bondholders, who had voting powers, were very unlikely to give up such a profitable income stream willingly, the UERL had one very important weapon to hand. The trust deed, by which authority the bonds had been issued in 1908, allowed the UERL to redeem the notes at any time before their 1948 expiry date and also (with the concurrence of bondholders) to alter the benefits conferred by the bonds. In July 1927 Ashfield's proposals were made known. In essence the bonds were no longer to be free of income tax and for ten years the UERL would refrain from redeeming the bonds at par; during this time there would be an option for the first two years to convert the bonds into ordinary shares at 22 shillings and after that either party could redeem the bonds at 103 per cent of their face value. After considering the response, the price for conversion was reduced to 21 shillings a share and the offer period extended to three years. The first bondholders' meeting on 6th August 1927 failed to achieve a quorum and was reconvened on 26th August where the proposal was lost on a show of hands. Ashfield required a poll be taken where the proposal was passed by votes to the value of £850,260 approving the resolution with only £199,210 against.

The number of 6% bonds affected amounted to £6,330,000 as additional bonds had been issued to deal with various challenges after 1908, including acquisition of the LGOC. In fact, the conversion offer was sufficiently attractive that by mid-1930 the number of outstanding bonds stood at only £414,270. These were compulsorily converted at 103 per cent on 2nd March 1931 by which time the UERL shareholding had risen to £10,700,990.[43]

It may be inferred from what has just been said that the District was now 'paying its way'. It is true it covered its operating costs, paid its finance costs and made financial provision for renewal of equipment on a like-for-like basis. What it could not do was to raise new cash easily for investment, or betterment. We shall see how this was addressed in the final chapters.

Staff and Organization

The Rt Hon Sir Edgar Speyer was not only a competent financier and good friend to London's underground railways but a generous philanthropist who amongst many other things supported affairs as diverse as Scott's polar expedition, the Proms, the National Society for the Prevention of Cruelty to Children and the Whitechapel Art Gallery. Though born in America and naturalized British in 1892, he had the misfortune to have German ancestors and family and in 1914 this became a problem. Almost as soon as war broke out, he was the victim of unprecedented paranoia and xenophobia and was effectively hounded out of the country, moving to America. By May 1915 he had gone and the chairmanship of the Underground passed to Lord George Hamilton. Hamilton remained chairman of the UERL and District until Stanley returned in 1919 when he became both chairman and managing director of the UERL, the railways it controlled and the LGOC. Henry Augustus Vernet became deputy chairman of all these concerns at the same time. As already noted, Stanley became Lord Ashfield in 1920.[44]

Throughout most of the 1920s the whole of the companies were in the safe hands of Lord Ashfield who exerted unprecedented influence and control. A major reorganization was announced in 1st February 1921 partly to reduce the administrative overhead and partly to streamline organization by further fusing together the administration of the various legally separate companies.

Two joint assistant managing directors reported to Ashfield, being H.E. Blain and F. Pick. The latter was noted earlier as one of the people brought to London in 1906 from the North Eastern Railway. Blain, also noted earlier, had been operating manager and assistant managing director in 1921. When he retired in 1924 to become chief agent of the Conservative Party, Pick became sole assistant managing director.

By the 1920s the separate organization of the District had virtually disappeared with all the senior railway officials sharing responsibilities across all four of the railways. John Pattinson Thomas was a name from the Yerkes era and was last noted moving to operating manager of the 'General' buses. As part of the 1919 reorganization he additionally took over as operating manager of the four railways, replacing the very competent H.E. Blain upon his promotion to assistant managing director. He lost responsibility for buses in 1921.

Reporting to Thomas was Mr J. Thornton, the superintendent of the line (a title used on many railways and in this case responsible for all the Underground railways). Thornton had for fourteen years previously been chief inspector of the District, though had started his railway career as a goods porter on the Caledonian Railway.[45] Thornton had replaced the popular W.E. Blake in 1919 following Blake's untimely death resulting indirectly from an injury sustained whilst helping out at a serious collision that year.

Below Thornton were two assistants. One dealt with so-called 'indoor' work which was essentially training and administration including recruitment, training, scheduling, policing and planning. The 'outdoor' assistant directly controlled day-to-day operations across all lines. To him reported several traffic superintendents, one of whom had sole responsibility for the District. The traffic superintendent was supported by a small number of 'control' staff to whom reported all the train and station staff.

By 1928 there were on the District 13 control staff, 43 stationmasters and inspectors, 152 booking clerks, 339 other station staff, 247 motormen, 282 guards and gatemen, 16 travelling ticket inspectors, 56 signalmen and 22 others.

Other names closely involved in the operation of the District were: W.A. Agnew (mechanical engineer), A.L. Barber (commercial manager), A.R. Cooper (chief engineer),

A selection of badges issued to District staff. All badges issued to operating grades were numbered so staff could be identified. Author's collection

District supervisory badges. There had been an earlier station master badge with the label at the bottom and the company initials in centre. The labels were of blue enamel. Author's collection

District station inspectors badge (foreman's badge similar with different label). There was also a divisional inspector's badge which bore no label. Author's collection

W.S. Every (signal engineer), S.A. Heaps (architectural officer), J.B. Mackinnon (superintendent of schedules) and S.J. Webb (passenger agent). Most of these people saw out the rest of their career with the Underground and, after 1933, London Transport.

The training of train staff involved an intimate knowledge of the equipment used on trains and even before electric services began it was recognized that there was a need for a specialist training facility where staff could be made familiar with the equipment. This led to a motorman's training school first at Mill Hill Park and later at West Brompton. Station staff on the District were less of a problem as the job involved a minimum of equipment and training could be given at stations.

As the Underground was welded together it became more necessary to have a uniform system of training across all the lines and in 1920 a central training school was established at Lambeth North, and this dealt with all the needs of the District. In addition to job-specific training the companies' doctor was located at Lambeth and all recruits had to pass a medical examination. The clothing store was also located in the premises.

This is Ealing Common depot where, on some date unknown, it was found necessary to photograph what appears to be the entire rolling stock staff. Roy Allen collection

Chapter Ten

TRAINS AND TRAIN SERVICES IN THE 1920s

Reinvigoration and the 1920 Stock Trains

Once the war was out of the way, the most immediate problem facing the District was shortage of serviceable rolling stock coupled with serious overcrowding in the central area, factors that were closely related since it was not possible to increase train services and overcrowding was causing delays. The war had greatly diminished the reliability of the fleet as maintenance was deferred, parts were difficult to obtain and labour had been reduced as skilled men had joined the forces (the introduction of the 8-hour day across the railway industry also meant that more skilled maintenance staff were needed and recruiting and training them was challenging).

In February 1919 Lord George Hamilton told shareholders:

> The prices of materials and labour is so high at the present moment that only the most vitally important works can be undertaken with any hope of securing an adequate return on capital expenditure. We have had a combination of difficulties to meet which were entirely beyond our control, which arose from war conditions and which during the past few months have been cumulative in their effect. We were practically prohibited from adding to our rolling stock. An arbitrary limitation was therefore imposed by Government upon the acquisition of fresh railway stock. Our old rolling-stock deteriorated, and with constant use and the perpetual overcrowding placed upon it a strain which necessitated an exceptional expenditure to maintain it in working order.[1]

In 1919 the fleet comprised the 14 experimental cars, 418 cars of the old wooden stock and 112 cars of the various batches of steel stock introduced just before the war, making 544 cars in all. Of these 40 cars were regarded as 'long-term' out of service and the performance of the others had deteriorated so that on a daily basis there were insufficient cars to match the reduced timetables and breakdowns were still common. In addition to the cars that were out of service, many of the indifferently-built wooden cars, the trailers in particular, were deteriorating badly. The train service became unreliable and it was found that the scheduled 40 trains an hour through the central area could not be delivered.

The District concluded the only practicable answer was to buy a large number of new cars, partly to replace the worst of the old ones and partly to allow services to be enhanced. So urgent was the need that it was discussed by the District on 12th November 1918, the day after the wartime armistice took place. It was decided the District needed a much-improved type of car as soon as deliveries and materials allowed. Getting the cars was not going to be easy. Frank Pick explained the problems at the time:

> There is great difficulty in placing rolling stock orders for passenger stock. Manufacturers are filled with orders, in some cases for five years ahead, for goods vehicles for which their works are laid out. War has occasioned a world shortage of rolling stock and it is hard to induce manufacturers to rearrange the work upon which they are engaged to take on work of a special character of underground passenger carriages.

Pick wanted the wartime machinery for prioritizing orders to continue as he felt the cars would be authorized, but the machinery was wound up.[2] 100 cars were finally ordered from the Metropolitan Carriage Wagon and Finance Co in summer 1919. Pick did not expect to get them very quickly owing to inability to 'secure us priority in the execution of the work and the supply of material'.[3]

The District went to a great deal of trouble to identify the most suitable door and seating layout and during early 1919 the board authorized mock ups being made so that options could be viewed. The District revealed it had 'built up' several cars in order that it might see what was the best type to order—the District wanted the world to know it was seeking best type of car that experience could produce.[4]

After painfully long delays, delivery was completed in August 1921 and the cars were formed up into twelve 8-car trains (with four spare cars). The 8-car formations were intended for use in the busy hours but could uncouple into 5-car and a 3-car portions at other times. The 1922 timetable shows ten of the new trains were required in service daily, generally timed to operate through the City at the very height of the peaks where they would be of most use.

The all-steel cars were 49ft 8ins long over end framing and built to the maximum possible width of 9ft 6¼ins at solebar level with sides tapering in to a slightly narrower width at roof level. The extra width meant it was unnecessary to fit continuous footboards along the car sides; these had been provided since 1912 in an attempt to reduce the gap between platform and car body. Each car had three sets of double-doors on each side of the car bodies but no doors at car ends; it was hoped these features would maximize carrying capacity and reduce loading times at busy stations. Although there were to be

A new District train on its way from Birmingham to Lillie Bridge, passing Northampton station. Behind the guards van there is a match wagon with District couplers at the far end, enabling this stock to be hauled. Trains were usually delivered this way although odd cars might be drawn as part of a scheduled freight train. London Underground Railway Society collection

Above: **New cars at about the time of delivery in 1921, strikingly different from older cars. Motor car 636 leads, with trailer behind. Destinations were to be shown by enamelled plates carried on the front of the train but 'Non Stop' or 'All Stations' was shown by a small swivelling plate adjusted from within the cab and visible through a small glass window.** Roy Allen collection

Below: **Interior of one of the new 1920 stock cars at time of delivery showing the original rather bland interior. Prominent in the ceiling are the troublesome air vents that were later sealed.** Author's collection

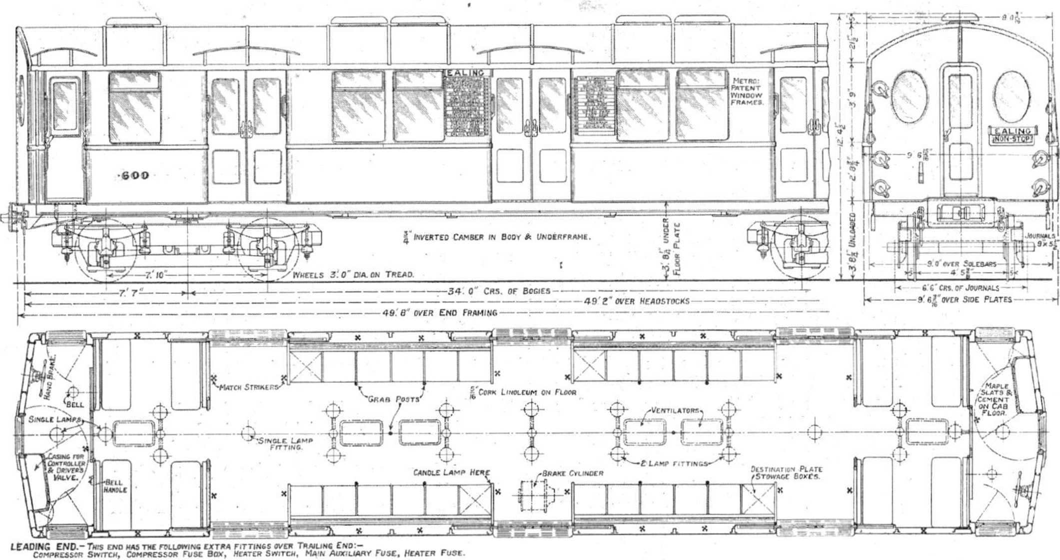

Outline general arrangement plan of 1920 stock showing car layout. Author's collection

only three motor cars on an 8-car train, each had all axles motored, unlike earlier cars which had axles on only one truck motored, and in consequence the control equipments were duplicated. New motors of the GE260 type, modified gearing and an additional motor bogie in the full length train, increased the nominal power from 1920hp to 2340hp and it was hoped this would address the concern that the existing trains were slightly under-powered. Unfortunately it was quickly found the new trains were rather over-powered and the higher acceleration and top speed was of no use so long as the new trains had to

Diagram showing arrangements of old stock (1905-1914) and the new stock trains. First class accommodation, car lengths and seating capacity are also indicated. Author's collection

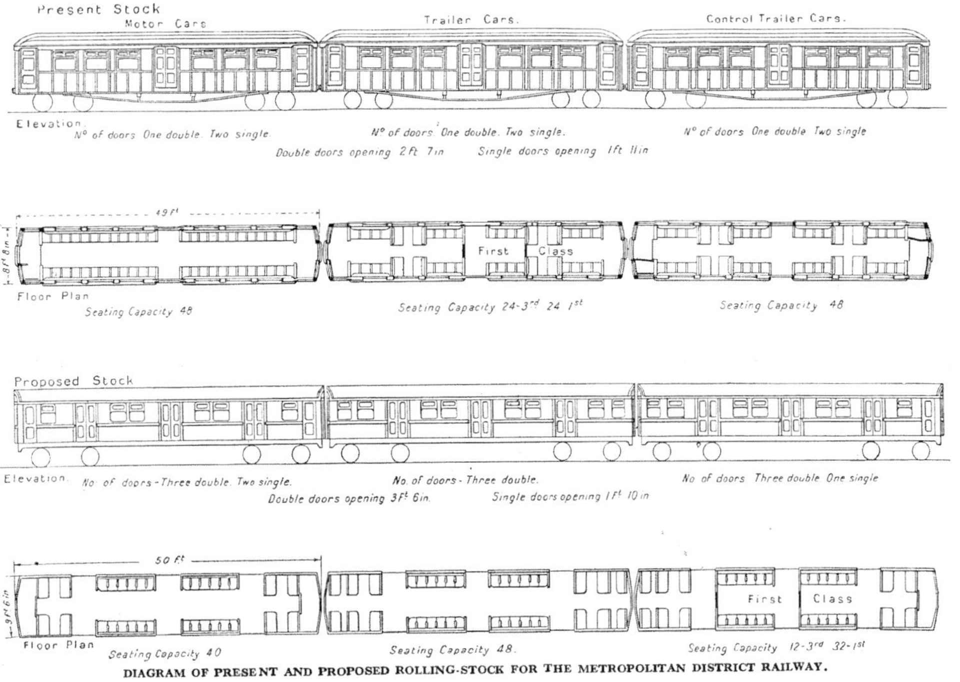

1920 stock trailer No 1003 in September 1922 after the cosmetic alterations had been made. This particular car was a composite trailer and was divided into sections by partitions. Just visible are the reupholstered seats, arm rests and the leather hand straps that replaced the free-standing vertical poles. LTM

interwork with so many of the old ones, and performance had to be reduced by removing the duplicate equipment and two motors from one motor car on each train.

The original composition was 40 motor cars, 12 control trailers and 48 trailers. The idea was to have motor cars at the outer ends of the 5-car portions and trailers between them; the 3-car portion had a motor car at the east end and a control trailer at the west end, this normally being the car to couple up. This arrangement, together with technical changes, meant that the trains would have to operate as a self-contained fleet, unlike the older cars which could at that time be coupled up in any formation as required. This was all a very different arrangement from the existing stock and for the whole of its time on the District system it had to be maintained as a separate fleet. The motor cars at first had driving controls in the compartments at both ends but the standard train formations quickly allowed one set to be removed as unnecessary (the control trailers had a cab only at one end). The cabs were separated from the saloons by a sliding door and could be used by passengers when not occupied by train staff (as before, the driving controls were shut away when not in use).

Following practice on older trains, non-stop display boards were fitted either side of the centre doors on all cars and continued to be of the swivelling plate type mounted one above the other, each bearing a station name on one side and blank on the other. There were so many stations that the list began by the left hand door and continued on the display on the right hand side. There was space for a destination board to be shown at the top of each left hand display, so that would have needed changing as well. It is perhaps of interest that amongst the potential non-stop stations were several east of Barking, anticipating by a decade the extension of services to Upminster.

Stylish, oval plate glass windows were installed in the ends of all cars (including the driver's windows) so one could see from one car to the next—a novel feature that predated by 70 years its reintroduction by London Underground. A great number of vertical grab poles were installed to make the work of standing passengers easier, but no hand-grabs were felt necessary. The steel floors were covered in cork linoleum. According to those present on the press viewing, ratchet-spring roller blinds were provided at each of the windows to reduce heat in summer. Fittings were of Florentine bronze, or were nickel plated. The roofs were of asbestos millboard, which photographs suggest were painted white. The interior surfaces of the carriage were for the first time of steel and descriptions of the finishes indicate the panels (and mouldings) were painted 'so as to resemble teak'. Presumably this meant some kind of brown; photographs suggest this was none too light in colour.[5]

Dissatisfaction with car ventilation on the 1914 Gloucester cars, with their Acme roof vents, caused a rethink and a completely new design was now attempted using ventilation holes along the centre line of the roof covered with what looks like an inverted rectangular tray, to keep out the weather. A narrow slit around all sides of this contrivance was intended to allow a moderate amount of air to pass beneath it in the hope that some of the resulting airflow would refresh the air inside the car.

First-class accommodation had to be provided in each portion of a full-length train. On the 3-car portion the control trailer was made a composite car with part of it divided off for first-class passengers. In turn this was also divided by a second partition into a smoking and non-smoking area. On the 5-car portion one of the trailers was subdivided in a similar way. Even the first-class seating lacked armrests, though individual seat cushions were provided, which photographs suggest were more comfortable than those in the rest of the train and are described as 'red plush'.

1920 stock Hounslow train in service at South Ealing in the 1920s. Old station name still in situ.
London Underground Railway Society collection

Third-class seats were covered in washable leather (it was actually a leather look-alike material coated with 'Pegamoid', a non-flammable cellulose-based substance, and described as having an 'old leather' finish). Cars each incorporated twenty 300W heaters that were located under the seats. 40 seats were available in motor cars and 48 in trailers (with control trailers, with a cab at only one end, seating 44). This seating arrangement meant that no seat was more than 9ft from a doorway.

The exterior paintwork of the previous District electric trains had been a bright red but these new trains were finished in a colour referred to as 'Engine Lake', which the *Railway Engineer* helpfully explains is a 'much deeper and more pleasing shade of red than the old-fashioned vermilion'. This seems to have been tested on a standard District car in 1919; according to the *Railway Magazine*:

> One car only, on the Metropolitan District Railway, has been painted English Lake outside and fitted with green curtains. This has been done as an experiment and in order to see whether this colour could be adopted in place of the familiar Post Office red which is the standard hue on the District line. The scheme has not been approved.[6]

It may not have been approved for the standard stock immediately, but seems to fit the description of the new cars, though the older stock did follow a little later.

In addition to reducing the power delivered by the new trains it was soon discovered that there was some adverse passenger reaction to the interior finishings, a pity, perhaps, given that two mock ups had been produced. Passengers found the interiors drab and unwelcoming, and the ventilation proved very draughty. The cars were rapidly modified. The clutter of grab-poles was completely cleared away and the usual longitudinal rails installed carrying the familiar leather straps. The roof ventilators had proved disastrous, probably because the airflows resulting from service conditions could not have been fully understood at that time: at any rate excessive draughts resulted and the opportunity was taken to seal these shut during the upgrading work (though the inverted trays remained fixed until the end of these cars' lives).

Recognizing the poor public reaction to the 'all steel' colour scheme as delivered, the District went out of its way to redeem itself. The well-known artist, Mr. Hall Thorpe,* was commissioned to plan 'pleasing and harmonious colour schemes' and several cars were decorated in order to show off the designs. Some were in grey, relieved with yellow, and were fitted with brown and gold moquette cushions. Some were in blue relieved with white, and fitted with brown plush cushions in the first-class compartments, and with brown and gold moquette cushions in the third class. Others were in green relieved with two shades of grey, the cushions being brown and green plush. All seats were fitted with moquette-covered arm rests, and were adjusted to be two inches wider. The floors were made more ornamental by the introduction of a kind of foot rest, breaking up the dull surface. Turning to the outside of the cars, these have been painted a deep brown, and the familiar Underground symbol 'London's Underground' appears on the side.[7] The description brown probably means the dark red colour about which no objection had been raised and which was later used on other stock.

We are invited to think one of the final internal colours selected for redecorating the trains, was blue and cream, but this is probably 'cerulean blue', or what Underground passengers for many years fondly remembered as the dark green and cream scheme used on most train interiors from the 1930s to the 1950s.

---

* John Hall Thorpe (1874-1947) was born in Victoria, Australia, and is best known for his woodcuts, but had strong views about the use of colour and interior decoration.

The staff magazine suggests that the successful internal redecoration of the 1920 cars drew attention to the drab appearance of some of the earlier stock and caused some upgrading of these cars too, at least in the first-class sections. An initial tranche of 23 first-class cars was dealt with in 1924 (the rest to follow) where the seats were more comfortably sprung and reupholstered throughout. Some were in brown plush, others in grey flowered moquette and the drab mahogany finishes that had 'prevailed for some years' gave way to bright and cheerful colours—yellow, green and brown.[8]

The contemporary press tells us that one of the 1920 cars had been equipped with noise eliminating devices, 'which are the outcome of experiments made by Professor A.M. Low'.[9] Archibald Low was an interesting man and a skilled communicator who perhaps could have achieved more if his fertile mind had not continuously been distracted by newly-found gadgets. He was interested in sound and was engaged by the Underground companies to find a reliable way of measuring and recording noise levels and suggesting possible solutions; these included ways of screening bogies so that track noise entering the passenger compartments was reduced. The shrouding was a partial success but was hated by the engineers as it complicated access to equipment and attracted dirt. The idea did not last.

1923 Rolling Stock

While the 1920 stock was on order the District reviewed the sorry position it was in after deferring the refurbishment of the older cars during the war, as a result of which they had deteriorated even faster. Retrieving the position required a determined effort to replace entirely the very worst trailer cars. This process was indirect and involved purchasing new motor cars, converting a number of existing (relatively strong) motor cars to trailers, refurbishment and strengthening of the better trailers and then disposing of the worst of the old ones. A number of new bogies would be obtained to replace the old and not wholly suitable bogies that were expensive to keep in running order.

Some thought was given to increasing the power of the main fleet to match the 1920 stock, which would involve substituting another motor car for a trailer, but the time was not felt right and existing train performance was accepted.

Fifty new motor car bodies were ordered from the Gloucester Wagon & Carriage Company in July 1923, together with motor bogies of a new design from both Gloucester and the Birmingham Railway Carriage and Wagon Co; these included ten extra for use on the older cars. Trailer bogies came from batches of another new design split between Leeds Forge and Birmingham and included a large number for replacing older unsatisfactory bogies. Delivery, again, was painfully slow, with no cars arriving for a year and the last car not arriving until December 1925.

The new motor cars were ordered without equipment as this was to be recovered from older rolling stock. 42 sets of control equipment (and 84 GE69 motors) were transferred from existing 1905 motor cars converted to trailers. Eight sets of equipment (and 16 motors) came from scrapped motor cars, which included the six experimental cars of 1903. In turn 42 of the worst trailers were scrapped (including the eight 1903 cars) whilst the 42 converted cars received new bogies.

From an operating point of view the new motor cars were entirely compatible with the older stock, rather than with the 1920 cars, with which they could not interwork. After they were delivered, the line had 317 motor cars, 272 trailers and 38 control trailers available for service.[10] Ten motor cars of the new stock were owned by the Midland Railway, as successors to the LTSR, to replace older vehicles.

Above: **Gloucester Carriage and Wagon Co workshops constructing the 1923 stock, several cars visible. In the foreground is an underframe (not yet turned right way up as it was more convenient to construct them upside down).** Roy Allen collection

Below: **Another part of the Gloucester workshops constructing District cars.** Roy Allen collection

Above: **One of the new Gloucester-built 1923 cars at manufacturers, being shown off. These were also known (with apparent indifference) as 1924 cars, it not being settled whether preference should be given to ordering or into-service date. These are the only cars to have quite such a flat front and 'boxy' look. The varnished wooden doors in an otherwise painted finish are particularly striking.** Roy Allen collection

Below: **A 1923 stock car upon delivery and before recovered electrical equipment was fitted. This is the trailing end (very similar to driving end). This is the last District stock to have windows at the guard's end and they were later removed.** Author's collection

The 1923 cars abandoned the smooth elliptical roofs and made a return to the clerestory type roof, probably because it was easier to provide ventilation. The design also reverted to the straight bodysides, requiring width to be reduced to 9ft and the reintroduction of 4-inch wide continuous exterior footboards. All cars had two pairs of sliding doors along each car side and a cab at each end with inward swinging side doors for staff use only. The driving cab was separated from saloon by a swing door and (for the first time) was only available for staff, whilst the guard's gangway (which had no saloon door) could be used by passengers when not occupied by the guard, though they could not use the side doors as they were locked. The door position was important. The 1920 stock showed advantages in increasing the overall door area and in having the doors evenly spread out. However, after some use in traffic it was felt that the doorways were slightly too narrow and discouraged people from using them two at a time, as had been hoped. The 1923 stock double-doorway were therefore about four inches wider (at over 4ft 4in clear) and symmetrically spaced to facilitate fast loading and unloading. This was felt the optimal arrangement because when used at the ends of 8-car trains both doorways would be likely to be accessible from the platform. In case the rear of the train stopped in tunnel owing to a particularly short platform, the double-doors nearest the cab had an indicator on one of the leaves giving a positive indication if it had been locked by staff; this was also fitted to later cars.[11]

Interior of 1923 stock car showing a degree of ornamentation and the heavy iron draught screens. Author's collection

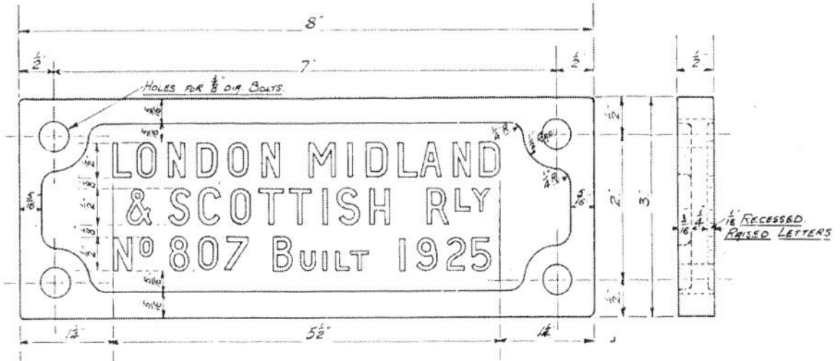

Left: **Ownership of many of the cars by the LMSR was sometimes indicated by paint but for a time cast metal plates were attached to the cars concerned. This is a drawing of a plate intended for a 1923 stock car (the last ones were not finished until 1925).** Author's collection

Below: **Plan and elevation of the new 1923 stock cars.** Author's collection

Bottom: **Elevation and vertical section through new 1923 stock cars.** Author's collection

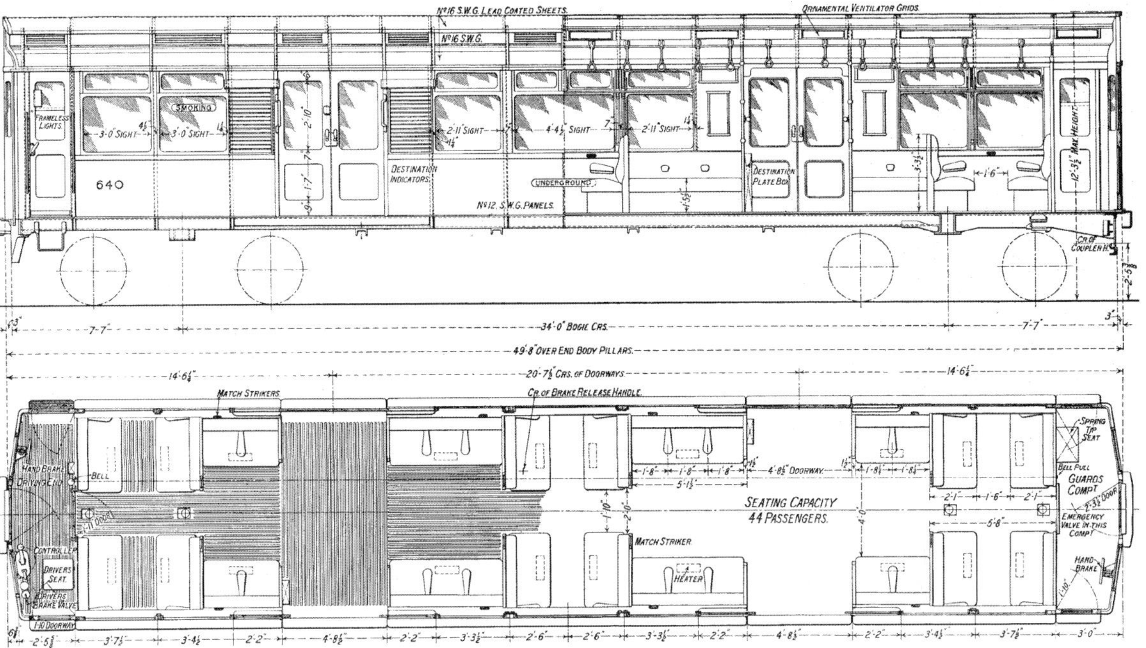

Fig. 2.—Elevation and Floor Plan of new Motor-Car, Metropolitan District Railway, constructed by the Gloucester Carriage & Wagon Co. Ltd.

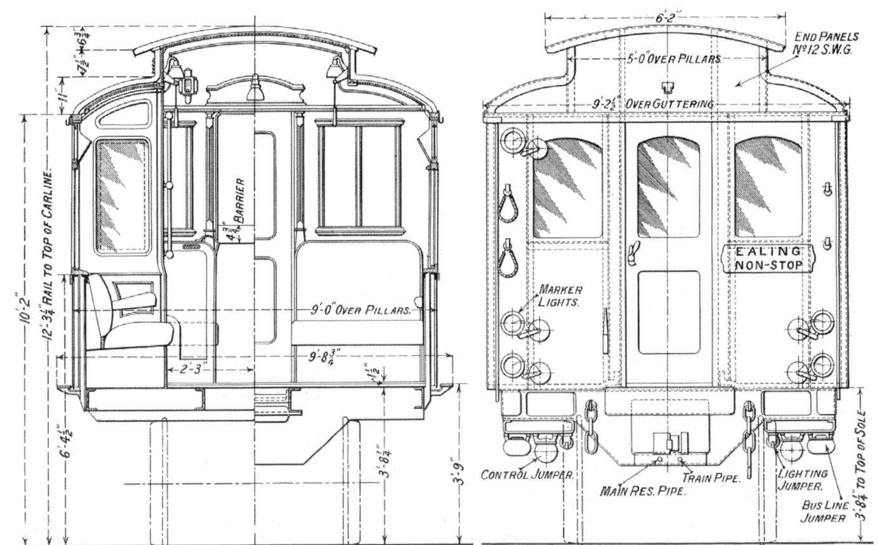

Fig. 4.—Section through Car, looking towards Guard's

View looking on Driver's Partition.

Fig. 5.—View of Driving End.

Photographs of the guard's areas of early electric cars are unusual. This view is of a 1923 stock car. Visible on the bulkhead on left (where there was an opening, but no door, to passenger saloon) are switches for lighting and heating. On right are original end windows, handbrake and rack for the spare destination plates. Roy Allen collection

A 1927 car shortly after delivery (this one owned by the LMSR). A great deal of thought has gone into tidying up (in particular) the front end. Obvious here are the darker doors, this time painted maroon instead of the earlier varnished wood. Just visible on the leading passenger door is the lock and its indicator, for use where trains were longer than the platforms. Author's collection

The interiors of the 1927 cars were less heavily ornamented and much lighter screens were used, making the cars feel more open. Many of the fittings and overall design approach were similar to the new tube cars being introduced and distinctive 'District' features were disappearing. Author's collection

Fleet Reorganization and the 1927 stock

Several matters caused the District to modify its approach in 1926. Factors included increasing unreliability of the earlier equipment which was now rather old-fashioned. Maintenance costs had to be contained whilst service requirements were rising to meet the needs of the developing suburbs. Whilst there was a possibility of some services transferring to the Piccadilly, new train service extension was likely in the east. All this called for a review.

To optimize the fleet the District decided to split the existing rolling stock into three groups. The newer cars (except for the 1920 stock) were upgraded and became part of the 'main line' fleet. For robustness, only the steel motor cars were included and most of the trailers were the old, wooden ones (either converted wood and metal motor cars or wooden cars rebuilt and reinforced); these cars were repaired and upgraded as necessary. The basic unit remained the 4-car train with a motor car at each end, to which extra two car (trailer-motor) sets could be added at the east end to form 6-car or 8-car trains.

The remainder of the main line stock would comprise the 1920 cars, which continued as a separate fleet with minimal modification, the trains divisible into 5-car and 3-car portions.

The small number of cars remaining comprised the 'local' stock, being the oldest cars in largely unmodified form. These were to operate the western branches and the Putney-High Street service. The 'local' stock comprised 37 motor cars and 18 control trailers of the old

1905 stock and trains of any length between one and six cars could be made up as necessary (two of the motor cars were middle motors that could function as a single car train). The opportunity was taken to replace their first-generation GE69 motors with the later GE212 motors recovered from other stock. Lacking the improvements made to the 'main line' cars, the 'local stock' had to be kept separate as the cars could no longer interwork.

This bold programme called for extensive modification or reconstruction of the fleet, a large amount of new equipment and over a hundred new steel cars. In turn a larger number of unreconstructed wooden trailers were disposed of.

The reorganization plan required 101 new motor cars, all ordered from the Birmingham Railway Carriage & Wagon Co in 1927. Of these, 81 were effectively replacements for older cars whilst 20 were for service improvement. Including the 1920 cars, this produced a fleet of 303 motor cars and 308 trailers for 'main line' services and 37 motor cars and 18 control trailers for the 'local' services. Only 91 cars had new bogies and ten cars reused serviceable bogies from withdrawn cars.

The 1927 cars had smoother lines and the clerestories curved down neatly at the ends. The door arrangements and general car layout was similar to the 1923 cars but internally the heavy partitions gave way to lighter glazed ones and the guard's cab became, in effect, part of the saloon with glazed partitions closing off the area when the guard needed it (lockable inward swinging side doors were retained for his use). The driving cab was a little larger than on the 1923 cars. As before, all the passenger doors were hand-operated. The first car was delivered in October 1928.

The upgrading of the older motor cars was largely of a technical nature and this brought them into line with the new 1927 cars with which they had to inter-work. The most important improvement was in the control apparatus and 263 sets of electro-magnetic control equipment were purchased from BTH together with the necessary WT54B traction motors; this was sufficient to equip the 101 new cars, the 50 1923 cars and the 112 earlier steel cars.

The new equipment incorporated 'automatic' acceleration where motor current was monitored when the driver demanded power and the resistances were cut out automatically at the optimal moment. The benefits included more consistent train operation and slightly faster average acceleration as the human element was removed.

The new equipment called for extensive rewiring and the opportunity was taken to improve lighting and heating circuits. Another troublesome item on the older cars had been the drawgear, which was prone to breaking and called for modification including addition of spring buffers, arranged so that there was one of these between each pair of cars. This modification work was substantially complete by 1930.

With changes to the wiring and couplers there was sense in altering the position of the inter-car air and cable connections from the existing rather inconvenient position under the coupler to the sides of the car ends where staff could get at them more easily. This loss of symmetry meant that it was no longer possible for cars to couple either way round, as the air-lines, auxiliary and control circuits could no longer be physically connected if a car was 'turned'. This complication (known as handing), meant that motor cars had for the first time to be designated 'east-facing' or 'west-facing' and modified in the correct numbers to produce the standard train formations required. Previously any imbalance in cars caused by accident, overhaul or heavy maintenance could be corrected by turning odd motor cars via the Cromwell Curve triangle, but now cars could only be turned in conjunction with major workshop attention.

The 1930 timetable required an 89-train evening service of 575 cars from a fleet of 681, this included 1x6-car traffic spare train. The trains comprised 27x8-car, 48x6-car, 1x7-car and 1x5-car trains on the 'main line' service and a number of 3-, 4-, 5- and 6-car trains on the 'local' services. Of the long trains, the 7-car and nine of the 8-car trains were of 1920 stock.

From 1927 the 1920 stock was progressively fitted with a new type of braking system. Called the electro-pneumatic (ep) brake, it was superimposed on the existing fail-safe Westinghouse brake and allowed air to enter or release from brake cylinders through electrically operated valves controlled by the driver's brake control handle. This brake became regarded as the normal brake and gave the driver better control of the train which improved stopping accuracy.

When complete the transformation resulted in the District having three different fleets of trains that could not be mixed, which was not ideal as it reduced flexibility and increased the number of spare cars needed. In 1926 the District began denoting each of its car types by means of a letter, the oldest cars being 'B' stock and the latest 1927 cars 'K' stock. As usage of the letter codes did not really catch on until the District had ceased to exist, usage here has been avoided.[12]

1905 wooden cars being rebuilt as part of the refurbishment programme. The photo shows not only the tremendous amount of work involved but also the way the cars were constructed in the first place.
Roy Allen collection

Acton Works

Trains must be maintained to ensure that they remain safe and reliable. Each night District cars were inspected, lubricated, cleaned and received any running repairs. For example, brake-blocks and pick-up shoes might need replacing or adjusting and minor faults could be fixed by a car examiner, including faults reported by drivers. Not all of these could be attended to in outlying sidings but the timetable was arranged so that trains should not out-stable on successive nights and should visit Ealing Common depot every two or three days. Sometimes trains that outstabled overnight could visit a large depot during the daytime to receive the necessary attention. In 1911 about 400 cars were put into service daily, 160 from Ealing Common depot (as Mill Hill Park depot had become) and 120 each from East Ham and Cromwell Road.

At intervals there was a 'shed day' at Ealing Common repair shop. Here, major inspection took place together with necessary changing of wearing or damaged parts. Particular attention was given to bogies and running gear, looking for flaws, defects, excessive wear and similar trouble and remedying whatever was required. The detailed inspection included springs and car height, bearings, motors, wheel profiles and so on. This could involve cars being lifted off their bogies and sometimes it was expedient to replace other parts while the body was separated. In 1911 the shed day averaged every 16 days but this had reduced to about 14 days by 1924.

In addition to regular inspections was heavy overhaul, which was undertaken on mileage basis. In 1911 motor cars were overhauled every 35,000 miles and trailers every 38,000 miles but by the early 1920s this had increased to 40,000 and 60,000 miles respectively, and then by stages to 50,000 and 70,000 and by 1931 to 80,000 and 90,000 miles.[13] Overhaul involved the car being stripped down, with running gear dismantled

Inside Acton Works in February 1924. 1903 motor car No 4 about to be lowered onto its own bogies after overhaul. The open platforms at trailing end contrast with the regular District stock. Author's collection

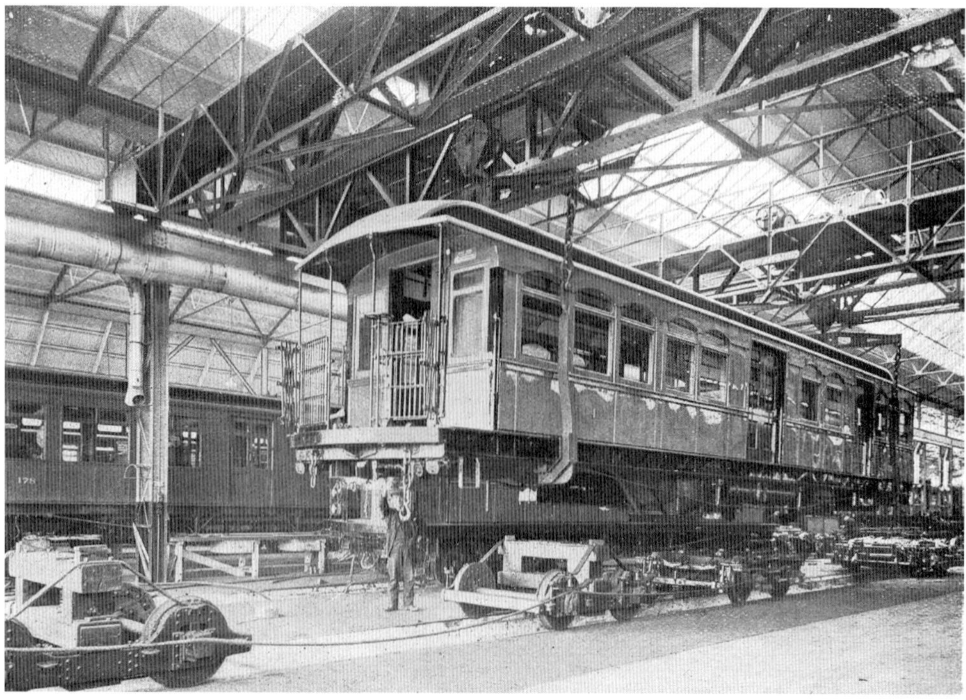

The fourteen 1903 experimental cars had outlived their welcome by 1925 when they were scrapped. This image, in unknown location, shows derelict cars awaiting destruction. Trailer car 303 nearest camera. Roy Allen collection

and electrical and brake equipment opened up for minute inspection and replacement of all worn parts. After re-assembly the cars were then completely repainted, inside and out, and looked almost new.

Not all the work was carried out at Ealing Common as it was found sensible to centralize it. For example, the repair of motor field coils for all the railways was undertaken at Golders Green depot (on the Hampstead Line) where special facilities were provided. A similar approach, also at Golders Green, was established for braking equipment where a dedicated test room was constructed and it was here that repairs and overhaul of drivers brake valves and triple valves was carried out, both precision pieces of equipment whose correct operation was essential.[14]

During 1919 and 1920, the expectation of extra rolling stock and arrears of wartime heavy maintenance threatened to overload the existing regime. The mechanical engineer suggested building a central overhaul works to undertake heavy overhaul for all the lines, relieving pressure on the local depots which were heavily occupied with routine maintenance. A large area of land at Acton Town was selected, just north of the LGOC's Chiswick Works. The facility was to be built in stages, the first stage to be capable of heavy overhaul of the District and Piccadilly stocks and a second, to be undertaken later, to add capacity to deal with the other lines. Construction work for Stage 1 began in December 1921 with work sufficiently advanced for overhauls to begin in December 1922. The official opening was on 1st January 1923.[15] The works concentrated on the intricate mechanical and electrical work required for heavy overhaul while the wood working, car body and paint shops were designed but not constructed; painting and car-body work was still carried out at Ealing Common where it continued for several more years. Cars were overhauled on a progressive system where the car-body and its bogies parted company on arrival with each subject to a succession of inspection, dismantling, repair and replacement before being married again at the end of the cycle. In 1924 the works was turning round seventeen cars per week which it was hoped shortly to increase to twenty. The two former District battery locomotives were adapted to move materials and parts under their own power between Acton Works and Ealing Common in the space between the cabs where the batteries had once been.

This 1925 view shows 1905 wooden trailer 349 (converted into a control trailer) displaying the metal-reinforced underframe to strengthen the car body. Author's collection

New 1927 stock car 573 outside Ealing Common depot contrasts with older cars to its rear. The car immediately behind is wooden composite trailer 1000, with its very obviously reinforced underframe. Roy Allen collection

By 1925, plans were in hand for the enlargement of Acton Works to deal with car-body work and painting, the transfer to Acton from Golders Green of the brake and motor overhaul work, and general expansion to deal with the cars from the remaining lines.[16] Enlargement was completed by 1930 but even from 1927 had been a key part of reconditioning the District Fleet. For many years the offices at Ealing Common depot had served all the various lines but in 1932 the mechanical engineer moved from Ealing to purpose-built offices at Acton Works.

Train Services

The train service became more reliable once the car repairs (and new cars) had begun to filter through and it became possible to restore pre-war services. Ongoing signalling and train despatch improvements also began to have a positive impact.

The following table summarizes the service improvements that were made during the 1920s (trains during busiest morning hour from each branch):

'Main Line' Trains – Morning Peak Hour (Eastbound)

Service	*1922*	*1925*	*1929*
Circle	10	10	8
Wimbledon	10*	11†	11*
Ealing	9	7	8
Richmond	5	5	5
Hounslow	5	6	8
South Harrow	1	1	1
Hammersmith	1	-	-
Total	**41**	**40**	**41**
Trains for east of Mansion House	31	29	34
Cars in service	452	518	557

* includes 2 from Putney Bridge
† includes 3 from Putney Bridge

The table shows that the maximum number of trains per hour had already been reached and increasing capacity was only reasonably possible by increasing train lengths, fine tuning the branch services to match demand and focusing on reliability. One can see from the increasing numbers of cars in service that trains were being strengthened, mainly from 6-car to 8-car.

The Richmond service was curiously slow to develop. Even after LNWR electric trains replaced steam from 1st October 1916, the section south of Gunnersbury retained its old LSWR mechanical signalling, which limited capacity. Moreover, a fast LNWR service could get passengers to Broad Street in 40 minutes in some comfort whilst a District took the same in theory but in rather less comfortable conditions. There was little incentive to increase District trains to Richmond.

The Wimbledon branch services had always been fairly busy and it is interesting to see how this traffic came to predominate. The District was a credible alternative for those wanting the City and not wanting the awful prospect of changing at Waterloo for a packed Waterloo & City train. Here, again, mechanical signalling and occasional LSWR trains restricted capacity, which had to be topped up by trains starting at Putney. In addition to the City trains there were also the local trains for High Street which started at Putney and which people for the City could use if they were happy to change at Earls Court.

The greatest proportionate increase was along the Hounslow line and it can be seen Hounslow trains have stolen paths from other routes. Much of the increase was by substituting through trains for the local ones, although there were still a few local trains in the busy hours connecting at Acton into trains from Ealing. Hounslow services were developing, partly at the expense of Ealing, as the areas around South Ealing and Osterley were built on, and the western side of Hounslow, where development had been quite slow. Evening services were similar in intensity, the main difference being the westbound composite trains which ran as 8-car sets of 1920 stock splitting into 5-car portions (for Hounslow) and 3-car portions (for South Harrow).

Even off-peak services were frequent, the summer 1925 timetable offering 28 trains an hour, mainly 4-car, though Inner Circles and 1920 stock trains were 5-cars. In a typical hour there were nine Inner Circles, eight trains from Ealing, seven from Wimbledon and four from Richmond. Of the Districts, nine went only to Mansion House, one to Whitechapel, five to Bow Road and just four to Barking.

Above: **Quite apart from scheduled services the District ran many special trains. This shows Stepney Green station 25th July 1925. A party of 1000 children from the East End Mission are on their way for a splendid day out in Eastcote. The party was carried each way by two special trains that travelled non-stop. Return departures were timed at about 6.30pm. This kind of arrangement was quite common.** LTM

Below: **This is the return journey showing a full length special District train at Eastcote awaiting the boarding of innumerable excited children. It is obvious why the District was heavily promoting this area as 'must-see' delightful open country.** Capital Transport collection

On Sundays the 1925 timetable offered six trains an hour from Ealing, two from Richmond and three from Wimbledon; with six Inner Circles this offered seventeen trains an hour as far as Charing Cross and eleven eastwards—six Inner Circle and five to Barking (the latter at irregular intervals). Again trains were mainly of four or five cars.[17]

The local services offered trains every half-hour to and from Uxbridge with extra trains from South Harrow providing a 15-minute service to Acton Town; in slack hours these had been just a single car in 1922 but had been improved to 2-car trains by 1925. Corresponding busy-hour train lengths had included some 2-car and 3-car trains, respectively, and some service enhancement.

In 1922 there was an irregular service on the Hounslow Line approximating to a train every ten minutes; these were 2-car trains. Some of the trains on the Hounslow and Harrow branches continued to South Acton which had a train roughly every 15 minutes. By 1925 the Hounslow service had improved to roughly a train every 8 minutes, still 2-car. In the peaks the odd shuttles still ran, this time as 3-car or 6-car trains. Until 1926 it was necessary for some Hounslow trains to start and finish at Hounslow Town as the Hounslow Barracks section was still single line, with limited capacity.

The LNWR service into and from Earls Court carried on at about 15 minute intervals but from 1923 it was operated by the newly-grouped LMSR. Between 4th January 1926 and 15th January 1927 a steam rail motor train operated one of the Willesden to Earls Court duties, covering one of several shortages of LMSR electric stock. Still in LNWR black and white livery, it is said to have caused something of a sensation at Earls Court.[18] During exhibitions at Olympia the service had for many years been augmented where required, often seeing extra LNWR/LMSR trains running along the Earls Court–Addison Road section. At the end of 1925, during the LMS electric stock shortage, the District lent it one train to work the enhanced service to Addison Road from 21st December until 23rd January for the International Circus and Christmas Fair; the existing LMS service also ran as normal. Something similar was also done for the ideal home exhibition between 2nd and 27th March 1926 and Building Trades Exhibition from 14th to 28th April.[19] The notices suggest District motormen were used, for a while assisted by LMSR 'pilot' staff.

When 8-car District trains began running, a problem arose at the ends of trains where doors were located in tunnels; at some stations even 7-car trains were too long. Although narrow catwalks were installed for emergencies the prospect of unconstrained passengers using them to board or alight from trains using the hand operated doors was considered extremely dangerous. Where trains were longer than the platforms, the 1915 instructions required drivers to stop with the middle door of the front car right at the platform end and for the front guard to watch this entrance very carefully, especially before the train started. At the rear, several doors might still be in the tunnel (almost certainly including the middle doors) and the guard was required to call out where the exit was and somehow discourage anyone trying to use any door farther back. Staff were specifically instructed not to stow luggage in the rear car of 8-car trains because of the difficulty getting it off.[20]

During the later 1920s all 8-car trains were either 1920 stock or tended to have 1923 or 1927 motor cars at the ends, and the door positions of the end cars differed. At many of the central London stations the platforms were still too short to accommodate all the doors on an 8-car train and the instructions by then required the leading and end doors of 1923/7 stock end cars to be physically locked out of use by the guard at the short platforms. This could only be done by the front or rear guard walking through the car and using his carriage key to lock the door before the train stopped and unlock it before arrival at the next 'long' station. On 1920 stock trains the middle doors as well as the end doors required locking.[21]

From 22nd May 1933 the District reduced the number of guards on 8-car trains to just one, who rode in the rear car, and this required procedures to be changed again. As before, at short platforms the drivers were expected to stop with the front car middle doors in the tunnel. During the time 8-car trains operated a member of the station staff at the tunnel stations had to be posted at the front to prevent passengers attempting to board via the catwalk that extended into the tunnel. The leading double doors on 1920 stock or later were supposed to be locked along the tunnel section. The guard had to lock (before arrival) so many of the rear doors as would not be fully in the platform at each station and also keep a careful lookout for anyone attempting to board beyond the platform limit.[22]

Early timetables for the 1920s indicate that the practice of non-stopping was still very extensive. It seems a fair generalization to suggest that the 1922 timetable showed the majority of trains in the busy hours did not call at one or more stations and that the pattern appears chaotic and must have been difficult to explain to passengers. As before, there is a hint that a few trains were designed to run 'express', within the severe limitations of a 2-track railway. The 8.27am from Hounslow Barracks missed out stations between South Ealing and Hammersmith and also Barons Court, Gloucester Road and South Kensington. This did the journey to Mansion House in 43 minutes, perhaps saving about four minutes on an all stations journey. Most non-stopping appears to have been to get trains across the many flat junctions efficiently and included missing out (as a minimum) combinations of stations either side of Earls Court and on the Barking line to manage junction work west of Whitechapel.

By 1930 there was slightly less non-stopping and evidence of some pattern to it so that trains from the various branches often followed a similar pattern, but it was still confusing and the non-stopping pattern at the east end remained baffling. This trend to reduce non-stopping continued very slowly until accelerated during World War II and from 1946 only five patterns remained.

Finally a word needs saying about operation during bad weather where trains might be slowed down by weather conditions with disruption to timetables, or possibly unable to run at all.

Fog was once quite common and discouraged drivers from operating at full speed as it became hard to see the signals, still semaphores in the open air. The Clayton fog machines were all very well but appallingly noisy and to keep the magazines charged with fresh detonators it still required staff to move about on the track when nobody could see them. At the start of the Great War, the Met experimented with lamp repeaters a standard distance ahead of a stop signal act as a guide to drivers. The signals were as much to indicate where the next stop signal was located as to announce the aspect it was showing. Although they were the only colour light signals in open-air sections, the letter F was printed on the lenses to make sure the signals were recognized for what they were. Several standard distances were tested but the best results were obtained with repeaters about 300 feet ahead of the stop signal, giving drivers enough time to stop and thus confidence to drive at a higher speed as they did not have to guess where the stop signals were. The District was keen to follow the lead here and engaged in its own experiments, which were broadly in agreement, and from 1919 began installing fog repeaters ahead of all automatic and semi-automatic signals and doing away with the Clayton machines and fog-men. These signals were switched off when it was not foggy.[23]

The other great challenge was ice on the current rails formed either of hoar frost (freezing damp air) or frozen rain. Ice was an insulator and could interrupt current supply to trains, especially short trains with fewer pick-up shoes. Snow was a problem if it accumulated and compacted or started to melt and refroze. Great reliance was placed on track staff to clear ice off current rails and from pointwork. A more general way of mitigating the effects of overnight snow or ice was to keep current on and run empty electric trains throughout the night along all open sections (including LTSR line east of Bromley). If circumstances warranted it, a steam engine was operated over badly affected sections of line; this was equipped with so-called sleet brushes (brushes with metal tines forced against the current rails). Two locos were fitted and these were effective for sweeping off snow and relatively loose ice when current was off. 100 of the motor cars were also fitted with sleet brushes for keeping the rails clear during the time ordinary services were operating (these were added as early as December 1905). Another mitigating measure was to run longer trains if there was a risk a short train might lose current. 1914 instructions show that the staff were given very clear instructions about exactly what conditions required what kind of response. These measures, though very staff intensive, appear to have kept services running well throughout all but the very worst weather.

Trains to Edgware Road

High Street Kensington was a relic of the intended outer circle route and was not an ideal terminus for District trains as many passengers wanted to go further, particularly to Paddington. In 1926 the Metropolitan completed a much-needed rearrangement of Edgware Road station as part of a plan for a new tube through north-west London to Kilburn, though this was not proceeded with. The rebuilt station had two island platforms with through and loop roads and could reverse part of the train service in either direction without fouling the main running lines. This new layout presented the opportunity to revisit the much-derided Inner Circle service. This was recast at 7½ minute intervals, with a slightly more generous running time that required only 14 trains, all now provided by the Metropolitan. The District's contribution (it was jointly liable for operating the inner circle) was to extend its Putney-High Street service to Edgware Road, thereby improving overall frequencies along the busy western side of the route. On Sundays frequencies were reduced to 10-minutes and the District continued to provide four trains (two in each direction) partly to keep District crews familiar with the route and partly to equalize the mileage operated.

Lillie Bridge

During the 1920s much of the Lillie Bridge site was used by the District's civil engineering staff, more particularly track staff who fabricated trackwork here and supplied materials throughout the line, often shifted by ballast train at night. This required an endless supply of heavy materials which were usually delivered by rail to the Warwick Road goods yard just south of Addison Road station. Materials would be conveyed by GWR and LMSR trains scheduled to run as required. Materials via the latter company would first arrive at its Brompton & Fulham yard where the loco had an hour's stand time in which, if goods were to be delivered or collected, it could make a trip into Lillie Bridge and back via the District's WLR access track. The GWR had a similar arrangement. Sometimes District engines would transfer vehicles to or from the Warwick Road yard using its own locos and the main line company would deal with them as convenient.

New rolling stock often came this way, delivered by main line railway and then received at Lillie Bridge yard before being conveyed to Ealing Common and all the 1923 and 1927 cars were received this way. Sometimes scrap cars were despatched via this route.[24]

District service loco L34 at Lillie Bridge around 1930, after fitting with enclosed cab. In background at left is an old District carriage still serving as a van, number 36. Author's collection

District Railway Diamond Jubilee

In 1928 the District celebrated its diamond jubilee, the 60th anniversary of the railway opening. The highlight was an exhibition at South Kensington station planned to run between 5th and 10th November 1928. This was so popular that it was extended to Sunday 11th, when on that day alone the attendance hit over 15,000. The total number of visitors was recorded as 96,375, which astonished all involved. Over 900 packs of postcards of District Railway cars were sold and 10,000 illustrated booklets were distributed giving details of the exhibits and the District's history.

The centrepiece of the exhibition was a display of rolling stock that was stabled in the bay road on the south side of the station, which was mostly under cover. The display comprised:

- Steam locomotive No 34 of 1881 vintage and retained for shunting at Lillie Bridge, though having just been fitted with an all-over cab.
- A 4-wheeled third class carriage, which included a guard's compartment. This had been a stores van with the compartments removed, but the exterior was restored and one compartment put back with a recreated interior.
- A District electric locomotive of 1905 used for hauling the LNWR trains and more recently for hauling the LMS Southend through trains.
- All-wood electric car No 914 (originally 262) of 1905 vintage. Though described as all-wood this car had a steel reinforced underframe and was originally a middle motor.
- All-steel car of 1920 vintage No 636 by Metropolitan Carriage, Wagon & Finance Co.
- A 1928 motor car of the type then still being delivered from the Birmingham Carriage & Wagon company.

The exhibits were accompanied by some officials and staff of the company who were on hand to explain things and answer questions. Engine drivers Membury and Spencer, and guards Doney and Shelton, had all worked for the company in steam days were happy to talk and reminisce to visitors.

Metropolitan District Railway
1868 – 1928

SEE THE
DIAMOND
JUBILEE
TRAIN

Showing imp
in rollin
th
Exhibition continued
on Sunday, 11th November
from 12 noon to 9 p.m.
to 10th
p.m.
on Free

AT
SOUTH KENSINGTON
STATION (PLATFORM No. 4)

Poster advertising the diamond jubilee train placed on display at South Kensington. LTM

The steam-hauled carriage was thought by District staff to have been a third-class brake carriage, No 8, built by Ashbury's in 1871, and the restored exterior bore this number. The recreated compartment was dressed as a 'smoker' and included a gas lamp (borrowed from the Met). The vehicle had been one of several used as stores vehicles and photos of a stores vehicle 'doctored' to look like a steam-era carriage suggest it might have been van No 20. Stores vehicles formed occasional trains running up and down the District to deliver station and depot stores and were loco-hauled. It has not proved possible to establish what happened to this vehicle after the display but, sadly, it was not preserved.[25]

This special train was prepared for subsequent exhibition at South Kensington and was photographed prior to transfer. LTM

Above: **District recreation of old steam-hauled carriage for 1928 Diamond Jubilee Exhibition. This had been a steam-age carriage, subsequently used as stores or tool van. One compartment only was restored. The carriage was not preserved and the authority is not known for its original number being 8.** Author's collection

Below: **Lord Ashfield and various District staff at South Kensington during the Diamond Jubilee display in 1928. Mr J Thornton is to Ashfield's right and divisional traffic superintendent Coole is next to him.** Author's collection

Chapter Eleven

CHANGES IN THE EAST

New signalling to Barking (but no Electrification beyond)

When District trains first used the LTSR, the signalling east of Campbell Road was entirely mechanical in operation and became a significant constraint as the electric train services were progressively increased to match demand. Along this section were eleven signal boxes using the Sykes lock-and-block system with all-mechanical signalling with mechanical trainstops on the electric lines. By the time the LMSR had taken charge in 1923 the position was almost intolerable, and nor was the District slow to explain how difficult it was to run its own services punctually west of Whitechapel when trains arriving from the Barking line were so prone to delay. Realizing action could be deferred no longer, the LMSR decided to install a 2-aspect colour light system between Campbell Road and Barking on the local lines only. Because of the large number of junctions all running signals were semi-automatic. Normally they operated automatically under track-circuit control but they were under the overriding control of the existing signal boxes when conflicting moves were required. The work was complicated by the need to allow for freight trains using these tracks, with their limited braking capacity. This challenge was answered by a device that had to be operated whenever a freight train was signalled; this lengthened the section ahead requiring to be clear before a 'proceed' aspect was given. The passing of the freight train released the device to allow a following electric train the normal distance.

Altogether 43 colour light signals with electric trainstops, 41 fog repeaters and 74 alternating-current track circuits were brought into use, the equipment being installed by LMSR staff using equipment from several suppliers. The first section converted was Campbell Road to West Ham on 18th July 1927 and the whole project was complete by 1929. After the new signalling was installed, the LMSR stated that running times had improved (a 6-minute reduction in running time was claimed between Bow Road and Upton Park) and the District was able to increase train services along this section from 5th March 1928 (the District claiming 21 trains an hour through to the central area). Whilst the new signalling was a marked improvement, the need for the local lines to handle goods trains and the fact of there being so many crossings and junctions was an ongoing source of delay not fixed until the 1950s.

The new signalling was, for robustness, dual-fed from the County of London Electric Supply Company and West Ham Corporation electricity supplies, the former via a new LMSR substation at Plaistow. It might be noted here that when the former company opened its new power station in River Road Barking in May 1925, the LMSR investigated the opportunity to take a bulk supply. The LMSR board was told on 17th December that switching to Barking from Lots Road would save £11,682 a year, though the cost of doing this was high. The estimate of £132,000 included construction of a bulk supply point at Dagenham, installation of new 11,000 volt cables and conversion of the three substations; the Barking supply was at 50 cycles per second whilst Lots Road was at 33⅓ cycles, requiring significant equipment alterations. The work was felt worthwhile and carried out in 1926/7. The bulk supply point at Dagenham and high voltage cables were part funded by the LMSR but when finished were the financial responsibility of the power company.[1] The Dagenham power intake was about three miles east of Barking and well located for further electrification, but at this stage no more was done.

A New Town Appears

The circumstances by which the LTSR electrified to Barking were set out in Chapter 4. To recap, the LTSR did not want to lose its new direct trains to the City and West End once the District electrified and also saw electrification of its own tracks towards Barking as a first stage in wider electrification of the LTSR; even in 1902 it was a busy line considered more suitable than many for large scale electrification. It irked Stride, the LTSR managing director, that in 1905 the press represented electrification east of Campbell Road as a District scheme when, as he carefully explained in correspondence, the LTSR was paying for it, had its own wider aspirations to electrify and was even paying the District to operate the trains.[2] Nevertheless, the arrangement suited both parties well. Unfortunately, the LTSR could not afford to electrify beyond Barking and there matters rested.

District poster explaining service increases owing to the new signalling on the Barking line. The District did not see fit to mention that this was an LMSR improvement for a train service the LMSR was paying for. At that time, the LMSR rarely mentioned the existence of the District whose trains carried all their passengers. LTM

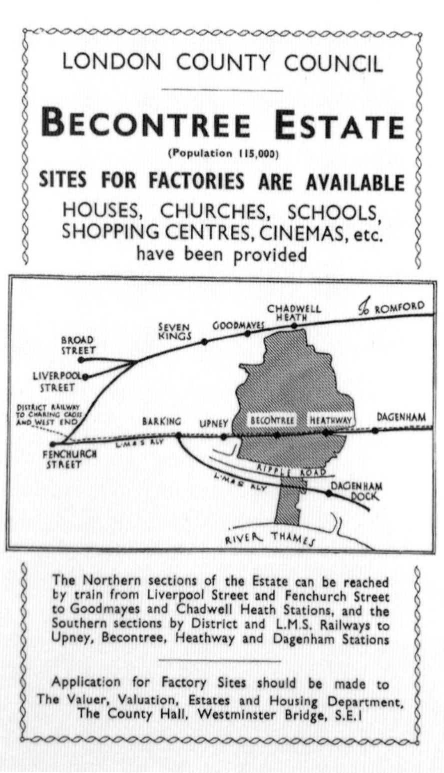

This advertisement for commercial space available within the new estate in its early days shows the lengths gone to by the LCC to provide jobs as well as homes. The importance of the LMS railway, running laterally across it near the centre, is perfectly obvious. The estate later swamped this line with traffic, the electric trains being provided by the District on behalf of the LMSR. Author's collection

When the Midland took over the LTSR in 1912 it was an express condition of Parliament that the whole of the former LTSR be electrified. Little was done before the Great War (which arrested the progress of many railway schemes) but matters were reviewed immediately afterwards. There were high hopes of proceeding with further electrification fairly quickly but the Midland became part of the vast LMSR in 1923 and we shall see that conditions had changed.

After the Great War, the government promoted a policy of 'homes for heroes', intended in part to ensure the men returning from the battlefields would be able to live in proper housing and partly to get rid of many of the country's slum areas—there was an enormous housing shortage. Some money was made available quite quickly but inevitably the task was immense and was thus a slow process, not helped by government reducing the funding owing to other pressures. Nevertheless, the 1919 Housing and Town Planning Act gave local authorities the job of building half a million new homes within three years. Local authorities were given some freedom in how they went about construction. The London County Council had an enormous housing need but virtually no suitable space within the county itself. The new Act allowed county councils to buy land outside their own areas and the LCC quickly identified suitable sites fairly close to London which could be used for its overspill. A key part of the thinking was that the new tenants were likely to have jobs and (at least at first) would need transport facilities to get to their existing place of employment. Since many of the run down areas from which the new tenants would come were in east and south-east London new estates were sought somewhere near a railway line also serving those areas.

For those Londoners living in the East End an estate constructed along the LTSR line was thought ideal. There was no suitably large area available west of Barking, but to its east much of the land was market garden and wholly undeveloped and it is here that the eyes of the LCC settled. As plans evolved, an estate ultimately housing 100,000 people was required and so emerged the Becontree estate.* The LCC agreed to develop the site in July 1919 and the compulsory purchase order was made in February 1920.

At first, the LCC was concerned to ensure that transport facilities were adequate. The former LTSR line ran right through the site of the estate and discussion with the Midland suggested that three new stations would be required. At this time the Midland was hoping shortly to proceed with electrification and be in a position to enhance train services as well. The LCC wanted government financial assistance to be given to the Midland to ensure the stations would be built and electrification would happen, but this idea was rejected. Government attitude was coloured by a feeling that railways ought to finance schemes that were to their own commercial advantage. The idea of making grants became more remote because of the serious financial depression that soon arose, which also meant scaling back funding for housing. The Midland, however, had no cash to throw at speculative facilities until the need actually arose, and in any case was heavily distracted by the looming amalgamation, required by the 1921 Railways Act. The outcome was that no extra transport facilities were provided as the first tenants arrived in 1921. In fact there was no convenient station at all until Gale Street opened on 28th June 1926, partly fulfilling the need. This was on one of the three sites the Midland had originally suggested and was located on a well-established highway, though from the point of view of where the early estate tenants had settled then Heathway might have been a better

* The name Becontree echoed the name of the historical Hundred – a subdivision of the County of Essex that lost importance when urban districts and other modern forms of local administration were created in 1894.

choice. Unfortunately the poor transport facilities discouraged occupation of the houses and the LCC went to much effort to find occupants.

The new estate was built on either side of the railway and was occupied piecemeal, depending in part on where existing sewerage facilities were located. Despite government cut-backs slow progress was made, though most of it came into use in 1925 and 1926 and it was not actually declared complete until 1936. When completed the estate was proclaimed as the world's largest housing estate and included over 25,000 houses and about 115,000 people (about the same as the City of Norwich). This was to have a profound effect on how the LMSR operated its Southend line and an equally profound impact on the District, as a vast extra traffic was delivered onto its system at Whitechapel. The most pain was felt between Whitechapel and Mark Lane owing to the awkward sequence of junctions that were already working to capacity.[3]

Electrification to Upminster Approved

When the LMSR took over the running in 1923, it was in no better financial position to electrify the whole of the former LTSR line than its predecessors, but it was perfectly obvious that between Barking and Upminster existing and potential developments

L.M.S. & DISTRICT RAILWAYS

CHEAP DAY RETURN TICKETS

TO

SOUTHEND-ON-SEA

(BENFLEET, LEIGH-ON-SEA or WESTCLIFF)

ARE ISSUED ON SUNDAYS, MONDAYS, THURSDAYS AND SATURDAYS, UNTIL FURTHER NOTICE, IN CONNECTION WITH THE TRAINS SPECIFIED BELOW :—

FROM	3rd Class Return.	FROM	3rd Class Return.	FROM	3rd Class Return.
Bow Road	3/6	Sloane Square ..	4/-	Chiswick Park ..	4/-
Mile End	3/6	South Kensington ..	4/-	Acton Town ..	4/-
Stepney Green ..	3/6	Gloucester Road ..	4/-	South Ealing ..	4/3
Whitechapel ..	3/6	High Street		Northfields ..	4/3
St. Marys	3/6	(Kensington) ..	4/-	Boston Manor ..	4/3
Aldgate East ..	3/6	Earls Court ..	4/-	Osterley	4/3
Mark Lane ..	3/6	West Brompton ..	4/-	Hounslow East ..	4/3
Monument.. ..	3/6	Walham Green ..	4/-	Hounslow Central ..	4/3
§Cannon Street ..	3/8	Parsons Green ..	4/-	Hounslow West ..	4/3
Mansion House ..	3/8	Putney Bridge ..	4/-	Ealing Common ..	4/3
Blackfriars	3/8	West Kensington ..	4/-	Ealing Broadway ..	4/3
Temple	3/8	Barons Court ..	4/-	North Ealing ..	4/3
Charing Cross ..	3/9	Hammersmith ..	4/-	Park Royal.. ..	4/3
Westminster ..	3/10	Ravenscourt Park ..	4/-	Alperton	4/3
St. James's Park ..	3/10	Stamford Brook ..	4/-	Sudbury Town ..	4/3
Victoria	4/-	Turnham Green ..	4/-	Sudbury Hill ..	4/3
				South Harrow ..	4/3

§ CANNON STREET STATION IS CLOSED ON SUNDAYS.

The Tickets are issued by, and in connection with, trains as follows from Ealing Broadway† :—

On SUNDAYS ... ... By all trains up to and including the 2.9 p.m.

On MONDAYS and THURSDAYS By all trains up to and including the 1.38 p.m.

On SATURDAYS ... ... By all trains up to and including the 9.43 a.m.

Available for return on day of issue only, by any ordinary train after 1.0 p.m.

† For times of Trains from other Stations see Timetables.

FOR CONDITIONS OF ISSUE SEE REVERSE SIDE.

UNDERGROUND

P.T.O.

This leaflet (one of many) shows the close commercial relationship forged between the District and the LMSR. In this case the leaflet promotes cheap-day travel to seaside resorts from District stations. Travel does not appear to be restricted to the Southend through trains. Capital Transport collection required urgent service improvements. Parliamentary powers, obtained in 1914, had authorized the Midland to acquire the land needed for widening the tracks east of Barking and these had already been used to buy a large proportion of what was needed, land in the area then being quite cheap. No physical works were done.

There was, at last, some movement in 1928, by which time overcrowding caused largely by the new estate had become a serious problem. Even so, only a reduced scheme was pressed forward for widening and electrification to Dagenham only, the eastern limit of the estate. This included rebuilding Dagenham station and providing a permanent station at Gale Street. It must be stressed that the investment problems of the LMSR at this time were similar to those of the Underground: they were commercial companies and no capital could be spent unless the extra revenue thereby created would at least pay for the cost of borrowing the money. In this case it meant that extra people would have to be carried. Since many of the people might be travelling on cheap workman's, or season tickets, and the likelihood of midday and evening leisure traffic was minimal, it was far from clear that there would be a financial return unless any scheme was kept to the bare minimum.

Fortunately, the position changed in 1929 because of the government's Development (Loan Guarantees and Grants) Act that was supposed to ease the latest, and most serious, financial depression by supporting capital works. No capital was to be provided, but the government would reimburse some of the interest costs, meaning that previously marginal schemes suddenly became affordable. In this light the LMSR decided to press ahead with electrification and widening as far as Upminster, and build additional stations at Upney and Heathway (and, later, Upminster Bridge). The widening works were authorized by the LMSR's 1930 Act. At the same time, it asked for release from its 1912 obligation to electrify the whole of the LTSR and Parliament acceded, leaving the requirement only in respect of the Barking-Upminster section.

The LMSR did not propose to operate its own electric trains at this stage, or electrify the tracks into Fenchurch Street, and took the view that electric trains should be provided by an arrangement with the District, easing the complications around offering through trains to the City, West End and beyond. Work was put in hand quickly, and Harold Arnold & Co undertook the widening work.

Power for the new electric lines was obtained from the County of London's supply by upgrading the existing bulk supply point in Dagenham, next to the new Heathway station. Here a new control room was built, which enabled the new unmanned substations at Upney, Heathway, Hornchurch and Upminster to operate automatically. Each substation was supplied at 11kV and had two 1.2MW converter units with room for a third; the units at Heathway and Upminster employed rotary converters while the other two used the latest mercury-arc equipment. In 1936, the older substations at Campbell Road, Plaistow and East Ham were fully automated and also supervised from Heathway control room.

Single-lens searchlight signals were deployed east of Barking and these could show one of three aspects (red, yellow or green) depending on track conditions. There were also two 4-aspect signals, the double-yellow (provisional caution) obtained by a second beam showing only a yellow light. Electric trainstops were provided at all signals. Signals working automatically were equipped with a small red marker light designed to indicate signal locations if the main beam failed and these were fed from an independent current supply. The marker light was suppressed if the main beam was showing clear. To avoid excessive delays where a signal remained at danger, a timing relay was actuated when a train arrived. If after one minute of a train stopping at a signal at danger, and if the track circuit immediately ahead were clear, then its marker light would change to yellow and the train stop would lower. This invited the driver to treat the signal as a calling-on signal and proceed with caution. After little more than four years, second thoughts about the wisdom of this resulted in the calling-on arrangement being removed. Drivers of detained trains were now required to telephone the signalman who, if permission were given for a train to proceed, would illuminate a 'P' sign at the signal authorizing the driver to proceed with great caution.[4]

Upminster Electrification comes into Service

The new electric tracks were available for trial running from 4th September 1932 and the new passenger services were introduced on 12th September. Trains from Upminster initially operated at about eight minute intervals in the busiest hours and twenty minutes off-peak (as the slack hours were now called). During the (mainly evening) peak-hours a few trains reversed at Dagenham and in addition LMSR trains on the 'through' lines often called at Upminster, Hornchurch, Becontree, Dagenham or Barking, but rarely more than one of these because of the limited track capacity. Early, late and off-peak trains stopped at more of the foregoing stations, and some at all of them, including East Ham, but they omitted stations further west until Burdett Road.

At Barking, few track alterations were required. The layout there had been a pair of tracks on the south side for the fast services, a pair on the north side for local and Tottenham & Hampstead services, and a pair of bay roads (platforms 4 and 5) in the centre of the station for electric services. On the extreme flanks of the station were up and down loop platforms, making eight in all. When electric trains were projected eastwards all that was necessary was to connect the tracks beyond already electrified platforms 2 and 3 to the new lines about quarter of a mile to the east. Terminating electric trains still used the bay roads. At Upminster the layout was completely rebuilt and included

Exterior of one the new 12-door trailers. These were built by the Union Construction Co, with bogies from Metropolitan Cammell, and came into service between March and October 1932. New techniques enabled these cars to be lighter than predecessors. LTM

Interior of one of the new 12-door trailer cars to supplement District services for the new Upminster service. These were all fitted with hand-worked doors and were referred to as the L stock in the new lettering scheme. The new end passenger doors had 2ft 2ins opening but the width of the main double doorways was slightly reduced. LTM

This view would have been very familiar to District users in the 1920s and 1930s and shows the partitioning in the composite trailers which divided the third class end from the two first class sections (one smoking and one non smoking). One can only imagine the challenge of restricting these sections to first class ticket holders and with what success this was achieved. LTM

One of the eight motor cars ordered for the Upminster improvements. These motor cars were all owned by the LMSR. LTM

Interior of one on the new motor cars built by the Underground's Union Construction Co in 1931/2. The styling was similar to the 1927 cars with a few further refinements, and the doors windows and seat layouts were slightly rearranged. Author's collection

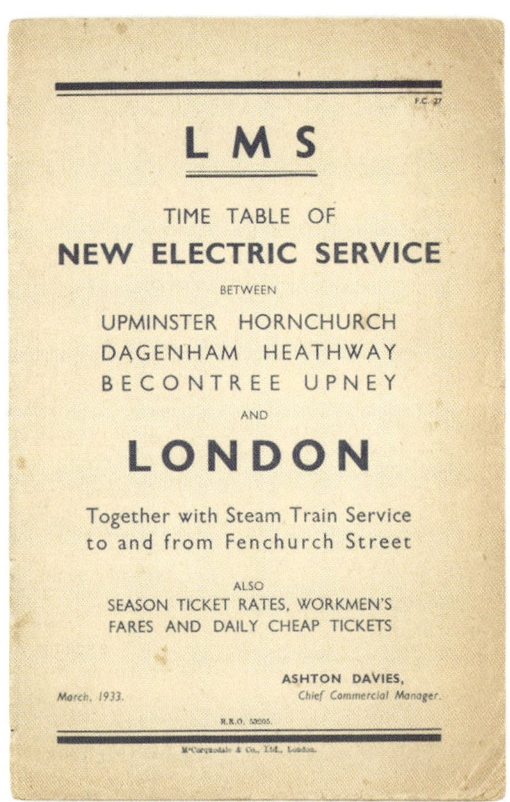
LMS

TIME TABLE OF

NEW ELECTRIC SERVICE

BETWEEN

UPMINSTER HORNCHURCH
DAGENHAM HEATHWAY
BECONTREE UPNEY

AND

LONDON

Together with Steam Train Service
to and from Fenchurch Street

ALSO

SEASON TICKET RATES, WORKMEN'S
FARES AND DAILY CHEAP TICKETS

ASHTON DAVIES,
Chief Commercial Manager.

March, 1933.

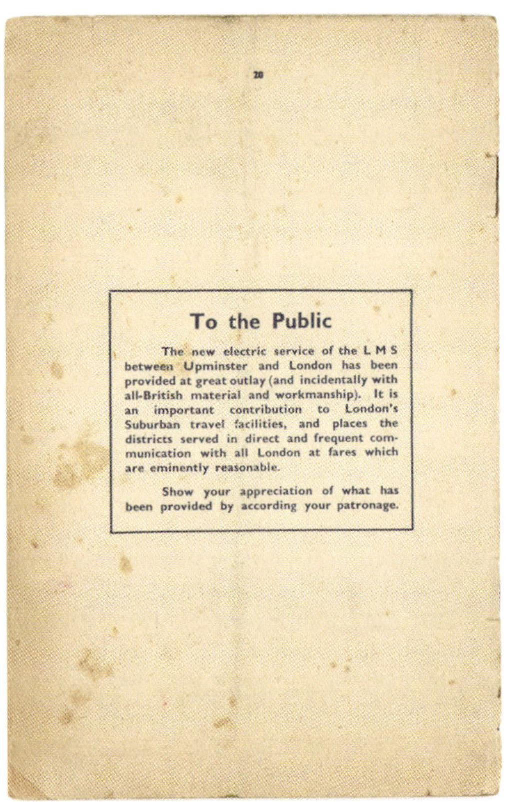
To the Public

The new electric service of the L M S between Upminster and London has been provided at great outlay (and incidentally with all-British material and workmanship). It is an important contribution to London's Suburban travel facilities, and places the districts served in direct and frequent communication with all London at fares which are eminently reasonable.

Show your appreciation of what has been provided by according your patronage.

Timetable leaflet presenting the new Upminster line electric services. The District isn't mentioned anywhere: they are mere contractors. John Liffen collection

three electrified platforms on the north side; the northernmost platform was usually used by the Romford branch trains but was shared with District trains in the peaks. The rearrangement destroyed the connection with the 1½-mile long tramway connected with some brick kilns near Bird Lane, which closed shortly afterwards. East of the station was an electrified traffic siding as well as a single-track link to six 500ft long electric stabling sidings a third of a mile to the east, in Cranham. These were intended for District trains to stable, reducing dead mileage to and from East Ham.[5]

The operation of electric trains to Upminster required more cars even though some cars were about to be released owing to changes at the west end of the line. 45 cars were ordered, eight motors and 37 trailers, this unequal combination was caused partly by the need to adjust imbalances elsewhere and partly because it offered an opportunity to replace yet more old wooden trailers. The car bodies were built by the Union Construction Company (an Underground subsidiary) at Feltham, but the bogies came from Metropolitan Cammell and the electro-magnetic control equipment from BTH.

The new cars were superficially similar to the 1927 ones but instead of the swing doors at the guard's position, single sliding doors were fitted enabling them to be used by passengers. In turn, this caused small alterations to the position of the double doors to even out spacing and this caused minor changes to window positions and seating. The trailers also had end doors and externally were like two motor car trailing ends back to back. Internally the trailers were all composites with the usual three sections divided by neat partitions, each with its swing connecting door.

Becontree (formerly Gale Street) station after reconstruction by LMSR in 1932. The District used the two electric tracks on north side and the two southern tracks were used by fast LMSR trains. A Hurst Nelson 1910 motor leads an eastbound train with 1931 composite trailer behind. As was often the case, an offside door has been left open. A striking feature of these doorways was the number of grab handles. LTM

Because of the increasing mileage being run by District trains over the LMSR, the number of cars owned by the latter was increased from 90 to 110 cars, comprising 57 motors and 53 trailers, equivalent to thirteen trains plus spares. These included all eight motors and ten trailers of the 1931 batch.[6] At first, the 1908 agreement between the District and LMSR was modified to reflect the extended services, but we shall see that this was replaced a couple of years later by an entirely fresh one.

The original stations along the widened section were at Dagenham, Hornchurch and Upminster, each of which had the usual side platforms. As is common with most widening schemes, the down platforms at these locations were widened and converted to islands and an additional down platform provided on the north (widened) side. Bridges were added, rebuilt or extended to provide access and other station improvements were carried out at the same time. The station buildings at Dagenham and Hornchurch were also rebuilt. Gale Street was rebuilt as a four-platform station in much the same way but more extensively, as it had not previously had a proper station building. 4-tracking required a replacement bridge over the line upon which a station building was erected with steps serving all platforms. The station acquired the name Becontree from 18th July 1932, though it was only one of three stations serving that estate, causing some criticism. Work was not complete until 12th September 1932.

Upney is representative of the smaller stations built by the LMSR along the Upminster line. These were all faced in brick. None of the stations made any obvious reference to the District, which provided the electric train services. There is not even a poster representing the UNDERGROUND. LTM

New stations, serving only the electric lines, were opened at Upney and Heathway (better-sited for the LCC estate) and these came into use with the widened lines. Upminster Bridge was added from 17th December 1934 and Elm Park from 13th May 1935. These stations were built on the newly-fashionable principle comprising an island platform to which access with the street was gained by a very long, sloping, covered ramp. Platforms were provided only on the local (electric) tracks but each was extraordinarily long, at 700ft, to accommodate full length main line trains if required: a full length District train required only 400ft. The new platforms at the existing stations were also lengthened and awnings covered 300ft lengths of platform where possible.

This view of Upney shows the long access ramp and the very long platforms—double the length of average District trains. The nearest tracks are the LMSR fast lines. LTM

View of the new ticket hall at the LMS's enlarged Upminster station. This station was equipped with a modern ticket booth as well as a wall ticket office. These stations were smart and well suited to their purpose, though modest compared with the extravagant designs that appealed to the Underground Group. LTM

The new and expanded stations were characteristic of the period and used brick extensively; very narrow bricks were used for decoration. The LMSR was coy about mentioning their architect which suggests the stations were designed in-house.* Details of the rebuilt surface building varied but all were single-storey with full-length canopies and a central entrance at street level. The ticket halls were equipped with passimeter-type ticket office booths and bookstalls but also had parcels offices doubling where required as booking offices. The stations, with pleasant buildings and wide and airy platforms were, and are still, very satisfactory today.

The LMSR paid for the capital works and the additional trains, built and electrified the new lines, ran the stations, sold the tickets, set the timetable and contracted with the District to operate the electric train service and appears to have taken the view that it should take all the credit, perhaps following Stride's attitude in 1905. The stations bore no obvious evidence that the District served them and Hornchurch station even carried a large sign above the entrance displaying 'LMS Electric' (though it appears to have been the only one to do so). Publicity was similar and timetables for the electric services made no overt reference to the District; the only clues were in the tabular work where the final destinations of the trains were reluctantly disclosed. This practice continued into London Transport days. On the District itself, the projection of District trains to Upminster was promoted as a joint service with the LMSR.

* The LMSR Architect was William Henry Hamlyn (1889-1968).

Chapter Twelve

CHANGES IN THE WEST

Opportunities in the West

Previous chapters have referred to improvements in the train services to the western branches and the doubling of the line to Hounslow West. It is now necessary to examine how a great scheme of infrastructure improvements slowly emerged to address the chaotic arrangement of branches upon which traffic was building up at differing rates but in all cases relentlessly. It was perfectly possible to serve four branches west of Hammersmith when traffic was very light but it was obvious this would become progressively more difficult as traffic grew. What nobody knew was at what point it would be impractical to funnel all this traffic through Earls Court. Some scheme was required that diverted some of this traffic in a different direction.

By 1926 there was sustained development along much of the Hounslow branch but still relatively little along the South Harrow line. Nevertheless, development on a large scale was looming and the existing services to Richmond and Ealing were already uncomfortably full with no very easy way of increasing them, given the limited capacity of the central section east of South Kensington.

An important factor in the way the west end of the District developed was the existence since 1911 of four tracks between Turnham Green and Studland Road (near Ravenscourt Park) along the section still owned by the LSWR. The objective of widening this section had been to reduce conflicting moves between the District's electric trains and the LSWR and GWR steam trains using this section but by an extraordinary twist of fate the GWR service between Richmond and Ladbroke Grove last ran on 31st December 1910

When the western improvements were announced in 1926, the staff cartoonist was inspired to represent the scene at Stamford Brook where the disused LSWR tracks were getting a little overgrown. Author's collection

On 20 August 1926 this picture was taken at Stamford Brook of a party of 500 children on an outing by special non-stop train to South Harrow. Such trips were then still very common. On the left are the derelict LSWR (by then Southern Railway) tracks remaining after what turned out to be the partly abortive widening. These beckoned redevelopment and a scheme was being drawn up. LTM

(before the works were even completed), and the LSWR service was soon reduced, then withdrawn altogether in 1916. Following this, the northern (unelectrified) tracks became derelict. This was far too tempting an opportunity simply to forget when the adjacent electrified lines were filling up.

The Met quickly considered electrifying the Grove Road (Hammersmith) to Acton Lane section of the LSWR and running Met electric trains from the City to Richmond. Discussions with the LSWR were promising and by 1914 that company was happy to entertain the Met running a service from which the LSWR would derive an income. This did not materialize for reasons covered shortly.

Central London Railway to Richmond?

The District and the Met were not the only railways interested in pushing west into the suburban belt, especially if through running over an existing railway might reduce costs.

The idea of sending the CLR to Richmond arose around 1912 when the section between Shepherds Bush and the terminus at Wood Lane was comparatively lightly used. It is true that the GWR's Ealing & Shepherds Bush Railway was being planned, by which CLR trains would reach Ealing Broadway, but even so there was still likely to be spare capacity east of Shepherds Bush. The CLR was then still independent and, like the District, saw great opportunities in the south-west for running over LSWR tracks via Richmond to places such as Twickenham, Sunbury and Chertsey, discussions about which were in an advanced state.[1]

On 26th November 1912, the CLR gave notice of the necessary bill it had prepared for the 1913 Session which set out the details of the 2½-mile link between Shepherds Bush (west of the station) and Gunnersbury (north of the station). Provisions were made for the CLR and LSWR to enter into the necessary agreements for through running trains, but the bill did not specify final destinations for the CLR trains. On 1st January 1913 ownership of the CLR passed to the UERL, which was less keen on the CLR competing for territory with the District and indicated that the extension (if it happened at all) would not involve CLR trains proceeding beyond Richmond, to the annoyance of those local authorities that were looking forward to through services to the West End and northern parts of the City.[2]

After the Great War the Underground noted how overcrowded District services had become compared with the CLR, where the west end was still only lightly used. This confirmed the pre-war idea that some extension of the CLR might relieve the District's busier western suburbs. It was by now apparent this could be done a great deal more cheaply than the pre-war scheme by placing the link at Shepherds Bush (where the disused LSWR station was close to the CLR station), rather than by lengthy new tunnelling. The necessary powers for this cheaper scheme were obtained in 1920.

Piccadilly West of Hammersmith?

Even before the CLR joined the Underground, the option of extending Piccadilly services westwards over the LSWR tracks had been considered as a low cost solution to District overcrowding. By simply extending the tracks beyond Hammersmith, to join the LSWR's northern pair at Studland Road, it was possible for Piccadilly trains to run west, improving capacity as well as reducing the heavy interchange traffic at Hammersmith. Before the Great War, Piccadilly trains were not heavily used at the Hammersmith end and there was scope to increase train services and carry a higher load. The Underground was keen to obtain all the traffic on offer irrespective of whether it came from the District or Piccadilly or both. Schemes were investigated from at least as early as 1912 and powers for a Piccadilly extension were obtained in 1913.

It was by no means a given that the LER would get these powers for, as mentioned earlier in this chapter, the Met was discussing electrification of the LSWR tracks to enable its own electric trains from Baker Street to reach Richmond via the junction at Grove Road. The Met already had running powers along this route and would undoubtedly oppose the LER's competing scheme. The LER felt the Met did not regard electrification of this line as a priority and persuaded it to enter into a 20-year agreement to desist from exercising its running powers for twenty years. In return, the Met would introduce a comprehensive system of through booking via Hammersmith and the District guaranteed the increase in income that was expected, adequately compensating the Met for not running its own through trains. Both companies were required to promote the through tickets and the agreement was formalized on 22 July 1914.[3]

With the Met now out of the way, The Underground was fully in control of developments west of Hammersmith as the LSWR was uninterested in developing its own services over the northern tracks. Because of the war, the inability to raise money and more pressing investment requirements, nothing was actually done on either the CLR or Piccadilly Line scheme, though it was unlikely both would proceed as the Richmond section did not have the capacity. Which to choose?

After the war, the District was busier than ever but some circumstances had changed and traffic patterns had altered. A review by the Underground of facilities in 1919 suggested the priorities in west London were as follows:

- Electrification of GWR west of Ealing Broadway and projection of both Central London and District trains.
- Electrification of LSWR tracks between Turnham Green and Hammersmith area and projection eastwards as a new relief tube line.
- Adjustment to stations at Wimbledon and Richmond and operation of District trains as a loop service via Kingston.
- Extension of District trains over Wimbledon & Sutton Railway (covered in an earlier chapter).

Importantly, neither the Piccadilly nor CLR connections with the now-disused LSWR tracks were regarded as a priority, though powers existed for both. A more comprehensive scheme was now preferred, where the disused tracks would become part of a new tube line. This would branch off the former LSWR line near Hammersmith and passing via High Street Kensington, Knightsbridge, Victoria, Trafalgar Square & Strand (joint), Holborn & British Museum (joint) and Mansion House & Bank (joint) with branches to Liverpool Street (through services to Brentwood and Ongar) and London Bridge (Dartford and Sevenoaks). No tunnel size was indicated but nevertheless some similarity with the modern conception of Crossrail is observed. The western destinations are not specified but given what the trains were to do in the east they would probably have served the LSWR and GWR destinations favoured in the other proposals just given, or something similar.

These suggestions were an indication of the Underground's thinking when considering London as a whole, but there was no question of a London-wide programme of this size being carried out quickly, or perhaps at all, and options were kept open. No progress was possible in the prevailing economic conditions.

In 1921, appalling unemployment caused the government to consider methods of stimulating jobs, including the encouragement of useful public works by large businesses. This was fraught with complication as the government wished to assist only schemes that were unlikely to proceed without assistance and not those which would at some point be carried out anyway; that was seen as public subsidy and at that time there was an ideological terror of being seen to be using public money that way.

The resulting government scheme was no more than to guarantee the interest payments of money borrowed for registered schemes. Because this made lending safer it resulted in a lower interest rate being applied which, in turn, made marginal schemes viable. The conditions included that the works be carried out entirely by British industry with British equipment.

The Underground was astonishingly quick to put improvement schemes forward and as this left no time to seek new powers it had to run with schemes for which there were already capital and construction powers. Most of the proposed works were to be carried out on the Hampstead Line but Ashfield was keen to include the simplified CLR link at Shepherds Bush and electrification of the LSWR tracks to Turnham Green. The Treasury was desperate to minimize the risk of having to pay out on the guarantee and felt the CLR extension was risky. As a result, the less expensive Piccadilly extension west of Hammersmith was substituted and approval was forthcoming. Unfortunately when accurate costs for the whole programme had been identified, and noting prices were rising for the larger schemes, the Underground had to find savings and the obvious candidate was the modest Piccadilly extension, which was deferred.

Although the scheme was not fully developed, contemporary reports (and the 1912 Act) suggests the Piccadilly Line would have passed underneath Hammersmith Broadway and climbed up either side of the LSWR viaduct to connect with the old tracks at the top. The northern LSWR lines would be electrified to Acton Lane, noting the tracks further west, towards Richmond, were already electrified. It was proposed to turn some of the extended trains round at Turnham Green as the Gunnersbury to Richmond section was already busy carrying District and LNWR trains. Platforms would also have been constructed on the northern tracks at Stamford Brook.

The Trade Facilities Act was renewed several times and the availability of relatively cheap money kept the Underground focussed on a small number of development schemes, principally the extension of the CSLR to Morden and the Charing Cross to Kennington link, and a large number of station reconstructions along the CLR. With all this work in hand, the extension of the Piccadilly westwards was not considered a priority, even though District train loadings were creeping up and it was obvious that at some point demand would considerably outstrip supply.

The Parliamentary powers for the works at Hammersmith were renewed in 1926, with additional authority to extend the duplicate tracks from Turnham Green about 1¼ miles to a point just west of Acton Town. By then housing developments in Ealing and beyond were demanding service improvements perhaps even more urgently than Richmond. At the same time an agreement was concluded with the Southern Railway (successors to the LSWR) that gave operational control of the stations, signalling and tracks between Studland Road and Turnham Green to the District and LER, though the Southern remained responsible for the viaduct, bridges and earthworks, and for the remainder of the route from Acton Lane to Richmond. It was expected that fast and slow services would operate each on its own set of tracks. The same act included additional widening work at Stamford Brook where it was still proposed to install an island platform on the northern tracks to match those on the southern.

It should be noted here that the Ealing & Shepherds Bush Railway opened in 1920 and allowed CLR trains to run to Ealing. With this and other developments in the Wood Lane area the traffic at the west end of the line looked likely to develop significantly and the appetite for a branch to Turnham Green and Richmond rapidly diminished and we hear no more of it.

Expansion Urgent

The Underground's stance was that extension of the Piccadilly westwards, to relieve the District, was inevitable. The question was not that it would happen, but how it was going to be paid for. The Underground could only finance extensions by borrowing money. Money borrowed was not free and interest would be payable from the date it was borrowed and this would be onerous until the works were complete and put into service. Even after that, it was essential that the extra fares revenue generated by the improved services exceeded the ongoing interest charges: in other words that the improvements would 'pay their way'. As a commercial company the directors could not recklessly proceed with schemes likely to make a loss. The challenge in this case was having confidence that the extra revenue generated would exceed interest charges thought likely to be around 5 per cent. This was by no means clear. It was not certain beyond doubt how fast new house-building would proceed, for example. Moreover, simply diverting existing passengers on full District trains to expensively-provided Piccadilly ones would generate minimal extra revenue by itself whilst pushing operating costs up. There was no doubt extra revenue would emerge, but so long as it seemed unlikely to hit 5 per cent the Underground was stuck, irrespective of the desire to 'do good'.

Meanwhile pressure for improvement mounted. Residential growth of Heston & Isleworth Urban District (which included Hounslow) had risen by only 3,500 in the ten

Above: **Park Royal station in the early 1920s with single car train of 1905 stock operating. The lack of development in this area is striking.** Author's collection

Below: **This south-looking view of Roxeth in 1927 shows some (quite old) development around South Harrow station, where a 2-car train stands. Two buses are waiting in the station forecourt; there is a small bus garage just to the north, on the corner of Northolt Road. There is little new development and the line passes through open country.** Alan A Jackson collection years from 1911 to 1921, but during the late 1920s it was obvious that growth had already exceeded this many times over and there was every reason to assume it would continue, perhaps even faster. This welcome traffic increase had been partly stimulated by existing post-electrification service improvement but without further modernization capacity improvement was difficult. The South Harrow line was worse; not only was housing sparse but competing services ate into the little traffic there was. There was no incentive for the Metropolitan's Uxbridge line traffic to divert to the District's moth-eaten shuttle; South Harrow and Sudbury Hill competed with Metropolitan and LNER services, Alperton and Sudbury Town with the London, Midland & Scottish, while Park Royal and North Ealing vied with the Great Western.

Meanwhile the Underground was increasingly preoccupied with the pressure to extend the Piccadilly Line northwards from Finsbury Park. This was no business of the District except that as the ideas resolved themselves into an extension to Cockfosters it was obvious the train frequency would be increased from the modest 24 trains an hour through the central area to at least 30 trains an hour. These trains would inevitably have to serve Hammersmith and the extra capacity further strengthened the argument for extending Piccadilly Line trains westwards to take unremitting pressure off the District.

Having renewed and extended the existing powers in 1926, the way was clear to extend the Piccadilly Line, subject to finding some way of paying for it. At this stage the proposed split of services on the western branches had not been clarified and even by 1929 some flexibility was apparent, though by this time it was known the Piccadilly was to augment services to South Harrow and Hounslow but not necessarily to the entire exclusion of the District. The running of Piccadilly trains to Richmond had not been ruled out entirely but in the meantime a proportion of the service would be thinned out at Turnham Green and these could be sent on to Richmond at some future date if required. In 1929, the District received parliamentary authority to widen the lines between Acton Town and Northfields so that fast services could continue at least as far as Northfields.

Although planning work proceeded, it was not possible to consider carrying out any work until the problem of finance had been overcome; it was still felt money could not be borrowed at less than 5 per cent and that was still too expensive. Circumstances changed in May 1929 when, in a climate of mounting unemployment, a Labour government was elected and within two months a Development (Loan Guarantees and Grants) Act was passed. As before, the intention was to stimulate great public works in the hope this would create employment. This time the mechanism was different from the old Trade Facilities Acts. These had guaranteed payments, making capital cheaper, but this time the government would actually rebate to those taking out loans part of the interest for a number of years, reducing the effective rate of the interest that had to be found.

The Underground quickly put together a package of work which, as with earlier schemes, included extensions, rolling stock, station reconstruction and other works and submitted this on 29th October. Having received favourable indications that the programme was compliant with the requirements, application was made to Parliament for the additional powers necessary and these were obtained in the London Electric, Metropolitan District, Central London and City & South London Railways Act 1930.

The rate of rebate decided by government was 3 per cent for fifteen years and the rate at which the bonds would have to be marketed was 5 per cent, so the effective rate of interest was 2 per cent, which would have been very cheap had it been the whole story. However, the rebate was only payable for goods and materials manufactured in the UK and did not extend to several substantial costs, the most expensive of which was land. Very roughly this meant that only about half of the programme was eligible for grant, so the effective rate of interest of the scheme as a whole was very approximately 3½ per cent. Even so, it made the extensions and improvements just about affordable (though as prices rose in the early 1930s some elements were dropped).

It might be noted that the Piccadilly Line was legally part of the London Electric Railway but that all the works to the west of Hammersmith were carried out by the District and the stations and tracks remained, as before, District freehold or leasehold property.

Reconstruction in Hand

Work on the western reconstruction began at the end of 1930. One of the more difficult tasks was the need to alter track and signalling between West Kensington and Hammersmith to suit a west/west/east/east pattern (from two pairs of east/west flows) while two operational railways still ran a full service. The Piccadilly's awkward depot link from Lillie Bridge also had to be maintained until the extensions had opened and the new depots became available. From December 1930 the works between Hammersmith and West Kensington began, with frequent temporary arrangements in force.

West of Hammersmith the object was to bring back into use the disused pair of Southern Railway tracks that ran parallel with the two electrified lines to Turnham Green. The eastbound District would need rerouting onto the most northerly of these old lines and the future Piccadilly would use the inner pair. West of Turnham Green the existing District embankment had to be widened from two to four tracks, as had the formation between Acton Town and Northfields; again the Piccadilly was to use the central pair. This was straightforward enough but a number of complicated junctions, and need for extensive stage-works, made this quite challenging.

The most difficult part of the works was the replacement of the existing seven platforms at Hammersmith by four new ones, in the form of two islands, within the existing cutting and without interfering with the train service. The first task was to demolish the northernmost platform, used for alighting Piccadilly passengers who had then to leave trains via the island. This created some working space and by stages the two Piccadilly tracks were spread more widely apart and the existing island rebuilt and widened. For many months the whole Piccadilly train service had to reverse in just one track, which was achieved without material reduction in service level, a very creditable performance.

Poster explaining that the major station works that were in hand were all part of the scheme to relieve unemployment. LTM

While that was in hand, work began on the District side of the station. An early move was to shift the eastbound platform and track north temporarily onto the former location of the southern Piccadilly arrivals platform which had been vacated during the stage-works. Shortly afterwards the Westbound loop was taken out of use so that side of the platform could be reconstructed, returning to service later in 1931 as the new Westbound District platform. These rearrangements allowed work to take place reconstructing the rest of the southern island platform and the eastbound District was eventually routed through its new northern face, releasing the space borrowed from the Piccadilly side of the station. Double track reversing of Piccadilly trains was restored only in March 1932 using the new northern island platform.

Between Hammersmith and Barons Court the flanking sidings were removed and the tracks slewed to the edges of the shallow cutting and a central siding was installed, accessible at both ends. From 5th June 1932 the connections at Barons Court were rearranged and the Piccadilly Line tracks were slewed south to run through the two middle platforms; the eastbound District was diverted further west to run through the northern platform and along the north side of the Piccadilly cutting. This necessarily coincided with the bringing into use of the new eastbound line all the way from Turnham Green to Hammersmith where District trains used the northern face of the northern island platform. Piccadilly trains now reversed in the two central platforms, using the new central siding to the east as a rather unusual crossover between the Piccadilly eastbound and westbound tracks.

Between Hammersmith station and Bradmore Lane, the 1877 covered way was only wide enough for the two existing District tracks but the scheme required four along this section. Two new tracks had to be laid in along the north side, which meant excavating a duplicate tunnel under the busy Broadway and the forecourt of Hammersmith (Met & GWR) station. The work was complicated by the immense number of utility services pipes and mains in the area, the tram tracks, the need to keep the traffic flowing and an underground public lavatory through which the new tunnel had to pass.

The new tunnel emerged at a point where the Southern's viaduct from Grove Road turned west, adjacent to the existing pair of District tracks, and there was just room to squeeze one of the two new tracks into the intervening space. The other track had to rise up on the north side of the old viaduct, which meant passing underneath it first. At this point it required piercing the viaduct structure on the curve and the loss of five arches which (though disused) were replaced by a bridge supported by concrete-clad girders. When the new tracks reached viaduct level they were connected up with the abandoned northern pair of tracks which were completely reconditioned, electrified and signalled. Little had to be done at Ravenscourt Park, except refurbishing the disused platforms. At Stamford Brook there had never been platforms on the northern tracks but since the outer track was to become the eastbound District it was necessary to provide one. Somewhat in contrast to the existing island platform a new platform was built on the north side with modern concrete walls and canopy, new stairs and a subway connecting with the existing station building. For economy, the idea of a platform on the eastbound Piccadilly track was abandoned.

The station at Turnham Green, like Ravenscourt Park, required little work doing to it but just east of the station it was necessary to install a goods loop between the old tracks requiring the embankment to be widened slightly.

West of Turnham Green there had only ever been two tracks towards Ealing and four were required now. Most of this section was elevated on embankment which had to be widened on the north side. Near Turnham Green some ingenuity was required to avoid excessive land take as the new tracks on the north side had to meet the old Southern lines at differing levels, the Southern lines from Richmond crossing beneath the District about a quarter mile west of the station. The eastbound (electrified) District track from Richmond also crossed beneath the District's line from Ealing about half a mile west of the station and this had to be realigned to accommodate the widened formation above. The solution was to drop the widened lines in level immediately east of the realigned underpass, occupied by the District's Richmond branch, so that it met the Southern tracks as they emerged from the bridge under the Ealing line before rising up to station level. One of the Southern tracks was removed between this junction and Acton Lane but the other was retained as a line for Kensington-bound goods trains. In the final arrangement, these would stand here out of the way awaiting a slot in the eastbound Piccadilly service and then trundle through the station into the second goods loop east of the station (already referred to) and then onto the eastbound District. The formation of the removed Southern track between Acton Lane and Turnham Green would remain available as part of the passive provision made to run Piccadilly trains to Richmond if this were ever required. The adjacent line, retained as the goods loop, was electrified briefly so that District trains from Richmond could reach Turnham Green whilst the alterations to the underpass further west were being made.

At Chiswick Park the future eastbound platform was required alongside the new northern set of rails and this was available from 17th January 1932 when the new eastbound track between Acton Town and Chiswick Park was brought into use. The westbound platform had to be rebuilt on its existing site but this would be very awkward to do whilst still serving trains. In any case the adjacent bridge across Acton Lane needed to be replaced by a bigger one, suggesting the need to build a temporary westbound platform. This was achieved by shifting the westbound line onto the widened formation round the back of the old eastbound platform, which was adapted to serve the re-routed westbound line. This temporary arrangement came into service on 24th January and

This view of Acton Town shortly before rebuilding looks west, into the 3-track station. LTM

This view of Acton Town (taken from a position a few yards to the right of previous view) shows the new platforms nearly complete early in 1932. The platform on the left had been the middle road and is temporarily in use for eastbound trains while the island on the right is completed. In the background is the new signalbox and in the distance the old substation which was enlarged at the west end. LTM

freed up a large working area on the old embankment allowing the permanent westbound platform to be built. This having been done, and the bridge replaced, the westbound track was restored to its old and final alignment on 15th May 1932 and the 'temporary' westbound platform removed, leaving behind it the large open space still rather visible today.

The work at Acton Town was equally intricate. First the westbound platform was taken out of use and all westbound trains used the middle road. This allowed the island platform to be widened on its south side and much of the reconstruction work effected. This work had been completed by December 1931 when the enlarged platform was restored to use. Following this, the eastbound platform was taken out of service and eastbound trains all ran through the middle road. This enabled the northern island platform to be demolished, though the actual track was left in place so that empty trains had access to and from the depot. North of this track, the coping for a new platform was constructed and in January the old track was shifted north and positioned alongside the new platform edge. This released space to construct the rest of the new island platform, the north face of which came into use for eastbound trains from 28th February. This having been done, the southern face of the northern island was completed with an additional track (future eastbound Piccadilly) inserted into the space next to what had been the middle road. This new platform and track came into use from 1st May 1932 and the former middle road (now serving the north face of the southern island) became the future Piccadilly Line westbound track.

West of Acton Town the objective was to continue the 4-tracking all the way to Northfields. Most of this was straightforward but the junction west of Acton Town and access to Ealing Common depot presented challenges. Before reconstruction, the tracks west of Acton Town comprised one pair of tracks towards Hounslow either side of which were the tracks to Ealing; the two Ealing tracks climbed up the sides of the deep cutting

This view of the Northfields area in May 1931 (looking west) shows the encroaching housing development which has built up heavily to east of Northfields. Land is already being cleared for the new railway depot but no work yet on the new station (the old station site is visible at centre of image west of Northfield Avenue. LTM

and where the two routes diverged the westbound Ealing line crossed the Hounslow tracks on the skew by means of a girder bridge. Ealing Common depot was on the north side adjacent to the eastbound line from Ealing and the depot outlet tracks (also on a steep gradient) met the main lines just outside Acton Town station.

The conversion of the existing 2-track line to Hounslow to four tracks was challenging given the existing arrangement and the desire that trains should be able to run to or from Ealing and Hounslow branches simultaneously from either platform. The only way of achieving this was for the two new tracks to flank the whole of the existing layout. On the westbound side this involved placing the new track alongside the Ealing line rising to the level of the bridge where the Ealing line crossed the existing Hounslow tracks. The new track, instead of going over the bridge, had now to drop rapidly to the level of the existing Hounslow route to clear the Tring Avenue overbridge. The work involved widening the cutting west of Acton Town without interfering with the existing service.

On the eastbound side, installation of the new track was much more complicated. For a start, the bridge carrying the Ealing line over the Hounslow branch had to be replaced as it was impractical to lengthen the sixty year old structure to cross three tracks rather than two. This was done by building the new bridge adjacent, but it left space if at some future date 4-tracking to Ealing was ever required. The next problem was to thread the new track (on the north side of the Hounslow branch) through the existing layout to

Above: **Looking west from the now-demolished footbridge at the eastern end of the new station at Northfields. In the foreground are the walkways to the footbridge from where long trackside gallery connected with the Weymouth Avenue exit.** Capital Transport collection

Below: **Northfields, Weymouth Avenue Exit. This view (taken after it was closed) shows that the design followed that of the other temporary buildings deployed for use whilst stations were being reconstructed. It was demolished in 1959.** Author's collection

connect with the new eastbound District platform at Acton Town station. The challenge here was the depot outlet ramp and the need to spread the Hounslow tracks apart to insert a reversing siding. The only way it everything could be fitted in was to trim back the cutting alongside the depot outlet, and eastbound line from Ealing, and install a near-vertical concrete walls. It was also necessary to construct a 450ft covered way underneath the depot throat emerging in steep concrete-lined cutting north of the depot outlet.

For the enhanced train services a new depot was required, primarily to service the Piccadilly Line but also for use by District trains still serving the Hounslow branch. The most convenient site was near Northfields station on the south side of the line but the existing 1908 station, west of the Northfield Avenue bridge, was really in the way and it was expedient to replace it with a modern one on the east side.

The new depot was planned with a capacity of 304 cars and included a 19-road car shed and 2-track lifting shop. Some District trains were to use the depot, reducing dead mileage and freeing up some space at Ealing Common for a few Piccadilly Line trains servicing the South Harrow line. The new depot was in part planned to allow the Piccadilly to withdraw from Lillie Bridge which was wholly unsuitable for servicing the much-enlarged line. It could neither house the larger fleet and the access difficulties at West Kensington would become intolerable with the enhanced services. The depot layout at Northfields allowed trains to enter and leave service at both ends, with the western connection just west of Boston Manor station. Some of the sheds were already complete by April 1932 and were used for storing and finishing work on some of the District's 1931 cars *en route* between Feltham and Acton where the traction equipment was to be installed.

The replacement station at Northfields was a substantial building set back from the road on the eastern side of the much-widened bridge and opening on 19th May 1932. It was designed with two island platforms, one for the eastbound and the other for the westbound pairs of tracks. However, construction involved numerous stage works caused partly by the complicated connections west of the platforms. At first only the northern island platform was used, together with a temporary station entrance to the south of the permanent building. In September, the westbound District service was diverted onto the new westbound line, through the new westbound local platform and through a short underpass west of the station allowing westbound trains to avoid conflicts with trains leaving the depot. The eastbound line was rerouted temporarily through the north side of this island.

From the end of October, the new eastbound District line track was brought into use between Ealing and Acton Town, including the new covered way, leaving the old centre pair of tracks out of use for reconditioning. The reorganization of the tracks between Acton Town and Boston Manor was completed on 18th December 1932 when what were to become the new Piccadilly tracks came into use and four tracks were available to the west end of Northfields station. Three new reversing sidings west of the station also came into service reflecting a belief during the planning process that the Piccadilly service would be substantially thinned out at Northfields, an assumption that was found only partially correct. The final connections to the depot came into service at the same time.

The reconstructed station brought the platforms at Northfields much closer to South Ealing, whose closure was considered. Northfields was given a secondary entrance at the eastern end of its platforms, a long concrete gallery linking them with Weymouth Avenue, only 200 yards from South Ealing station entrance and less than 70 yards from the western end of South Ealing's platforms. A tiny auxiliary entrance was built on the bridge, in style like the temporary entrances installed at many of the other stations that served during reconstruction; by road it was only 325 yards from the station entrance at

South Ealing and much closer to the platforms at South Ealing than the one at Northfields to which it was connected.

Closure of South Ealing was dependent on two main factors, neither implemented. First there was a plan to open another station at Ascott Avenue, in the long stretch between Acton Town and South Ealing. The second was maintenance of an interchange with local buses, which Weymouth Avenue could not immediately offer. With this vacillation about what to do at South Ealing the minimum possible work was done there. New tracks were laid around the back of the old platforms by trimming back the base of the cutting, but on the resulting island platforms only temporary sheltering was provided on the eastbound platform and none on the westbound. The widening caused the destruction of the existing station building, and both footbridge and replacement building were temporary (the latter, in the standard style, remaining 'temporary' for the next six decades).*

The branch towards South Acton was a problem as the modernization scheme required the whole of the train service from the Hounslow, Ealing and South Harrow branches to proceed towards Hammersmith. Because of the very light traffic using South Acton, the District concluded that a shuttle service from Acton Town would be sufficient and that economies could be made by reducing the line to a single track. Since Acton Town would have to be rebuilt anyway, it was easy enough to add another platform for the exclusive use of the shuttle. The line was singled from 14th February 1932 and the shuttle service was introduced the same day using the new 100ft long platform on the north side of the station to which it was connected by overbridge.

At first, the shuttle service was run by an ordinary 2-car train but from 24th April 1933 a single 1905 motor car was allocated to this service. This had a driving position at both ends and duplicated braking equipment. Only the centre doors were available to passengers; these were air-operated and interlocked with the control circuit so a train could not be moved with passengers able to board or alight. The doors were operated by the driver and no guard was provided. This was the first attempt to use air-operated doors on the District since 1908. In case of emergency, a pair of bare copper wires was suspended by insulators on posts alongside the branch to which, if there were a problem, the driver could clip a portable telephone handset and discharge traction current, asking for assistance if necessary from substation staff answering the call. This feature was actually available from 22nd January.[4] The car, number 37, was one of the two motor cars that had previously operated single car trains along the South Harrow line. When this special car was not available, a normal motor and control trailer pair was allocated, together with a guard. At South Acton the signal box was closed and buffers installed about 200ft along the existing platform, though trains always stopped at the west end.

In addition to the new depot at Northfields five stabling sidings were constructed on land south of the station at South Harrow to avoid dead mileage; these were located more or less where the old 1903 car shed had been and retained for a possible goods yard. There had been the usual uncertainty about what to do here. One plan included four open and four covered sidings and another plan no sidings at all. The issue was partly affected by whether Piccadilly Line trains would go beyond South Harrow to Rayners Lane or Uxbridge, an issue still not resolved at the end of the District's life.

---

* The eastbound island platform was given a contemporary awning and shelter in 1936 but continuing indecision resulted it retaining the "temporary" wooden station ticket hall which had been erected while the widening work proceeded—it survived until 1989 when a pleasant modern station building and short westbound shelter were erected—it was the Weymouth Avenue entrance at Northfields which was not to survive, being closed after traffic on 3rd May 1942, the concrete support structure remaining an intriguing site today.

Latest Signalling and Power Systems

Power supplies had to be upgraded for the enhanced services. A new substation and control room was built at Alperton, the substation coming into service on 20th January 1933 and the control room on 13th March. The latter controlled further new substations at Sudbury Hill (29th January 1933, allowing Sudbury Town to be closed), North Ealing (11th December 1932) and Northfields (18th December 1932). New substations also opened at Barons Court (19th March 1933) and Chiswick Park (27th June 1932), the former remotely controlled from the existing District substation at Earls Court and the latter from Ravenscourt Park. The existing substations at Hounslow East and Acton Town were retained and the latter somewhat enlarged. Power was normally obtained from Lots Road although a bulk supply could be obtained from the Met at Neasden via an under-street tie-line to Alperton for distribution when necessary. All the new equipment employed the latest mercury arc rectifiers. We have noted earlier that Lots Road had just been re-equipped and capacity increased with these extensions in mind.

Two-aspect coloured light signalling was installed where there were new signal boxes, but elsewhere a curious mixture of coloured light and electro-pneumatic semaphore signals were to be found. On the South Harrow branch the pioneering automatic signalling with semaphore arms was replaced by new coloured light signalling (commissioned between October and December 1932), but semaphores were retained at North Ealing and South Harrow for some years more. Semaphores were also retained along the whole of the Hammersmith to Acton Town section, including the new sections of track. New signal boxes were built at Hammersmith, Acton Town and Northfields, with signal cabins elsewhere retained.

At South Harrow the old mechanical cabin was retained, perhaps incongruously, to deal with the much-enhanced train service. A new facing crossover was installed to enable Piccadilly trains to reverse west to east in either platform, and further connections

New station building under construction at Hounslow West in March 1931, existing station building visible on right, Bath road in foreground. LTM

Hounslow West in March 1931, new station building visible in background. The train on left is in original 1883 platform, the island platform dating from 1926. The old station building (still then in use) is out of shot on the left and the island platform is accessed via a walkway behind the buffers. The near (wooden) car presents another useful view of a heavily reinforced underframe. LTM

1931 poster explaining the work of rebuilding Hounslow West is nearly complete. LTM

were laid in to serve the new stabling sidings. An issue arose about what to do about the through District service to Uxbridge and with no agreement with the Met about replacing them with Piccadilly trains a District shuttle train was the only option, shuttling between Uxbridge and South Harrow. It was hardly convenient to reverse trains at South Harrow from both directions but to ease the pain a traffic siding was installed between the stabling sidings and eastbound line and the shuttle usually turned around there. It is likely the old box was retained until the permanent train service (and hence track layout) had been agreed.

New Train Services

In the early 1920s it was not at all clear how the joint District and Piccadilly services would function west of Hammersmith. The few references hint that some Piccadilly trains might serve any of the western branches, including Richmond, with no indication that any District trains would be withdrawn. Non-stopping would be adopted to speed up some services. At this stage, of course, it was quite unknown where, when or in what density, housebuilding would occur and, except in general terms, what level of train service improvement was called for.

By 1929 it had been decided to extend 4-tracking to Northfields and install reversing facilities at Turnham Green. By 1930, it was proposed to operate a 2-minute Piccadilly peak service east of Turnham Green where a quarter of the service would turn. West of Acton Town, an 8-minute service was planned for South Harrow (or Rayners Lane) and 4-minutes to Northfields with half of those projected to Hounslow. The fast (Piccadilly) trains were to call only at Hammersmith, Turnham Green, Acton Town and Northfields. A 7½-minute District service would also operate to Hounslow with the Ealing service improved. Two 'up' morning and five 'down' evening District trains would also operate

Above: **Sudbury Town in 1931 with the previously stark platforms being transformed. On the right is evidence of the house-building that has already taken place near the station.** LTM

Above: **Platforms at the new Park Royal station on 8th July 1931, two days after it replaced the old station further north. Works are clearly far from complete and the permanent station building has yet to be erected. The automatic semaphore signal on the right is newly installed.** LTM

Below: **The temporary station building at Park Royal had to do service until 1936 when an impressive permanent station was built. It was part of the arrangement for moving the station that the developers donated free land on which they would themselves build a permanent station to fit in with the surrounding estate.** LTM

Northfield Avenue just before the Great War. Some development is in hand and the local Route 80 bus route helps enlarge the station catchment. Capital Transport collection

along the South Harrow line, seemingly in an attempt to perpetuate the existing through trains.[5]

By 1931 plans were more refined and the 2-minute Piccadilly service was to continue to Acton Town, where a third of the trains would turn. The balance was to be split equally between Hounslow and South Harrow. Trains would now non-stop Turnham Green and the idea of installing reversing sidings here, or a link towards Richmond, was dropped though passive provision was made (and is still available today). Proposals for District services did not contemplate great change along Ealing and Hounslow branches, but the District 'local' shuttle trains were no longer necessary during the peaks. By now there was a question-mark about what was going to happen along the South Harrow branch but some kind of District service at the height of the peak had not been ruled out. The need to make provision for a temporary Uxbridge-South Harrow shuttle was becoming evident.[6]

The new works crept into use gradually. The first public indication was a notice that from 8th February 1932 certain local trains to Hounslow and South Harrow would no longer carry first-class accommodation owing to the infiltration of Piccadilly tube stock onto the District's shuttle services so crews could be trained. Two weeks later first-class accommodation was abandoned completely between North Ealing and South Harrow.

On 4th July 1932 the whole of the District service between Acton Town and South Harrow was withdrawn and replaced by through Piccadilly Line trains, one in three being extended westwards beyond Hammersmith along the two central tracks intended for 'fast' trains. From the same date, Piccadilly trains connected at South Harrow (rather inconveniently) into a continuing District shuttle between South Harrow and Uxbridge. The shuttle operated half-hourly turning at South Harrow either in the traffic siding or sometimes in the eastbound platform. Depending on traffic conditions, it was of between two and four cars of District stock. The first westbound working on weekdays started at Acton Town, for Uxbridge, in passenger service as a District train throughout. On Sundays it began at Ealing Common and split into two short trains at South Harrow, one of them proceeding to direct to Uxbridge and the other forming the next working. Return depot workings were empty or staff workings. This inconvenient arrangement ceased in October 1933 when the whole service to Uxbridge was operated by Piccadilly stock.

Interior of the new station booking hall at Northfields in May 1933. On its new site the station building profoundly improves the station facilities. LTM

4-tracking was ready from Acton Town to Northfields on 18th December 1932, and from 9th January 1933 additional Piccadilly trains were projected beyond Hammersmith as far as Northfields, calling only at Acton Town. From 13th March, Piccadilly trains were projected to Hounslow West, with compensating reductions to District services in the peaks.

Off-peak services on the Hounslow branch were a little eccentric. The through Piccadilly Line trains (as in peaks) did not call at South Ealing which was still regarded as a District station (like Ravenscourt Park), and public timetables instructed South Ealing passengers to catch a District train. The District had long since operated only a shuttle service to Acton Town during the off-peak and this arrangement was continued in an idiosyncratic way by using 2-car sets of Piccadilly stock, shown meticulously in the working timetables as District trains and ignored entirely in most passenger timetables. However, at the extremes of the day these shuttles continued to comprise District stock.

The new train services meant that South Harrow line stations now had a through service to central London and simple cross-platform interchange at Hammersmith for those actually needing a District destination. Housing development along this line had finally begun more or less when work started on the improvements, but once opened it became rampant and by the time the District became part of London Transport houses threatened to occupy virtually all the available land in one near-continuous belt. Even houses a 20-minutes or more walk away from a station were in reach as feeder bus services to the various stations improved, together with through road-rail season tickets. Most of the new estates quickly found themselves on convenient new bus routes.

On the then-busier Hounslow branch it was a broadly similar story. Passengers now had a choice of central London destinations and the thinning of District trains allowed services to Ealing and Richmond to be strengthened. Again new housebuilding appeared on a large scale, dragging Ealing further southwards and producing a near-seamless belt of housing virtually obliterating the various disparate communities that had previously existed. Hounslow itself was slower to respond but, when the Piccadilly got there, accelerated development followed.

New Stations

Several District stations were rebuilt during this period, the designs influenced by Charles Holden's architectural practice—several buildings are now listed. Along the Hounslow and Ealing routes, Northfields (1933), Ealing Common (1931), Acton Town (1932), Chiswick Park (1932) and Hammersmith (1932) were all totally rebuilt. Hammersmith retained only its 1906 façade onto the Broadway, but a new façade was built facing Queen Caroline Street and the whole of the booking hall remodelled. Hounslow West (1931) and Boston Manor (1934) were rebuilt only at ticket hall level, and Stamford Brook's new eastbound platform was completed in the new style, but the existing island and ticket hall were left alone. The old Osterley & Spring Grove station was closed, replaced by a new Holden-style station on The Great West Road, a little farther west. The former station building in Thornbury Road closed after 24th March 1934 but the building still stands and represents the only surviving Hounslow & Metropolitan Railway building; some thought was given to providing a footpath to the new station but the cost was not felt justified. At Hammersmith, Acton Town, Ealing Common and along the Hounslow branch platforms were built or altered to 'compromise' height, half way between the car floor levels of tube and surface stock, giving a rather high step up into District's trains.

Along the South Harrow line, the existing tin sheds were impossible to adapt to modern needs. New station buildings were required on an appropriate scale for the emerging suburbs that threatened to cover all the green space developers could lay their hands on. Development along the branch really only began in the late 1920s but was clearly accelerating and the District needed the facilities to attract as much of the resulting new traffic as it could. The first rebuilt station was Sudbury Town, something of a prototype, and this was the first of Holden's tall brick box designs, unveiled in July 1931. Sudbury Hill and Alperton followed in 1932, together with corresponding platform reconstruction—as on the Hounslow line, platforms were altered to compromise height since when the stations were planned the train service mix was still uncertain. The more substantial station at North Ealing was not much altered, though the great mass of brick incorporated in the adjacent substation somewhat diminished the rural feel; for a similar reason Sudbury Hill is dominated by its new substation. Nor, for the moment, was anything done at South Harrow where new development was a little slower. There was much hand-wringing about how to deal with South Harrow and how many platforms it should have and plans were examined for reversing sidings and even a 3-track station, but with the creation of London Transport looming nothing was done and the old station, tucked away, had to continue, quite unmodified, for a couple more years.

Most of the stations had new or improved facilities for interchange with the rapidly increasing local bus services that could infiltrate the sprawling estates to bring traffic to the Underground. Park Royal was in a rather different situation. This had been built as a temporary station to serve the Royal Agricultural showground, intended to be the permanent home of the Royal Agricultural Society. The showground occupied a very large area between Twyford Abbey Road and the GWR's Birmingham line. The idea was not

Acton Town is representative of the brick and geometric concrete style favoured by Charles Holden's architectural school and used widely on the District's western improvements. The new building was completed in 1932 and also has an entrance in Bollo Lane. LTM

a success and after 1905 the show left the grounds and maps suggest that even from the elevated station it was not possible to see the nearest house. The showground space was well connected by rail and found a use during the Great War as National Filling Factory No 3, known as Perivale; here munitions (mainly detonators) were filled with explosives. Afterwards the buildings were adapted for industrial use and were soon supplemented by new factories. By 1932 this had become London's largest trading estate with 73 factories, employing 13,500 people. From the District's point of view, this was unhelpful because the workers tended to live locally and not need the Underground. Meanwhile the land was sterilized from the point of view of housing, diminishing the possibility of gaining new season ticket holders. But there was pressure to build east of Hanger Hill as far as the new Western Avenue and the District was persuaded that it would be better to move Park Royal station further south rather than rebuild on the existing, and rather inaccessible, site. Such an idea was made even more attractive by the developer's offer of free land. The new station was opened in temporary form in July 1931 and the permanent station building followed in 1936.

The job of station reconstruction was complicated because the new buildings had often to be on the site of the old ones and the station had to remain fully functional in the meantime. In most cases the answer was to provide one or more temporary buildings nearby. The ticket office had to remain at street level and a standard design of temporary ticket office and station entrance was created. This usually gave access to an existing stairway or bridge behind, but sometimes these too had to be provided on a temporary basis or as an advanced part of the completed work. In most cases the temporary ticket office was removed as soon as the new station building was available but at Northfields the temporary building survived about another half century as a hut occupied by a charity.

Chapter Thirteen

THE END OF THE DISTRICT RAILWAY

The long road towards integration

While the District's network of services adapted to meet London's suburban expansion, the organization of passenger transport in London was about to change. The Underground had long believed that fragmented control meant poor co-ordination and difficulty in raising funds for much-needed improvements and extensions. A single traffic authority for London had been urged for many years by virtually anybody who had gone into the matter, including two Royal Commissions; Lord Ashfield had more recently pushed the idea, but governments had not considered the matter urgent. The best Ashfield had achieved was in 1924 when the Underground Group's co-ordinated bus services were under attack from large numbers of independent bus operators, popularly known as pirate buses, which skimmed off the meagre profits from all the services. To the dismay of some, the government heavily regulated bus operation in London through the London Traffic Act 1924 and this made the operation of buses by anyone but a large operator very difficult. It did not extinguish independent operators but it propped up the practical monopoly already held by the Underground in many parts of London and Ashfield wanted to go further.

Ashfield had a difficult line to hold as the Underground and its subsidiaries were private companies whose shareholders and bondholders had their money tied up in the companies and would be affected by any transfer to a public body. Ashfield and his co-directors were under a legal duty to act in the best interest of their shareholders and were therefore not free to act against their interests. Nor were they free to make improvements and extensions to the system simply to aid the public at large unless, in their reasonable opinion, there would be a return on the capital spent building them—or, at least, there would not be a loss. Funding improvements was therefore very hard to achieve when borrowing costs were high and government still did not see its way towards using public money to support private business.

Lord Ashfield always stated publicly that the existing structure made further investment in the network nearly impossible to finance without assistance. If direct financial support were not forthcoming then he felt a statutory transport monopoly was the answer. This was hoped to reduce costs, make borrowing money a little cheaper, and by eliminating competition it would mean opportunists (as he viewed them) could not skim off the profits. It would also facilitate better planning and improved co-ordination of resources (reducing wasteful competition). Towards the end of the 1920s a political consensus was emerging that some kind of central authority was needed. During this awkward period, the Underground board (from whom the District took its direction) was probably at its most formidable; in 1929 its eighteen directors included seven privy councillors, seven peers, several holding senior army rank, various lawyers and a sitting MP. It was likely they would be able to obtain some kind of satisfaction during any parliamentary squabbles.

In whatever form this central authority might take, it was clear that the Underground was so big that its culture and practices would dominate the new body. Moreover the

Underground (or perhaps, more accurately, Ashfield) was also to be influential in its design. Ashfield's personal involvement was crucial in guiding the existing stockholders. If they were to co-operate, they needed to have their financial positions looked after and be satisfactorily compensated.

The Metropolitan Railway, with whom the Underground had usually been on very friendly terms, rather resented the Underground's assumption of the moral high ground in all this, especially as it would clearly mean the end of the Met as the rather individualistic, almost paternal, company that it had become. It felt it was doing a good job for its own catchments and didn't need to adopt the Underground's more uniform and extravagant way of doing things.

The difference in attitude is perhaps shown by the debates about what to do about Rayners Lane, a station entirely the property of the Met. The Met also enjoyed support from the 1929 Development (Loan Guarantees and Grants) Act and resignalled the Uxbridge branch with automatic signals as far east as Eastcote. The Met had hoped then to rebuild Rayners Lane station to handle the new housing going up; resignalling the station and junction was expected to be included then. The government declined to support this reconstruction as it felt housing numbers were speculative and without them rebuilding would produce no new passengers, increasing risk of default on the loan guarantee. The District had wanted to improve its own services to Uxbridge and with new Piccadilly Line trains in the offing wanted to send those through to Uxbridge (or at least to Rayners Lane). The Met fully recognized that the existing station hut was hopelessly inadequate and was happy to consider station reconstruction even without government support, but the Underground was demanding facilities far in excess of anything the Met felt was necessary—the Met was always careful with money. Agreement was impossible to reach and with a new transport body inevitable the matter was simply left and the old wooden station remained with its restrictive mechanical signalling. In consequence, in 1932, shiny new Piccadilly Line trains reached only South Harrow and there was a moth-eaten District shuttle to carry people beyond. There were other examples where the difference in attitude of the two companies was just as stark. In this climate, the Met felt it better not to spend its own money on schemes that the new organization would probably carry out itself.

London Transport came into existence in 1933, but first it is necessary to see what else was happening in the District's last days.

London Passenger Transport.

A

BILL

To provide for the establishment of a Passenge Transport Board for the London Traffic Area and for the transfer to that Board of various transport undertakings and interests; to make other provisions with respect to traffic in the said area; and for purposes connected with the matters aforesaid.

Presented by Mr. Herbert Morrison, supported by Mr. Secretary Clynes, Mr. William Graham, Mr. Solicitor-General and Mr. Pethick-Lawrence.

Ordered, by The House of Commons, *to be Printed*, 12 *March* 1931.

LONDON:
PUBLISHED BY HIS MAJESTY'S STATIONERY OFFICE.

To be purchased directly from
H.M. STATIONERY OFFICE at the following addresses:
Adastral House, Kingsway, London, W.C. 2;
120, George Street, Edinburgh; York Street, Manchester;
1, St. Andrew's Crescent, Cardiff; 15, Donegall Square West, Belfast;
or through any Bookseller.

Printed by Eyre and Spottiswoode, Ltd.,
East Harding Street, E.C. 4,
Printers to the King's most Excellent Majesty.

[*Price* 1s. 3*d*. *Net*.]

[Bill 109]

This was the London Passenger Transport Bill, introduced in 1931. This document greatly preoccupied the directors of the District and other Underground companies and meant the end of the District Railway company was in sight. Author's collection

Cuts in Wages

The dreadful recession that began in 1930 quickly affected travel habits and reduced the income of the Underground railways, including the District, which responded by finding economies. An early casualty was the generous attitude previously held with regard to staff who had, for some reason, become redundant. Hitherto they had been kept on the books and kept occupied until suitable permanent positions became available but this was no longer possible; towards the end of 1931 some 377 staff were let go, with another 188 shortly afterwards and the risk of yet more to come.[1]

This early move was considered insufficient to balance the books and the board proposed a temporary reduction in earnings of all staff by 2½ per cent and an additional wage reduction of a further 2½ per cent for that portion of their earnings over 40 shillings a week. For those with earnings in excess of £750 a year yet another 2½ per cent slice would be taken. This temporary measure would apply to all 45,000 staff, including officers and directors, and earnings would be restored as soon as possible. Understandably, the trades unions gave this proposal lukewarm support but the reductions were introduced from 3rd September 1932 with the important provision that they would never result in weekly wages falling below 50 shillings. The matter was complicated by comparable cuts proposed by the main line railways and this led to some industrial relations turbulence. Ashfield regretted having to implement this reduction but pointed out the Underground always tried to pay its staff well. It might also be noted that during a similar crisis in 1928 the main line and Met railways had resorted to something similar but the Underground companies had managed to avoid making cuts. The pay reductions remained until after the formation of London Transport and were progressively withdrawn between August 1934 and June 1935.[2]

A New Engineering Depot

As the District began preparing for absorption within London Transport there were still pressing matters to get on with. One of these was the enlarging engineering organization based on Lillie Bridge required to handle the extended and busier system, particularly at the west end of the line. Some of the existing workshop and office buildings were now quite old and no longer efficient. Meanwhile the District also owned the adjacent land on the western side (north of Empress Hall), formerly part of the exhibition grounds but no longer used. In addition, there was the old Piccadilly car shed, representing further possible engineering space now it was no longer needed by Piccadilly trains (they departed in March 1933 when Northfields depot opened). Wholesale reconstruction of the whole site was called for, with the intention of becoming a central engineering depot for all the lines and with space for further expansion later.

The new buildings were built mainly on the old exhibition grounds on the west side of the existing yard and over half the space was given over to all manner of stores, divided departmentally into areas for substations, cables, timber and general stores. There was then a large machine shop, whose work was mainly fabricating rails and track parts. Next to that was a signals workshop where signalling equipment could be overhauled. Routine overhaul was considered vital for virtually anything containing sensitive moving parts. A vast area was left open. Much of this was storage space for rails and sleepers, with a workshop adjacent to the latter whose sole job was to fit iron chairs accurately to the sleepers so they could be delivered to site ready-chaired. A sizeable space was left available as the crossing layout ground, where complex trackwork could be assembled and adjusted accurately before disassembly to enable it to be moved by train to site. Covering the whole of the open area was a goliath crane, enabling track components to be moved

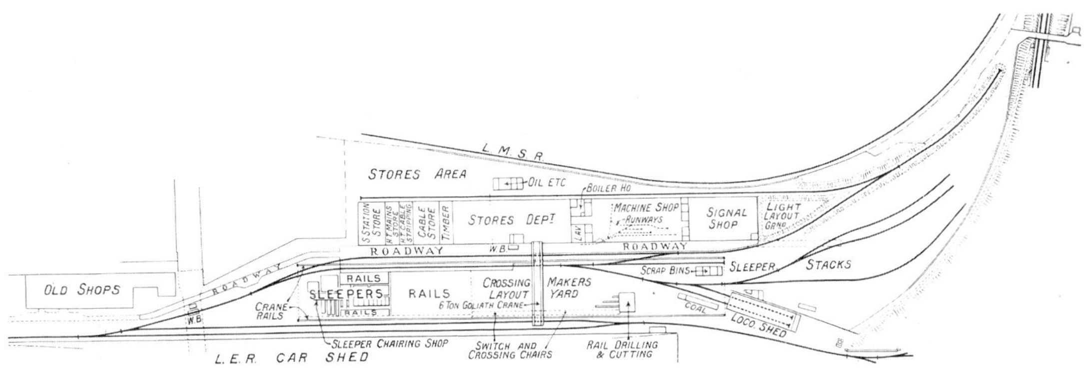

This is a plan of the new engineering depot at Lillie Bridge, built largely on the site of the old District works (used only for engineering infrastructure since 1905). Lillie Road is to left and exit towards District tracks bottom right. West Kensington is at top right but actual connection District tracks not shown. This part of the works was completed in 1932. Author's collection

about efficiently. The crane was also useful for unloading the stores trains which brought materials into the depot direct from the WLR.

In 1931 the District concluded the old tank locomotives were no longer suitable for the work they had to carry out, and would be even less suitable for the enlarged depot. The answer was to buy two brand new tank locomotives from the Hunslet Engine Company. These had a 0-6-0 wheel arrangement, a boiler pressure of 200lb, weighed 44 tons and were comparatively low machines with a maximum height of 12ft 3ins. These were well-suited to the work at Lillie Bridge and for the odd trips to Ealing Common, East Ham and the Warwick Road goods yard to exchange stores (and presumably coal) wagons with the main line system. They also appeared on ballast trains when required.

By 1931 the old Beyer Peacock yard locomotives were life expired and the District invested in two powerful Hunslet Tank locomotives, primarily for use in the yard at Lillie Bridge, which was being expanded. This shows one of them (No L30) probably at maker's factory before the full Underground livery was applied. Roy Allen collection

Most of the new work was available from 1932 but was not completed until the following year. Later stages of the scheme were much modified and did not proceed until 1937, after London Transport was formed and the nature of the projected Underground extensions was known. Notable improvements saw an expansion of the track fabrication area, a new engine shed and conversion of part of the old Piccadilly shed into a rail welding shop.[3]

London Transport

On 1st July 1933 the Metropolitan District, London Electric, Central London, City & South London and Metropolitan railways and various bus and tram concerns were absorbed by the newly-created London Passenger Transport Board, a public corporation more generally known as London Transport. The District and the routes over which its trains operated were henceforth promoted as London Transport's District Line. The takeover of the old companies did not alter the ownership (or joint ownership) of the main line companies over which the Underground operated and (as before 1933) more District mileage was owned by the main lines than by London Transport. Nevertheless, one would not know this from the publicity put out by the new organization where District trains served London extensively without reference to main line involvement. On a day-to-day basis very little changed on the District.

The consideration paid by London Transport to District stockholders of all classes was £15,542,695, all of it in the form of newly-issued London Transport stock, the majority of it paying reasonable rates of fixed interest. It may be useful to explain here that whilst the Underground held a controlling interest in the District, by far the majority of the District's securities were actually held by private individuals or institutions (the 1929 capital of £14.9 million was owned £3.3 million by the Underground and £11.6 million by institutions or private individuals); this had been a factor in not attempting to amalgamate the railways before 1933, the effort required would have been very complex given that at a practical level the companies were already being run as a single organization.

Although no cash was paid to any holder of District securities, there was an expectation the new stock would be tradeable and also generate a regular return. There were several types of London Transport stock relevant to District shareholders, as follows:

- 'A' Stock payable in exchange for debenture and rentcharge stocks; there were two types of 'A' stock, one paying 4½ per cent and the other 5 per cent.
- 'B' Stock to be exchanged for guaranteed and preference stocks paying 5 per cent.
- 'C' Stock to be exchanged for ordinary shares and whilst there was no guarantee of any return there were some conditions that will be covered shortly.

Where existing stocks paid an amount different from the rates of equivalent new stock then the amount of stock exchanged would be varied pro rata so that the practical effect was to continue the existing payment.

The amount of stock exchanged was as follows:

£100 6% perpetual debenture stock to receive £120 5% 'A' Stock;
£100 4% perpetual and prior lien debenture stock to receive £88. 17s 9d 4½% 'A' Stock;
£100 3% consolidated rentcharge stock to receive £66 13s 4d 4½ 'A' Stock;
£100 5% redeemable debenture stock to receive £100 'A' Stock;
£100 4% Midland rentcharge stock to receive £88. 17s 9d 4½% 'A' Stock;
£100 4% guaranteed stock to receive £80 5% 'B' Stock;
£100 4½% first preference stock to receive £90 5% 'B' Stock;
£100 5% second preference stock to receive £100 5% 'B' Stock;
£100 Ordinary stock to receive £92 10s 0d of 'C' Stock.

All of the stocks were redeemable, at London Transport's option, for their face value after various periods from 1955 to 1985 but other than this distant promise, and the need to pay the interest in the meantime, the new board merely replaced the old company certificates for the new ones with no exchange of cash.

District Shareholders do alright, but only just

The question arises whether the District shareholders were better or worse off as a result of London Transport taking over. This imponderable cannot invite a definite answer, although ordinary shareholders at the time felt the District was at last becoming a financial success and did not want to be robbed of their reward just as it was being delivered. The new structure had somehow to reflect this.

In the District's last decade, the rising traffic and constant attack on costs resulted in all of the common fund companies, including the District, finally paying a respectable dividend on their ordinary shares. The amounts paid to District ordinary shareholders were:

1921	**1922**	**1923**	**1924**	**1925**	**1926**	**1927**	**1928**	**1929**	**1930**	**1931**	**1932**
1%	3%	3½%	3½%	3½%	3½%	4%	5%	5%	5%	4½%	3%

In being asked to consent to the setting up of London Transport in 1931/2 the District ordinary shareholders rather had their expectations set by the dividends paid in the good years 1929-31. The replacement London Transport 'C' stock, like ordinary shares, was guaranteed no dividend but District shareholders were induced to believe there was a reasonable chance they would receive at least 5 per cent, and this secured their co-operation in the face of the economic depression evident at the time. In fact the 'C' stock on no occasion paid as much as this, which must have been a disappointment.

The 1933 Act defined a 'standard' rate of dividend for 'C' stock of 5 per cent for the first two years of London Transport and 5½ or 6 per cent thereafter but there was no obligation to pay this if the money to do so were not there. Paying the 'standard' rate proved quite unachievable—it never exceeded 4½ per cent—and war broke out shortly after the 1938-9 dividend was declared, at only 1½ per cent. With such a low return, the stock value drifted down to under 75 and then the low 60s. Some former District shareholders must have wondered whether their support for London Transport had been justified but we can never know what would have happened had the District carried on. After nationalization in 1948 the 'C' stock was swapped at market value for British Transport Stock guaranteeing 3 per cent and surviving District shareholders were probably content to have certainty of payment for the first time. The 1933 Act provided a sanction if the 'standard' rate were not paid for three consecutive years but this simply amounted to giving not less than 5 per cent of the 'C' stock holders the right to appoint a receiver. This was a fairly toothless provision that would have done as much harm as good and though London Transport was in breach after 1936 it was never suggested such drastic action be taken.

What was the problem? One problem was that the bringing together of staff from so many organizations exposed serious inconsistencies in terms and conditions. The unions saw to it that the tendency was to raise pay and conditions to the level of the best, pushing up costs to the surprise of those involved who had promised that costs would fall. We then have extensions made taking time for traffic to build up (but creating instant extra costs), difficulty raising fares owing to the complex processes needed and finally the ongoing depression which though less dire in the late 1930s looked as though it might come back.

The creation of London Transport also created reorganization costs which might also have been underestimated.

The control of London Transport was a little curious and seemed to make the new board rather detached from the consequences of their actions. The London Transport stockholders had no control over the board and were unable to influence the appointment of directors and senior managers, or anything else. The board was not even appointed by the minister—such was the terror of political interference—but by a body of appointing trustees. These trustees were sound members of the establishment required to select suitable individuals for their particular experience: it is little surprise to find that Lord Ashfield and Frank Pick were put in charge, guaranteeing a degree of continuity. Instead of working in the interests of the shareholders, as any normal company, the new board was required to function for the public good as set out in the 1933 Act.

Unfortunately, whilst its credit was good, London Transport could only raise money by issuing more stock or by borrowing it. This was a problem as Section 3(4) of the Act required the board to operate the business so as to balance its books. In turn, this meant that new railway schemes had to be at least sufficiently remunerative to recover the cost of borrowing the money. This was not only exceedingly challenging, it had been precisely the problem since before the Great War and put London Transport in not much better a position than the District had been for most of its history.

The District's guaranteed and preference shareholders suffered no great inconvenience by the transfer of their interests to London Transport but it is a moot point whether the ordinary shareholders were so satisfied since the capital value of their District shares was linked to market confidence in there being a reasonable dividend. The value of the ordinaries had been static at about 74 or 75 until May 1931 but fell in value while the bill was under consideration in Parliament, falling to a low of 52 in April 1932, though recovering slightly before vesting day. At the beginning of October 1933, 3-months after vesting day, 'C' stock was trading at 84 which by curious coincidence was more or less the value of the District stock in 1930/31 if one allows for the rates at which the stock was swapped. In terms of the value of capital, the District shareholders had initially come through all right.

The UERL itself was not taken over by London Transport as it also had interests in businesses which were not relevant to public transport in London. The shares it had held in the various transport subsidiaries were exchanged for London Transport stock as though it was any other shareholder. The 1933 Act did require the UERL's non-transport subsidiaries to be disposed of and for the UERL (and the London & Suburban Traction Company) to be closed down. Once the shares had been swapped for London Transport stock they were sold on the open market for cash, which was used to liquidate the UERL's various debts. The remaining subsidiaries, such as the North Metropolitan Power Supply Company (which generated and distributed electricity to large area north and east of London) and Associated Equipment Company (which made buses and other road vehicles), became independent companies the sale of which recompensed the UERL shareholders and bondholders. Lord Ashfield was appointed liquidator in August 1933 and the UERL was wound up on 24th May 1935, its task complete.[4]

The London Passenger Transport Pool

A major feature of the 1933 Act, and one frequently overlooked, was the mechanism for co-ordinating the operations and development of the main line railways in London, since these did not become part of LT even though their operations were frequently interconnected. The Act established the London Passenger Transport Pool into which the revenues of LT were paid together with all revenue generated by the main line railways that related to journeys wholly within the London Passenger Transport Area (a vast district about twice the size of today's greater London). The actual amount paid in excluded agreed expenses incurred in operating those services. The pooled revenue was then distributed to the contributors in agreed proportions relating to the results in earlier years adjusted to reflect subsequent changes. The dynamics of this encouraged cooperation between LT and the main lines rather than competitive schemes that would only benefit one party. To supervise the pool and co-ordinate development a standing joint committee was set up by the Act which to a degree became the transport planning authority for public transport within London and the home counties.

It is beyond the scope of this chapter to explore the successes of the standing joint committee, but if one considers it to have parallels with the 1915 Underground pooling scheme then one gets a flavour. In particular, it simplified the accounting arrangements between the LMSR and the District and greatly facilitated the projection of Underground electric trains over other main line railways.

The LMSR-owned Electric Cars

During the latter part of 1933, London Transport renegotiated the agreement with the LMSR for provision of trains along the Barking line to reflect altered conditions. As part of this, London Transport agreed to buy the 90 cars operated under the 1908 agreement, and the further 20 cars purchased for the Upminster extension, for their current book value of £202,934. London Transport also agreed to replace the life expired element of these for an agreed price of £167,066. To avoid the sudden cost of doing this the LMSR agreed to loan London Transport the sum of £370,000 indefinitely and to charge 5 per cent interest on the balance; London Transport was authorized to pay some or all of it off whenever it chose. The agreement was signed on 30th December 1933 but was retroactive to 1st January 1933 which is why the cars appeared to have been transferred from the District to London Transport on 1st July 1933 (even though on that date nobody had an inkling that this would happen!).

The new agreement completely replaced the 1908 operating arrangements and provided that:

- London Transport would provide an electric train service to Barking and Upminster to a timetable agreed between the parties.
- In doing this London Transport would endeavour to meet the traffic requirements of the LMSR but the LMSR would accept additional trains reflecting the nature of the London Transport requirements further west.
- Trains would be staffed by London Transport but be subject to the LMSR rulebook.
- Sheds and stabling accommodation for the trains working this service would be provided by the company on whose property they were erected.
- The LMSR to pay London Transport for provision of the above services (the cost is based on cost per car mile operated including depreciation, maintenance and train staff).
- The LMSR to provide the carriages for the Southend through trains and London Transport to provide loco haulage and train staff to Barking.
- If the agreement is terminated the LMSR shall buy back the 110 cars or their replacement.

The new agreement simplified the arrangements dating back to 1908. Although the transfer and loan arrangements look complicated, the outcome was that London Transport obtained full control of the cars for an annual charge of 5% of their value. Since this was offset by the increased charges now paid by the LMSR (now freed of their maintenance and renewal costs), there was little, if any, actual extra cost or burden on either party.[5]

The Legacy

The District became an important part of the London Transport network and some simple statistics for the year ending 1932 might give some flavour:

No of stations owned:	37
No of stations served:	72
Passengers carried (ordinary tickets)	75,643,292 (of which 988,186 first-class)
Passengers carried (workmen)	25,064,704
Passengers carried (seasons)	25,779,176 (of which 2070 first class)
Total passengers carried	126,487,172
Average daily passengers carried:	372,569
Capital employed:	£16,208,159
Route miles (owned or leased)	25m 58ch (of which 58ch is share in ELR)
Route miles (run over):	66m 40ch (of which 7m 17ch jointly owned or worked and 34m 23ch are foreign lines over which running powers exercised).
No of cars owned:	564 (283 motors, 113 3rd trailers, 168 composite trailers)
Car miles in passenger service:	24,361,489
Passenger locos:	7
Service locos:	3
Steam locos:	2
Various service and stores vehicles:	69

A few things might be said of the District's last year or so. It might be thought that the forthcoming absorption by London Transport would be a distraction but the reality was that the District had already ceased to have direction of its own and was already functioning as part of the larger Underground Group. To that extent it was very much business as usual.

We have seen that the District modernized and expanded. By 1932 virtually all the central area stations had been rebuilt, or at least heavily renovated and improved. The western extensions work had also resulted in many stations being renovated or completely rebuilt. The station stock was therefore in comparatively good condition although some of the jointly-owned City Line stations called for improvement. The exhibition hall that had been fashioned out of the large space at Charing Cross was in use frequently, often for third party events or for exhibitions promoting UK industry. The Underground Group itself used the space on occasion and more than one exhibition was held showing off all the Underground's safety equipment. This included a model railway and examples of full sized signals and other apparatus.

Other infrastructure was also in a reasonably good state and the electrification works had stood up well. For example the power station at Lots Road and the electrical supply system was being kept up to date. Signalling was subject to continuous improvement and was keeping up with train service demands and the early direct current track circuits were being replaced by more reliable alternating current versions. Work was in hand to replace some of the early moving-spectacle tunnel signals with less maintenance-hungry colour light versions. The signalling was less than thirty years old and little of it could be thought life-expired.

Above: **As the days of the District Railway came to a close there were still a small number of 1905 motor cars in service on the 'local' services, of which this survivor is one (image after 1932). Apart from the shifting of the upper marker light to the offside window these cars had been much repaired but had not otherwise been heavily modified.** Author's collection

Below: **This is one of the many original 1905 motor cars still in use in the late 1920s after complete refurbishment and conversion to trailer. This was originally French motor car No 38.** Author's collection

The rolling stock had aged less well, and we have seen the trouble the original all-wood cars had given. By the end of the District the majority of these cars had been scrapped and a significant proportion relegated to the various short 'local' services. Figures for April 1932 show 55 cars restricted to local services with a further 81 were used as trailers in main line

Above: **The exhibition space built into the ticket hall at Charing Cross continued to be used until the 1970s. The Design in British Goods exhibition was held in April 1932. This display case promotes the design excellence promoted by the Design & Industries Association, of which the Underground's Frank Pick was president. The last exhibition in District days appears to have been the Hydrogenation exhibition, in May 1933.** LTM

Below: **The District experimented with direction-finding aids at various times and this image from Charing Cross (December 1932) shows an interesting idea tested at a number of central area stations, but not one pursued. The world appears to end at Whitechapel.** LTM

trains. This totals just 136 cars of the total District fleet of 638 cars and represents just a third of the original 1905 fleet with further cars destined for early retirement too. The work involved in keeping these cars in shape was heavy and expensive.

The District 'brand' (a term not then used) had been subsumed by the name 'UndergrounD', which featured prominently on station exteriors together with the 'bullseye' symbol or, latterly, the updated version using a bar and circle device. Where cross-modal promotions were made (for example bus-rail seasons) then the Train-Omnibus-Tram (or T.O.T.) promotional name was used. The name District Railway was certainly not banished (it was vital on directional signage), but it received little promotional prominence and certainly not the heavy line branding with extensive use of green ink, paint and enamel that can be seen everywhere today. It is true that green had been used as a distinguishing colour on the underground diagram since 1923 but this was just to distinguish it from the other lines and seems not to have been used at all as a promotional tool.

Conclusion

By most criteria, the District was a useful and successful railway. It helped relieve London traffic; it helped develop the London suburbs; it was a boon to the East End workmen, who used the workmen's tickets in huge quantities; it was the main east-west railway, which became the core of the Underground system in the 1920s. It was an innovative railway constantly trying and testing potentially useful ideas, usually at someone else's risk. It was comparatively reliable, apart, perhaps, from the dismal Inner Circle service. The staff were loyal and the quality of the managers and engineers seemingly very good.

There are, however, criteria by which is was not successful. Financially it was for many years a basket case. Companies are supposed to make money for their shareholders and the hopelessly over-extended District singularly failed to do this for most of its life. For many years, it teetered on the edge of bankruptcy. Even allowing for the consequential difficulty of raising money for investment, one cannot overlook the company's static and ineffectual board of directors. They were dominated for so many years by Forbes, who was ultimately responsible for studied inaction in so many areas, at least in part caused by the huge number of calls on his time by other weighty concerns. One would not go so far as to say the District did nothing during Forbes' time, for it plainly did. What it did not do was to fix the finances and aggressively target the most lucrative markets. Once Forbes had gone, and the much-needed American investment had become effective, the District improved and showed what it was really capable of. In the end, it was rather successful.

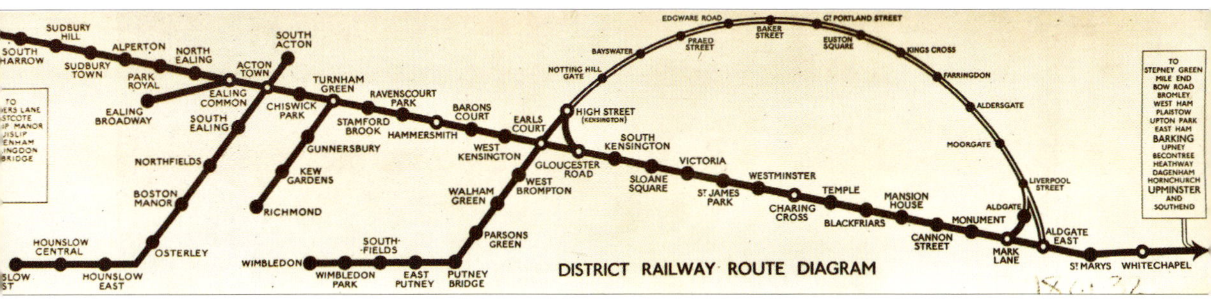

This is the route diagram placed in each of the District cars during the 1920s and until the end of the railway (this image dated 1932). Its resemblance to some vile insect was observed by the staff magazine which could not resist a parody. LTM

Appendix One

LIFE AFTER THE DISTRICT

The New Order

The formal name 'London Passenger Transport Board' was hardly euphonious and the abbreviation 'LPTB' was not much better, and the name 'London Transport' quickly lodged in the public mind, at least in part because this name appeared on the sides of trains and buses and on publicity. It will be convenient to use the abbreviation 'LT' from this point, notwithstanding later changes in the status of the organization.

The creation of LT resulted in the consolidation of head office departments and the end (administratively at least) of any functions specifically serving only the District, including marketing and engineering. The obvious exception was the train service which was for historical reasons difficult to alter in any significant way and today, eight decades after the end of the District Railway, operates remarkably unchanged. While unified management simplified the irksome administration of the former eastern and western

Looking west from the Warwick Road Bridge (Earls Court) around 1935 one sees at far left the branch towards Putney whilst a Hammersmith-bound train enters the 1914 tunnel under the Putney line. Meanwhile work is in hand all around to construct the new Earls Court exhibition hall, the forecourt of which will cover the space visible here. Author's collection

joint lines, previously shared with the Met, the Whitechapel & Bow Joint Committee continued as before. The running of District trains along the LMSR and Southern railways also carried on uninterrupted.

LT was quick to resolve several train service annoyances that the Underground had been unable to sort out. The first was the working of Piccadilly Line trains beyond South Harrow. The earlier hope that Piccadilly trains should be projected only to an improved Rayners Lane interchange station gave way to a scheme for sending through trains all the way to Uxbridge, addressing the rapid suburban development in the area. It was necessary to adjust Met platform heights to suit both tube and surface stock but from 23rd October 1933 a through Piccadilly service to Uxbridge replaced the District's South Harrow-Uxbridge shuttle. It was not possible to run many trains until the old mechanical signalling at Rayners Lane had been replaced, achieved in 1935. Another early improvement was to tidy up the train services along the Hounslow branch, with all Piccadilly Line trains calling at South Ealing and District trains running through to Hounslow only in peak hours.

LT established an active public relations organization that constantly fed a grateful press with stories about its activities and aspirations. It took credit shamelessly for a stream of new works that had been started under the old regime, particularly the completion of the government-supported schemes. One example was the link from the west end of the platforms at Monument to the south end of the platforms at Bank, on what was later called the Northern Line; this involved a lengthy passage and deep flight of escalators, which came into use on 18th September 1933, completing plans developed by the pre-1933 Underground. Interchange from the District to the Central London Railway was also possible by walking the entire length of the Northern platforms and an equally long and dreary subway. Curiously, Monument continued to enjoy a separate name although the District name boards were altered to 'Monument for Bank' (to this day continuing to puzzle users of what is quite clearly now one station).

At Earls Court, following work initiated by the District Railway, a large new exhibition hall by C. Howard Crane was built on the triangle of railway land west of the station and this opened in September 1937. To improve access, a new concourse was constructed beneath the District platforms extending from the top of the existing escalators to a new flight of escalators that emerged within the exhibition building, a small ticket office being included in the area at the head of the escalators. At the same time the existing walkway from Warwick Road was replaced by a new covered (but unglazed) concrete walkway built alongside. This included a rotunda at the Warwick Road end that incorporated a small ticket booth whilst at the east end the walkway ended at a new bridge over the tracks leading to modernized platforms. The new escalators were ready when the exhibition hall opened and station reconstruction was completed on 14th October.[1]

In December 1934, LT and the LMSR concluded a joint investigation into traffic on the Barking Line, already heavily overloaded and with developments further east threatening to make matters worse. The main constraint was the crossing of the District and the Met services on the flat (west of Aldgate East and east of St Mary's), where Met trains still ran onto the ELR. A commendable 36 trains an hour was operated in each direction along this short section of line, despite the two junctions; of these, 27 were District and nine were Met trains between Hammersmith and the ELR. This bottleneck required five District Line trains to be turned east to west at Mansion House in the evening peak, not doing anything for the overcrowded trains east of Cannon Street.

Analysis showed that most Met passengers continued along the Whitechapel route rather than to ELR destinations; indeed their need to change trains at Aldgate East was contributing to delay and overcrowding. The answer was to switch at least some of the Met trains towards Barking, which would increase capacity through the bottleneck to 39 trains an hour by reducing conflicting junction working at St Mary's and passenger delays at Aldgate East. The Southern (which had an interest in the ELR) did not want all the Met trains withdrawn without testing the result, so it was proposed to maintain four trains an hour to the ELR and run eight through to Barking, in theory increasing that service from 27 to 35 trains an hour. As part of this scheme, improved interchange at Whitechapel was necessary between the District and ELR platforms where ELR local services would be improved to make up the loss of through trains.

A preliminary service began on 30th March 1936, comprising a morning working from Hammersmith (Met) to East Ham and back, and an evening trip from Hammersmith (Met) to Plaistow and back. The new timetable proper came into use from 4th May 1936 with eight 6-car trains an hour scheduled between Hammersmith (Met) and Barking during rush hours, and District services recast to accommodate them. Off peak, the Met trains reversed at Whitechapel.

The much-increased service required some track alterations at Barking. A new up loop was provided through platform 5, so either platform 3 or 5 could be used for up local services as traffic required. This left platform 4 to accommodate reversing trains without fouling movements in the other direction. In the peaks, several District trains were extended from Barking to Dagenham where from 24th November 1935 a new electrified bay road and a stabling siding was made available. Part of the scheme included an additional substation at Tower Hill.

These improvements were found insufficient and the track layout at Aldgate East was the main culprit. The solution was to rebuild Aldgate East station on a new site about a train's length to the east. This released space into which the eastern arm of the triangular junction could be extended, so that 8-car trains could stand on any part of the triangular junction without the rear end fouling the path of a train proceeding along another route. The resited station was opened on 31st October 1938 and in the following four weeks the old platforms were removed and the new tracks, junction work and signalling laid in. The entire southern curve linking Aldgate East and Minories Junction was replaced by a new tunnel slightly to the south (a substation was later built in the old one). All was ready on 27th November when the new track and signalling was commissioned. St Mary's station was partly superseded by the eastern entrance to the new station and was closed after traffic on 30th April 1938.

In fact sending Met trains to Barking to ease the pressure on the District was a very successful move and it was not long before through trains to the ELR ceased so that trains along the Barking line could be maximised; this also reduced conflicts at the junction at St Mary's. These enhancements left the Met slightly short of trains and four more (plus spare cars) were needed. For convenience, LT purchased similar cars to the District's 1931-type cars and 28 were purchased from the Birmingham Railway Carriage & Wagon Co, half motors and half trailers; these were made up into the usual 4+2 formation and ran as 4-car sets off peak. They were equipped with electro-pneumatic brakes and two sets were equipped with air-operated doors: both were novel features on the sub-surface lines at that time. The guard would usually release the doors and had responsibility for closing them, but once released each door set could be opened individually by passengers operating a locally situated push button. The system was called 'passenger door control' and its future development was to hinge upon the success of these trains. The guard could open all doors himself during busy times.

In addition, LT also purchased a further 26 trailers, of similar design, from Metropolitan Cammell as a contribution towards replacing the remaining 78 wooden trailers of 1905 origin. As these had to be compatible with other District trains they at first lacked electro-pneumatic brakes and air doors.

New Trains for the District

During the mid-1930s LT concluded that the District rolling stock should be modernized to incorporate electro-pneumatic braking, which had been successfully applied to the 1920 fleet and which would increase capacity. There was also a view that the adoption of air-worked doors controlled by the guard was essential, rather than perpetuating the handworked arrangements that were less safe and which caused delays. The 1910-14 cars were not suitable for conversion to air door operation and, allowing for the further culling of old wooden cars, it was decided to retain a small hand-doored fleet using these motor cars working with the 1931-35 trailers. This would leave a main fleet of 173 motor cars (built 1923-35) to be converted, for which an equivalent number of new trailers would be needed. To get the right combination of cars, 183 trailers were ordered, together with 25 new motor cars, and this was sufficient for the 46 assorted 6- or 8-car trains needed for service and spare cars. The 1920 stock continued to provide eleven 8-car trains for service and the balance (using the oldest motor cars, just described) would carry on with the hand-operated doors cars until the motor cars were life expired.

All the new cars were ordered from Gloucester Railway Carriage & Wagon Co. These were flair-sided vehicles, had elliptical roofs and were quite unlike any previous cars on the District, though they were similar to the new fleets of cars just purchased for the Met and long-term standardization was in mind (not in fact achieved until 2017). Each car had two pairs of double doors along each car side and a single doorway at one end. At the other end was a hinged cab door which provided entry to the driving cab on motor cars but was sealed shut on the trailers, the interior space being used for extra seating; this novel arrangement anticipated the eventual conversion of the trailers to driving motor cars. All cars had 600 volt power bus lines and auxiliary equipment, and the motor cars had the District's standard BTH control equipment (some recovered from existing stock). The motor cars and 58 of the trailers were designated third class, while 125 trailers were composite 1st/3rd, and had a doored partition separating the two sections. It was intended to scrap all the rotting 1905 cars but the Second World War somewhat disrupted plans and several of these survived hostilities, with three remaining in service until 1948.

It will be helpful to mention here that in 1926 the District introduced a classification scheme which made it easier to refer to the confusing variety of cars it then operated. The classification scheme may have been useful to the engineers but was rarely used by anybody else until LT days. LT found the scheme rather convenient and it was later expanded to include all stock operated along the sub-surface lines (and is still in use today).

Class	**Description**
B	Unrebuilt cars of 1905 origin
C	1910 Hurst Nelson cars
D	1912 Metropolitan Amalgamated cars
E	1913/14 cars from Gloucester
F	1920 Metropolitan Cammell (incompatible with other cars)
G	1923/4 cars from Gloucester
H	Rebuilt 1905 cars

The scheme was extended as later cars were delivered:

K	1927/8 cars
L	1931/2 cars
M	1935 cars (for Met's Barking service)
N	1935 cars (for District)
O	1936 cars for Met (Hammersmith & City)
P	1937-8 cars for Met (Main)

The new District cars were designated Q stock and were delivered mainly between 1938 and 1940. On delivery, they had to be married up with older motor cars already modified with electro-pneumatic brakes and air-operated doors, which required control panels for the guards installing in the trailing ends of motor cars and much alteration to the wiring. The new Q stock cars were delivered already wired for the modified brakes and doors. The older cars converted to run with the new trailers also became known as Q stock and operated as a single fleet.

The self-contained F stock (1920) fleet was reformed at the same time into 11 8-car trains (plus spares) now arranged into two 4-car sets, each containing one double-equipped motor, one single-equipped motor and two trailers. This work required conversion of the control trailers into motor cars, mainly by using equipment from former double-equipped motor cars. Air doors were fitted at the same time but the fleet had still to operate self-contained because of wiring and coupler differences.

The District during World War 2

Early in the battle of Britain, on the night of 7th September 1940, heavy bombing in the East End caused damage at West Ham and near Campbell Road and major damage at Plaistow where a train was hit, causing considerable destruction. The bombing continued for days and on 9th September destruction rained down upon Monument, Aldgate East, Bow Road and Parsons Green. And so it went on, repair gangs being constantly at work and the railway generally being patched up within hours. Some bombing caused much longer shutdowns. Parsons Green to Earls Court shut for a week, Charing Cross to Mansion house two weeks (with a later 1-week closure) and St James's Park to Sloane Square closed for three weeks; but this overlooks the sheer volume of interruptions of up to a day or two and individual station closures of longer duration. Several sites were hit more than once, such as Whitechapel, which was very badly damaged.

Sloane Square ticket hall had been entirely reconstructed in the early days of the war, with up escalators linking each platform to the ticket hall from 27th March 1940. On 12th November 1940 the station building, ticket hall, staff canteen and new escalators were demolished by a 1500kg high explosive bomb, the wreckage falling onto the last coach of a departing train and destroying it. In all, 42 people were killed. The entire section of railway was closed for twelve days and a temporary station building came into service from 2nd December.

Later in the war, the V weapons began to cause new damage and further service disruption and by 1945 the Underground was heavily patched up. The whole system suffered from much-reduced maintenance caused by loss of staff to the war effort, diversion of resources to cope with air raid damage, and difficulty in getting components and supplies; in a sense this began the maintenance backlog which lasted decades. To try and protect stations from bomb blast outside, many had blast walls built just beyond station entrances which did nothing for their appearance, but these were removed

Lots Road power station on 10th August 1944 showing the wartime devastation of nearby property along Upcerne Road. The power station received one direct hit, with a second bomb landing unexploded in the adjacent dock and, despite searches, not being found. Damage was limited and under different circumstances could have had a devastating effect on services. LTM

quickly after hostilities finished. In addition, large signs were removed as a potential aid to enemy aircraft and lighting was reduced to support blackout requirements. Trains were blacked out by a combination of window netting (which also protected against glass splinters) and severely reduced lighting during air raids.

After the War

With war out of the way, the District Line settled down for a few years. The main problem was the same as that after the previous war, which was increasing traffic and lack of modern serviceable rolling stock. After tediously lengthy analysis and debate with government officials about the number of railway cars they would permit to be built in Britain, and what meagre allocation LT might get, we see the birth of the R stock which differed from earlier trains in having all cars motored. This stock was constructed in several batches but in nearly all cases the driving motor cars were created by converting Q stock trailers. These received motors, electrical equipment and a driving cab in the space provided for it at the designated end of the cars. New non-driving motor cars (NDMs) were built from new, at first of a similar all-steel design but with later cars of lighter aluminium alloy. The aluminium cars, when painted, looked the same as the all-steel ones but were lighter and appealed to the government which was still trying to direct scarce steel supplies to goods being exported. The NDMs were all built without provision for driving cabs and had adjusted door positions with single-leaf doors at both ends. The stock came into use mainly between 1950 and 1953 and allowed large numbers of very old cars to be scrapped, including the last of the cars still employing hand-worked doors.

The authorities running the exhibition halls at Olympia were concerned by the abolition of the LMSR train service along the WLR to Earls Court, abandoned after heavy bombing in 1940. The railway link was important for access to events and the service had usually been augmented when large shows were put on. In post-war conditions there was no prospect of a regular service being restored but LT agreed that it would be a simple job to run a shuttle service to Addison Road during exhibitions, trains starting at Earls Court or High Street Kensington where they would connect with the rest of the system. Exhibition trains first operated on 20th December 1946, the first time that District trains had served Olympia on their own account (Addison Road was renamed Kensington Olympia at the same time). At the Olympia end, the existing electrification system was unusable but it was only necessary to couple up the conductor rail on the approach tracks to the District tracks south of Earls Court Junction to be able to run trains, which normally used the south end of the long down main platform.

In 1958 arrangements were made to segregate the (by now established) shuttle service from the main line tracks, as frequent exhibition train movements rather got in the way of the heavy goods traffic. This was achieved by appropriating a bay road on the western side of the station and rearranging the tracks to make room for a quarter-mile of single-line electric track between the station and the former Earls Court Junction. This came into use on 3rd March and allowed the LT service to operate quite independently.

Below: **East Ham (or Little Ilford) depot had been used by District trains since 1905, although it had been enlarged more than once. This image was taken shortly before closure when the new depot at Upminster was opened.** Alan A Jackson

Segregation of frequent LT services from main line trains (especially goods trains) had been an aspiration for a while east of Campbell Road where many junctions and heavy goods traffic wrought havoc with the frequent District trains, which impacted adversely along the whole line. During the late 1950s, money was finally found to do this very expensive piece of work, the whole lot being paid for by British Railways, which had inherited the infrastructure. The work was precipitated by the proposed electrification of the former LTSR line on the overhead system which itself required extensive track modification (this was completed in November 1961, nearly half a century after the Midland Railway promised to do it).

The plan was to eliminate virtually all the flat junction connections with the slow lines and, where functionality was lost, rerouting goods trains by completely different routes. This having been done, the slow lines would be used exclusively by District trains and LT signalling would be installed (at main line cost). Barking proved a challenge and required a series of flyovers and flyunders to separate LT services and introduce cross platform interchange. The District sidings at East Ham had to go and new sidings were installed east of Barking, together with a new depot at Upminster. A flat crossing was unavoidable at Upminster to allow Romford branch trains access to the main line tracks and this was fully signalled (as was a freight yard access near Dagenham). The works were finally complete in 1960, but it was another decade until ownership of the track, staffing and intermediate stations (excepting Barking and Upminster) were transferred to LT.

The South Acton branch had never generated much traffic and its usefulness was further reduced in 1932 when it became a shuttle running only to Acton Town. The meagre traffic was impossible to develop further and in June 1958 the Sunday service was withdrawn and the future of the branch was in doubt. London Transport felt the line was not worth keeping and the last train ran on 28th February 1959. In 1964, falling traffic levels saw the withdrawal of the rush hour District trains along the Hounslow branch. In turn, this meant District Line trains no longer stabling at Northfields, nor Piccadilly Line trains at Ealing Common depots.

The junctions at the Minories and Aldgate East continued to restrict the number of peak hour trains east of Mansion House but during the early 1960s increasing traffic in the City required more trains. In addition, the interchange between Tower Hill and Fenchurch Street was poor and required something better. LT considered reusing the old Tower of London station. By re-using the wide, open cutting here it was possible to relocate Tower Hill station to the east side of Trinity Square and at the same time create a 3-platform station incorporating a central reversing road. This shortened the interchange with Fenchurch Street and allowed most of the trains reversing at Mansion House to be extended to Tower Hill. The new station opened in 1967 and reversing facilities were brought into use in 1968 with a bay road using part of the former westbound track. At the same time the northern bay road at Mansion House was removed, leaving only the central bay, intended for use mainly when the service was adrift. This, too, was removed in 2016 as it was very little used.

With traffic dwindling, the uncoupling of 2-car east end portions was abandoned in 1972 and the rolling stock was progressively rearranged as permanent 7-car sets (with a few of 6-cars) instead of 6-car off peak and 6-car and 8-car during the peaks. This had the advantage of removing the need for passengers to use the catwalks in the tunnels where there were still short platforms. New trains, the D stock, were introduced from 1979 in 6-car formations but with individual cars longer than previous so train lengths were not much altered. 6-car trains of another type, the C stock, were used on the Edgware Road to Wimbledon line as shorter trains were needed because of restricted platform lengths.

Above: **South Acton station closed in February 1959 and this shows the old station shortly after the track was removed, local boys appear delighted to have discovered this new playground. The short section of useable platform can clearly be seen.** London Underground Railway Society collection

Both of these stocks were, in turn, replaced by London Underground's new 'S' stock trains, conversion being completed in 2017 in advance of resignalling and introduction of automatic train operation. From the mid-1990s traffic on the whole of the Underground began increasing substantially, particularly off-peak, with frequent services operating through central London throughout the day. This makes more efficient use of expensive infrastructure but puts the system under stress, which it is hoped conversion of the District Line to automatic operation will relieve.

The general appearance of many District stations has altered little since the 1930s although interior changes have been more obvious, particularly those resulting from the new ticketing system in the 1980s. The meagre facilities at South Ealing and Hounslow East have been replaced by new stations. Property developments have seen new station buildings at Hammersmith, Fulham Broadway, Gloucester Road and Mansion House, with the booking office at Ealing Broadway merged with that of the main line station (though the old District station building still stands, as it does also at Fulham Broadway). System development has also seen new stations required at Westminster, Blackfriars, Cannon Street, Monument, Tower Hill, Aldgate East (described earlier), Whitechapel and Mile End. At platform level most stations have been modernized to an extent, but still the station entrances display a certain permanence. There are few early District stations in their original form, though West Brompton and North Ealing are pleasant examples, and the exteriors of Stepney Green and Bow Road are relatively unspoilt. The Underground took over East Putney, Southfields and Wimbledon Park in 1994 and although they were not built by the District they are substantially unaltered since opening.

Just as this story began with a desire to introduce a circular railway around London, so it will end with some more words on that subject. LT did not like the Inner Circle service at all. It was infrequent, notoriously unreliable, troublesome to manage (especially when it was disorganized) and a scheduling nightmare that required concessions from other services so it could function at all. Many of these horrors arose from the trains having neither a terminus nor any track of their own. The service (especially the clockwise one) also crossed nearly every flat junction the sub-surface lines had to offer, almost guaranteeing delays. The service was not even heavily used but, of course, it served virtually all of the London termini and could hardly be abandoned. Moreover statute compelled it to continue.

LT considered several schemes for reducing the number of flat junctions, all appallingly expensive. Powers were obtained in 1935 to disengage from the statutory commitment to run it as a continuous service and at the same time to build a flying junction at Cromwell Road, but this was not treated as a priority. The possibility of breaking the circle with overlapping sections was also looked at but more urgent schemes, and the war, postponed action. Some relief was obtained in 1957 when track between South Kensington and High Street was rearranged to avoid the particularly inconvenient flat junction at South Kensington. Under LT, the Inner Circle service was operated as part of the Metropolitan Line and had no separate existence although all regular passengers knew how it functioned. It was not until 1948 that the Underground diagram first disclosed the existence of the Inner Circle Line, and the following year when it appeared in yellow, with the prefix 'Inner' dropped (forty years after the last of the other 'Circles' ceased). It was not until 2009 that the root cause of Circle Line irregularity was tackled, with the present form of the Line introduced and continuous all-round trains abandoned after 125 years.

Below: **This was a familiar scene at Parsons Green, where trains were strengthened for the peak service and reduced afterwards. A 2-car (usually) set was worked out of sidings into platform and a service train was brought up behind (seen here) and coupled up. In this view the extra cars are both motors but usually it was a motor car (leading) and trailer. This practice ceased in 1972.** John Gillham

Appendix Two

UERL DIRECTORS

The directors of the Metropolitan District Railway have been given in Volume 1 but it will be evident from this volume that after 1902 they were increasingly influenced by the Underground Electric Railways Company of London Ltd (the UERL). The UERL never had a majority financial interest in the District but it owned enough voting shares to exert control, especially as there were no other substantial interests to challenge this position (even had they wanted to). Practical control was exerted by appointing a number of directors from the UERL itself and by pooling all the departmental resources with the UERL's other transport concerns. Financial pooling from 1915 meant that for all practical purposes there was only a single transport business and from the early 1920s it is doubtful if any specifically 'District' policies could be identified—at least, none of any significance.

Because control of the District became substantially exerted by the policies of the UERL it has been necessary also to record the various UERL directors, and those of the earlier Metropolitan District Electric Traction Company, set up to electrify the District. Those directors listed below who were also at some time directors of the District are noted by an *. In passing one might note the drift from the clutch of important international bankers on the board in the early years to senior and very influential representatives of the British establishment later on. The board must have been one of the most influential in the country: one had almost to be a peer or a privy councillor to be considered.

Directors of the Metropolitan District Electric Traction Co (registered July 1901)

(Directors appointed by subscribers to the company)
Charles Tyson Yerkes (Chairman)
Cecil Grenfell (London)
Patrick Calhoun (New York)
Walter Abbott (Old Colony Trust, Boston)
Murray Griffith (Metropolitan District Railway), appointed subsequently

Directors of the Underground Electric Railways Company of London Ltd (registered 9th April 1902)

1902 Subscribers to the Underground Company, one share each:

Mr E.S. Speyer, Mr W.H. Brown, Mr A.N. Smith, Mr H.G. Leith, Mr C.T. Yerkes, Mr W.E. Mandelick and Mr A.J. Kent.

Initial directors were: Charles Yerkes, Walter Abbott, Edgar Speyer, William H. Brown (of Speyer Bros) as set out on Memorandum of Association. In 1903 it was decided to raise the maximum number of directors from seven to fifteen.

Charles Tyson Yerkes* (Chairman). Died in office 1902-1905
Walter Abbott* (Old Colony Trust), Boston 1902-1908
Frank Dawes (Bircham and Co.) London 1902-1910
Lord Farrer (Right Hon). Director of Midland Railway Company 1902-1933
Maj Ernest St Clair Pemberton RE, Norwich 1902-1903
Charles James Cater Scott (Chairman of the London and India Docks Co). Died in office .. 1902-1931
Charles Ainsworth Spofford* (US railroad magnate residing in London till 1905) 1902-1909
Edgar Speyer, (Sir Edgar from 1906)(Chairman from 1906), Speyer Bros, London 1903-1915
James Speyer (Speyer & Co), New York 1903-1912
Robert H. McCurdy (Mutual Life Insurance Company of New York) 1903-1906
James A Blair (Blair and Co), New York 1903-1909
James H Hyde (vice-president of the Equitable Life Insurance Society), New York 1903-1905
T Jefferson Coolidge Jnr (chairman of the Old Colony Trust Company), Boston 1903-1908
Leonore F Loree (President Baltimore & Ohio RR), USA 1903-1912
Jhr Henry Teixeira de Mattos (Teixeira de Mattos Brothers), Amsterdam 1903-1915
Hon Sydney G Holland (Viscount Knutsford from 1914), Royston. Died in office 1904-1931
William Hugh Kemsley 1905-1905
Lord George Hamilton* (Deputy chairman 1910-15 then chairman to 1919), London 1905-1926
Sir James Clifton Robinson* (London United Tramways), London. Died in office 1905-1910
Ralegh Buller Phillpots, London 1905-1907
Sir George Stegmann Gibb (Deputy chairman and MD) 1906-1910
Albert Henry Stanley* (Managing director from 1910, Sir Albert 1914) 1908-1916
Col Millard Hunsiker (US Steel Company) 1908-1909
William Barclay Parsons, New York 1908-1912
Jacob G Metcalfe, New York 1908-1912
William Corwin Burton* (Resident director from 1916), J.G. White & Co 1908-1919
Henry Augustus Vernet* (Deputy chairman from 1919), London 1910-1933
Rt Hon Sir Algernon West (formerly London County Council), London 1910-1919
Lieut-Col Sir Herbert Jekyll, (formerly Board of Trade, Rly Dept), London 1912-1932
Charles Beilby Stuart-Wortley (Lord Stuart of Wortley from 1916; died 1926) 1912-1926
William Mitchell Acworth* (Sir William from 1921; died 1925), London 1912-1925
Rt Hon Lord Southborough (Former Permanent Secretary and Lord of Admiralty) 1918-1933
James Devonshire (Sir James from 1920), power engineer, London 1919-1933
Lionel Robinson, Stockbroker, London. Died in office 1919-1922
Sir Albert Stanley (2nd term)(Chairman and MD)(Lord Ashfield from 1921) 1919-1933
Rt Hon Lord Colwyn* (Banker), London 1921-1933
Maj Gen Sir Frederick Sykes MP (former Chief of Air Staff), London 1922-1928
Rt Hon Sir Robert Stevenson Horne MP (later, chairman of the GWR), London 1923-1933
Rt Hon Edwin Samuel Montagu* (politician), London, Died in office 1923-1924
Rt Hon Earl of Bessborough (politician and businessman), London 1925-1931
Rt Hon Lord Newton (politician and diplomat), London 1925-1933
Brig-Gen Arthur Melland Asquith (businessman and son of former PM), London 1926-1933
Solomon Barnato Joel (Diamond and gold mining business), London Died in office 1926-1931
Gordon Leith (partner with J.P. Morgan, once connected with Speyer Bros), London 1926-1933
Edward Robert Peacock (director Barings, previously Bank of England), London 1926-1929
Sir Max Julius Bonn (Banker), London 1927-1933
Frank Pick* (Managing director from 1928) 1928-1933
Evelyn B Baring (Banker, Managing director Barings), London 1929-1933

Appendix Three

DISTRICT POWER SIGNALLING

Manually Controlled (or Semi-Automatic) Signals

The Americans who electrified the District believed that swift electric trains could only operate reliably in conjunction with power-operated signalling, operating fully automatically wherever possible. Where switching between tracks was necessary, automation would have to be supplemented by power-controlled points and signals under manual control from some nearby control point (the Americans called these 'towers' on their elevated electric lines but in London they continued to be called signal boxes).

The question arose as to the equipment that would be used by the new 'power' signalmen (power-controlled points had been avoided on the experimental South Harrow line) and the use of miniature lever frames became the preferred solution. The need was to be able to control the outdoor equipment quickly, safely and economically from signal boxes from which some or all of the trains might not be visible. The equipment had also to integrate seamlessly with the track-circuit operated fully-automatic signalling that would be installed between junctions.

Earls Court East was typical of the various new power signal boxes. The frame is equipped with bells to describe the trains, and four pushes are visible. Within a few months the automatic train describers were installed on the instrument shelf and used instead. Author's collection

Above: **Earls Court East cabin spanned the yard east of the station. The line on left is eastbound line and adjacent line (with train) is the siding, which survived in this form until 1966. The two tracks on the right are the two westbound lines, that from High Street emerging from the dip. Access to the cabin appears to have been via gallery fixed to right hand retaining wall. This view also gives some idea of the scale of the high voltage power distribution system.** Author's collection

Below: **A close up of two of the elecro-pneumatic signals at South Kensington, the one on the left an ordinary stop signal and the other a shunt signal.** Roy Allen collection

The chosen means of control was the 'Style B' miniature lever frame made by the Westinghouse Brake Company. This design was a development of an interlocking frame devised by the Union Switch company in America with which Westinghouse (with McKenzie & Holland) had a commercial arrangement. This frame provided a means of combining the security of mechanical interlocking with the ability to control outdoor equipment through a system of reliable electrical contacts. It also incorporated some electrical locking so that track circuit occupation by a train would prevent unsafe moves being set up. The equipment vastly reduced the space required compared with an all-mechanical system of equivalent functionality. The mechanical work performed by the outdoor equipment would be performed by compressed air, controlled by electrically-operated valves; this was already the system arranged to be used by the automatic signals and was very suitable for moving points.

The original Union Switch frames had been operated by small pivoted levers at the ends of rotating shafts, and these had to be rotated from side to side to operate the equipment; the British market was horrified by this crude means of control, as a result of which Westinghouse, in the UK, installed a row of miniature levers, with small catch handles, along the front of the frame, the fore-and-aft movement being converted to the required rotary movement inside the equipment. There were only a few of these early 'Style A' frames installed in the UK before an improved type, the 'Style B' appeared in 1903, first used on the North Eastern Railway. It was eminently suited to the needs of the UERL and a list of the District installations follows. Using American practice each installation was allocated a code which appeared on the signal box instead of the customary name, and also on signal identification plates before the lever number. Codes were allocated from Earls Court beginning at EA, working eastwards, and WA working westwards. Some gaps were left in the two series, for example ED and WH, presumably to allow for possible later additions.

The signal box at South Kensington was on a rather narrow site and elevated. This is the rear (which has been bricked up apart from a small lookout). The signals control the junction between the District route (to the left) and Inner Circle route (to the right). Roy Allen collection

Location	Code	Number	Levers	Into Service	Out of Service (last day)
Mill Hill Park	WL	29	47	11 June 1905	23 Jan 1932
Putney Bridge	WG	46	15	17 Sept 1905	19 Nov 1960*
Parsons Green	WF	47	39	17 Sept 1905	8 Oct 1960
Earls Court East	EA	45	27	26 Nov 1905	8 Aug 1936
Earls Court West	WA	31	27	26 Nov 1905	19 Sept 1936
Cromwell Road	EC	32	47	7 Jan 1906	20 June 1936
South Kensington	EE	56	23	14 Jan 1906	27 July 1957
Mansion House	EJ	59	35	25 Feb 1906	1 Sept 1939†
Hammersmith	WD	53	39	16 June 1906	2 May 1931
Minories	EK	60	7	15 July 1906	27 Feb 1909
Aldgate East	EL	61	15	15 July 1906	6 Oct 1928†
West Kensington West	WC	57	39	28 Oct 1906	14 Apr 1962‡
Whitechapel	EN	85	51	25 Feb 1907	17 Nov 1951†
West Kensington East	WB	54	39	31 May 1908	2 Oct 1948¶
Turnham Green	WK	114	23	3 Dec 1911	30 Oct 1931
Hounslow West	WX	151	15	28 Nov 1926	25 Mar 1972
Ealing Common	WM	Rec'd	23	10 Mar 1925	5 Nov 1960
Hammersmith	WD	Rec'd	43	3 May 1931	4 Jan 1964
Northfields	WR	Rec'd	71	4 Sept 1932	20 July 1974
Acton Town (Style 'N')	WL	171	119	24 Jan 1932	11 Jul 1965

Rec'd means frame recovered from elsewhere and reused, perhaps with modification.
* Putney Bridge frame moved to new box in July 1910
† Frame changed but signal box remained open
‡ This box was re-inspected in May 1908 when it took over control of the Midland goods junction at West Kensington.
¶ The reason for delay here unclear for plans were inspected in 1906 and there is some evidence the box was built soon afterwards. The early plans show a quite different track layout and settling this may have caused the delay.

The Acton Town frame (the largest on the Underground) was of a new style developed by what had become the Westinghouse Brake and Saxby Signal Co and adapted to Underground requirements as the Style 'N'. This was later used in large numbers by London Transport. It still used miniature levers but incorporated numerous design improvements including a device to prevent a lever damaging the interlocking despite determined efforts to shift a lever that was locked. The new frame was installed in a new signal box and the old installation removed. Prior to adoption of the new frame old frames were recovered and rebuilt. At Ealing Common rebuilt equipment was installed in the old signal box whilst at Hammersmith and Northfields new signal boxes were required as the old boxes were unsuitable or in the way.

District power signal boxes were usually constructed anew but to conventional design with brick bases containing relays and electrical equipment and a fully glazed operating floor containing the interlocking frame. There were some interesting variations on this theme. For example, at Earls Court East and West Kensington West the signal boxes were mounted on gantries above the railway and the relay rooms were adjacent. At South Kensington, a full sized operating floor was provided above a rather narrow brick relay room as there was only limited space.

Converted Signal Boxes

Where it was not worthwhile installing a miniature power frame the existing District mechanical frames were adapted and the following list indicates where this was done.

Location	Code	Levers	Note
Bow Road	EP	29	1902 frame adapted
Charing Cross	EH	9 or more	Opened 1906/12†
St James's Park	EG	11 or more	Frame resited in tunnel c1912
High Street (Ken)	EB	22	Assumed control of Met signals 1926
Chiswick Park	WK	10	Out of use by 1910
South Acton	WQ	15	Out of use 1932
Ealing Common	WM	16	Out of use 1925 (replaced by power frame)
Hanger Lane Junction	WO	18	Closed 1925. Control to Ealing Common
Ealing Broadway	WP	43	Closed 1952. Control to new box.
South Harrow	WV	30	Closed 1957
Northfields	WR	11 or more	Opened 1919. Closed 1932
Osterley	WR	19	Closed 1915-1919
Hounslow Town (old)	WS	20	Closed 1909
Hounslow Town (new)	WS	22	Opened 1909. Closed 1923
Hounslow Barracks	WT	10	Probably closed around 1906-7
Heston-Hounslow (1)	WT	7	Open 1910-1912 only
Heston-Hounslow (2)	WT	?	Open 1912-1913 only
Heston-Hounslow (3)	WT	6	Open 1913-1923 only
Heston-Hounslow (4)	WT	22	Open 1923 (probably frame from Hounslow Town)

† The sparse evidence suggests an 'emergency' crossover installed in 1906 (without signals) controlled by a 2-lever frame and that in 1912 the frame was enlarged and crossover was fully signalled.

At these locations the mechanical connections between the full-size frame and the points and point locks were retained, but the actual running signals were replaced by standard electro-pneumatic signal arms. Operation was achieved through electric contact breakers connecting to the controlling levers and the addition of electric lever locks to prevent unsafe lever movements, depending on which track circuits were occupied. Several of these mechanical installations outlived the District Railway.

Unmanned Signal Boxes

At many intermediate signal boxes it was necessary to provide signalmen at only certain times or in the event of an emergency; normally signals could be left to operate automatically merely by leaving the levers over in the frame, though drivers received no indication whether a box was manned or not. This arrangement was satisfactory at quiet locations but at busier places, and where miniature frames were located, there were difficulties. The electric locking of the miniature frames was normally arranged so that no signal could clear a second time without the lever being fully replaced and pulled off again; this was a safeguard against a busy signalman overlooking the passage of a train such that another took the route without him noticing (possibly sending a train the wrong way). At the cabins that were not manned during the whole of the traffic day, or where it was convenient to have certain signals operating automatically anyway, the through signals that had sometimes to work completely automatically had to have this 'stick' facility removed.

After the Great War, where new frames were arranged to have any signals operate automatically, it was thought better to leave the stick facility in use when the signal box were staffed and cut it out only when it was closed. This was achieved by introducing a so-called 'king' lever. Once the required signal levers had been pulled over the king lever was operated, locking the selected signal levers reverse in the frame and cutting out the 'stick' function so those signals worked purely automatically. This was found a satisfactory method of operation and king levers were gradually retro-fitted on other frames where levers had to be left reversed for any reason.

A shortcoming of these early conversions was that where one of these 'controlled' signals was actually working automatically 'in king', a driver being detained at the signal had no idea whether this was a decision of some signalman, or because there was a train ahead or whether the signal had failed. Whatever the cause, the driver was compelled to follow the rules for detention at a controlled signal and this could cause great delay where the signal box was actually unstaffed. From 1926, whenever a new king lever was installed, this shortcoming was addressed by adding a small illuminated 'A' sign at the signals affected to show when they were operating automatically. When illuminated, it meant that if the signal remained at danger a driver could treat the signal as purely automatic and follow the simpler rules that applied. Again, the alteration worked well and these 'A' signs were retro-fitted at existing sites, improving service resilience.

There were many shunting signals required on the District and a 'dwarf' semaphore design was produced for this purpose by Westinghouse that used a small compressed air motor with semaphore arm (with the usual red and green coloured aspects visible at night). These signals were not for many years provided with train stops. To the right may be seen a double-arm version (there was a separate arm for each route). This view is at Mill Hill Park and a 1905 stock train is visible in background. Author's collection

Automatic Signalling

Stop Signals

Between signal boxes, the signalling was arranged to operate completely automatically, often for quite long distances within which many trains might be moving. The signalling circuits were a development of the direct current system first trialled on the South Harrow line but a number of features had been improved, such as the electro-pneumatic motor used on the semaphore arms. The need for electro-pneumatic rising spectacle colour-light signals for use in tunnels, where space was restricted, has been described in Chapter 3.

In addition to starting and home signals there was at first an intermediate signal between stations, or perhaps more than one in the longer sections, and this alone much-increased the line capacity, allowing more frequent services to run. Over time, further signals were added where found necessary. Continual improvements to improve train running in the light of experience also involved repositioning of some signals and the reduction of some of the section lengths where this could be done safely.

There was always scepticism about whether the ambitious District timetables actually produced the stated throughput of trains. This is an example of a headway chart from January 1926 (after multiple home signals installed) showing the actual service one day. 40 trains ran in one hour during the morning peak and 41 during the evening. This may have been a particularly good day but even a small average shortfall in this throughput would still have produced a very frequent service. Traffic Notice 6, 1926, in Author's collection

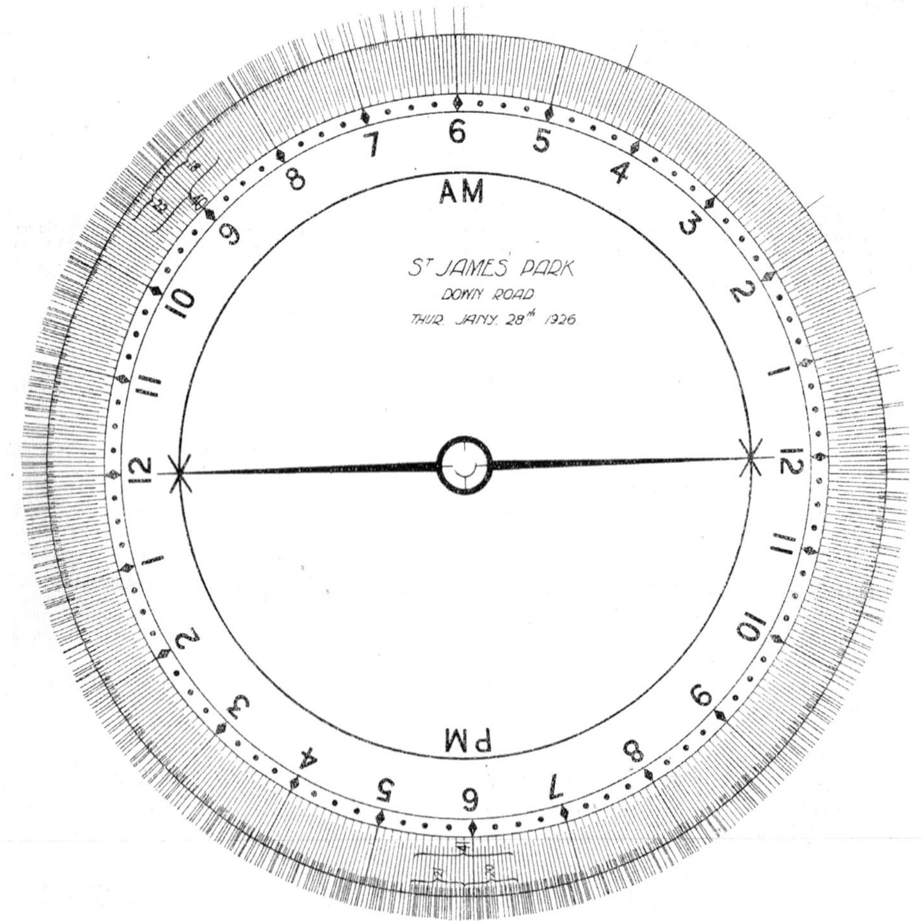

A District electro-pneumatic automatic signal. The air valve is at the top of the post and the motor arm at rear. These automatic signals later had a horizontal white stripe painted along the arm.
Author's collection

A close up view of a District Railway tunnel signal. To show clear, a compressed air motor pushed the spectacle upwards, so placing the green lens in front of the lamp. When the air was released, the spectacle fell to show the red aspect. These signals were very reliable. Although 2-aspect colour light signals had been introduced for new work before the Great War, 200 of the old type were still in operation in August 1945 and the last was replaced in 1946.
Author's collection

It was then found expedient to add extra home signals to reduce delays at busy stations where stopping times were unduly long. To achieve the timetable the standard station stop time had not to exceed twenty seconds but this was quite impossible at many central stations—two and, later, three home signals were found necessary to maintain intervals at many of the busier locations. For a 90-second service, during which a train might be stationary in the platform for thirty seconds, it was necessary to have four home signals, successively clearing ahead of a train behind one just pulling away. The idea was to reduce the possibility of a train having to stop in the tunnel behind a train in the platform that was already pulling away and would soon leave the platform vacant. Careful positioning of signals and introduction of extra home signals reduced minimum headways by up to ten seconds and greatly aided the operation of trains reliably at up to 40 an hour.

Repeater Signals

At platforms, the conductors sometimes found it difficult to see the starting signal and this became a source of delay as the train staff would not want to send the bell signal to start the train unless the starting signal were clear. To improve punctual departures a number of special repeater signals were quickly installed along the central area platforms where they could be seen by the rear conductor and other staff. These took the form of electric lanterns that showed a yellow* or green light that corresponded with the starting signal, green meaning the starting signal was 'clear'. These became known as platform repeaters.

The new signalling already included a few repeater signals along the running lines; these were occasionally found necessary in open sections where visibility of particular stop signals was restricted. According to contemporary descriptions these were at first only 'sparingly' provided; they were also painted red and the arms were distinguishable from electro-pneumatic stop signals only by the familiar notched end. These also carried a red light for viewing at night; when staff saw a red light they were expected to know from their training what sort of signal it was and whether to treat it as a warning signal or to stop at it. There were not, at first, expected to be any rising spectacle repeater signals on the District, where they would have been very difficult to identify.

The use of red arms and lights for 'distant' signals as well as stop signals had for some years been causing the British railway industry to agonize about the self-evident possibility of dangerous confusion. In fact, those worrying about the matter had already noticed both the use of yellow lights by the District in its new platform repeaters, and also its use on the New York subway, and this encouraged discussion about the possible use of yellow for signals giving a 'warning' indication, though lunar white had been looked at as an alternative. Moreover, yellow was known already on the Yerkes tube lines which needed repeating signals in tunnels (long range visibility was very poor in sharply-curved tube tunnels) and the tubes employed yellow Kopp's glass lenses in their rising spectacle repeating signals. Despite the obvious advantage of using a different colour for signals giving only a warning indication, no firm course of action had been agreed by the industry as a whole.

* We call this aspect 'yellow' now, but in fact the colours were once a great deal more orange and have become lighter now, conforming to national standards. Historical works occasionally use the name orange. The actual colour also depended on the light source behind the lens, and early electric lamp types were variable and would have influenced perceived colour. The important factor was that it would not be confused with red, green or white.

Even before all the automatic signalling was completed through the central area there was a debate with the railway inspectorate about signal positioning, the District contending the positions could not be altered and in June 1906 suggested installing tunnel repeaters where better sighting was unachievable; these, they particularly noted, would use the orange glass (just described) for the caution aspect. The inspectorate reluctantly agreed to this and the repeaters were installed. Shortly afterwards the District unilaterally decided that yellow was a far better colour for a warning signal and from March responded by painting the semaphore repeater signal arms yellow and replacing the red lenses with yellow ones.[1] Within a few years, other British railways grasped the nettle and made exactly the same changes.

When the District began running non-stop trains it was considered necessary to give drivers more warning about the state of the line ahead as it could not be assumed a driver would necessarily be slowing down in the same places, or at all. Where the necessary sighting distance was not available for faster moving trains repeating signals were added, including a number of tunnel signals. Some of the extra home signals also required repeating and the result was an ongoing stream of minor signal improvements which carried on throughout the District's life.

Technical Development

Naturally there were technical improvements to the system, not least because the direct current track circuits were not sufficiently reliable and could still be affected by traction interference. After detailed investigation, the answer was to install alternating current track circuits fed through condensers (which blocked traction current) and using vane relays that were inoperable by direct current, more sensitive and safer. The first of these on the District was installed at Acton Town in 1922. Coincident with this was the installation of miniature colour light signal heads for new work in the tunnel sections which slowly superseded the electro-pneumatic light signals, already much diminished by the end of the District era. These had the advantage of having no moving parts to maintain and more efficient lenses. Even so, as late as 1936, there were still as many as 42 full-sized electro-pneumatic semaphore stop or repeater signals between Earls Court West and Minories Junction. The District was never in a hurry to install long-range colour light signals in the open sections even though the Underground had used them successfully from 1923; even when the line west of Hammersmith was resignalled in 1931-32 many new semaphores were installed rather than having a mixture of the two types. The last was actually replaced only as late as 1953 (at Hanger Lane Junction).

In Chapter 3 reference was made to installation of calling-on signals to allow a train to enter an occupied section, usually to couple up, but an unusual arrangement was installed briefly at Earls Court. The problem here was the eastbound line from Putney, as the home signal was even further away from the platform than usual as it had also to protect the flat junction at the west end of the station. By 1913 the District had thought of a way around this and installed a 'calling-on' signal arm at that home signal, which had to be maintained at danger if a westbound Richmond or Ealing train were using the junction. In this circumstance, the signalman could lower the calling-on arm (which was not locked by the conflicting move) and this would allow the train to proceed to a new inner home signal even though the junction, only 164ft ahead, was in use; enabling a train to move forward this way brought it very close to the station saving valuable seconds when the platform cleared.[2] The calling-on arm was a distinctive shape and was prevented from being operated until an approaching train had been brought to a stand; it was felt the

Hanger Lane Junction in 1953. These were the last of the old electro-pneumatic semaphore signals still in operation and were due for replacement. The new colour light signal has already been erected in front, with its route indicator. The old signals were removed after traffic on 21st November. Ahead is the bridge over the GWR.
Brian Hardy collection

driver would know he had to proceed at great caution into a section that was (or might be) occupied. The arrangement did not last long: not because it was not effective but because the flat junction was soon replaced by the flyover arrangement still in use today. This District innovation was a precursor to later use of speed controlled signals to constrain speed and allow trains to close up to improve headways.

The security of the automatic signalling system was dependent upon the satisfactory operation of the automatic trainstop and the corresponding trip-cocks on the leading car of each train. From 1921, automatic testing apparatus came into service at Charing Cross on both roads. As each train approached the station the leading positive pick-up shoe engaged with a short section of current rail that 'armed' the equipment and illuminated a purple lamp at the leading end of the platform. A correctly positioned trip-cock arm would operate a mechanical treadle placed on the track and extinguish the lamp. The tester was located about 250ft before the light and comprised a ramp-operated switch located so as to engage with the tripcock arm without 'tripping' it. If the trip-cock arm was not in position the lamp remained alight and the driver had to investigate the reason and report the matter. Later installations of tripcock testers were similar but were 'armed' by the operation of a track circuit rather than a pick up shoe.

Similar apparatus had already been tested at Charing Cross (both roads) from the summer of 1916 but had evidently proved unsatisfactory. The automatic testing is reported to have replaced an earlier regime where every train was tested in service once a day; this was done at a central area station by arranging for it to pass a trainstop held at danger to ensure the brakes were immediately applied. This was quickly found to be very annoying to passengers and resulted in the development of the equipment just described.[3]

Later Developments

After the early 1920s, it becomes increasingly futile to identify signalling developments on the District separately from what was happening on the Underground as a whole. The whole of the signalling function across the associated companies was run as a single operation and the resulting practices carried on undiminished when London Transport was created. So far as the signalling actually deployed on the District is concerned a few highlights can be identified.

The first amongst these is the introduction (modest at first) of centralization, which meant the control of one location by a signal box further away. In 1934 it was arranged that the signals at West Kensington West could be controlled by the East signal box, releasing staff. A bigger scheme came into service in 1936 when a new signal box at Cromwell Road was arranged to control an area previously operated by four of the 1905/6 signal boxes. During the 1950s a system of automated control was introduced where signal frames were operated automatically by a device called a programme machine; this incorporated timetable information pre-punched onto plastic rolls and did away with the need for locally-based signalmen. By the late 1970s programme machines had been installed at all junctions west of Minories (except on main line railway tracks used by District trains). Minories and Aldgate East were worked by a new signalbox at Aldgate and east of Whitechapel signalling was controlled by area signal boxes at Barking and Upminster which controlled numerous junctions along that long stretch of line by means of push-button control desks (first tried at Ealing Broadway in 1952). At Whitechapel the old 1905 cabin was left in service, though it did have a new lever frame in 1952. To supervise the train service a central control room was constructed above the rotunda at the Warwick Road entrance to Earls Court and from here all train movements between Tower Hill,

Shown at left is a guard using his flag to operate the earlier type of train starting device; this requiring pulling down a tensioned wire that operated a bell at the leading end of the train (in earshot of the driver) when it was safe to depart. Shown at right is a later version where the guard placed the brass ferule of his flag against two wires, completing an electric circuit that operated the bell, as before. Their introduction is referred to on Page 270. LTM (left), Author's collection (right)

Ealing and Putney Bridge could be monitored; where necessary supervisory staff could intervene with the programme machine operation and re-route or re-time trains.* Earls Court station was listed Grade II in 1984 and includes the control room, described as 'of no merit' without explaining it was a control room and not an architectural fad. Whether it gets removed after its closure we shall have to wait and see.

During the 1940s and 1950s the oldest of the original automatic signalling was replaced and all the semaphore arms disappeared, replaced by standard colour light signals. To improve headways at peak times there was an innovation in the central area called speed-controlled signalling, involving up to six home signals. Where a heavily-loaded train was delayed in a platform, this signalling allowed the following train to close up right behind. To enable this to be done safely the following train was presented with successively lower speed limit signs and equipment was installed to check the train was slowing down accordingly. If speed was reduced correctly the home signals cleared successively at which point one of two things happened. Either the first train began to move out, in which case the speed limit was withdrawn and the remaining signals cleared successively, or the first train did not move immediately and the following train was

* At the time of publication of this volume, Whitechapel was still in service but was expected to survive only another year or so. The control room at Earls Court is in a similar position with control about to be moved to Hammersmith as the new automatic train control system is introduced.

brought to rest very close behind it and was ready to move into the platform as soon as it was safe to do so (the train would stop 200ft closer to the platform than it would otherwise have done). The signal engineer claimed that in heavy traffic the equipment would save trains ten seconds at each station. Moreover a 40 trains-per-hour service was required but even under favourable conditions no more than 39 trains were achievable (often less) with a 30-second station stop. The signal engineer stated new equipment might allow 44 trains an hour to run but more probably would indulge some stations stops of up to 38 seconds, which seemed unavoidable at certain places. In fact the loss of heavy very early workman's traffic had the effect of concentrating the peaks (especially in the morning) and the speed controlled signalling probably achieved no more than to mitigate the effects of very heavy boarding traffic, especially at Victoria and Charing Cross. Most central stations had this equipment installed by the early 1960s but in the face of what had become gradually diminishing traffic, train services began to be reduced and the high maintenance cost of this special signalling was then felt unjustified the additional equipment was removed.

Finally it is worth mentioning that the 1906 train describer system and the novel District train indicators on the platforms remained in full service until the 1970s and the technology was found compatible with that of the programme machines which were half a century newer. The equipment did then gradually fall out of use and all the old signs have gone except for a set on working display at Earls Court, though in far from original condition. The new train indicators are modern dot-matrix displays so ubiquitous these days.

Appendix Four

DISTRICT TRAIN HEADCODES

Since the early days of the District, giving staff certainty about the destination of approaching trains was achieved by means of a headcode, an arrangement of up to five lamps particular to each possible destination and visible at a distance. This was so useful the idea was perpetuated in the new electric trains, with modification caused by the central door which meant moving one of the lamp positions.

On the new trains, each code position comprised a white reflector with a lamp in front. The lamps could not be switched individually, so unwanted code positions were at first obscured by a metal cap, put in position by train staff as required. This was awkward and required trainmen leaning out of the cab or getting onto the track and from about 1910 permanent metal shutters were installed that could be swivelled into place by a handle within the cab. The top lamp (in the roof dome) could not be adapted and was moved to a position in the top offside window. From the 1927 stock these 'marker lights' were grouped together beneath the offside window, The last stock to be fitted with these was the R stock as technology rendered marker lights unnecessary. Staff became very familiar with these codes and the signalmen used them all the time as the train description apparatus was labelled not with the names of the destinations but with the headcode arrangement.

Examples of the codes follow; those given are 1901, 1907 and 1930.

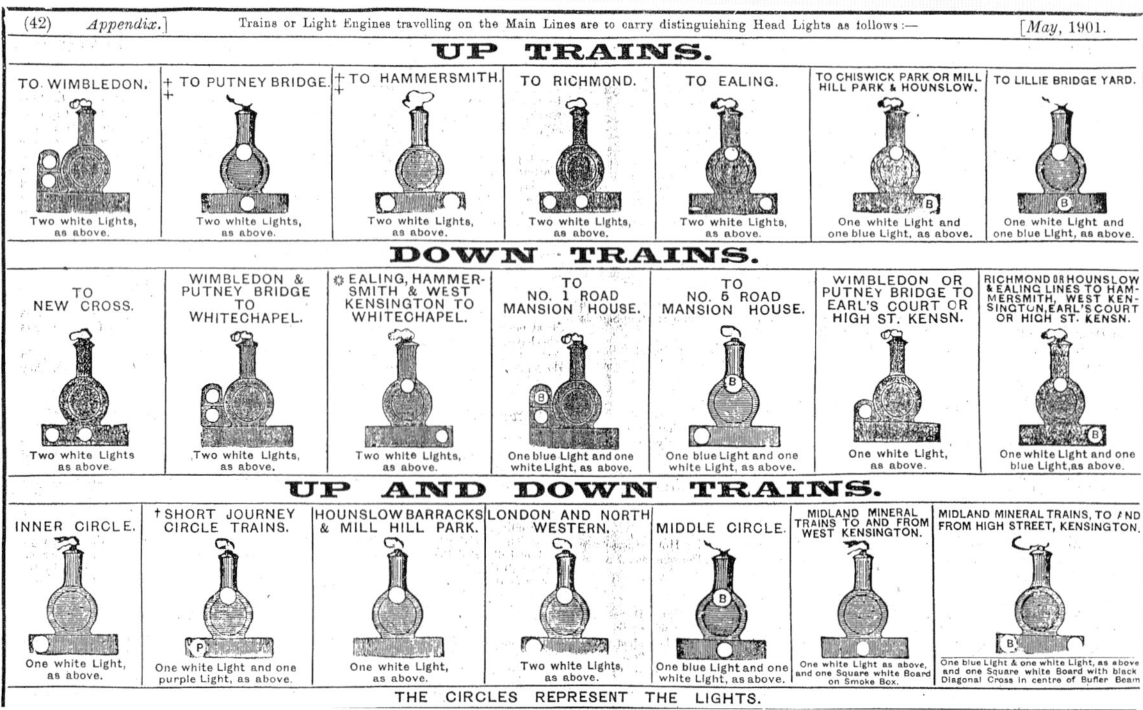
(42) *Appendix.*] Trains or Light Engines travelling on the Main Lines are to carry distinguishing Head Lights as follows :— [*May*, 1901.

UP TRAINS.

TO WIMBLEDON.	† TO PUTNEY BRIDGE.	† TO HAMMERSMITH.	TO RICHMOND.	TO EALING.	TO CHISWICK PARK OR MILL HILL PARK & HOUNSLOW.	TO LILLIE BRIDGE YARD.
Two white Lights, as above.	Two white Lights, as above.	Two white Lights, as above.	Two white Lights, as above.	Two white Lights, as above.	One white Light and one blue Light, as above.	One white Light and one blue Light, as above.

DOWN TRAINS.

TO NEW CROSS.	WIMBLEDON & PUTNEY BRIDGE TO WHITECHAPEL.	✲ EALING, HAMMERSMITH & WEST KENSINGTON TO WHITECHAPEL.	TO NO. 1 ROAD MANSION HOUSE.	TO NO. 5 ROAD MANSION HOUSE.	WIMBLEDON OR PUTNEY BRIDGE TO EARL'S COURT OR HIGH ST. KENSN.	RICHMOND OR HOUNSLOW & EALING LINES TO HAMMERSMITH, WEST KENSINGTON, EARL'S COURT OR HIGH ST. KENSN.
Two white Lights as above.	Two white Lights, as above.	Two white Lights, as above.	One blue Light and one white Light, as above.	One blue Light and one white Light, as above.	One white Light, as above.	One white Light and one blue Light, as above.

UP AND DOWN TRAINS.

INNER CIRCLE.	† SHORT JOURNEY CIRCLE TRAINS.	HOUNSLOW BARRACKS & MILL HILL PARK.	LONDON AND NORTH WESTERN.	MIDDLE CIRCLE.	MIDLAND MINERAL TRAINS TO AND FROM WEST KENSINGTON.	MIDLAND MINERAL TRAINS, TO AND FROM HIGH STREET, KENSINGTON.
One white Light, as above.	One white Light and one purple Light, as above.	One white Light, as above.	Two white Lights, as above.	One blue Light and one white Light, as above.	One white Light as above, and one Square white Board on Smoke Box.	One blue Light & one white Light, as above and one Square white Board with black Diagonal Cross in centre of Buffer Beam

THE CIRCLES REPRESENT THE LIGHTS.

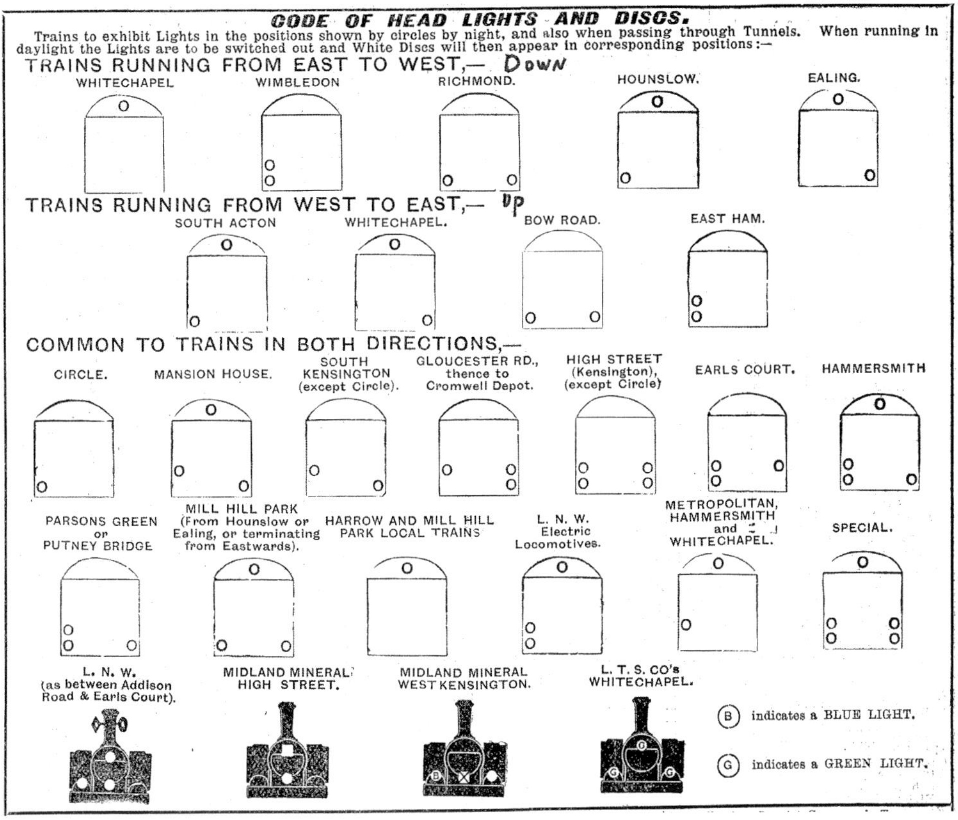

CODE OF HEAD LIGHTS AND DISCS.
Trains to exhibit Lights in the positions shown by circles by night, and also when passing through Tunnels. When running in daylight the Lights are to be switched out and White Discs will then appear in corresponding positions:—
TRAINS RUNNING FROM EAST TO WEST,— Down
WHITECHAPEL
WIMBLEDON
RICHMOND.
HOUNSLOW.
EALING.
TRAINS RUNNING FROM WEST TO EAST,— Up
SOUTH ACTON
WHITECHAPEL.
BOW ROAD.
EAST HAM.
COMMON TO TRAINS IN BOTH DIRECTIONS,—
CIRCLE.
MANSION HOUSE.
SOUTH KENSINGTON (except Circle).
GLOUCESTER RD., thence to Cromwell Depot.
HIGH STREET (Kensington), (except Circle)
EARLS COURT.
HAMMERSMITH
PARSONS GREEN or PUTNEY BRIDGE
MILL HILL PARK (From Hounslow or Ealing, or terminating from Eastwards).
HARROW AND MILL HILL PARK LOCAL TRAINS
L. N. W. Electric Locomotives.
METROPOLITAN, HAMMERSMITH and WHITECHAPEL.
SPECIAL.
L. N. W. (as between Addison Road & Earls Court).
MIDLAND MINERAL HIGH STREET.
MIDLAND MINERAL WEST KENSINGTON.
L. T. S. CO's WHITECHAPEL.
(B) indicates a BLUE LIGHT.
(G) indicates a GREEN LIGHT.

HEADLIGHT CODE FOR TRAINS RUNNING FROM EAST TO WEST.
PUTNEY
WIMBLEDON
RICHMOND
EALING
NORTHFIELDS
HOUNSLOW CENT
HOUNSLOW WEST
SOUTH HARROW
UXBRIDGE
HEADLIGHT CODE FOR TRAINS RUNNING FROM WEST TO EAST.
BARKING
EAST HAM
PLAISTOW CHARING + SUNS
BOW ROAD *
MANSION HOUSE
EDGWARE ROAD
HIGH STREET
TURNHAM GREEN
SOUTH ACTON
* WHEN A TRAIN RUNS FROM UXBRIDGE TO BOW ROAD IT MUST CARRY WHITECHAPEL HEADLIGHTS AS FAR AS SOUTH HARROW
HEADLIGHT CODE FOR TRAINS RUNNING IN EITHER DIRECTION.
EALING COM
ACTON TOWN
HAMMERSMITH
PARSONS GN.
EARLS COURT
GLOSTER ROAD
STH KENS'TON
ALDGATE E
WHITECHAPEL
CIRCLE
THRO' SOUTHEND
LM&S

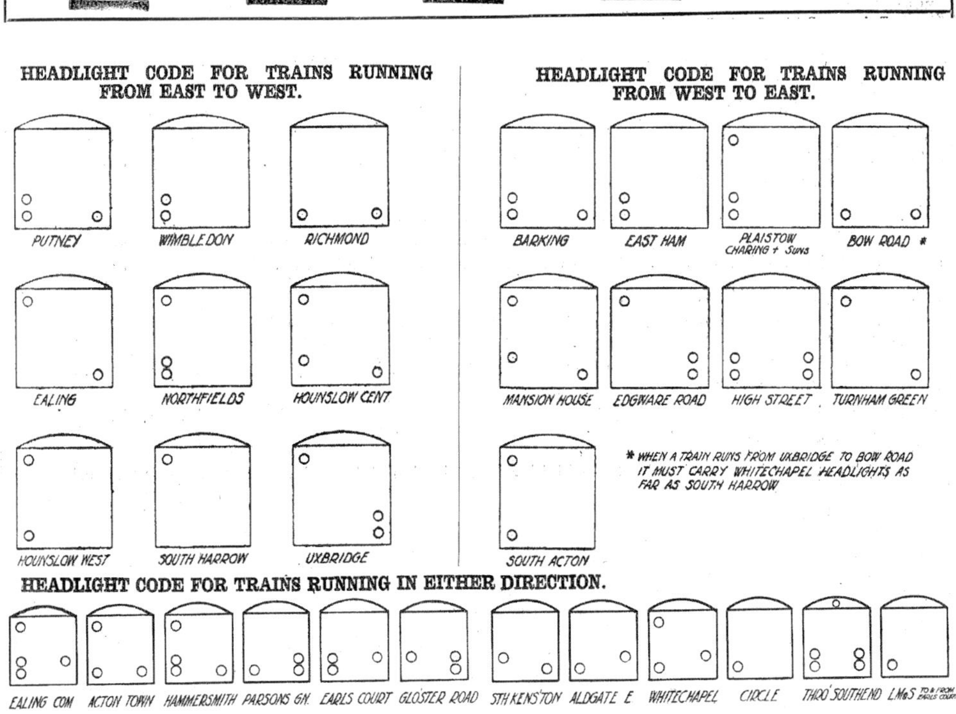

Appendix Five

STATISTICS

Passenger Numbers						Revenue				
Year	1st Class	2nd & 3rd Cl	Workmen	Seasons	**Total**	1st	2nd & 3rd Cl	Workmen	Seasons	**Total**
1902	2,975,187	39,313,518		4,725,826	**47,014,531**	49,468	283,871		37,755	**87,223**
1903	2,924,823	42,056,773		5,057,975	**50,039,571**	46,257	286,157		37,909	**368,037**
1904	3,127,747	43,448,735		4,591,310	**51,167,792**	46,939	287,483		31,970	**365,066**
1905	3,634,145	45,001,631		2,912,641	**51,548,417**	53,991	298,335		20,810	**362,284**
1906	3,363,920	48,683,292		3,015,212	**55,062,424**	47,777	334,483		21,055	**367,167**
1907	2,728,997	45,038,715		3,467,845	**51,235,557**	39,024	341,753		26,204	**399,711**
1908	2,413,371	53,008,642		5,708,295	**61,130,308**	34,002	395,426		43,221	**472,649**
1909	2,270,405	57,136,368		7,445,528	**66,852,301**	32,605	424,409		57,773	**514,787**
1910	2,209,246	61,289,206		9,234,160	**72,732,612**	32,631	455,163		72,740	**560,534**
1911	2,333,754	67,733,640		11,333,498	**81,400,892**	33,069	492,402		88,726	**614,197**
1912	2,373,228	70,547,813		13,082,118	**86,003,159**	33,624	517,309		101,737	**652,670**
From 1913 the number of workman's tickets is separated out. Prior to that included in 3rd class ordinaries										
1913	2,325,147	56,709,913	15,661,272	14,742,000	**89,438,332**	33,712	471,952	64,331	116,171	**686,166**

Year	1st	3rd	Workmen	Seasons	**Total**	Revenue	Government Compensation	**Total**
1914	Detail not available. During the years of government financial control the District was excused from providing detail of passenger numbers and revenue					817,456		**817,456**
1915						934,125		**934,125**
1916						1,026,411		**1,026,411**
1917						1,122,068		**1,122,068**
1918	2,500,000	85,675,563	20,992,107	25,680,427	**134,848,097**	1,341,939	302,619	**1,644,558**
1919	2,633,921	92,312,815	22,095,147	25,401,190	**142,443,073**	1,565,568	566,370	**2,131,938**
1920	2,335,124	92,985,055	24,338,296	28,040,865	**147,699,340**	1,767,267	705,347	**2,472,614**

Passenger Numbers						Revenue						
Date	1st	3rd	Workmen	Seasons	**Total**	1st	3rd	Workmen	Seasons	Sub-total	Other	**Total**
1921	1,877,202	78,245,542	22,524,130	27,666,850	**130,313,724**	43,126	1,090,890	171,435	353,618	1,659,069	191,512	**1,850,581**
1922	1,728,449	76,292,811	22,488,263	27,666,850	**128,176,373**	40,353	1,004,293	178,872	321,056	1,544,574	231,590	**1,776,164**
1923	1,741,604	77,367,596	23,050,281	24,800,050	**126,959,531**	36,732	984,591	171,042	310,391	1,502,756	214,963	**1,717,719**
1924	1,606,702	78,935,376	23,104,404	23,555,750	**127,202,232**	33,393	948,931	177,522	273,648	1,433,494	216,028	**1,649,522**
1925	1,508,595	77,729,448	23,567,904	23,063,608	**125,869,555**	30,997	941,409	175,974	279,964	1,428,344	206,434	**1,634,778**
1926	1,371,194	71,052,603	22,379,968	22,177,788	**116,981,553**	28,416	954,960	172,061	292,457	1,447,894	192,771	**1,640,665**
1927	1,384,463	75,531,040	24,110,052	22,646,652	**123,672,207**	28,854	1,006,293	186,856	301,926	1,523,929	195,923	**1,719,852**
1928	1,347,007	78,208,598	25,407,869	24,190,250	**129,153,724**	28,844	995,216	197,698	309,217	1,530,975	19,353	**1,550,328**
1929	1,307,052	80,040,735	27,226,128	25,252,562	**133,826,477**	27,779	1,023,140	211,411	323,514	1,585,844	19,694	**1,605,538**
1930	1,242,323	81,822,029	27,732,950	26,221,456	**137,018,758**	26,180	900,843	217,536	301,451	1,446,010	18,883	**1,464,893**
1931	1,109,187	79,266,351	26,537,201	26,211,998	**133,124,737**	23,120	905,669	212,193	311,263	1,452,245	18,620	**1,470,865**
1932	988,186	74,655,106	25,064,704	25,779,176	**126,487,172**	20,872	904,982	205,496	323,482	1,454,832	18,912	**1,473,744**
1933 to June	498,031	36,929,166	12,234,180	13,506,856	**63,168,233**	10,483	494,445	106,674	185,162	796,764	7,928	**804,692**

District route mileage owned, leased and worked over				
Year ending (1933 is correct to June)	1903	1913	1923	1933
Lines owned by MDR	17m 60ch	24m 47ch	24m 68ch	25m 0ch
Partly owned	3m 58ch	1m 54ch	1m 54ch	1m 54ch
Jointly Leased	3m 14ch	2m 10ch	2m 10ch	5m 43ch
Worked	6m 39ch	-	-	-
Other lines worked over	27m 8ch	26m 47ch	26m 34ch	34m 23ch
TOTAL	**58m 19ch**	**54m 78ch**	**55m 6ch**	**66m 40ch**

NOTES ON SOURCES FOR VOLUME 2

The early history of the District in the twentieth century suffers from the same constraints pointed out in Volume 1. There are a comparatively small number of original sources to draw from and these say little about policy and yield detail inconsistently; there remained the great pre-occupation with keeping the company afloat. The most helpful source remain the shareholders' meetings where the reports and the records of what was said (widely reported in newspapers) shed at least some light on what the directors had in mind. As before, it has been necessary to trawl a very wide range of contemporary material to weave any kind of satisfactory thread from this material. But then the story changes dramatically. The Americans arrive and control of the District shifts and is quickly subsumed into what colloquially was known as the Underground Group, or just 'the combine'. It may be thought by some that it was not until 1933 that transport in London was co-ordinated but this is not so: a great deal was done in the previous decade and I argue the process began before the Great War and had made considerable progress by 1923, by which time the various companies within 'the combine' were for most practical purposes being run as a single operation. Since this book is about the District Railway it has been a great challenge to filter out material from what became a much more plentiful supply of original sources so as to maintain a coherent history of the District without getting dragged into the policies and politics of 'the combine' which is really another subject area. Of course, the emergence of 'the combine' as a pre-eminent local transport operator in London cannot avoid establishing the context within which the District operated, and there has been a risk that picking out snippets of District history from programmes and policies applying to the wider network is a bit artificial. Nevertheless there is a wealth of original material relating to the development of the Underground network that exist as reports, lectures, programmes of works, evidence given in Parliament and so on that help illuminate this interesting period.

As before, the former BTHR records at the National Archives and London Metropolitan Archives have proved essential, with incidental material in private collections, including my own (upon which I have relied for technical and operational information). My set of T.O.T. staff magazine (1922-33) has proved a useful source, with its predecessor pamphlets of which there is a substantial set at the LT Museum. The railway and national press have been trawled and found a useful source of material, together with contemporary engineering journals and books. Helpful background was provided by 'A History of London Transport, Volume II,' Theo Barker & Michael Robbins, Allen & Unwin 1974. Once more useful background has been found in Alan Jackson's book 'London's Metropolitan Railway', David & Charles, 1986 which, from the Met's rich historical resources, illuminates its relationship with the District (abbreviated in endnotes to 'Jackson'). Also very helpful is Peter Kay's three volumes on the London, Tilbury & Southend Railway, upon which I have relied for background about what that railway was doing at the time the District projected its trains over that line. These were published by the author 1996 (Vol 1, pre 1836-93), 1997 (Vol 2, 1893-1912), 2010 (Vol 3, 1912-1939) and are referred in endnotes as 'Kay'. For dates and name changes I have relied once more on H.V. Borley's 'Chronology of London Railways', Railway & Canal Historical Society 1982 and Doug Rose's 'The London Underground – A Diagrammatic History' now in its ninth edition (June 2016). Specific reliance on the former is indicated here as 'Borley'. Some early material was also found in a 'History of the Metropolitan District Railway to June 1908' by Alexander Edmonds, London Transport 1974, referred to in endnotes as 'Edmonds'.

ENDNOTES

Chapter 1: Facing up to Electrification

[1] Charles Yerkes to UERL shareholders reported in *Railway News* 22 October 1904

[2] *Pond & Wright*, Paul Hadley and *Railway News* for 20 June 1896

[3] See, for example, *The Railway Times* 19 September 1896.

[4] *The Railway Times* 10 October 1896

[5] A good summary is given in *Great Central,* Volume II, George Dow, 1962, pp332-5

[6] See report of meeting in *Railway Times* 4 March and 12 August 1899

[7] *The Railway Times* 14 November 1896

[8] Jackson (Met Ry)

[9] LMA (Acc1297/Met/10/75)

[10] See evidence given to committee examining the bill, *Railway Times*, 21 July 1900.

[11] Jackson (Met Ry)

[12] This list is from *A History of London Transport,* Volume II, p58, Barker & Robbins amplified by *Steam to Silver*, J. Graeme Bruce p29. However, a very comprehensive review of the entire tendering process, the specification and the proposals received (with commentary) are found in *Traction & Transmission* Vol 2, 1901 pp240 etc.

[13] *Tramway & Railway World* 6 December 1900, based on story in Daily Express.

[14] *Railway News*, 23 November 1900.

[15] MDR Minutes, various but see for example 14 March 1901. The chain of events is also described at length in Edmonds, p188 etc.

[16] *Electrical Review* 1 March 1901 and *Traction & Transmission* Vol 1, 1901 pp60

Chapter 2: The Americans

[1] *Robber Baron, The Life of Charles Tyson Yerkes*, John Franch, University of Illinios Press 2006, mainly chap 24

[2] See meeting report in *Railway News* 8 June 1901 and Franch, pp289.

[3] *Rails Through the Clay*, Alan A. Jackson and Desmond Croome, Allen & Unwin 1962

[4] *Railway News* 5th March 1902

[5] See *The Times* 10 and 25 April 1902

[6] *Railway News* 19 April 1902

[7] *The Railway Times* 10 August and 27 October 1901

[8] Report of half-year shareholders' meeting held on 16 August 1901 and board meeting of 5 September 1901.

[9] *The Railway Times* 1 August 1900.

[10] *The Railway Times* 27 October 1900.

[11] *Electrical Review* 8 April 1904

[12] *Ring Up Britain* edited by Neil Johannessen includes a useful discourse about Forbes's work with the NTC.

[13] Select Committee examining the MDR bill 1901 (reported in *Electrical Review* 5 July 1901) and Section 9 of the MDR Act 1901

[14] Useful data is given in *Electrical Traction*, Vol II (Alternating Current), Wilson and Lydall, Arnold 1907.
[15] *The Engineer*, 3 January 1896
[16] TNA MT6/1227/1
[17] *The Electrician* 22 May 1903
[18] *Tramway & Railway World*, 14 May 1903.
[19] *Daily Mail* 12 March 1903, *Herapath's Railway Journal*, Vol 65 1903 p236 specifically give date and *Railway Times*, Vol 83, (and other journals) makes observations consistent with this.
[20] *Financial Times* 22 March 1903
[21] *Railway Magazine* Vol 13 Jul-Dec 1903, p344 (October)
[22] *The Electrician*, 1 May 1903 and *Street Railway Journal*, Vol 22, 1903.
[23] See, for example, *Street Railway Journal*, 9 May 1903.
[24] See, *Electrical Engineer*, Vol 32, 3 July 1903 and MDR Notice to Staff 20 June 1903
[25] *The Times*, 23 March 1903
[26] TNA MT6/1548/3
[27] *Street Railway Journal*, 17 August 1901.
[28] *The Electrician*, 1 May 1903
[29] *Electrical Review* 5 June 1903
[30] TNA MT6/1548/3
[31] Good descriptions of the apparatus on these trains are given in *The Electrician* 24 April and 1 May 1903
[32] *Electrical Review* 17 April 1903
[33] *The Times* 17 June 1903
[34] *The Electrical Engineer* 3 July 1903
[35] MDR public timetable for July 1903 and statements in a number of newspapers.
[36] *The Times* 7 August 1903 reporting District shareholders' meeting on 6 August. See also Way & Works Committee Minute 6835 of 18 June 1903 and *Railway News* Vol 79 (1903 Pt I) p961
[37] MDR Way and Works Committee Minute 6835 18 June 1903, MDR Notice GO27 of [20] June 1903 relating to proposed opening of line on 22nd, and Railway News 20 June 1903. For *The Financier* report see the *Railway News* 28 May 1904. Equipment alteration stated in *Steam to Silver*, Graeme Bruce, Capital Transport 1984, p31
[38] UER Way and Works Committee Minutes and see *The Electrical Engineer* for 10 July 1903
[39] UER Way and Works Committee Minutes
[40] *The Times*, 27 November and 15 December 1903
[41] Report of shareholders' meeting in *Railway News*, 13 February 1904
[42] MDR Board minute 5420 15 December 1904

Chapter 3: Modernization At Last
[1] *London Gazette* 27 November 1900
[2] *London Gazette* 22 November 1901 and GNPBR Act 1902 as passed. See also reports of the parliamentary committees on this bill, eg the reports in *Electrical Review* 1 August 1902.
[3] *Railway News* 29 October 1904
[4] See the *Electrical Engineer* 25 April and 27 June 1890.
[5] *Railway News* 21 February 1903
[6] *Railway Magazine* Vol 12, January-June 1903
[7] MDR WTTs No 4, 6 and 7, 1903-4
[8] *Railway Times* 22 February 1902

[9] *Railway News* 15 February 1902 and 7 June 1902
[10] *Railway News* 27 February 1904.
[11] *Railway News* 6 August 1904.
[12] Edmonds pp236
[13] *Railway News* 3 Sept 1904
[14] Way and Works Committee Min 7108, 21 April 1904
[15] *Railway Times* 22 December 1906
[16] *Street Railway Journal*, Vol 29, 4 May 1907.
[17] TNA MT6/1227/1
[18] UER Way and Works Committee Minutes
[19] *Railway Times* 17 June 1905
[20] *Street Railway Journal*, Vol 30, 7 December 1907.
[21] Several references to this but see in particular *The Railroad Gazette* Vol XXXV No 45 (1903).
[22] UER Minute 325, 9 February 1904
[23] *Automatic Signalling on the Underground Railways of London*, Westinghouse Brake Co Signalling Pamplet No 9 1906.
[24] *Tramway & Railway World*, 9 February 1905
[25] *50 Years of Railway Signalling* (Golden Jubilee of The Institution of Railway Signal Engineers), O.S. Nock 1962.
[26] A good description of the arrangements are given in *Engineering* 25 May and 1 June 1906 where reference to the train description 'being installed' is given. The original announcement is in *The Electrician* 3 November 1905 but a picture appears in *Illustrated London News* for 14 October 1905.
[27] *Daily Illustrated Mirror* 6 February 1904 (interview), *Street Railway Journal* 21 November 1903 (interview)
[28] *Street Railway Journal*, 4 March 1905
[29] TNA MT6/1227/1
[30] *Street Railway Journal*, 6 August 1904
[31] *Railway News* 22 August 1903 and 6 February 1904
[32] Good descriptions appear in *Street Railway Journal* 4 March 1905 and *Tramway & Railway World* February 1905
[33] UER minutes 31 May 1904 for 5050 car curtains and fittings at 13/3 each
[34] *Railway Times* 23 December 1905
[35] *Railway Magazine* Vol 20, March 1907 and MDR Board Minute 5894 20 June 1906
[36] *Railway Magazine* Vol 20, April 1907
[37] For example, advertisement in *Railway News* 26 October 1907, MDR and Taff Vale Ry minutes (various)
[38] Metropolitan District Railway Chronology.
[39] *Railway News* 6 August 1904
[40] *Electrical Review* June 1906
[41] Appendix to MDR WTT 56, 1st June 1915.
[42] *Railway News* 13 February 1904
[43] UER Works Committee minute 83 of 21 September 1906
[44] *Metropolitan District Railway Electrification*, *Tramway & Railway World*, February 1905
[45] Edmonds pp60
[46] *Street Railway Journal*, Vol 30, 7 December 1907
[47] *Railway Magazine* Vol 20, 1907, pp343-4
[48] *The Times* 22 September 1909

Chapter 4: Running the New Services

[1] *The Times*, 10 February 1905, and Edmonds, page 230.

[2] *The Times* 30 March 1905.

[3] *The Memories and Writings of a London Railwayman*, H.V. Borley, RCHS, p120

[4] *Railway & Travel Monthly* July 1915

[5] *The Memories and Writings of a London Railwayman*, H.V. Borley, RCHS, p120 tends to support this use for the loop.

[6] *Railway Times*, 1 July 1905

[7] District and Metropolitan Railways official chronologies and Edmonds, pp231.

[8] *The Times* 20 October 1905.

[9] MDR timetable notes for 1907. WTTs 25. 2 April and 27, 1 October 1907. Met Ry company Chronology entries for Inner Circle, Jackson pp183.

[10] *The Engineer* 8 Nov 1907

[11] MDR timetable notes for 1908

[12] MDR timetable for June 1903

[13] MDR Working Timetables 25 (2 April 1907) and MDR Schedules notebook.

[14] Speed at shareholders' meeting 19 February reported in *Railway News* 24 February 1906

[15] *Railway Engineer*, April 1907

[16] See letter by W.E. Blake to *The Times* 1 April 1914.

[17] *Railway Times* 11 February 1905

[18] *Street Railway Journal*, 17 August 1901

[19] MDR Special Notice to Electric Trainmen dated 4th September 1905

[20] *Railway Engineer*, September 1906

[21] *Electrical Review* 1 Dec 1905 repeating what it had observed in an unnamed daily newspaper

[22] *Electrical Review* 5 April 1907

[23] *Electrical Review* 13 April 1906 and confirmed *Tramway & Railway World* 10 May 1906. See also detail in the *Railway Engineer* June 1906.

[24] *Electrical Review* 31 Aug 1906 but also referred to in *Street Railway Journal* 12 January 1907

[25] *Railway Magazine* Vol 20, June 1907 and MDR Board 10 April 1907, Min 6272.

[26] *Railway Magazine* Vol 28, February 1911

[27] *Railway News* 5 May 1906

[28] *Railway News*, 1 April 1905.

[29] Parliamentary question from Timothy Davies MP reported in *Railway Times* 24 March 1906.

[30] Norman McKillop, *The Lighted Flame* (a history of ASLEF), Nelson 1950

[31] UER Minutes 5284 and 5311 2 June and 14 July 1903 and MDR Way & Works Committee Minute 7215 8 September 1904.

[32] *Tramway & Railway World*, February 1905.

[33] *Tramway & Railway World*, 10 August 1905.

[34] Parliamentary question by Mr Will Thorne to the President of the Board of Trade, *Electrical Review* 1 June 1906.

[35] See report of Amalgamated Society of Railway Servants, reported in *Electrical Review* 6 October 1905

[36] Edmonds pp194

[37] *The West London Railway and the WLER*, H.V. Borley and R.W. Kidner, Oakwood Press 1975

[38] *Railway Magazine*, Vol 31, 1912.
[39] Kay, Vol 2
[40] *Steam to Silver*, 2nd edition, J Graeme Bruce, Capital Transport 1983
[41] *Railway Magazine* May 1909, Kay, Vol 2, and OS mapping 1920 and 1938.

Chapter 5: Money and Managers
[1] *The Robber Baron*, John Franch, 2006, Urbana and Chicago, Chap 25.
[2] MDR Minute book for 1902, minutes 4710 and 4847
[3] *Tramway & Railway World*, 13 October 1904 and 8 December 1904.
[4] *New York Times*, 16 January 1901, *Kansas City Times*, 5 May 1910, *The Times*, 17 January 1934
[5] *Western Electrician*, 16 June 1900
[6] *London United Tramways: A History 1894-1933*, Geoffrey Wilson. *The Engineer*, 10 August 1926
[7] Reported in *New York Times*, 7 February 1943
[8] *The Seven From Chicago*, a paper by J.P. Thomas prepared 1970 for the London Underground Railway Society
[9] *Railway Times* 6 April 1901
[10] *Railway News* 31 May 1902, though *The Times* 30 May 1902 covers change and gives a number of examples
[11] Correspondence in authors collection relating to the complexity of the fares and listing 28 particular agreements.
[12] *Railway News* 2 Dec 1905
[13] *Tramway & Railway World* February 1903 reports Perks having stated £1.1 - £1.2 million but this increased slightly later.
[14] These were also recited in Edmonds, pp189 and 221.
[15] UERL shareholder reports give detail of all the stock it had accumulated.
[16] *Rails Through the Clay*, Jackson & Croome, Allen & Unwin 1962, pp90-92
[17] *Street Railway Review*, Vol 16 No 1, 15 January 1906
[18] *Chicago Daily Tribune* 21 April 1910 and *The Robber Baron*, John Franch, 2006, Urbana and Chicago
[19] A useful commentary is given in Barker & Robbins, Vol II, pp139
[20] Report in *Railway News* 18 April 1908
[21] *Railway News* 12 December 1908
[22] *Railway News* 1 August 1908
[23] *The Man Who Built London Transport, a Biography of Frank Pick*, Christian Barman, David & Charles 1979
[24] A brief commentary of Stanley's move is given in *The Man Who Built London Transport, a Biography of Frank Pick*, Christian Barman, David & Charles 1979
[25] *Philadelphia Inquirer*, 23 October 1921
[26] *Railway Times* 18 August 1906 and 30 November 1907
[27] *The Times* 6 October 1906 and *Railway Magazine* Vol 34, February 1914.
[28] *Electrical Review*, 8 May 1914
[29] *Railway Times* 27 July 1907
[30] *A History of London Transport, Part 2*, Barker & Robbins
[31] *Railway Magazine* October 1912 and LGOC bus maps in Author's collection

Chapter 6: Infrastructure Improvements
[1] *Tramway & Railway World*, February 1905 and *Railway Times* 21 October 1905
[2] *Illustrated London News* 14 October 1905

[3] *Underground Architecture*, David Lawrence, Capital Transport 1994
[4] MDR board minute 7817 of 19 June 1911
[5] *Underground Architecture*, David Lawrence, Capital Transport 1994
[6] *Railway Magazine*, April 1914 (Advert)
[7] *The Times* 12 and 25 January 1911 and MDR Notebook
[8] *Railway Magazine* December 1913.
[9] MDR reconstruction plans of 1909 are signed by George Sherrin.
[10] *Railway Magazine*, Vol 33 1913 p446 and *Underground Architecture*, David Lawrence, Capital Transport 1994
[11] *The Railway Engineer* March 1920
[12] *Railway Magazine*, Vol 33, 1913
[13] *Railway Times* 17 June 1911
[14] *Railway Times* 7 January 1911
[15] *Railway Times* 17 June 1911
[16] *Electrical Review* 8 December 1911, *London Gazette* 21 November 1911 and MDR Act 1912
[17] *Electrical Review*, 8 September 1911
[18] *Facts About London's Underground, No 1, The Power House*, London's Underground June 1924, further informed by *Garcke's Manual of Electrical Undertakings* 1920/21 and 1921/22, and *Rails Through The Clay*, Alan A Jackson and Desmond F Croome, 1963.
[19] *Electrical Review*, 13 May 1921
[20] *Electrical Review*, 24 June 1921
[21] *The Times* 22 Jan 1913, citing paper given to Institution of Civil Engineers.
[22] *Railway Magazine*, Vol 37 1915 Pt II, pp349
[23] *Railway and Travel Monthly*, Vol 3, 1911 pp259.

Chapter 7: Train Service Development
[1] District Railway timetable notebook and *Railway Magazine* Vol 28, February 1911. See also shareholders report given in February 1911 recorded in *Railway Times* 11 February 1911. WTT 59 5 Jan 1914 shows 40 trains.
[2] *Electrical Review* Vol 69 1911
[3] MDR Working Timetables 27 (1st October 1907) and 28 (16th December 1907)
[4] *Bulletin of the International Railway Congress Association*, Vol 21, 1907.
[5] MDR Working Timetable 29 (1st April 1908)
[6] *Railway Magazine* 1910, Vol 27, pp349, MDR timetables 1 June and 1 October 1910
[7] *Railway Magazine*, August 1914
[8] *Railway Magazine* April 1918
[9] Much of this from District Rly WTTs 29 (1st April 1908) and 32 (1 January 1909).
[10] MDR Minute 7435 9 February 1910
[11] MDR Minute 7927 7 December 1911
[12] MDR WTTs, several dates during 1907 and 1908
[13] *Railway Magazine* September 1909.
[14] *Railway and Travel Monthly*, Vol 4, January 1912 pp83.
[15] *Railway and Travel Monthly*, Vol 2, May 1911 pp366.
[16] MDR Working Timetable 53 (5th January 1914)
[17] MDR Minute 8179 of 12 December 1912
[18] MDR Minute 8072 of 20 June 1912
[19] MDR Minute 7831 of 27 July 1911
[20] MDR Working Timetable 28 (16th December 1907)

[21] *Railway and Travel Monthly*, Vol 1, November 1910 pp614.
[22] *Railway Magazine* February 1915.
[23] *Railway News* 17 August 1907 referring to shareholders' meeting.
[24] Jackson (Met Ry)
[25] *Railway Magazine* Vol 25, September 1909.
[26] *Railway Magazine* Vol 26, April 1910.

Chapter 8: The Great War and its Aftermath
[1] *Railway Magazine* May 1911
[2] *Middlesex Times* 9 December 1911
[3] *Railway Magazine*, January 1908.
[4] *Street Railway Journal* 21 Nov 1903 and *Daily Illustrated Mirror* 6 February 1904
[5] *Electrical Review* 9 February 1906
[6] MDR Minute 6058 and 6510 of 24 October 1906 and 16 October 1907
[7] *Railway Times*, 23 September 1905
[8] MDR Board Minutes 6081 (24 October 1906), 6699 (29 January 1908),
[9] *Railway Engineer* Vol 30, April 1909
[10] Reported in *Electrical Review* 5 August 1910
[11] *Financial Times* 26 February 1910 and *The Times* 4 January 1911
[12] MDR Minutes 7747 and 7784 of 16 March and 27 April 1911
[13] *Scientific American*, Vol 103, 6 August 1910
[14] *Workhorses of the Underground*, J. Graeme Bruce, Capital Transport 1987
[15] MDR Board 7805, 18 May 1911
[16] *Railway Times* 1 February 1913
[17] MDR Board 8458 of 14 May 1914 and *The West London Railway and WLER*, H.V. Borley and R.W. Kidner, Oakwood Press.
[18] See OS mapping of period for initial and modified track layouts and maintenance agreement at TNA Rail791/493
[19] *Railway Magazine* Vol 25, September 1909
[20] *Locomotive Magazine* Volume 18 No. 233 (15 January 1912)
[21] Kay, Vol 3 and *Railway & Travel Monthly*, Vol 4, 1912
[22] Kay, Vol 3 and District WTT No 58 (1915)
[23] Kay, Vol 3
[24] District Railway WTT No 100, 23 June 1930.
[25] MDR Train Service Notebook
[26] MDR Working Timetable 29 (1st April 1908)
[27] MDR Train Service Notebook
[28] MDR Train Service Notebook
[29] MDR Working Timetable 32 (1st January 1909)
[30] Kay, Vol 3 (and subsequent correspondence with him and Brian Hardy with MDR traffic notice confirming operation)
[31] *Railway Magazine* Vol 27, October 1910
[32] Various MDR timetables 1914-1925.
[33] TNA File MT6/1895/5
[34] *Railway & Travel Monthly*, Vol 4, 1912
[35] Edwin A. Pratt, *British Railways and the Great War*, Selwyn & Blount, 1921
[36] MDR Events and Occurrences 1916-1920 in Author's collection, and *The Times* 1 February 1918
[37] Edwin A. Pratt, *British Railways and the Great War*, Selwyn & Blount, 1921, and also TOT War Record (reprinted in 'Truth' 17 December 1919)

[38] Sandra Gittins, *The Great Western Railway in the First World War*, The History Press 2010
[39] See, in particular, Hansard for 25 March 1920 and 1st July 1920, though the issue was alluded to on other occasions too.
[40] A useful summary of this is given in *The Times* 25 June 1920
[41] *Railway Magazine* March 1915 and June 1919
[42] *Railway & Travel Monthly*, Vol 11 December 1915 p412
[43] Edwin A. Pratt, *British Railways and the Great War*, Selwyn & Blount, 1921
[44] *A History of London Transport*, Barker & Robbins, Vol II, 1974 pp199.
[45] *Electrical Review*, 2 March 1917
[46] *Railway Magazine* Vol 40 April 1917 and *Railway & Travel Monthly*, Volume 14, April 1917
[47] TOT War Record (reprinted in 'Truth' 17 December 1919)
[48] Daily reports in the *Manchester Guardian* 5-8 February 1919.

Chapter 9: The Roaring 'Twenties
[1] Information from UK Population Statistics (UK Statistical Office)
[2] *Electric Railway Journal* Feb 7th 1914 Vol 43 pp301 and *Rails Through the Clay*, Alan Jackson and Desmond Croome, Allen & Unwin 1962
[3] *Electric Railway Journal* 6 June 1914 Vol 43
[4] *London Gazette* 19 November 1909
[5] *Railway News*, 10 October 1908 and see *Wimbledon and Sutton Railway* by Geoffrey Wilson, Merton Historical Society bulletin 167 September 2008.
[6] See *Wimbledon and Sutton Railway* by Geoffrey Wilson, Merton Historical Society bulletin 167 September 2008 and *The Wimbledon & Sutton Railway*, Alan A Jackson, Railway Magazine December 1966.
[7] Evidence to Select Committee on the bill, 8 April, *Railway Times*, 16 April 1910
[8] Deposited Plans for 1909-1910 bill, *Railway News*, 10 October 1908
[9] Much assistance was rendered by *The Wimbledon & Sutton Railway*, Alan A Jackson, Railway Magazine December 1966. See also Wimbledon & Sutton Railway Act 1913
[10] Alan A Jackson, *London Railway Record*, July 2000, based on report on the W&SR by J.G.White & Co to Sir Albert Stanley, dated 12 October 1914 in Merton archives.
[11] *Railway & Travel Monthly* July 1913 and *Railway Magazine* 1913 Vol 33.
[12] Traffic Notice 25 1928, but general pattern established from runs of traffic notices and publicity material.
[13] *TOT Magazine*, September & October 1925, Traffic Notice 39/1925
[14] *Electric Railway Journal*, Vol 43, 6 June 1914
[15] *Railway Magazine* January 1915
[16] *The Times* 6 January 1928
[17] *TOT Magazine*, November 1929
[18] *TOT Magazine* August 1925 and March 1926.
[19] *Railway Magazine*, April 1929.
[20] *Electric Railway Journal* 26 February 1927 and *TOT Magazine* January 1926
[21] *TOT Magazine* April 1923
[22] Edmonds
[23] District Railway Official Record of Events
[24] Edmonds (though the references are not very clear). *Railway & Travel Monthly*, Vol 2, 1911, pp436.
[25] *TOT Magazine*, January 1923
[26] *The Times*, 25 January 1911.
[27] See *The Builder*, 22 February 1925, pp340-3

[28] *TOT Magazine*, August 1924.
[29] *TOT Magazine*, January 1927
[30] *TOT Magazine*, November and December 1922.
[31] *TOT Magazine*, June 1928
[32] TNA Rail1007/14
[33] TNA MT6/2183/1 and 2183/2
[34] *TOT Magazine* November 1923 and Underground Traffic Notices 1921-1924.
[35] *TOT Magazine* March 1927 and Underground Traffic Notices 1927-1928
[36] *Illustrated London News* 3 January 1920.
[37] *Railway & Travel Monthly*, July 1921
[38] *Railway Magazine*, November 1928
[39] *Railway Magazine*, December 1927
[40] *Garke's Manual of Electrical Undertakings* Vol 39 1936-7, and *Lots Road Generating Station*, London Transport 1965 and *90-Years of Power*, J.M. Burgess, London Underground Ltd 1995.
[41] Minor incidents from MDR incident log and Wimbledon accidents from Ministry of Transport inspecting officers reports of 1 November 1920 and 13 October 1927
[42] Lord Ashfield speech to shareholders reported in *Financial Times* 16 March 1927. See also summary of events in Jackson & Croome, Chapter 10.
[43] Lord Ashfield speech to shareholders reported in *Financial Times* 7 and 27 August 1927. See also summary of events in Jackson & Croome, Chapter 10.
[44] *The Times* 31 May 1919 relates to his return to the Underground. Also covered in Barker & Robbins. Speyer's departure is covered in Barker & Robbins in footnote on page 71.
[45] *Commercial Motor*, 21 October 1919

Chapter 10: Trains and Train Services in the 1920s

[1] District Railway Shareholders' meeting February 1919 reported in *The Times* 22 February 1919
[2] *Select Committee on Transport (Metropolitan Area)* 1919, Appendix 14 paras 50-52.
[3] *Select Committee on Transport (Metropolitan Area)* 1919, Evidence of Frank Pick q4036-4050.
[4] *Select Committee on Transport (Metropolitan Area)* 1919, Evidence of H.E.Blain q5368-9. MDR board minutes 9290 and 9293 of 10 April and 8 May 1919.
[5] A detailed description of this stock is given in *The Railway Engineer*, March 1921.
[6] *Railway Magazine* Vol 44 1919, pp188
[7] *Railway Magazine* Vol 51 November 1922.
[8] *TOT Magazine* July 1924
[9] *Railway Magazine* Vol 51 Octber 1922, p323.
[10] *Steam to Silver*, Graeme Bruce, Capital Transport 1984, p82.
[11] These cars were widely described in railway press, but see, in particular, *The Railway Engineer*, November 1924.
[12] *TOT Magazine* August 1926
[13] *The Overhaul Works of London's Underground*, Acton, August 1932
[14] *TOT Magazine* February 1924 and *Tramway & Railway World* 2 February 1911 Vol 29.
[15] *TOT Magazine* June 1924 and District Railway Record of Events
[16] *TOT Magazine* May 1925
[17] MDR WTT No 78 (1st May 1922)
[18] J.B. Atkinson, *The West London Joint Railways*, Ian Allan 1984
[19] Traffic Notices 52 1925, 9 1926, and MDR Schedules notebook.

[20] Appendix to MDR WTT No 58, 1 June 1915.
[21] Traffic Notice No 27 of 1930
[22] Supplement to Traffic Notice No 20, 1933
[23] TNA MT6 2565/3
[24] J.B. Atkinson, *The West London Joint Railways*, Ian Allan 1984 (see, particularly pp79 and associated note 8)
[25] *TOT Magazine* December 1928 and *MDR Diamond Jubilee 1868-1928* illustrated booklet, 1928.

Chapter 11: Changes in the East
[1] *LMS Journal* No 20, November 2007, pp29
[2] See, for example, cross letter in *The Times* 22 August 1905
[3] The history of the estate is well documented and sources here include: *Semi-Detached London* by Alan A Jackson, Second Edition, Wild Swan 1991 and *History of the London County Council 1889-1930* by Sir Gwilym Gibbon and Reginald W Bell. MacMillan 1939
[4] *Railway Magazine*, November 1932; Traffic Notices 18 1936 and 9 1937, LMSR Instructions for working trains over electrified lines, Midland division, 1 March 1937.
[5] *Victoria County History of Essex*, Vol 7; *Railway Magazine*, November 1932
[6] *Steam to Silver*, Graeme Bruce, Capital Transport 1984, p89, confirmed by Agreement between LPTB and LMSR dated 30 December 1933 in Author's collection.

Chapter 12: Changes in the West
[1] *Rails Through the Clay*, Alan A. Jackson and Desmond Croome, Allen & Unwin 1962, Chapter 7
[2] *London Gazette*, 26 November 1913
[3] Heads of Agreement between Met, District and LER 22 July 1914 in Author's collection
[4] Underground traffic notices 7/1932, 3/1933 and 16/1933 (with supplement)
[5] *Operating Manager's Personal Letters* No 8, 29 November 1929 and No 10, 15 October 1930
[6] *Operating Manager's Personal Letter* No 11, 30 March 1931

Chapter 13: The End of the District Railway
[1] Lord Ashfield speech to shareholders reported in *The Times* 26 February 1932.
[2] This distressing period is described in Chap 18 of *The Railwaymen* (the history of the NUR) by Philip Bagwell, Allen & Unwin 1963
[3] This mostly drawn from *The Railway Engineer* November 1933 and *London Railway Record* No 80 July 2014.
[4] *London Gazette*, 1 August 1933 and 24 May 1935
[5] Agreement between LPTB and LMSR dated 30 December 1933 in Author's collection.

Chapter 14: Life After The District
[1] *Pennyfare* Vol IV No 11

Appendix 3: District Power Signalling
[1] MDR Traffic Notice 17 March 1907 and *The Railway Engineer* May 1907 (which hints the job had been completed).
[2] *The Railway Engineer*, January 1913.
[3] *Railway & Travel Monthly*, August 1916 and *Railway Engineer* September 1921

INDEX

Page numbers in *italics* refer to illustrations and maps.